Natural Language Processing and Text Mining

T0137747

Anne Kao and Stephen R. Poteet (Eds)

Natural Language Processing and Text Mining

 Springer

Anne Kao, BA, MA, MS, PhD
Bellevue, WA98008, USA

Stephen R. Poteet, BA, MA, CPhil
Bellevue, WA98008, USA

British Library Cataloguing in Publication Data
A catalogue record for this book is available from the British Library

ISBN-13: 978-1-84996-558-3   e-ISBN-13: 978-1-84628-754-1

Printed in the United States of America   (MVY)

9 8 7 6 5 4 3 2 1

Springer Science+Business Media, LLC
springer.com

List of Contributors

Jan W. Amtrup
Kofax Image Products
5465 Morehouse Dr, Suite 140
San Diego, CA 92121, USA
Jan_Amtrup@kofax.com

John Atkinson
Departamento de Ingeniera In-
formtica
Universidad de Concepción
P.O. Box code: 160-C
Concepción, Chile
atkinson@inf.udec.cl

Chutima Boonthum
Department of Computer Science
Old Dominion University
Norfolk, VA 23529, USA
cboont@cs.odu.edu

Janez Brank
J. Stefan Institute
Jamova 39, 1000
Ljubljana, Slovenia
janez.brank@ijs.si

Stephen W. Briner
Department of Psychology, Institute
for Intelligent Systems
University of Memphis
Memphis, TN 38152, USA
sbriner@memphis.edu

Razvan C. Bunescu
Department of Computer Sciences
University of Texas at Austin
1 University Station C0500
Austin, TX 78712-0233, USA
razvan@cs.utexas.edu

Kiel Christianson
Department of Educational Psychol-
ogy
University of Illinois
Champaign, IL 61820, USA
kiel@uiuc.edu

Navdeep Dhillon
Insightful Corporation
1700 Westlake Ave N, Suite 500
Seattle, WA 98109, USA
infact@insightful.com

Oren Etzioni
Department of Computer Science
University of Washington
Seattle, WA 98125-2350, USA
etzionig@cs.washington.edu

Bernd Freisleben
Department of Mathematics and
Computer Science
University of Marburg
Hans-Meerwein-Str.
D-35032 Marburg, Germany
freisleb@informatik.uni-marburg.de

Marko Grobelnik
J. Stefan Institute
Jamova 39, 1000
Ljubljana, Slovenia
marko.grobelnik@ijs.si

Renu Gupta
Center for Language Research
The University of Aizu
Aizu-Wakamatsu City
Fukushima 965-8580, Japan
renu@u-aizu.ac.jp

Martin Hoof
Department of Electrical Engineering
FH Kaiserslautern
Morlauterer Str. 31
D-67657 Kaiserslautern, Germany
m.hoof@et.fh-kl.de

Youcef-Toumi Kamal
Dept. of Mechanical Engineering
Massachusetts Institute of Technology
Cambridge, MA 02139, USA
youcef@mit.edu

Anne Kao
Mathematics and Computing
Technology
Boeing Phantom Works
Seattle, WA 92107, USA
anne.kao@boeing.com

Krzysztof Koperski
Insightful Corporation
1700 Westlake Ave N, Suite 500
Seattle, WA 98109, USA
infact@insightful.com

Irwin B. Levinstein
Department of Computer Science
Old Dominion University
Norfolk, VA 23529, USA
ibl@cs.odu.edu

Jisheng Liang
Insightful Corporation
1700 Westlake Ave N, Suite 500
Seattle, WA 98109, USA
infact@insightful.com

Ying Liu
Singapore MIT Alliance
National University of Singapore
Singapore 117576
mpeliuy@nus.edu.sg

Han Tong Loh
Dept. of Mechanical Engineering
National University of Singapore
Singapore 119260
mpelht@nus.edu.sg

Giovanni Marchisio
Insightful Corporation
1700 Westlake Ave N, Suite 500
Seattle, WA 98109, USA
infact@insightful.com

Philip M. McCarthy
Department of Psychology, Institute
for Intelligent Systems
University of Memphis
Memphis, TN 38152, USA
pmmccrth@memphis.edu

Danielle S. McNamara
Department of Psychology, Institute
for Intelligent Systems
University of Memphis
Memphis, TN 38152, USA
dsmcnamr@memphis.edu

Dunja Mladenić
J. Stefan Institute
Jamova 39, 1000
Ljubljana, Slovenia
dunja.mladenic@ijs.si

Raymond J. Mooney
Department of Computer Sciences
University of Texas at Austin
1 University Station C0500
Austin, TX 78712-0233, USA
mooney@cs.utexas.edu

Eni Mustafaraj
Department of Mathematics and
Computer Science
University of Marburg
Hans-Meerwein-Str.
D-35032 Marburg, Germany
eni@informatik.uni-marburg.de

Thien Nguyen
Insightful Corporation
1700 Westlake Ave N, Suite 500
Seattle, WA 98109, USA
infact@insightful.com

Lubos Pochman
Insightful Corporation
1700 Westlake Ave N, Suite 500
Seattle, WA 98109, USA
infact@insightful.com

Ana-Maria Popescu
Department of Computer Science
University of Washington
Seattle, WA 98125-2350, USA
amp@cs.washington.edu

Stephen R. Poteet
Mathematics and Computing
Technology
Boeing Phantom Works
Seattle, WA 92107, USA
stephen.r.poteet@boeing.com

Jonathan Reichhold
Insightful Corporation
1700 Westlake Ave N, Suite 500
Seattle, WA 98109, USA
infact@insightful.com

Vasile Rus
Department of Computer Science,
Institute for Intelligent Systems
University of Memphis
Memphis, TN 38152, USA
vrus@memphis.edu

Mauritius A. R. Schmidtler
Kofax Image Products
5465 Morehouse Dr, Suite 140
San Diego, CA 92121, USA
Maurice_Schmidtler@kofax.com

Lothar M. Schmitt
School of Computer Science &
Engineering
The University of Aizu
Aizu-Wakamatsu City
Fukushima 965-8580, Japan
L@LMSchmitt.de

Shu Beng Tor
School of Mechanical and Aerospace
Engineering
Nanyang Technological University
Singapore 117576
msbtor@ntu.edu.sg

Carsten Tusk
Insightful Corporation
1700 Westlake Ave N, Suite 500
Seattle, WA 98109, USA
infact@insightful.com

Dan White
Insightful Corporation
1700 Westlake Ave N, Suite 500
Seattle, WA 98109, USA
infact@insightful.com

Preface

The topic this book addresses originated from a panel discussion at the 2004 ACM SIGKDD (Special Interest Group on Knowledge Discovery and Data Mining) Conference held in Seattle, Washington, USA. We the editors organized the panel to promote discussion on how text mining and natural language processing, two related topics originating from very different disciplines, can best interact with each other, and benefit from each other's strengths. It attracted a great deal of interest and was attended by 200 people from all over the world. We then guest-edited a special issue of ACM SIGKDD Explorations on the same topic, with a number of very interesting papers. At the same time, Springer believed this to be a topic of wide interest and expressed an interest in seeing a book published. After a year of work, we have put together 11 papers from international researchers on a range of techniques and applications.

We hope this book includes papers readers do not normally find in conference proceedings, which tend to focus more on theoretical or algorithmic breakthroughs but are often only tried on standard test data. We would like to provide readers with a wider range of applications, give some examples of the practical application of algorithms on real-world problems, as well as share a number of useful techniques.

We would like to take this opportunity to thank all our reviewers: Gary Coen, Ketty Gann, Mark Greaves, Anne Hunt, Dave Levine, Bing Liu, Dragos Margineantu, Jim Schimert, John Thompson, Rod Tjoelker, Rick Wojcik, Steve Woods, and Jason Wu. Their backgrounds include natural language processing, machine learning, applied statistics, linear algebra, genetic algorithms, web mining, ontologies and knowledge management. They complement the editors' own backgrounds in text mining and natural language processing very well. As technologists at Boeing Phantom Works, we work on practical large scale text mining problems such as Boeing airplane maintenance and safety, various kinds of survey data, knowledge management, and knowledge discovery, and evaluate data and text mining, and knowledge management products for Boeing use. We would also like to thank Springer for the opportunity to interact with researchers in the field and for publishing this book and especially Wayne Wheeler and Catherine Brett for their help and encouragement at every step. Finally, we would like to offer our special thanks to Jason Wu. We would not have been able to put all the chapters together into a book without his expertise in LaTeX and his dedication to the project.

Bellevue, Washington, USA   *Anne Kao*

April 2006   *Stephen R. Poteet*

Contents

1

Overview

Anne Kao and Stephen R. Poteet

1.1 Introduction

Text mining is the discovery and extraction of interesting, non-trivial knowledge from free or unstructured text. This encompasses everything from information retrieval (i.e., document or web site retrieval) to text classification and clustering, to (somewhat more recently) entity, relation, and event extraction. Natural language processing (NLP), is the attempt to extract a fuller meaning representation from free text. This can be put roughly as figuring out who did what to whom, when, where, how and why. NLP typically makes use of linguistic concepts such as part-of-speech (noun, verb, adjective, etc.) and grammatical structure (either represented as phrases like noun phrase or prepositional phrase, or dependency relations like subject-of or object-of). It has to deal with anaphora (what previous noun does a pronoun or other back-referring phrase correspond to) and ambiguities (both of words and of grammatical structure, such as what is being modified by a given word or prepositional phrase). To do this, it makes use of various knowledge representations, such as a lexicon of words and their meanings and grammatical properties and a set of grammar rules and often other resources such as an ontology of entities and actions, or a thesaurus of synonyms or abbreviations.

This book has several purposes. First, we want to explore the use of NLP techniques in text mining, as well as some other technologies that are novel to the field of text mining. Second, we wish to explore novel ways of integrating various technologies, old or new, to solve a text mining problem. Next, we would like to look at some new applications for text mining. Finally, we have several chapters that provide various supporting techniques for either text mining or NLP or both, or enhancements to existing techniques.

1.2 Approaches that Use NLP Techniques

The papers in our first group deal with approaches that utilize to various degrees more in-depth NLP techniques. All of them use a parser of some sort or another, one of them uses some morphological analysis (or rather generation), and two of them use other lexical resources, such as WordNet, FrameNet, or VerbNet. The first three use off-the-shelf parsers while the last uses their own parser.

Popescu and Etzioni combine a wide array of techniques. Among these are NLP techniques such as parsing with an off-the-shelf parser, MINIPAR, morphological rules to generate nouns from adjectives, and WordNet (for its synonymy and antonymy information, its IS-A hierarchy of word meanings, and for its adjective-to-noun pertain relation). In addition, they use hand-coded rules to extract desired relations from the structures resulting from the parse. They also make extensive and key use of a statistical technique, pointwise mutual information (PMI), to make sure that associations found both in the target data and in supplementary data downloaded from the Web are real. Another distinctive technique of theirs is that they make extensive use of the Web as a source of both word forms and word associations. Finally, they introduce relaxation labeling, a technique from the field of image-processing, to the field of text mining to perform context sensitive classification of words.

Bunescu and Mooney adapt Support Vector Machines (SVMs) to a new role in text mining, namely relation extraction, and in the process compare the use of NLP parsing with non-NLP approaches. SVMs have been used extensively in text mining but always to do text classification, treating a document or piece of text as an unstructured bag of words (i.e., only what words are in the text and what their counts are, not their position with respect to each other or any other structural relationships among them). The process of extracting relations between entities, as noted above, has typically been presumed to require parsing into natural language phrases. This chapter explores two new kernels for SVMs, a subsequence kernel and a dependency path kernel, to classify the relations between two entities (they assume the entities have already been extracted by whatever means). Both of these involve using a wholly novel set of features with an SVM classifier. The dependency path kernel uses information from a dependency parse of the text while the subsequence kernel treats the text as just a string of tokens. They test these two different approaches on two different domains and find that the value of the dependency path kernel (and therefore of NLP parsing) depends on how well one can expect the parser to perform on text from the target domain, which in turn depends on how many unknown words and expressions there are in that domain.

Mustafaraj et al. also combine parsing with statistical approaches to classification. In their case they are using an ensemble or committee of three different classifiers which are typically used with non-NLP features but the features they use are based on parse trees. In addition, their application requires a morphological analysis of the words in their domain, given the nature of German, their target language. They explore the use of off-the-shelf POS taggers and morphological analyzers for this purpose, but find them falling short in their domain (a technical one, electrical fault diagnosis), and have to result to hand coding the morphological rules. Another couple of NLP resources that they utilize are FrameNet and VerbNet to find relevant verbs and relationships to map into their knowledge-engineering categories, but this is used off-line for analysis rather than in on-line processing. Finally, they use active learning to efficiently train their classifiers, a statistical technique that is relatively new to text mining (or data mining in general, for that matter).

Marchisio et al. utilize NLP techniques almost exclusively, writing their own parser to do full parsing and using their novel indexing technique to compress complex parse forests in a way that captures basic dependency relations like subject-of, object-of, and verb-modification like time, location, etc., as well as extended relations involving the modifiers of the entities involved in the basic relations or other entities associated with them in the text or in background knowledge. The index allows them to rapidly access all of these relations, permitting them to be used in document search, an area that has long been considered not to derive any benefit from any but surface NLP techniques like tokenization and stemming. This entails a whole new protocol for search, however, and the focus of their article is on how well users adapt to this new protocol.

1.3 Non-NLP Techniques

Boontham et al. discuss the use of three different approaches to categorizing the free text responses of students to open-ended questions: simple word matching, Latent Semantic Analysis (LSA), and a variation on LSA which they call Topic Models. LSA and Topic Models are both numerical methods for generating new features based on linear algebra and ultimately begin with a representation of the text as a bag of words. In addition, they use discriminant analysis from statistics for classification. Stemming and soundex (a method for correcting misspelling by representing words in a way that roughly corresponds to their pronunciation) are used in the word matching component. Stemming is the only NLP technique used.

McCarthy et al. also use LSA as their primary technique, employing it to compare different sections of a document rather than whole documents and develop a "signature" of documents based on the correlation between different sections.

Schmidtler and Amtrup combine an SVM with a Markov chain to determine how to separate sequences of text pages into distinct documents of different types given that the text pages are very noisy, being the product of optical character recognition. They do a nice job of exploring the different ways they might model a sequence of pages, in terms both of what categories one might assign to pages and how to combine page content and sequence information. They use simple techniques like tokenization and stemming, but not more complex NLP techniques.

Atkinson uses a technique that is very novel for text mining, genetic algorithms (GAs). Genetic algorithms are typically used for solving problems where the features can be represented as binary vectors. Atkinson adapts this to text representations by employing a whole range of numerical and statistical methods, including LSA and Markov chains, and various metrics build on these. However, other than some manually constructed contexts for rhetorical roles, he uses no true NLP techniques.

1.4 Range of Applications

The papers in this book perform a wide range of applications, some more traditional for text mining and some quite novel.

Marchisio et al. take a novel approach to a very traditional application, simple search or document retrieval. They introduce a new paradigm, taking advantage of the linguistic structure of the documents as opposed to key words. Their end-user is the average user of a web search engine.

There are several variants on information extraction.

Bunescu and Mooney look at extracting relations, which, along with entity extraction, is an important current research area in text mining. They focus on two domains, bioinformatics and newspaper articles, each involving a completely different set of entities and relations. The former involves entities like genes, proteins, and cells, and relations like protein-protein interactions and subcellular localization. The latter involves more familiar entities like people, organizations, and locations and relations like "belongs to," "is head of," etc.

Mustafaraj et al. focus on extracting a different kind of relation, the roles of different entities relevant to diagnosis in the technical domain of electrical engineering. These roles include things like "observed object," "symptom," and "cause." In the end, they are trying to mark-up the text of diagnostic reports in a way to facilitate search and the extraction of knowledge about the domain.

Popescu and Etzioni's application is the extraction of product features, parts, and attributes, and customers' or users' opinions about these (both positive and negative, and how strongly they feel) from customer product reviews. These include specialized entities and relations, as well as opinions and their properties, which do not quite fit into these categories.

Atkinson ventures into another novel extraction paradigm, extracting knowledge in form of IF-THEN rules from scientific studies. The scientific domain he focuses on in this particular study is agricultural and food science.

The remaining applications do not fit into any existing text mining niche very well. Schmidtler et al. need to solve a very practical problem, that of separating a stack of pages into distinct documents and labeling the document type. Complicating this problem is the need to use optical character recognition, which results in very noisy text data (lots of errors at the character level). To help overcome this, they utilize whatever sequential information is available in several ways: in setting up the categories (not just document type but beginning/middle/end of document type); in using the category of preceding pages as input in the prediction of a page, and in incorporating knowledge about the number of pages in each document type and hard constraints on the possible sequencing of document types.

McCarthy et al. investigate the use of LSA to compare the similarity of the different sections of scientific studies as a contribution to rhetorical analysis. While the tool is at first blush useful primarily in the scientific field of discourse analysis, they suggest a couple of practical applications, using it to help classify different types of documents (genre and field) or, by authors, to assess how their document measures up to other documents in the same genre and field.

Finally, Boonthum et al. explore the use of various text mining techniques in pedagogy, i.e., to give feedback to students based on discursive rather than categorical (i.e., true-false or multiple choice) answers. In the end, it is a kind of classification problem, but they investigate a method to adapt this quickly to a new domain and set of questions, an essential element for this particular application.

1.5 Supporting Techniques

In addition to various approaches using text mining for some application, there are several papers that explore various techniques that can support text mining (and frequently other data mining) techniques.

Liu et al. investigate a new means of overcoming one of the more important problems in automatic text classification, imbalanced data (the situation where some categories have a lot of examples in the data and other categories have very few examples in the data). They explore various term weighting schemes inspired by the TFIDF metric (term frequency / inverse document frequency) used traditionally in document retrieval in feature selection, and demonstrate that the resulting weighted features show improved performance when used with an SVM.

Brank et al. do a nice survey and classification of approaches to evaluating ontologies for their appropriateness for different domains and tasks, and propose their own metric. Ontologies are an important component for many NLP and text mining applications (e.g., topic classification, entity extraction) and, while the method they propose is based on graph theoretic principles rather than on text mining, many of the other approaches they survey utilize text mining principles as part of the evaluation (or part of the automatic or semi-automatic generation) of ontologies for a particular domain.

Finally, the final chapter by Schmitt et al. is rather different from the other chapters, being more of a tutorial that can benefit students and seasoned professionals alike. It shows how to construct a broad range of text mining and NLP tools using simple UNIX commands and sed and awk (and provides an excellent primer on these in the process). These tools can be used to perform a number of functions, from quite basic ones like tokenization, stemming, or synonym replacement, which are fundamental to many applications, to more complex or specialized ones, like constructing a concordance (a list of terms in context from a corpus, a set of documents to be used for training or analysis) or merging text from different formats to capture important information from each while eliminating irrelevant notations (e.g., eliminating irrelevant formatting mark-up but retaining information relevant both to the pronunciation and kanji forms of different Japanese characters. This information is not only useful for people working on UNIX (or Linux), but can be fairly easily adapted to Perl, which shares much of the regular expression language features and syntax of the UNIX tools, sed and awk.

1.6 Future Work

With the increased use of the Internet, text mining has become increasingly important since the term came into popular usage over 10 years ago. Highly related and specialized fields such as web mining and bioinformatics have also attracted a lot of research work. However, more work is still needed in several major directions. (1) Data mining practitioners largely feel that the majority of data mining work lies in data cleaning and data preparation. This is perhaps even more true in the case of text mining. Much text data does not follow prescriptive spelling, grammar or style rules. For example, the language used in maintenance data, help desk reports, blogs, or email does not resemble that of well-edited news articles at all. More studies on how and to what degree the quality of text data affects different types of text mining algorithms, as well as better methods to 'preprocess' text data would be very beneficial. (2) Practitioners of text mining are rarely sure whether an algorithm demonstrated to be effective on one type of data will work on another set of data. Standard test data sets can help compare different algorithms, but they can never tell us whether an algorithm that performs well on them will perform well on a particular user's dataset. While establishing a fully articulated natural language model for each genre of text data is likely an unreachable goal, it would be extremely useful if researchers could show which types of algorithms and parameter settings tend to work well on which types of text data, based on relatively easily ascertained characteristics of the data (e.g., technical vs. non-technical, edited vs. non-edited, short news vs. long articles, proportion of unknown vs. known words or jargon words vs. general words, complete, well-punctuated sentences vs. a series of phrases with little or no punctuation, etc.) (3) The range of text mining applications is now far broader than just information retrieval, as exhibited by some of the new and interesting applications in this book. Nevertheless, we hope to see an even wider range of applications in the future and to see how they drive additional requirements for text mining theory and methods. In addition, newly emerging fields of study such as link analysis (or link mining) have suggested new directions for text mining research, as well. Our hope is that between new application areas and cross-pollination from other fields, text mining will continue to thrive and see new breakthroughs.

2

Extracting Product Features and Opinions from Reviews

Ana-Maria Popescu and Oren Etzioni

2.1 Introduction

The Web contains a wealth of opinions about products, politicians, and more, which are expressed in newsgroup posts, review sites, and elsewhere. As a result, the problem of "opinion mining" has seen increasing attention over the past three years from [1, 2] and many others. This chapter focuses on product reviews, though we plan to extend our methods to a broader range of texts and opinions.

Product reviews on Web sites such as amazon.com and elsewhere often associate meta-data with each review, indicating how positive (or negative) it is using a 5-star scale, and also rank products by how they fare in the reviews at the site. However, the reader's taste may differ from the reviewers'. For example, the reader may feel strongly about the quality of the gym in a hotel, whereas many reviewers may focus on other aspects of the hotel, such as the decor or the location. Thus, the reader is forced to wade through a large number of reviews looking for information about particular features of interest.

We decompose the problem of review mining into the following main subtasks:

I. Identify product features. In a given review, features can be *explicit* (*e.g.,* "the *size* is too big ") or *implicit* (*e.g.,* "the scanner is slow" refers to the "scanner speed").

II. Identify opinions regarding product features. For example, "the size is *too big*" contains the opinion phrase *"too big,"* which corresponds to the "size" feature.

III. Determine the polarity of opinions. Opinions can be *positive* (*e.g.,* "this scanner is *so great"*) or *negative* (*e.g.,* "this scanner is a *complete disappointment"*).

IV. Rank opinions based on their strength. For example, *"horrible"* is a stronger indictment than *"bad."*

This chapter introduces OPINE, an unsupervised information extraction system that embodies a solution to each of the above subtasks. Given a particular product and a corresponding set of reviews, OPINE outputs a set of *product features*, accompanied by a list of associated *opinions*, which are ranked based on strength.

Our contributions are as follows:

1. We describe OPINE's novel use of a *relaxation labeling* method to find the semantic orientation of words in the context of given product features and sentences.

2. We compare OPINE with the review mining system of Hu and Liu [2] and find that OPINE's precision on the *feature extraction* task is 22% higher than that of Hu and Liu, although its recall is 3% lower. We show that 1/3 of OPINE's increase in precision comes from the use of its *feature assessment* mechanism on review data while the rest is due to Web statistics.

3. While many other systems have used extracted opinion phrases in order to determine the polarity of sentences or documents, OPINE reports its precision and recall on the tasks of *opinion phrase extraction* and *opinion phrase polarity extraction* in the context of known product features and sentences. On the first task, OPINE has a precision of 79% and a recall of 76%. On the second task, OPINE has a precision of 86% and a recall of 89%.

4. Finally, OPINE ranks the opinion phrases corresponding to a particular property based on their strength and obtains an accuracy of 73%.

The remainder of this chapter is organized as follows: Section 2.2 introduces the basic terminology; Section 2.3 gives an overview of OPINE, and describes and evaluates its main components; Section 2.4 describes related work; and Section 2.5 describes our conclusions and future work.

2.2 Terminology

A *product class* (*e.g.*, Scanner) is a set of *products* (*e.g.*, Epson1200). OPINE extracts the following types of *product features*: *properties, parts, features of product parts, related concepts, parts* and *properties of related concepts* (see Table 2.1 in subsection 2.3.2 for examples in the Scanner domain). *Related concepts* are concepts relevant to the customers' experience with the main product (*e.g.*, the company that manufactures a scanner). The relationships between the main product and related concepts are typically expressed as verbs (*e.g.*, "the company *manufactures* scanners") or prepositions ("scanners *from* Epson"). Features can be *explicit* ("good `scan quality`") or *implicit* ("good scans" implies good `ScanQuality`).

OPINE also extracts *opinion phrases*, which are adjective, noun, verb or adverb phrases representing customer opinions. Opinions can be *positive* or *negative* and vary in *strength* (*e.g.*, "fantastic" is stronger than "good").

2.3 OPINE Overview

This section gives an overview of OPINE (see Figure 2.1) and describes its components and their experimental evaluation.

Given product class C with instances I and corresponding reviews R, OPINE's goal is to find a set of (feature, opinions) tuples $\{(f, o_i, ...o_j)\}$ such that $f \in F$ and $o_i, ...o_j \in O$, where:

a) F is the set of product class features in R.

b) O is the set of opinion phrases in R.

c) f is a feature of a particular product instance.

d) o is an opinion about f in a particular sentence.

d) the opinions associated with f are ranked based on opinion strength.

Input: product class C, reviews R.
Output: set of [feature, ranked opinion list] tuples
R' ← parseReviews(R);
E ← findExplicitFeatures(R', C);
O ← findOpinions(R', E);
CO ← clusterOpinions(O);
I ← findImplicitFeatures(CO, E);
RO ← rankOpinions(CO);
$\{(f, o_i, ...o_j)...\}$←outputTuples(RO, I ∪ E);

Fig. 2.1. OPINE Overview.

The steps of our solution are outlined in Figure 2.1 above. OPINE parses the reviews using MINIPAR [3] and applies a simple pronoun-resolution module to the parsed review data. OPINE then uses the data to find *explicit* product features. OPINE's *Feature Assessor* and its use of Web *Point-wise Mutual Information* (PMI) statistics are vital for the extraction of high-quality features (see 2.3.3). OPINE then identifies *opinion phrases* associated with explicit features and finds their polarity. OPINE's novel use of relaxation labeling techniques for determining the semantic orientation of potential opinion words in the context of given features and sentences leads to high precision and recall on the tasks of *opinion phrase extraction* and *opinion phrase polarity extraction* (see 2.3.5).

Opinion phrases refer to *properties*, which are sometimes *implicit* (*e.g.*, "tiny phone" refers to the size of the phone). In order to extract implicit properties, OPINE first clusters opinion phrases (*e.g.*, *tiny* and *small* will be placed in the same cluster), automatically labels the clusters with property names (*e.g.*, *Size*) and uses them to extract *implicit* features (*e.g.*, PhoneSize). The final component of our system is the ranking of opinions which refer to the same property based on their strength (*e.g.*, *fantastic* > (*almost*, *great*) > *good*). Finally, OPINE outputs a set of (feature, ranked opinions) tuples for each identified feature.

2.3.1 The KnowItAll System

OPINE is built on top of KnowItAll, a Web-based, domain-independent information extraction system [4]. Given a set of relations of interest, KnowItAll instantiates relation-specific generic extraction patterns into extraction rules which find candidate facts. KnowItAll's Assessor then assigns a probability to each candidate. The Assessor uses a form of *Point-wise Mutual Information* (PMI) between phrases that is estimated from Web search engine hit counts [5]. It computes the PMI between each fact and *automatically generated discriminator phrases* (*e.g.*, "is a scanner" for the isA() relationship in the context of the Scanner class). Given fact f and discriminator d, the computed PMI score is:

$$\text{PMI}(f, d) = \frac{\text{Hits}(d + f)}{\text{Hits}(d) * \text{Hits}(f)}$$

For example, a high PMI between "Epson 1200" and phrases such as "is a scanner" suggests that "Epson 1200" is a Scanner instance. The PMI scores are converted to binary features for a Naive Bayes Classifier, which outputs a probability associated with each fact [4].

2.3.2 Finding Explicit Features

OPINE extracts *explicit* features for the given product class from parsed review data. The system recursively identifies the *parts* and the *properties* of the given product class and their parts and properties, in turn, continuing until no more such features are found. The system then finds *related concepts* and extracts their meronyms (parts) and properties. Table 2.1 shows that each feature type contributes to the set of final features (averaged over seven product classes).

Table 2.1. Explicit Feature Information

Explicit Features	Examples	% Total
Properties	ScannerSize	7%
Parts	ScannerCover	52%
Features of Parts	BatteryLife	24%
Related Concepts	ScannerImage	9%
Related Concepts' Features	ScannerImageSize	8%

Table 2.2. Meronymy Lexical Patterns   Notation: $[C]$ = product class (or instance) $[M]$ = candidate meronym $(*)$ = wildcard character

$[M]$ of (*) $[C]$	$[M]$ for (*) $[C]$
$[C]$'s M	$[C]$ has (*) $[M]$
$[C]$ with (*) $[M]$	$[M]$ (*) in (*) $[C]$
$[C]$ come(s) with (*) $[M]$	$[C]$ contain(s)(ing) (*) $[M]$
$[C]$ equipped with (*) $[M]$	$[C]$ endowed with (*) $[M]$

In order to find parts and properties, OPINE first extracts the noun phrases from reviews and retains those with frequency greater than an experimentally set threshold. OPINE's *Feature Assessor*, which is an instantiation of KnowItAll's Assessor, evaluates each noun phrase by computing the PMI scores between the phrase and *meronymy discriminators* associated with the product class (see Table 2.2). OPINE distinguishes parts from properties using WordNet's IS-A hierarchy (which enumerates different kinds of properties) and morphological cues (*e.g.*, "-iness", "-ity" suffixes).

Given a target product class C, OPINE finds concepts related to C by extracting frequent noun phrases as well as noun phrases linked to C or C's instances through verbs or prepositions (*e.g.*, "The scanner *produces* great images"). *Related concepts* are assessed as described in [6] and then stored as product features together with their parts and properties.

2.3.3 Experiments: Explicit Feature Extraction

The previous review mining systems most relevant to our work are those in [2] and [7]. We only had access to the data used in [2] and therefore our experiments include a comparison between OPINE and Hu and Liu's system, but no direct comparison between OPINE and IBM's SentimentAnalyzer [7] (see the related work section for a discussion of this work).

Hu and Liu's system uses association rule mining to extract frequent review noun phrases as features. Frequent features are used to find potential opinion words (only adjectives) and the system uses WordNet synonyms and antonyms in conjunction with a set of seed words in order to find actual opinion words. Finally, opinion words are used to extract associated infrequent features. The system only extracts explicit features.

On the five datasets used in [2], OPINE's precision is 22% higher than Hu's at the cost of a 3% recall drop. There are two important differences between OPINE and Hu's system: a) OPINE's Feature Assessor uses PMI assessment to evaluate each candidate feature and b) OPINE incorporates Web PMI statistics in addition to review data in its assessment. In the following, we quantify the performance gains from a) and b).

a) In order to quantify the benefits of OPINE's Feature Assessor, we use it to evaluate the features extracted by Hu's algorithm on review data. The Feature Assessor improves Hu's precision by 6%.

b) In order to evaluate the impact of using Web PMI statistics, we assess OPINE's features first on reviews, and then on reviews in conjunction with the Web. Web PMI statistics increase precision by an average of 14.5%.

Overall, 1/3 of **OPINE**'s precision increase over Hu's system comes from using PMI assessment on reviews and the other 2/3 from the use of the Web PMI statistics.

In order to show that OPINE's performance is robust across multiple product classes, we used two sets of 1,307 reviews downloaded from tripadvisor.com for Hotels and amazon.com for Scanners. Two annotators labeled a set of unique 450 OPINE extractions as *correct* or *incorrect*. The inter-annotator agreement was 86%. The extractions on which the annotators agreed were used to compute OPINE's precision, which was 89%. Furthermore, the annotators extracted explicit features from 800 review sentences (400 for each domain). The inter-annotator agreement was 82%. OPINE's recall on the set of 179 features on which both annotators agreed was 73%.

Table 2.3. Precision Comparison on the Explicit Feature Extraction Task. OPINE's precision is 22% better than Hu's precision; Web PMI statistics are responsible for 2/3 of the precision increase. All results are reported with respect to Hu's.

Data	Hu	Hu Assess(Reviews)	Hu Assess(Reviews,Web)	OPINE (Reviews)	OPINE
D_1	0.75	+0.05	+0.17	+0.07	**+0.19**
D_2	0.71	+0.03	+0.19	+0.08	**+0.22**
D_3	0.72	+0.03	+0.25	+0.09	**+0.23**
D_4	0.69	+0.06	+0.22	+0.08	**+0.25**
D_5	0.74	+0.08	+0.19	+0.04	**+0.21**
Avg	0.72	+0.06	+ 0.20	+0.07	**+0.22**

Table 2.4. Recall Comparison on the Explicit Feature Extraction Task. OPINE's recall is 3% lower than the recall of Hu's original system (precision level = 0.8). All results are reported with respect to Hu's.

Data	Hu	Hu Assess(Reviews)	Hu Assess(Reviews,Web)	OPINE (Reviews)	OPINE
D_1	0.82	-0.16	-0.08	-0.14	**-0.02**
D_2	0.79	-0.17	-0.09	-0.13	**-0.06**
D_3	0.76	-0.12	-0.08	-0.15	**-0.03**
D_4	0.82	-0.19	-0.04	-0.17	**-0.03**
D_5	0.80	-0.16	-0.06	-0.12	**-0.02**
Avg	0.80	-0.16	-0.07	-0.14	**-0.03**

2.3.4 Finding Implicit Features

We now address the extraction of *implicit features*. The system first extracts *opinion phrases* attached to explicit features, as detailed in 2.3.5. Opinion phrases refer to *properties* (*e.g.*, "clean" refers to "cleanliness"). When the property is *implicit* (*e.g.*, "clean room"), the opinion is attached to an explicit feature (*e.g.*, "room"). OPINE examines opinion phrases associated with explicit features in order to extract implicit properties. If the opinion phrase is a verb, noun, or adverb, OPINE associates it with Quality; if the opinion phrase is an adjective, OPINE maps it to a more specific property. For instance, if "clean" and "spacious" are opinions about hotel rooms, OPINE associates "clean" with Cleanness and "spacious" with Size.

The problem of associating adjectives with an implied property is closely related to that of finding adjectival scales [8]. OPINE uses WordNet synonymy and antonymy information to group the adjectives in a set of initial clusters. Next, any two clusters A_1 and A_2 are merged if multiple pairs of adjectives (a_1, a_2) exist such that $a_1 \in A_1$, $a_2 \in A_2$ and a_1 is *similar to* a_2 (an explanation of adjective similarity is given below). For example, $A_1 = \{$ "intuitive"$\}$ is merged with $A_2 = \{$ "understandable", "clear"$\}$.

Clusters are labeled with the names of their corresponding properties (see Table 2.6). The property names are obtained from either WordNet (*e.g.*, *big* is a value of *size*), or from a name-generation module which adds suffixes (*e.g.*, "-iness", "-ity") to adjectives and uses the Web to filter out non-words and highly infrequent candidate names. If no property names can be found, the label is generated based ona djectives: "beIntercontinental," "beWelcome," etc.

Adjective Similarity The adjective similarity rules in Table 2.5 consist of WordNet-Based rules and Web-Based rules. WordNet relationships such as $pertain(adjSynset, nounSynset)$ and $attribute(adjSynset, nounSynset)$ are used to relate adjectives to nouns representing properties: if two adjectives relate to the same property or to related properties, the two adjectives are similar. In addition to such WordNet-based rules, OPINE bootstraps a set of lexical patterns (see 2.3.7 for details) and instantiates them in order to generate search-engine queries which confirm that two adjectives correspond to the same property. Given clusters A_1 and A_2, OPINE instantiates patterns such as "a_1, (*) even a_2 " with $a_1 \in A_1$ and $a_2 \in A_2$ in order to check if a_1 and a_2 are similar. For example, hits *("clear, (*) even intuitive")* > 5, therefore "clear" is similar to "intuitive."

Table 2.5. WordNet-Based and Web-Based Adjective Similarity Rules. Notation: s_1, s_2 = **WordNet synsets**

adj_1 and adj_2 are similar if
$\exists s_1, s_2$ s.t. $pertain(adj_1, s_1), attribute(adj_2, s_2), isA(s_1, s_2)$
$\exists s_1, s_2$ s.t. $pertain(adj_1, s_1), pertain(adj_2, s_2), isA(s_1, s_2)$
$\exists s_1, s_2$ s.t. $attribute(adj_1, s_1), attribute(adj_2, s_2), isA(s_1, s_2)$
$\exists p \in \{$ "$[X], even[Y]$", "$[X], almost[Y]$", ...$\}$ s.t. $hits(p(adj_1, adj_2)) > t, t = threshold$

Table 2.6. Examples of Labeled Opinion Clusters

Quality: *like, recommend, good, very good, incredibly good, great, truly great*
Clarity: *understandable, clear, straightforward, intuitive*
Noise: *quiet, silent, noisy, loud, deafening*
Price: *inexpensive, affordable, costly, expensive, cheap*

Given an explicit feature f and a set of opinions associated with f which have been clustered as previously described, OPINE uses the opinion clusters to extract *implicit features*. For example, given f=Room and opinions *clean, spotless* in the *Cleanness* cluster, OPINE generates the implicit feature RoomCleanness. We evaluated the impact of *implicit feature extraction* in the Hotels and Scanners domains.[1] Implicit features led to a 2% average increase

---

[1] Hu's datasets have few implicit features and Hu's system doesn't handle implicit feature extraction.

in precision and a 6% increase in recall, mostly in the Hotel domain, which is rich in adjectives (*e.g.,* "*clean room,*" "*soft bed*").

2.3.5 Finding Opinion Phrases and Their Polarity

This subsection describes how OPINE extracts potential opinion phrases, distinguishes between opinions and non-opinions, and finds the *polarity* of each opinion in the context of its associated feature in a particular review sentence.

OPINE uses explicit features to identify potential opinion phrases. Our intuition is that an opinion phrase associated with a product feature will occur in its vicinity. This idea is similar to that of [9] and [2], but instead of using a window of size k or the output of a noun phrase chunker, OPINE takes advantage of the dependencies computed by the MINIPAR parser. Our intuition is embodied by a set of *extraction rules*, the most important of which are shown in Table 2.7. If an explicit feature is found in a sentence, OPINE applies the extraction rules in order to find the heads of potential opinion phrases. Each head word, together with its modifiers, is returned as a potential opinion phrase.

Table 2.7. Domain-Independent Rules for Potential Opinion Phrase Extraction. Notation: po=potential opinion, M=modifier, NP=noun phrase, S=subject, P=predicate, O=object. Extracted phrases are enclosed in parentheses. Features are indicated by the typewriter font. The equality conditions on the left-hand side use *po*'s head.

Extraction Rules	Examples
if $\exists(M, NP = f) \rightarrow po = M$	(expensive) `scanner`
if $\exists(S = f, P, O) \rightarrow po = O$	`lamp` has (problems)
if $\exists(S, P, O = f) \rightarrow po = P$	I (hate) this `scanner`
if $\exists(S = f, P) \rightarrow po = P$	`program` (crashed)

Table 2.8. Dependency Rule Templates For Finding Words w**,** w' **with Related Semantic Orientation Labels** Notation: v,w,w'=words; f, f'=feature names; dep=dependent; m=modifier

Rule Templates	Example Rules
$dependent(w, w')$	$modifier(w, w')$
$\exists v$ s.t. $dep(w, v), dep(v, w')$	$\exists v$ s.t. $m(w, v), object(v, w')$
$\exists v$ s.t. $dep(w, v), dep(w', v)$	$\exists v$ s.t. $m(w, v), object(w', v)$
$\exists f, f'$ s.t. $dep(w, f), dep(w', f'), dep(f, f')$	$\exists f, f'$ s.t. $m(w, f), m(w', f'), and(f, f')$

OPINE examines the potential opinion phrases in order to identify the actual opinions. First, the system finds the semantic orientation for the lexical head of each potential opinion phrase. Every phrase whose head word has a *positive* or *negative* semantic orientation is then retained as an *opinion phrase*.

In the following, we describe how OPINE finds the semantic orientation of words.

Context-Specific Word Semantic Orientation

Given a set of *semantic orientation (SO) labels* ({*positive, negative, neutral*}), a set of reviews and a set of tuples (w, f, s), where w is a potential opinion word associated with feature f in sentence s, OPINE assigns a SO label to each tuple (w, f, s). For example, the tuple (*sluggish, driver*, "I am not happy with this sluggish driver") will be assigned a *negative* SO label [2].

OPINE uses the three-step approach below to label each (w, f, s) tuple:

1. Given the set of reviews, OPINE finds a SO label for each word w.

2. Given the set of reviews and the set of SO labels for words w, OPINE finds a SO label for each (w, f) pair.

3. Given the set of SO labels for (w, f) pairs, OPINE finds a SO label for each (w, f, s) input tuple.

Each of these subtasks is cast as an unsupervised collective classification problem and solved using the same mechanism. In each case, OPINE is given a set of *objects* (words, pairs or tuples) and a set of *labels* (SO labels); OPINE then searches for a *global* assignment of labels to objects. In each case, OPINE makes use of *local constraints* on label assignments (*e.g.*, conjunctions and disjunctions constraining the assignment of SO labels to words [10]).

A key insight in OPINE is that the problem of searching for a *global* SO label assignment to words, pairs, or tuples while trying to satisfy as many *local* constraints on assignments as possible is analogous to labeling problems in computer vision (*e.g.*, model-based matching). OPINE uses a well-known computer vision technique, *relaxation labeling* [11], in order to solve the three subtasks described above.

Relaxation Labeling Overview

Relaxation labeling is an unsupervised classification technique which takes as input:

a) a set of *objects* (*e.g.*, words)

b) a set of *labels* (*e.g.*, SO labels)

c) initial probabilities for each object's possible labels

d) the definition of an object o's *neighborhood* (a set of other objects which influence the choice of o's label)

e) the definition of *neighborhood features*

f) the definition of a *support function* for an object label

The influence of an object o's neighborhood on its label L is quantified using the *support function*. The support function computes the probability of the label L being assigned to o as a function of o's *neighborhood features*.

---

[2] We use "word" to refer to a potential opinion word w and "feature" to refer to the word or phrase which represents the explicit feature f.

Examples of features include the fact that a certain *local constraint* is satisfied (*e.g.*, the word *nice* participates in the conjunction *and* together with some other word whose SO label is estimated to be *positive*).

Relaxation labeling is an iterative procedure whose output is an assignment of labels to objects. At each iteration, the algorithm uses an *update equation* to reestimate the probability of an object label based on its previous probability estimate and the features of its neighborhood. The algorithm stops when the global label assignment stays constant over multiple consecutive iterations.

We employ relaxation labeling for the following reasons: a) it has been extensively used in computer-vision with good results and b) its formalism allows for many types of constraints on label assignments to be used simultaneously. As mentioned before, constraints are integrated into the algorithm as neighborhood features which influence the assignment of a particular label to a particular object.

OPINE uses the following sources of constraints:

a) *conjunctions* and *disjunctions* in the review text

b) manually supplied *syntactic dependency rule templates* (see Table 2.8). The templates are automatically instantiated by our system with different dependency relationships (premodifier, postmodifier, etc.) in order to obtain syntactic dependency rules which find words with related SO labels.

c) automatically derived *morphological relationships* (*e.g.*, "wonderful" and "wonderfully" are likely to have similar SO labels).

d) WordNet-supplied *synonymy, antonymy, IS-A* and *morphological* relationships between words. For example, *clean* and *neat* are synonyms and so they are likely to have similar SO labels.

Each of the SO label assignment subtasks previously identified is solved using a relaxation labeling step. In the following, we describe in detail how relaxation labeling is used to find SO labels for words in the given review sets.

Finding SO Labels for Words

For many words, a word sense or set of senses is used throughout the review corpus with a consistently positive, negative or neutral connotation (*e.g.*, "great," "awful," etc.). Thus, in many cases, a word w's SO label in the context of a feature f and sentence s will be the same as its SO label in the context of other features and sentences. In the following, we describe how OPINE's relaxation labeling mechanism is used to find a word's dominant SO label in a set of reviews.

For this task, a word's *neighborhood* is defined as the set of words connected to it through conjunctions, disjunctions, and all other relationships previously introduced as sources of constraints.

RL uses an *update equation* to re-estimate the probability of a word label based on its previous probability estimate and the features of its neighborhood (see **Neighborhood Features**). At iteration m, let $q(w, L)_{(m)}$ denote the support function for label L of w and let $P(l(w) = L)_{(m)}$ denote the probability that L is the label of w. $P(l(w) = L)_{(m+1)}$ is computed as follows:

RL Update Equation [12]

$$P(l(w) = L)_{(m+1)} = \frac{P(l(w) = L)_{(m)}(1 + \alpha q(w, L)_{(m)})}{\sum_{L'} P(l(w) = L')_{(m)}(1 + \alpha q(w, L')_{(m)})}$$

where $L' \in \{pos, neg, neutral\}$ and $\alpha > 0$ is an experimentally set constant keeping the numerator and probabilities positive. RL's output is an assignment of dominant SO labels to words.

In the following, we describe in detail the initialization step, the derivation of the support function formula and the use of neighborhood features.

RL Initialization Step OPINE uses a version of Turney's PMI-based approach [13] in order to derive the initial probability estimates $(P(l(w) = L)_{(0)})$ for a subset S of the words (since the process of getting the necessary hitcounts can be expensive, S contains the top 20% most frequent words). OPINE computes a *SO score* $so(w)$ for each w in S as the difference between the PMI of w with positive keywords (*e.g.*, "excellent") and the PMI of w with negative keywords (*e.g.*, "awful"). When $so(w)$ is small, or w rarely co-occurs with the keywords, w is classified as *neutral*. Otherwise, if $so(w) > 0$, w is *positive*, and if $so(w) < 0$, w is *negative*. OPINE then uses the labeled S set in order to compute prior probabilities $P(l(w) = L)$, $L \in \{pos, neg, neutral\}$ by computing the ratio between the number of words in S labeled L and $|S|$. These probabilities will be used as initial probability estimates associated with the labels of the words outside of S.

Support Function The support function computes the probability of each label for word w based on the labels of objects in w's neighborhood N.

Let $A_k = \{(w_j, L_j)|w_j \in N\}$, $0 < k \leq 3^{|N|}$ represent one of the potential assignments of labels to the words in N. Let $P(A_k)_{(m)}$ denote the probability of this particular assignment at iteration m. The *support* for label L of word w at iteration m is :

$$q(w, L)_{(m)} = \sum_{k=1}^{3^{|N|}} P(l(w) = L|A_k)_{(m)} * P(A_k)_{(m)}$$

We assume that the labels of w's neighbors are independent of each other and so the formula becomes:

$$q(w, L)_{(m)} = \sum_{k=1}^{3^{|N|}} P(l(w) = L|A_k)_{(m)} * \prod_{j=1}^{|N|} P(l(w_j) = L_j)_{(m)}$$

Every $P(l(w_j) = L_j)_{(m)}$ term is the estimate for the probability that $l(w_j) = L_j$ (which was computed at iteration m using the RL update equation).

The $P(l(w) = L|A_k)_{(m)}$ term quantifies the influence of a particular label assignment to w's neighborhood over w's label. In the following, we describe how we estimate this term.

Neighborhood Features Each type of word relationship which constrains the assignment of SO labels to words (synonymy, antonymy, conjunction, morphological relations, etc.) is mapped by OPINE to a neighborhood feature. This mapping allows OPINE to simultaneously use multiple independent sources of constraints on the label of a particular word. In the following, we formalize this mapping.

Let T denote the type of a word relationship in R and let $A_{k,T}$ represent the labels assigned by A_k to neighbors of a word w which are connected to w through a relationship of type T . We have $A_k = \bigcup_T A_{k,T}$ and

$$P(l(w) = L|A_k)_{(m)} = P(l(w) = L|\bigcup_T A_{k,T})_{(m)}$$

For each relationship type T, OPINE defines a *neighborhood feature* $f_T(w, L, A_{k,T})$ which computes $P(l(w) = L|A_{k,T})$, the probability that w's label is L given $A_{k,T}$ (see below). $P(l(w) = L|\bigcup_T A_{k,T})_{(m)}$ is estimated combining the information from various features about w's label using the sigmoid function $\sigma()$:

$$P(l(w) = L|A_k)_{(m)} = \sigma(\sum_{i=1}^{j} f_i(w, L, A_{k,i})_{(m)} * c_i)$$

where $c_0, ...c_j$ are weights whose sum is 1 and which reflect OPINE 's confidence in each type of feature.

Given word w, label L, relationship type T and neighborhood label assignment A_k, let N_T represent the subset of w's neighbors connected to w through a type T relationship. The feature f_T computes the probability that w's label is L given the labels assigned by A_k to words in N_T. Using Bayes's Law and assuming that these labels are independent given $l(w)$, we have the following formula for f_T at iteration m:

$$f_T(w, L, A_{k,T})_{(m)} = P(l(w) = L)_{(m)} * \prod_{j=1}^{|N_T|} P(L_j|l(w) = L)$$

$P(L_j|l(w) = L)$ is the probability that word w_j has label L_j if w_j and w are linked by a relationship of type T and w has label L. We make the simplifying assumption that this probability is constant and depends only on T, L and L_j, not on the particular words w_j and w. For each tuple (T, L, L_j), $L, L_j \in \{pos, neg, neutral\}$, OPINE builds a probability table using a small set of bootstrapped positive, negative and neutral words.

Finding (Word, Feature) SO Labels

This subtask is motivated by the existence of frequent words which change their SO label based on associated features, but whose SO labels in the context of the respective features are consistent throughout the reviews (*e.g.*, in the Hotel domain, "hot water" has a consistently positive connotation, whereas "hot room" has a negative one).

In order to solve this task, OPINE initially assigns each (w, f) pair w's SO label. The system then executes a relaxation labeling step during which syntactic relationships between words and, respectively, between features, are used to update the default SO labels whenever necessary. For example, *(hot, room)* appears in the proximity of *(broken, fan)*. If "room" and "fan" are conjoined by *and*, this suggests that "hot" and "broken" have similar SO labels in the context of their respective features. If "broken" has a strongly negative semantic orientation, this fact contributes to OPINE's belief that "hot" may also be negative in this context. Since *(hot, room)* occurs in the vicinity of other such phrases (*e.g.*, *stifling kitchen*), "hot" acquires a negative SO label in the context of "room".

Finding (Word, Feature, Sentence) SO Labels

This subtask is motivated by the existence of (w,f) pairs (*e.g.*, *(big, room)*) for which w's orientation changes depending on the sentence in which the pair appears (*e.g.*, " I hated the big, drafty room because I ended up freezing" vs. "We had a big, luxurious room").

In order to solve this subtask, OPINE first assigns each (w, f, s) tuple an initial label which is simply the SO label for the (w, f) pair. The system then uses syntactic relationships between words and, respectively, features in order to update the SO labels when necessary. For example, in the sentence "I hated the big, drafty room because I ended up freezing.", "big" and "hate" satisfy condition 2 in Table 2.8 and therefore OPINE expects them to have similar SO labels. Since "hate" has a strong negative connotation, "big" acquires a negative SO label in this context.

In order to correctly update SO labels in this last step, OPINE takes into consideration the presence of *negation modifiers*. For example, in the sentence "I don't like a large scanner either," OPINE first replaces the *positive* (w, f) pair *(like, scanner)* with the *negative* labeled pair *(not like, scanner)* and then infers that "large" is likely to have a negative SO label in this context.

After OPINE has computed the most likely SO labels for the head words of each potential opinion phrase in the context of given features and sentences, OPINE can extract opinion phrases and establish their polarity. Phrases whose head words have been assigned *positive* or *negative* labels are retained as *opinion phrases*. Furthermore, the polarity of an opinion phrase o in the context of a feature f and sentence s is given by the SO label assigned to the tuple $(head(o), f, s)$.

2.3.6 Experiments

In this section we evaluate OPINE's performance on the following tasks: finding SO labels of words in the context of known features and sentences (*word*

SO label extraction); distinguishing between opinion and non-opinion phrases in the context of known features and sentences (*opinion phrase extraction*); finding the correct polarity of extracted opinion phrases in the context of known features and sentences (*opinion phrase polarity extraction*).

We first ran OPINE on 13,841 sentences and 538 previously extracted features. OPINE searched for a SO label assignment for 1756 different words in the context of the given features and sentences. We compared OPINE against two baseline methods, **PMI++** and **Hu++**.

PMI++ is an extended version of [1]'s method for finding the SO label of a word or a phrase. For a given (word, feature, sentence) tuple, **PMI++** ignores the sentence, generates a phrase containing the word and the feature (*e.g.*, "clean room") and finds its SO label using PMI statistics. If unsure of the label, **PMI++** finds the orientation of the potential opinion word instead. The search engine queries use domain-specific keywords (*e.g.*, "clean room" + "hotel"), which are dropped if they lead to low counts. **PMI++** also uses morphology information (*e.g.*, *wonderful* and *wonderfully* are likely to have similar semantic orientation labels).

Hu++ is a WordNet-based method for finding a word's context-independent semantic orientation. It extends Hu's adjective labeling method [2] in order to handle nouns, verbs and adverbs and in order to improve coverage. Hu's method starts with two sets of positive and negative words and iteratively grows each one by including synonyms and antonyms from WordNet. The final sets are used to predict the orientation of an incoming word. **Hu++** also makes use of WordNet IS-A relationships (*e.g.*, *problem* IS-A *difficulty*) and morphology information.

Experiments: Word SO Labels

On the task of finding SO labels for words in the context of given features and review sentences, OPINE obtains higher precision than both baseline methods at a small loss in recall with respect to **PMI++**. As described below, this result is due in large part to OPINE's ability to handle context-sensitive opinion words.

We randomly selected 200 (word, feature, sentence) tuples for each word type (adjective, adverb, etc.) and obtained a test set containing 800 tuples. Two annotators assigned positive, negative and neutral labels to each tuple (the inter-annotator agreement was 78%). We retained the tuples on which the annotators agreed as the gold standard. We ran **PMI++** and **Hu++** on the test data and compared the results against OPINE's results on the same data.

In order to quantify the benefits of each of the three steps of our method for finding SO labels, we also compared OPINE with a version which only finds SO labels for words and a version which finds SO labels for words in the context of given features, but doesn't take into account given sentences. We have learned from this comparison that OPINE's precision gain over **PMI++**

Table 2.9. Finding Word Semantic Orientation Labels in the Context of Given Features and Sentences. OPINE's precision is higher than that of **PMI++** and **Hu++**. All results are reported with respect to **PMI++**.

Word POS	PMI++		Hu++		OPINE	
	Precision	Recall	Precision	Recall	Precision	Recall
Adjectives	0.73	0.91	+0.02	-0.17	**+0.07**	**-0.03**
Nouns	0.63	0.92	+0.04	-0.24	**+0.11**	**-0.08**
Verbs	0.71	0.88	+0.03	-0.12	**+0.01**	**-0.01**
Adverbs	0.82	0.92	+0.02	-0.01	**+0.06**	**+0.01**
Avg	0.72	0.91	+0.03	-0.14	**+0.06**	**-0.03**

Table 2.10. Extracting Opinion Phrases and Opinion Phrase Polarity in the Context of Known Features and Sentences. OPINE's precision is higher than that of **PMI++** and **Hu++**. All results are reported with respect to **PMI++**.

Measure	PMI++	Hu++	OPINE
Opinion Extraction: Precision	0.71	+0.06	**+0.08**
Opinion Extraction: Recall	0.78	-0.08	**-0.02**
Opinion Polarity: Precision	0.80	-0.04	**+0.06**
Opinion Polarity: Recall	0.93	+0.07	**-0.04**

and **Hu++** is mostly due to its ability to handle context-sensitive words in a large number of cases.

Although **Hu++** does not handle context-sensitive SO label assignment, its average precision was reasonable (75%) and better than that of **PMI++**. Finding a word's SO label is good enough in the case of strongly positive or negative opinion words, which account for the majority of opinion instances. The method's loss in recall is due to not recognizing words absent from Word-Net (*e.g.*, "depth-adjustable") or not having enough information to classify some words in WordNet.

PMI++ typically does well in the presence of strongly positive or strongly negative words. Its main shortcoming is misclassifying terms such as "basic" or "visible" which change orientation based on context.

Experiments: Opinion Phrases

In order to evaluate OPINE on the tasks of *opinion phrase extraction* and *opinion phrase polarity extraction* in the context of known features and sentences, we used a set of 550 sentences containing previously extracted features. The sentences were annotated with the opinion phrases corresponding to the known features and with the opinion polarity. The task of *opinion phrase polarity extraction* differs from the task of *word SO label assignment* above as follows: the polarity extraction for opinion phrases only examines the assignment of *pos* and *neg* labels to phrases which were found to be opinions (that is, not *neutral*) after the *word SO label assignment* stage is completed.

We compared OPINE with **PMI++** and **Hu++** on the tasks of interest. We found that OPINE had the highest precision on both tasks at a small loss in recall with respect to **PMI++**. OPINE's ability to identify a word's SO label in the context of a given feature and sentence allows the system to correctly extract opinions expressed by words such as "big" or "small," whose semantic orientation varies based on context.

OPINE's performance is negatively affected by a number of factors: parsing errors lead to missed candidate opinions and incorrect opinion polarity assignments; other problems include sparse data (in the case of infrequent opinion words) and complicated opinion expressions (*e.g.*, nested opinions, conditionals, subjunctive expressions).

2.3.7 Ranking Opinion Phrases

OPINE clusters opinions in order to identify the properties to which they refer. Given an opinion cluster A corresponding to some property, OPINE ranks its elements based on their *relative strength*. The probabilities computed at the end of the relaxation-labeling scheme generate an initial opinion ranking.

Table 2.11. Lexical Patterns Used to Derive Opinions' Relative Strength.

$a, (*)$ *even* b	$a, (*)$ *not* b
$a, (*)$ *virtually* b	$a, (*)$ *almost* b
$a, (*)$ *near* b	$a, (*)$ *close to* b
$a, (*)$ *quite* b	$a, (*)$ *mostly* b

In order to improve this initial ranking, OPINE uses additional Web-derived constraints on the relative strength of phrases. As pointed out in [8], patterns such as "a_1, (*) even a_2" are good indicators of how strong a_1 is relative to a_2. To our knowledge, the sparse data problem mentioned in [8] has so far prevented such strength information from being computed for adjectives from typical news corpora. However, the Web allows us to use such patterns in order to refine our opinion rankings. OPINE starts with the pattern mentioned before and bootstraps a set of similar patterns (see Table 2.11). Given a cluster A, queries which instantiate such patterns with pairs of cluster elements are used to derive constraints such as:

$c_1 = (strength(deafening) > strength(loud))$,
$c_2 = (strength(spotless) > strength(clean))$.

OPINE also uses synonymy and antonymy-based constraints, since synonyms and antonyms tend to have similar strength:

$c_3 = (strength(clean) = strength(dirty))$.

The set S of such constraints induces a constraint satisfaction problem (CSP) whose solution is a ranking of the cluster elements affected by S (the remaining elements maintain their default ranking). In the general case, each constraint would be assigned a probability $p(s)$ and OPINE would solve a probabilistic CSP as described in [14]. We simplify the problem by only using constraints supported by multiple patterns in Table 2.11 and by treating them as hard rather than soft constraints. Finding a strength-based ranking of cluster adjectives amounts to a topological sort of the induced constraint graph. In addition to the main opinion word, opinion phrases may contain *intensifiers* (*e.g., very*). The patterns in Table 2.11 are used to compare the strength of modifiers (*e.g., strength(very) > strength(somewhat)*) and modifiers which can be compared in this fashion are retained as *intensifiers*. OPINE uses intensifier rankings to complete the adjective opinion rankings (*e.g.,* "very nice" is stronger than "somewhat nice"). In order to measure OPINE's accuracy on the opinion ranking task, we scored the set of adjective opinion rankings for the top 30 most frequent properties as follows: if two consecutive opinions in the ranking are in the wrong order according to a human judge, we labeled the ranking as incorrect. The resulting accuracy of OPINE on this task was 73%.

2.4 Related Work

The review-mining work most relevant to our research is described in [2], [15] and [7]. All three systems identify product features from reviews, but OPINE significantly improves on the first two and its reported precision is comparable to that of the third (although we were not able to perform a direct comparison, as the system and the data sets are not available). [2] doesn't assess candidate features, so its precision is lower than OPINE's. [15] employs an iterative semi-automatic approach which requires human input at every iteration. Neither model explicitly addresses *composite* (feature of feature) or *implicit* features. [7] uses a sophisticated feature extraction algorithm whose precision is comparable to OPINE's much simpler approach; OPINE's use of meronymy lexico-syntactic patterns is inspired by papers such as [16] and [17]. Other systems [18, 19] also look at Web product reviews but they do not extract opinions about particular product features.

Recognizing the subjective character and polarity of words, phrases or sentences has been addressed by many authors, including [13, 20, 10]. Most recently, [21] reports on the use of spin models to infer the semantic orientation of words. The chapter's global optimization approach and use of multiple sources of constraints on a word's semantic orientation is similar to ours, but the mechanism differs and the described approach omits the use of syntactic information. Subjective phrases are used by [1, 22, 19, 9] and others in order to classify reviews or sentences as positive or negative. So far, OPINE's focus has been on extracting and analyzing opinion phrases corresponding to specific features in specific sentences, rather than on determining sentence or review polarity. To our knowledge, [7] and [23] describe the only other systems which address the problem of finding context-specific word semantic orientation. [7] uses a large set of human-generated patterns which determine the final semantic orientation of a word (in the context of a product feature) given its prior semantic orientation provided by an initially supplied word list. OPINE's approach, while independently developed, amounts to a more general version of the approach taken by [7]: OPINE automatically computes both the prior and final word semantic orientation using a relaxation labeling scheme which accommodates multiple constraints. [23] uses a supervised approach incorporating a large set of features in order to learn the types of linguistic contexts which alter a word's prior semantic orientation. The paper's task is different than the one addressed by OPINE and [7], as it involves open-domain text and lacks any information about the target of a particular opinion.

[13] suggests using the magnitude of the PMI-based SO score as an indicator of the opinion's strength while [24, 25] use a supervised approach with large lexical and syntactic feature sets in order to distinguish among a few strength levels for sentence clauses. OPINE's unsupervised approach combines Turney's suggestion with a set of strong ranking constraints in order to derive opinion phrase rankings.

2.5 Conclusions and Future Work

OPINE is an unsupervised information extraction system which extracts fine-grained features, and associated opinions, from reviews. OPINE's use of the Web as a corpus helps identify product features with improved precision compared with previous work. OPINE uses a novel relaxation-labeling technique to determine the semantic orientation of potential opinion words in the context of the extracted product features and specific review sentences; this technique allows the system to identify customer opinions and their polarity with high precision and recall. Current and future work includes identifying and analyzing opinion sentences as well as extending OPINE's techniques to open-domain text.

2.6 Acknowledgments

We would like to thank the members of the KnowItAll project for their comments. Michael Gamon, Costas Boulis, and Adam Carlson have also provided valuable feedback. We thank Minquing Hu and Bing Liu for providing their data sets and for their comments. Finally, we are grateful to Bernadette Minton and Fetch Technologies for their help in collecting additional reviews. This research was supported in part by NSF grant IIS-0312988, DARPA contract NBCHD030010, ONR grant N00014-02-1-0324 as well as gifts from Google and the Turing Center.

References

1. Turney, P.D.: Thumbs up or thumbs down? semantic orientation applied to unsupervised classification of reviews. In: Procs. of ACL. (2002) 417–424

2. Hu, M., Liu, B.: Mining and Summarizing Customer Reviews. In: Procs. of KDD, Seattle, WA (2004) 168–177
3. Lin, D.: Dependency-based evaluation of MINIPAR. In: Procs. of ICLRE'98 Workshop on Evaluation of Parsing Systems. (1998)
4. Etzioni, O., Cafarella, M., Downey, D., Kok, S., Popescu, A., Shaked, T., Soderland, S., Weld, D., Yates, A.: Unsupervised named-entity extraction from the web: An experimental study. Artificial Intelligence **165**(1) (2005) 91–134
5. Turney, P.D.: Mining the Web for Synonyms: PMI-IR versus LSA on TOEFL. In: Procs. of the Twelfth European Conference on Machine Learning (ECML), Freiburg, Germany (2001) 491–502
6. Popescu, A., Yates, A., Etzioni, O.: Class extraction from the World Wide Web. In: AAAI-04 Workshop on Adaptive Text Extraction and Mining. (2004) 68–73
7. Yi, J., Nasukawa, T., Bunescu, R., Niblack, W.: Sentiment Analyzer: Extracting Sentiments about a Given Topic Using Natural Language Processing Techniques. In: Procs. of ICDM. (2003) 1073–1083
8. Hatzivassiloglou, V., McKeown, K.: Towards the automatic identification of adjectival scales: clustering adjectives according to meaning. In: Procs. of ACL. (1993) 182–192
9. Kim, S., Hovy, E.: Determining the sentiment of opinions. In: Procs. of COLING. (2004)
10. Hatzivassiloglou, V., McKeown, K.: Predicting the semantic orientation of adjectives. In: Procs. of ACL/EACL. (1997) 174–181
11. Hummel, R., Zucker, S.: On the foundations of relaxation labeling processes. In: PAMI. (1983) 267–287
12. Rangarajan, A.: Self annealing and self annihilation: unifying deterministic annealing and relaxation labeling. In: Pattern Recognition, 33:635-649. (2000)
13. Turney, P.: Inference of Semantic Orientation from Association. In: CoRR cs. CL/0309034. (2003)
14. Fargier, H., Lang, J.: A constraint satisfaction framework for decision under uncertainty. In: Procs. of UAI. (1995) 167–174
15. Kobayashi, N., Inui, K., Tateishi, K., Fukushima, T.: Collecting Evaluative Expressions for Opinion Extraction. In: Procs. of IJCNLP. (2004) 596–605
16. Berland, M., Charniak, E.: Finding parts in very large corpora. In: Procs. of ACL. (1999) 57–64
17. Almuhareb, A., Poesio, M.: Attribute-based and value-based clustering: An evaluation. In: Procs. of EMNLP. (2004) 158–165
18. Morinaga, S., Yamanishi, K., Tateishi, K., Fukushima, T.: Mining product reputations on the web. In: Procs. of KDD. (2002) 341–349
19. Kushal, D., Lawrence, S., Pennock, D.: Mining the peanut gallery: Opinion extraction and semantic classification of product reviews. In: Procs. of WWW. (2003)
20. Riloff, E., Wiebe, J., Wilson, T.: Learning Subjective Nouns Using Extraction Pattern Bootstrapping. In: Procs. of CoNLL. (2003) 25–32s
21. Takamura, H., Inui, T., Okumura, M.: Extracting Semantic Orientations of Words Using Spin Model. In: Procs. of ACL. (2005) 133–141
22. Pang, B, L.L., Vaithyanathan, S.: Thumbs up? sentiment classification using machine learning techniques. In: Procs. of EMNLP. (2002) 79–86
23. Wilson, T., Wiebe, J., Hoffmann, P.: Recognizing Contextual Polarity in Phrase-Level Sentiment Analysis. In: Procs. of HLT-EMNLP. (2005)

24. Wilson, T., Wiebe, J., Hwa, R.: Just how mad are you? finding strong and weak opinion clauses. In: Procs. of AAAI. (2004) 761–769
25. Gamon, M.: Sentiment classification on customer feedback data: Noisy data, large feature vectors and the role of linguistic analysis. In: Procs. of COLING. (2004) 841–847

3

Extracting Relations from Text: From Word Sequences to Dependency Paths

Razvan C. Bunescu and Raymond J. Mooney

3.1 Introduction

Extracting semantic relationships between entities mentioned in text documents is an important task in natural language processing. The various types of relationships that are discovered between mentions of entities can provide useful structured information to a text mining system [1]. Traditionally, the task specifies a predefined set of entity types and relation types that are deemed to be relevant to a potential user and that are likely to occur in a particular text collection. For example, information extraction from newspaper articles is usually concerned with identifying mentions of people, organizations, locations, and extracting useful relations between them. Relevant relation types range from social relationships, to roles that people hold inside an organization, to relations between organizations, to physical locations of people and organizations. Scientific publications in the biomedical domain offer a type of narrative that is very different from the newspaper discourse. A significant effort is currently spent on automatically extracting relevant pieces of information from Medline, an online collection of biomedical abstracts. Proteins, genes, and cells are examples of relevant entities in this task, whereas subcellular localizations and protein-protein interactions are two of the relation types that have received significant attention recently. The inherent difficulty of the relation extraction task is further compounded in the biomedical domain by the relative scarcity of tools able to analyze the corresponding type of narrative. Most existing natural language processing tools, such as tokenizers, sentence segmenters, part-of-speech (POS) taggers, shallow or full parsers are trained on newspaper corpora, and consequently they incur a loss in accuracy when applied to biomedical literature. Therefore, information extraction systems developed for biological corpora need to be robust to POS or parsing errors, or to give reasonable performance using shallower but more reliable information, such as chunking instead of full parsing.

In this chapter, we present two recent approaches to relation extraction that differ in terms of the kind of linguistic information they use:

1. In the first method (Section 3.2), each potential relation is represented implicitly as a vector of features, where each feature corresponds to a *word sequence* anchored at the two entities forming the relationship. A relation extraction system

is trained based on the subsequence kernel from [2]. This kernel is further generalized so that words can be replaced with word classes, thus enabling the use of information coming from POS tagging, named entity recognition, chunking, or Wordnet [3].

2. In the second approach (Section 3.3), the representation is centered on the shortest *dependency path* between the two entities in the dependency graph of the sentence. Because syntactic analysis is essential in this method, its applicability is limited to domains where syntactic parsing gives reasonable accuracy.

Entity recognition, a prerequisite for relation extraction, is usually cast as a sequence tagging problem, in which words are tagged as being either outside any entity, or inside a particular type of entity. Most approaches to entity tagging are therefore based on probabilistic models for labeling sequences, such as Hidden Markov Models [4], Maximum Entropy Markov Models [5], or Conditional Random Fields [6], and obtain a reasonably high accuracy. In the two information extraction methods presented in this chapter, we assume that the entity recognition task was done and focus only on the relation extraction part.

3.2 Subsequence Kernels for Relation Extraction

One of the first approaches to extracting interactions between proteins from biomedical abstracts is that of Blaschke *et al.*, described in [7, 8]. Their system is based on a set of manually developed rules, where each rule (or frame) is a sequence of words (or POS tags) and two protein-name tokens. Between every two adjacent words is a number indicating the maximum number of intervening words allowed when matching the rule to a sentence. An example rule is *"interaction of (3) <P> (3) with (3) <P>"*, where '<P>' is used to denote a protein name. A sentence matches the rule if and only if it satisfies the word constraints in the given order and respects the respective word gaps.

In [9] the authors described a new method ELCS (Extraction using Longest Common Subsequences) that automatically learns such rules. ELCS' rule representation is similar to that in [7, 8], except that it currently does not use POS tags, but allows disjunctions of words. An example rule learned by this system is *"- (7) interaction (0) [between | of] (5) <P> (9) <P> (17) ."* Words in square brackets separated by '|' indicate disjunctive lexical constraints, i.e., one of the given words must match the sentence at that position. The numbers in parentheses between adjacent constraints indicate the maximum number of unconstrained words allowed between the two.

3.2.1 Capturing Relation Patterns with a String Kernel

Both Blaschke and ELCS do relation extraction based on a limited set of matching rules, where a rule is simply a sparse (gappy) subsequence of words or POS tags anchored on the two protein-name tokens. Therefore, the two methods share a common limitation: either through manual selection (Blaschke), or as a result of a greedy learning procedure (ELCS), they end up using only a subset of all possible anchored sparse subsequences. Ideally, all such anchored sparse subsequences would be used as features, with weights reflecting their relative accuracy. However, explicitly creating for each sentence a vector with a position for each such feature is infeasible, due to the high dimensionality of the feature space. Here, we exploit dual learning algorithms that process examples only via computing their dot-products, such as in Support Vector Machines (SVMs) [10, 11]. An SVM learner tries to find a hyperplane that separates positive from negative examples and at the same time maximizes the separation (margin) between them. This type of max-margin separator has been shown both theoretically and empirically to resist overfitting and to provide good generalization performance on unseen examples.

Computing the dot-product (i.e., the kernel) between the features vectors associated with two relation examples amounts to calculating the number of common anchored subsequences between the two sentences. This is done efficiently by modifying the dynamic programming algorithm used in the string kernel from [2] to account only for common sparse subsequences constrained to contain the two protein-name tokens. The feature space is further prunned down by utilizing the following property of natural language statements: when a sentence asserts a relationship between two entity mentions, it generally does this using one of the following four patterns:

• [FB] Fore–Between: words before and between the two entity mentions are simultaneously used to express the relationship. Examples: 'interaction of $\langle P_1 \rangle$ with $\langle P_2 \rangle$,' 'activation of $\langle P_1 \rangle$ by $\langle P_2 \rangle$.'

• [B] Between: only words between the two entities are essential for asserting the relationship. Examples: '$\langle P_1 \rangle$ interacts with $\langle P_2 \rangle$,' '$\langle P_1 \rangle$ is activated by $\langle P_2 \rangle$.'

• [BA] Between–After: words between and after the two entity mentions are simultaneously used to express the relationship. Examples: '$\langle P_1 \rangle - \langle P_2 \rangle$ complex,' '$\langle P_1 \rangle$ and $\langle P_2 \rangle$ interact.'

• [M] Modifier: the two entity mentions have no words between them. Examples: *U.S. troops* (a ROLE:STAFF relation), *Serbian general* (ROLE:CITIZEN).

While the first three patterns are sufficient to capture most cases of interactions between proteins, the last pattern is needed to account for various relationships expressed through noun-noun or adjective-noun compounds in the newspaper corpora.

Another observation is that all these patterns use at most four words to express the relationship (not counting the two entity names). Consequently, when computing the relation kernel, we restrict the counting of common anchored subsequences only to those having one of the four types described above, with a maximum word-length of four. This type of feature selection leads not only to a faster kernel computation, but also to less overfitting, which results in increased accuracy.

The patterns enumerated above are completely lexicalized and consequently their performance is limited by data sparsity. This can be alleviated by categorizing words into classes with varying degrees of generality, and then allowing patterns to use both words and their classes. Examples of word classes are POS tags and generalizations over POS tags such as Noun, Active Verb, or Passive Verb. The entity type can also be used if the word is part of a known named entity. Also, if the sentence is segmented into syntactic chunks such as noun phrases (NP) or verb phrases (VP), the system may choose to consider only the head word from each chunk, together with the type of the chunk as another word class. Content words such as nouns and verbs can also be related to their synsets via WordNet. Patterns then will consist of sparse subsequences of words, POS tags, generalized POS tags, entity and chunk types, or WordNet synsets. For example, 'Noun of $\langle P_1 \rangle$ by $\langle P_2 \rangle$' is an FB pattern based on words and general POS tags.

3.2.2 A Generalized Subsequence Kernel

Let $\Sigma_1, \Sigma_2, ..., \Sigma_k$ be some disjoint feature spaces. Following the example in Section 3.2.1, Σ_1 could be the set of words, Σ_2 the set of POS tags, etc. Let $\Sigma_\times = \Sigma_1 \times \Sigma_2 \times ... \times \Sigma_k$ be the set of all possible feature vectors, where a feature vector would be associated with each position in a sentence. Given two feature vectors $x, y \in \Sigma_\times$, let $c(x, y)$ denote the number of common features between x and y. The next notation follows that introduced in [2]. Thus, let s, t be two sequences over the finite set $\Sigma_\times$, and let $|s|$ denote the length of $s = s_1...s_{|s|}$. The sequence $s[i{:}j]$ is the contiguous subsequence $s_i...s_j$ of s. Let $\mathbf{i} = (i_1, ..., i_{|\mathbf{i}|})$ be a sequence of $|\mathbf{i}|$ indices in s, in ascending order. We define the length $l(\mathbf{i})$ *of the index sequence* $\mathbf{i}$ *in* s as $i_{|\mathbf{i}|} - i_1 + 1$. Similarly, $\mathbf{j}$ is a sequence of $|\mathbf{j}|$ indices in t.

Let $\Sigma_\cup = \Sigma_1 \cup \Sigma_2 \cup ... \cup \Sigma_k$ be the set of all possible features. We say that the sequence $u \in \Sigma_\cup^*$ is a (sparse) subsequence of s if there is a sequence of $|u|$ indices $\mathbf{i}$ such that $u_k \in s_{i_k}$, for all $k = 1, ..., |u|$. Equivalently, we write $u \prec s[\mathbf{i}]$ as a shorthand for the component-wise '$\in$' relationship between u and $s[\mathbf{i}]$.

Finally, let $K_n(s, t, \lambda)$ (Equation 3.1) be the number of weighted sparse subsequences u of length n common to s and t (i.e., $u \prec s[\mathbf{i}]$, $u \prec t[\mathbf{j}]$), where the weight of u is $\lambda^{l(\mathbf{i})+l(\mathbf{j})}$, for some $\lambda \leq 1$.

$$K_n(s, t, \lambda) = \sum_{u \in \Sigma_\cup^n} \sum_{\mathbf{i}:u \prec s[\mathbf{i}]} \sum_{\mathbf{j}:u \prec t[\mathbf{j}]} \lambda^{l(\mathbf{i})+l(\mathbf{j})} \qquad (3.1)$$

Let $\mathbf{i}$ and $\mathbf{j}$ be two index sequences of length n. By definition, for every k between 1 and n, $c(s_{i_k}, t_{j_k})$ returns the number of common features between s and t at positions i_k and j_k. If $c(s_{i_k}, t_{j_k}) = 0$ for some k, there are no common feature sequences of length n between $s[\mathbf{i}]$ and $t[\mathbf{j}]$. On the other hand, if $c(s_{i_k}, t_{j_k})$ is greater than 1, this means that there is more than one common feature that can be used at position k to obtain a common feature sequence of length n. Consequently, the number of common feature sequences of length n between $s[\mathbf{i}]$ and $t[\mathbf{j}]$, i.e., the size of the set $\{u \in \Sigma_\cup^n | u \prec s[\mathbf{i}], u \prec t[\mathbf{j}]\}$, is given by $\prod_{k=1}^n c(s_{i_k}, t_{j_k})$. Therefore, $K_n(s, t, \lambda)$ can be rewritten as in Equation 3.2:

$$K_n(s, t, \lambda) = \sum_{\mathbf{i}:|\mathbf{i}|=n} \sum_{\mathbf{j}:|\mathbf{j}|=n} \prod_{k=1}^n c(s_{i_k}, t_{j_k}) \lambda^{l(\mathbf{i})+l(\mathbf{j})} \qquad (3.2)$$

We use λ as a decaying factor that penalizes longer subsequences. For sparse subsequences, this means that wider gaps will be penalized more, which is exactly the desired behavior for our patterns. Through them, we try to capture head-modifier dependencies that are important for relation extraction; for lack of reliable dependency information, the larger the word gap is between two words, the less confident we are in the existence of a head-modifier relationship between them.

To enable an efficient computation of K_n, we use the auxiliary function K_n' with a definition similar to K_n, the only difference being that it counts the length from the beginning of the particular subsequence u to the end of the strings s and t, as illustrated in Equation 3.3:

$$K_n'(s, t, \lambda) = \sum_{u \in \Sigma_\cup^n} \sum_{\mathbf{i}:u \prec s[\mathbf{i}]} \sum_{\mathbf{j}:u \prec t[\mathbf{j}]} \lambda^{|s|+|t|-i_1-j_1+2} \qquad (3.3)$$

An equivalent formula for $K_n'(s,t,\lambda)$ is obtained by changing the exponent of λ from Equation 3.2 to $|s| + |t| - i_1 - j_1 + 2$.

Based on all definitions above, K_n is computed in $O(kn|s||t|)$ time, by modifying the recursive computation from [2] with the new factor $c(x,y)$, as shown in Figure 3.1. As in [2], the complexity of computing $K_i'(s,t)$ is reduced to $O(|s||t|)$ by first evaluating another auxiliary factor $K_i''(s,t)$. In Figure 3.1, the sequence sx is the result of appending x to s (with ty defined in a similar way). To avoid clutter, the parameter λ is not shown in the argument list of K and K', unless it is instantiated to a specific constant.

$$K_0'(s,t) = 1, \; for \; all \; s,t$$
$$K_i'(s,t) = 0, \; if \; \min(|s|,|t|) < i$$
$$K_i''(s,\emptyset) = 0, \; for \; all \; i,s$$
$$K_i''(sx,ty) = \lambda K_i''(sx,t) + \lambda^2 K_{i-1}'(s,t) \cdot c(x,y)$$
$$K_i'(sx,t) = \lambda K_i'(s,t) + K_i''(sx,t)$$
$$K_n(s,t) = 0, \; if \; \min(|s|,|t|) < n$$
$$K_n(sx,t) = K_n(s,t) + \sum_j \lambda^2 K_{n-1}'(s,t[1:j-1]) \cdot c(x,t[j])$$

Fig. 3.1. Computation of subsequence kernel.

3.2.3 Computing the Relation Kernel

As described at the beginning of Section 3.2, the input consists of a set of sentences, where each sentence contains exactly two entities (protein names in the case of interaction extraction). In Figure 3.2 we show the segments that will be used for computing the relation kernel between two example sentences s and t. In sentence s, for instance, x_1 and x_2 are the two entities, s_f is the sentence segment before x_1, s_b is the segment between x_1 and x_2, and s_a is the sentence segment after x_2. For convenience, we also include the auxiliary segment $s_b' = x_1 s_b x_2$, whose span is computed as $l(s_b') = l(s_b) + 2$ (in all length computations, we consider x_1 and x_2 as contributing one unit only).

The relation kernel computes the number of common patterns between two sentences s and t, where the set of patterns is restricted to the four types introduced in Section 3.2.1. Therefore, the kernel $rK(s,t)$ is expressed as the sum of four sub-kernels: $fbK(s,t)$ counting the number of common fore–between patterns, $bK(s,t)$ for between patterns, $baK(s,t)$ for between–after patterns, and $mK(s,t)$ for modifier patterns, as in Figure 3.3. The symbol $\mathbb{1}$ is used there as a shorthand for the indicator function, which is 1 if the argument is true, and 0 otherwise.

The first three sub-kernels include in their computation the counting of common subsequences between s_b' and t_b'. In order to speed up the computation, all these

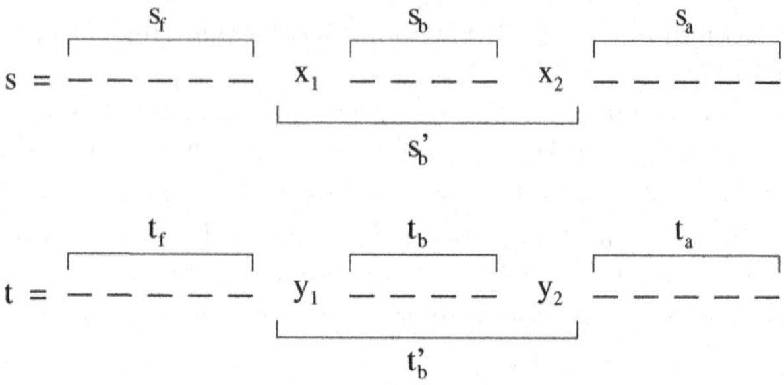

Fig. 3.2. Sentence segments.

$$rK(s,t) = fbK(s,t) + bK(s,t) + baK(s,t) + mK(s,t)$$

$$bK_i(s,t) = K_i(s_b, t_b, 1) \cdot c(x_1, y_1) \cdot c(x_2, y_2) \cdot \lambda^{l(s'_b) + l(t'_b)}$$

$$fbK(s,t) = \sum_{i,j} bK_i(s,t) \cdot K'_j(s_f, t_f), \quad 1 \le i,\ 1 \le j,\ i+j < fb_{max}$$

$$bK(s,t) = \sum_i bK_i(s,t), \quad 1 \le i \le b_{max}$$

$$baK(s,t) = \sum_{i,j} bK_i(s,t) \cdot K'_j(s_a^-, t_a^-), \quad 1 \le i,\ 1 \le j,\ i+j < ba_{max}$$

$$mK(s,t) = \mathbb{1}(s_b = \emptyset) \cdot \mathbb{1}(t_b = \emptyset) \cdot c(x_1, y_1) \cdot c(x_2, y_2) \cdot \lambda^{2+2},$$

Fig. 3.3. Computation of relation kernel.

common counts are calculated separately in bK_i, which is defined as the number of common subsequences of length i between s'_b and t'_b, anchored at x_1/x_2 and y_1/y_2 respectively (i.e., constrained to start at x_1 in s'_b and y_1 in t'_b, and to end at x_2 in s'_b and y_2 in t'_b). Then fbK simply counts the number of subsequences that match j positions before the first entity and i positions between the entities, constrained to have length less than a constant fb_{max}. To obtain a similar formula for baK we simply use the reversed (mirror) version of segments s_a and t_a (e.g., s_a^- and t_a^-). In Section 3.2.1 we observed that all three subsequence patterns use at most 4 words to express a relation, therefore the constants fb_{max}, b_{max} and ba_{max} are set to 4. Kernels K and K' are computed using the procedure described in Section 3.2.2.

3.3 A Dependency-Path Kernel for Relation Extraction

The pattern examples from Section 3.2.1 show the two entity mentions, together with the set of words that are relevant for their relationship. A closer analysis of

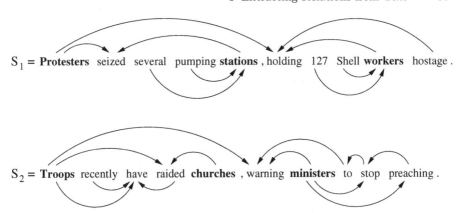

S_1 = **Protesters** seized several pumping **stations** , holding 127 Shell **workers** hostage .

S_2 = **Troops** recently have raided **churches** , warning **ministers** to stop preaching .

Fig. 3.4. Sentences as dependency graphs.

these examples reveals that all relevant words form a shortest path between the two entities in a graph structure where edges correspond to relations between a word (head) and its dependents. For example, Figure 3.4 shows the full dependency graphs for two sentences from the ACE (Automated Content Extraction) newspaper corpus [12], in which words are represented as nodes and word-word dependencies are represented as directed edges. A subset of these word-word dependencies capture the predicate-argument relations present in the sentence. Arguments are connected to their target predicates either directly through an arc pointing to the predicate ('troops → raided'), or indirectly through a preposition or infinitive particle ('warning ← to ← stop'). Other types of word-word dependencies account for modifier-head relationships present in adjective-noun compounds ('several → stations'), noun-noun compounds ('pumping → stations'), or adverb-verb constructions ('recently → raided').

Word-word dependencies are typically categorized in two classes as follows:

- **[Local Dependencies]** These correspond to local predicate-argument (or head-modifier) constructions such as 'troops → raided', or 'pumping → stations' in Figure 3.4.
- **[Non-local Dependencies]** Long-distance dependencies arise due to various linguistic constructions such as coordination, extraction, raising and control. In Figure 3.4, among non-local dependencies are 'troops → warning', or 'ministers → preaching'.

A Context Free Grammar (CFG) parser can be used to extract local dependencies, which for each sentence form a dependency tree. Mildly context sensitive formalisms such as Combinatory Categorial Grammar (CCG) [13] model word-word dependencies more directly and can be used to extract both local and long-distance dependencies, giving rise to a directed acyclic graph, as illustrated in Figure 3.4.

3.3.1 The Shortest Path Hypothesis

If e_1 and e_2 are two entities mentioned in the same sentence such that they are observed to be in a relationship R, then the contribution of the sentence dependency

Table 3.1. Shortest Path representation of relations.

Relation Instance	Shortest Path in Undirected Dependency Graph
S_1:protesters AT stations	**protesters** $\rightarrow$ seized $\leftarrow$ **stations**
S_1:workers AT stations	**workers** $\rightarrow$ holding $\leftarrow$ protesters $\rightarrow$ seized $\leftarrow$ **stations**
S_2:troops AT churches	**troops** $\rightarrow$ raided $\leftarrow$ **churches**
S_2:ministers AT churches	**ministers** $\rightarrow$ warning $\leftarrow$ troops $\rightarrow$ raided $\leftarrow$ **churches**

graph to establishing the relationship $R(e_1, e_2)$ is almost exclusively concentrated in the shortest path between e_1 and e_2 in the undirected version of the dependency graph.

If entities e_1 and e_2 are arguments of the same predicate, then the shortest path between them will pass through the predicate, which may be connected directly to the two entities, or indirectly through prepositions. If e_1 and e_2 belong to different predicate-argument structures that share a common argument, then the shortest path will pass through this argument. This is the case with the shortest path between 'stations' and 'workers' in Figure 3.4, passing through 'protesters,' which is an argument common to both predicates 'holding' and 'seized'. In Table 3.1, we show the paths corresponding to the four relation instances encoded in the ACE corpus for the two sentences from Figure 3.4. All these paths support the LOCATED relationship. For the first path, it is reasonable to infer that if a PERSON entity (e.g., 'protesters') is doing some action (e.g., 'seized') to a FACILITY entity (e.g., 'station'), then the PERSON entity is LOCATED at that FACILITY entity. The second path captures the fact that the same PERSON entity (e.g., 'protesters') is doing two actions (e.g., 'holding' and 'seized') , one action to a PERSON entity (e.g., 'workers'), and the other action to a FACILITY entity (e.g., 'station'). A reasonable inference in this case is that the 'workers' are LOCATED at the 'station'.

In Figure 3.5, we show three more examples of the LOCATED (AT) relationship as dependency paths created from one or two predicate-argument structures. The second example is an interesting case, as it illustrates how annotation decisions are accommodated in our approach. Using a reasoning similar with that from the previous paragraph, it is reasonable to infer that 'troops' are LOCATED in 'vans,' and that 'vans' are LOCATED in 'city'. However, because 'vans' is not an ACE markable, it cannot participate in an annotated relationship. Therefore, 'troops' is annotated as being LOCATED in 'city,' which makes sense due to the transitivity of the relation LOCATED. In our approach, this leads to shortest paths that pass through two or more predicate-argument structures.

The last relation example is a case where there exist multiple shortest paths in the dependency graph between the same two entities – there are actually two different paths, with each path replicated into three similar paths due to coordination. Our current approach considers only one of the shortest paths, nevertheless it seems reasonable to investigate using all of them as multiple sources of evidence for relation extraction.

There may be cases where e_1 and e_2 belong to predicate-argument structures that have no argument in common. However, because the dependency graph is always connected, we are guaranteed to find a shortest path between the two entities. In general, we shall find a shortest sequence of predicate-argument structures with target predicates $P_1, P_2, ..., P_n$ such that e_1 is an argument of P_1, e_2 is an argument of P_n, and any two consecutive predicates P_i and P_{i+1} share a common argument (where by "argument" we mean both arguments and complements).

---

(1) He had no regrets for **his** actions in **Brcko**.

his $\rightarrow$ actions $\leftarrow$ in $\leftarrow$ **Brcko**

(2) U.S. **troops** today acted for the first time to capture an alleged Bosnian war criminal, rushing from unmarked vans parked in the northern Serb-dominated **city** of Bijeljina.

troops $\rightarrow$ rushing $\leftarrow$ from $\leftarrow$ vans $\rightarrow$ parked $\leftarrow$ in $\leftarrow$ **city**

(3) Jelisic created an atmosphere of terror at the **camp** by killing, abusing and threatening the **detainees**.

detainees $\rightarrow$ killing $\leftarrow$ Jelisic $\rightarrow$ created $\leftarrow$ at $\leftarrow$ **camp**
detainees $\rightarrow$ abusing $\leftarrow$ Jelisic $\rightarrow$ created $\leftarrow$ at $\leftarrow$ **camp**
detainees $\rightarrow$ threatning $\leftarrow$ Jelisic $\rightarrow$ created $\leftarrow$ at $\leftarrow$ **camp**
detainees $\rightarrow$ killing $\rightarrow$ by $\rightarrow$ created $\leftarrow$ at $\leftarrow$ **camp**
detainees $\rightarrow$ abusing $\rightarrow$ by $\rightarrow$ created $\leftarrow$ at $\leftarrow$ **camp**
detainees $\rightarrow$ threatening $\rightarrow$ by $\rightarrow$ created $\leftarrow$ at $\leftarrow$ **camp**

Fig. 3.5. Relation examples.

3.3.2 Learning with Dependency Paths

The shortest path between two entities in a dependency graph offers a very condensed representation of the information needed to assess their relationship. A dependency path is represented as a sequence of words interspersed with arrows that indicate the orientation of each dependency, as illustrated in Table 3.1. These paths, however, are completely lexicalized and consequently their performance will be limited by data sparsity. The solution is to allow paths to use both words and their word classes, similar with the approach taken for the subsequence patterns in Section 3.2.1.

The set of features can then be defined as a Cartesian product over words and word classes, as illustrated in Figure 3.6 for the dependency path between 'protesters' and 'station' in sentence S_1. In this representation, sparse or contiguous subsequences of nodes along the lexicalized dependency path (i.e., path fragments) are included as features simply by replacing the rest of the nodes with their corresponding generalizations.

Examples of features generated by Figure 3.6 are "protesters $\rightarrow$ seized $\leftarrow$ stations," "Noun $\rightarrow$ Verb $\leftarrow$ Noun," "PERSON $\rightarrow$ seized $\leftarrow$ FACILITY," or "PERSON $\rightarrow$ Verb $\leftarrow$ FACILITY." The total number of features generated by this dependency path is $4 \times 1 \times 3 \times 1 \times 4$.

$$\begin{bmatrix} \text{protesters} \\ \text{NNS} \\ \text{Noun} \\ \text{PERSON} \end{bmatrix} \times [\rightarrow] \times \begin{bmatrix} \text{seized} \\ \text{VBD} \\ \text{Verb} \end{bmatrix} \times [\leftarrow] \times \begin{bmatrix} \text{stations} \\ \text{NNS} \\ \text{Noun} \\ \text{FACILITY} \end{bmatrix}$$

Fig. 3.6. Feature generation from dependency path.

For verbs and nouns (and their respective word classes) occurring along a dependency path we also use an additional suffix '(-)' to indicate a negative polarity item. In the case of verbs, this suffix is used when the verb (or an attached auxiliary) is modified by a negative polarity adverb such as 'not' or 'never.' Nouns get the negative suffix whenever they are modified by negative determiners such as 'no,' 'neither' or 'nor.' For example, the phrase "He never went to Paris" is associated with the dependency path "He $\rightarrow$ went(-) $\leftarrow$ to $\leftarrow$ Paris."

As in Section 3.2, we use kernel SVMs in order to avoid working explicitly with high-dimensional dependency path feature vectors. Computing the dot-product (i.e., kernel) between two relation examples amounts to calculating the number of common features (i.e., paths) between the two examples. If $x = x_1 x_2 ... x_m$ and $y = y_1 y_2 ... y_n$ are two relation examples, where x_i denotes the set of word classes corresponding to position i (as in Figure 3.6), then the number of common features between x and y is computed as in Equation 3.4.

$$K(\mathbf{x}, \mathbf{y}) = \mathbb{1}(m = n) \cdot \prod_{i=1}^{n} c(x_i, y_i) \tag{3.4}$$

where $c(x_i, y_i) = |x_i \cap y_i|$ is the number of common word classes between x_i and y_i.

This is a simple kernel, whose computation takes $O(n)$ time. If the two paths have different lengths, they correspond to different ways of expressing a relationship – for instance, they may pass through a different number of predicate argument structures. Consequently, the kernel is defined to be 0 in this case. Otherwise, it is the product of the number of common word classes at each position in the two paths. As an example, let us consider two instances of the LOCATED relationship, and their corresponding dependency paths:

1. 'his actions in **Brcko**' (**his** $\rightarrow$ actions $\leftarrow$ in $\leftarrow$ **Brcko**).
2. 'his arrival in **Beijing**' (**his** $\rightarrow$ arrival $\leftarrow$ in $\leftarrow$ **Beijing**).

Their representation as a sequence of sets of word classes is given by:

1. $x = [x_1\ x_2\ x_3\ x_4\ x_5\ x_6\ x_7]$, where $x_1 = \{\text{his, PRP, PERSON}\}$, $x_2 = \{\rightarrow\}$, $x_3 = \{\text{actions, NNS, Noun}\}$, $x_4 = \{\leftarrow\}$, $x_5 = \{\text{in, IN}\}$, $x_6 = \{\leftarrow\}$, $x_7 = \{\text{Brcko, NNP, Noun, LOCATION}\}$
2. $y = [y_1\ y_2\ y_3\ y_4\ y_5\ y_6\ y_7]$, where $y_1 = \{\text{his, PRP, PERSON}\}$, $y_2 = \{\rightarrow\}$, $y_3 = \{\text{arrival, NN, Noun}\}$, $y_4 = \{\leftarrow\}$, $y_5 = \{\text{in, IN}\}$, $y_6 = \{\leftarrow\}$, $y_7 = \{\text{Beijing, NNP, Noun, LOCATION}\}$

Based on the formula from Equation 3.4, the kernel is computed as $K(x, y) = 3 \times 1 \times 1 \times 1 \times 2 \times 1 \times 3 = 18$.

3.4 Experimental Evaluation

The two relation kernels described above are evaluated on the task of extracting relations from two corpora with different types of narrative, which are described in more detail in the following sections. In both cases, we assume that the entities and their labels are known. All preprocessing steps – sentence segmentation, tokenization, POS tagging, and chunking – were performed using the OpenNLP[1] package. If a sentence contains n entities ($n \geq 2$), it is replicated into $\binom{n}{2}$ sentences, each containing only two entities. If the two entities are known to be in a relationship, then the replicated sentence is added to the set of corresponding positive sentences, otherwise it is added to the set of negative sentences. During testing, a sentence having n entities ($n \geq 2$) is again replicated into $\binom{n}{2}$ sentences in a similar way.

The dependency graph that is input to the shortest path dependecy kernel is obtained from two different parsers:

- The CCG parser introduced in [14][2] outputs a list of functor-argument dependencies, from which head-modifier dependencies are obtained using a straightforward procedure (for more details, see [15]).
- Head-modifier dependencies can be easily extracted from the full parse output of Collins' CFG parser [16], in which every non-terminal node is annotated with head information.

The relation kernels are used in conjunction with SVM learning in order to find a decision hyperplane that best separates the positive examples from negative examples. We modified the LibSVM[3] package by plugging in the kernels described above. The factor λ in the subsequence kernel is set to 0.75. The performance is measured using *precision* (percentage of correctly extracted relations out of the total number of relations extracted), *recall* (percentage of correctly extracted relations out of the total number of relations annotated in the corpus), and *F-measure* (the harmonic mean of *precision* and *recall*).

3.4.1 Interaction Extraction from AIMed

We did comparative experiments on the AIMed corpus, which has been previously used for training the protein interaction extraction systems in [9]. It consists of 225 Medline abstracts, of which 200 are known to describe interactions between human proteins, while the other 25 do not refer to any interaction. There are 4084 protein references and around 1000 tagged interactions in this dataset.

The following systems are evaluated on the task of retrieving protein interactions from AIMed (assuming gold standard proteins):

- [**Manual**]: We report the performance of the rule-based system of [7, 8].
- [**ELCS**]: We report the 10-fold cross-validated results from [9] as a Precision-Recall (PR) graph.
- [**SSK**]: The subseqeuence kernel is trained and tested on the same splits as ELCS. In order to have a fair comparison with the other two systems, which use only lexical information, we do not use any word classes here.

---

[1] URL: http://opennlp.sourceforge.net
[2] URL:http://www.ircs.upenn.edu/~juliahr/Parser/
[3] URL:http://www.csie.ntu.edu.tw/~cjlin/libsvm/

• [**SPK**]: This is the shortest path dependency kernel, using the head-modifier dependencies extracted by Collins' syntactic parser. The kernel is trained and tested on the same 10 splits as ELCS and SSK.

The Precision-Recall curves that show the trade-off between these metrics are obtained by varying a threshold on the minimum acceptable extraction confidence, based on the probability estimates from LibSVM. The results, summarized in Figure 3.7, show that the subsequence kernel outperforms the other three systems, with a substantial gain. The syntactic parser, which is originally trained on a newspaper corpus, builds less accurate dependency structures for the biomedical text. This is reflected in a significantly reduced accuracy for the dependency kernel.

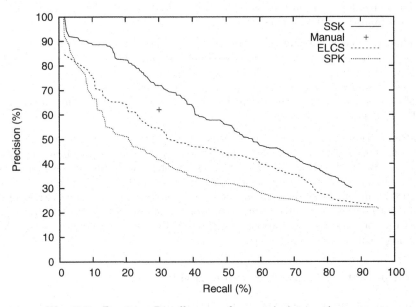

Fig. 3.7. Precision-Recall curves for protein interaction extractors.

3.4.2 Relation Extraction from ACE

The two kernels are also evaluated on the task of extracting top-level relations from the ACE corpus [12], the version used for the September 2002 evaluation. The training part of this dataset consists of 422 documents, with a separate set of 97 documents reserved for testing. This version of the ACE corpus contains three types of annotations: coreference, named entities and relations. There are five types of entities – PERSON, ORGANIZATION, FACILITY, LOCATION, and GEO-POLITICAL ENTITY – which can participate in five general, top-level relations: ROLE, PART, LOCATED, NEAR, and SOCIAL. In total, there are 7,646 intra-sentential relations, of which 6,156 are in the training data and 1,490 in the test data.

A recent approach to extracting relations is described in [17]. The authors use a generalized version of the tree kernel from [18] to compute a kernel over relation examples, where a relation example consists of the smallest dependency tree containing the two entities of the relation. Precision and recall values are reported for the task of extracting the five top-level relations in the ACE corpus under two different scenarios:

– [**S1**] This is the classic setting: one multi-class SVM is learned to discriminate among the five top-level classes, plus one more class for the no-relation cases.

– [**S2**] One binary SVM is trained for *relation detection*, meaning that all positive relation instances are combined into one class. The thresholded output of this binary classifier is used as training data for a second multi-class SVM, trained for *relation classification*.

The subsequence kernel (SSK) is trained under the first scenario, to recognize the same five top-level relation types. While for protein interaction extraction only the lexicalized version of the kernel was used, here we utilize more features, corresponding to the following feature spaces: Σ_1 is the word vocabulary, Σ_2 is the set of POS tags, Σ_3 is the set of generic POS tags, and Σ_4 contains the five entity types. Chunking information is used as follows: all (sparse) subsequences are created exclusively from the chunk heads, where a head is defined as the last word in a chunk. The same criterion is used for computing the length of a subsequence – all words other than head words are ignored. This is based on the observation that in general words other than the chunk head do not contribute to establishing a relationship between two entities outside of that chunk. One exception is when both entities in the example sentence are contained in the same chunk. This happens very often due to noun-noun ('U.S. troops') or adjective-noun ('Serbian general') compounds. In these cases, the chunk is allowed to contribute both entity heads.

The shortest-path dependency kernel (SPK) is trained under both scenarios. The dependencies are extracted using either Hockenmaier's CCG parser (SPK-CCG) [14], or Collins' CFG parser (SPK-CFG) [16].

Table 3.2 summarizes the performance of the two relation kernels on the ACE corpus. For comparison, we also show the results presented in [17] for their best performing kernel K4 (a sum between a bag-of-words kernel and a tree dependency kernel) under both scenarios.

Table 3.2. Extraction Performance on ACE.

(Scenario) Method	Precision	Recall	F-measure
(S1) K4	70.3	26.3	38.0
(S1) SSK	73.9	35.2	47.7
(S1) SPK-CCG	67.5	37.2	48.0
(S1) SPK-CFG	**71.1**	**39.2**	**50.5**
(S2) K4	67.1	35.0	45.8
(S2) SPK-CCG	63.7	41.4	50.2
(S2) SPK-CFG	**65.5**	**43.8**	**52.5**

The shortest-path dependency kernels outperform the dependency kernel from [17] in both scenarios, with a more substantial gain for SP-CFG. An error analysis revealed that Collins' parser was better at capturing local dependencies, hence the increased accuracy of SP-CFG. Another advantage of shortest-path dependency kernels is that their training and testing are very fast – this is due to representing the sentence as a chain of dependencies on which a fast kernel can be computed. All of the four SP kernels from Table 3.2 take between 2 and 3 hours to train and test on a 2.6GHz Pentium IV machine.

As expected, the newspaper articles from ACE are less prone to parsing errors than the biomedical articles from AIMed. Consequently, the extracted dependency structures are more accurate, leading to an improved accuracy for the dependency kernel.

To avoid numerical problems, the dependency paths are constrained to pass through at most 10 words (as observed in the training data) by setting the kernel to 0 for longer paths. The alternative solution of normalizing the kernel leads to a slight decrease in accuracy. The fact that longer paths have larger kernel scores in the unnormalized version does not pose a problem because, by definition, paths of different lengths correspond to disjoint sets of features. Consequently, the SVM algorithm will induce lower weights for features occurring in longer paths, resulting in a linear separator that works irrespective of the size of the dependency paths.

3.5 Future Work

There are cases when words that do not belong to the shortest dependency path do influence the extraction decision. In Section 3.3.2, we showed how negative polarity items are integrated in the model through annotations of words along the dependency paths. Modality is another phenomenon that is influencing relation extraction, and we plan to incorporate it using the same annotation approach.

The two relation extraction methods are very similar: the subsequence patterns in one kernel correspond to dependency paths in the second kernel. More exactly, pairs of words from a subsequence pattern correspond to pairs of consecutive words (i.e., edges) on the dependency path. The lack of dependency information in the subsequence kernel leads to allowing gaps between words, with the corresponding exponential penalty factor λ. Given the observed similarity between the two methods, it seems reasonable to use them both in an integrated model. This model would use high-confidence head-modifier dependencies, falling back on pairs of words with gaps, when the dependency information is unreliable.

3.6 Conclusion

Mining knowledge from text documents can benefit from using the structured information that comes from entity recognition and relation extraction. However, accurately extracting relationships between relevant entities is dependent on the granularity and reliability of the required linguistic analysis. In this chapter, we presented two relation extraction kernels that differ in terms of the amount of linguistic information they use. Experimental evaluations on two corpora with different types of discourse show that they compare favorably to previous extraction approaches.

3.7 Acknowledgment

This work was supported by grants IIS-0117308 and IIS-0325116 from the NSF. We would like to thank Arun Ramani and Edward Marcotte for their help in preparing the AIMed corpus.

References

1. R. J. Mooney, R. C. Bunescu, Mining knowledge from text using information extraction, SIGKDD Explorations (special issue on Text Mining and Natural Language Processing) 7 (1) (2005) 3–10.
2. H. Lodhi, C. Saunders, J. Shawe-Taylor, N. Cristianini, C. Watkins, Text classification using string kernels, Journal of Machine Learning Research 2 (2002) 419–444.
3. C. D. Fellbaum, WordNet: An Electronic Lexical Database, MIT Press, Cambridge, MA, 1998.
4. L. R. Rabiner, A tutorial on hidden Markov models and selected applications in speech recognition, Proceedings of the IEEE 77 (2) (1989) 257–286.
5. A. McCallum, D. Freitag, F. Pereira, Maximum entropy Markov models for information extraction and segmentation, in: Proceedings of the Seventeenth International Conference on Machine Learning (ICML-2000), Stanford, CA, 2000.
6. J. Lafferty, A. McCallum, F. Pereira, Conditional random fields: Probabilistic models for segmenting and labeling sequence data, in: Proceedings of 18th International Conference on Machine Learning (ICML-2001), Williamstown, MA, 2001, pp. 282–289.
7. C. Blaschke, A. Valencia, Can bibliographic pointers for known biological data be found automatically? protein interactions as a case study, Comparative and Functional Genomics 2 (2001) 196–206.
8. C. Blaschke, A. Valencia, The frame-based module of the Suiseki information extraction system, IEEE Intelligent Systems 17 (2002) 14–20.
9. R. Bunescu, R. Ge, R. J. Kate, E. M. Marcotte, R. J. Mooney, A. K. Ramani, Y. W. Wong, Comparative experiments on learning information extractors for proteins and their interactions, Artificial Intelligence in Medicine (special issue on Summarization and Information Extraction from Medical Documents) 33 (2) (2005) 139–155.
10. V. N. Vapnik, Statistical Learning Theory, John Wiley & Sons, New York, 1998.
11. N. Cristianini, J. Shawe-Taylor, An Introduction to Support Vector Machines and Other Kernel-based Learning Methods, Cambridge University Press, 2000.
12. National Institute of Standards and Technology, ACE – Automatic Content Extraction, http://www.nist.gov/speech/tests/ace (2000).
13. M. Steedman, The Syntactic Process, MIT Press, Cambridge, MA, 2000.
14. J. Hockenmaier, M. Steedman, Generative models for statistical parsing with combinatory categorial grammar, in: Proceedings of the 40th Annual Meeting of the Association for Computational Linguistics (ACL-2002), Philadelphia, PA, 2002, pp. 335–342.
15. R. C. Bunescu, R. J. Mooney, A shortest path dependency kernel for relation extraction, in: Proceedings of the Human Language Technology Conference and Conference on Empirical Methods in Natural Language Processing (HLT/EMNLP-05), Vancouver, BC, 2005, pp. 724–731.

16. M. J. Collins, Three generative, lexicalised models for statistical parsing, in: Proceedings of the 35th Annual Meeting of the Association for Computational Linguistics (ACL-97), 1997, pp. 16–23.
17. A. Culotta, J. Sorensen, Dependency tree kernels for relation extraction, in: Proceedings of the 42nd Annual Meeting of the Association for Computational Linguistics (ACL-04), Barcelona, Spain, 2004, pp. 423–429.
18. D. Zelenko, C. Aone, A. Richardella, Kernel methods for relation extraction, Journal of Machine Learning Research 3 (2003) 1083–1106.

Mining Diagnostic Text Reports by Learning to Annotate Knowledge Roles

Eni Mustafaraj, Martin Hoof, and Bernd Freisleben

4.1 Introduction

Several tasks approached by using text mining techniques, like text categorization, document clustering, or information retrieval, operate on the document level, making use of the so-called bag-of-words model. Other tasks, like document summarization, information extraction, or question answering, have to operate on the sentence level, in order to fulfill their specific requirements. While both groups of text mining tasks are typically affected by the problem of data sparsity, this is more accentuated for the latter group of tasks. Thus, while the tasks of the first group can be tackled by statistical and machine learning methods based on a bag-of-words approach alone, the tasks of the second group need natural language processing (NLP) at the sentence or paragraph level in order to produce more informative features.

Another issue common to all previously mentioned tasks is the availability of labeled data for training. Usually, for documents in real world text mining projects, training data do not exist or are expensive to acquire. In order to still satisfy the text mining goals while making use of a small contingent of labeled data, several approaches in machine learning have been developed and tested: different types of active learning [16], bootstrapping [13], or a combination of labeled and unlabeled data [1]. Thus, the issue of the lack of labeled data turns into the issue of selecting an appropriate machine learning approach.

The nature of the text mining task as well as the quantity and quality of available text data are other issues that need to be considered. While some text mining approaches can cope with data noise by leveraging the redundancy and the large quantity of available documents (for example, information retrieval on the Web), for other tasks (typically those restricted within a domain) the collection of documents might not possess such qualities. Therefore, more care is required for preparing such documents for the text mining task.

The previous observations suggest that performing a text mining task on new and unknown data requires handling all of the above mentioned issues, by combining and adopting different research approaches. In this chapter, we present an approach to extracting knowledge from text documents containing diagnostic problem solving situations in a technical domain (i.e., electrical engineering). In the proposed approach, we have combined techniques from several areas, including NLP, knowledge engineering, and machine learning to implement a learning framework for annotating cases with knowledge roles. The ultimate goal of the approach is to discover interesting problem solving situations (hereafter simply referred to as cases) that can be used by an experience management system to support new engineers during their working activities. However, as an immediate benefit, the annotations facilitate the retrieval of cases on demand, allow the collection of empirical domain knowledge, and can be formalized with the help of an ontology to also permit reasoning. The experimental results presented in the chapter are based on a collection of 500 Microsoft Word documents written in German, amounting to about one million words. Several processing steps were required to achieve the goal of case annotation. In particular, we had to (a) transform the documents into an XML format, (b) extract paragraphs belonging to cases, (c) perform part-of-speech tagging, (d) perform syntactical parsing, (e) transform the results into XML representation for manual annotation, (f) construct features for the learning algorithm, and (g) implement an active learning strategy. Experimental results demonstrate the feasibility of the learning approach and a high quality of the resulting annotations.

The chapter is organized as follows. In Section 4.2 we describe our domain of interest, the related collection of documents, and how knowledge roles can be used to annotate text. In Section 4.3 we consider work in natural language processing, especially frame semantics and semantic role labeling, emphasizing parallels to our task and identifying how resources and tools from these domains can be applied to perform annotation. Section 4.4 describes in detail all the preparatory steps for the process of learning to annotate cases. Section 4.5 evaluates the results of learning. Section 4.6 concludes the chapter and outlines areas of future work.

4.2 Domain Knowledge and Knowledge Roles

4.2.1 Domain Knowledge

Our domain of interest is predictive maintenance in the field of power engineering, more specifically, the maintenance of insulation systems of high-voltage rotating electrical machines. Since in many domains it is prohibitive to allow faults that could result in a breakdown of the system, components of the system are periodically or continuously monitored to look for changes in the expected behavior, in order to undertake predictive maintenance actions when necessary. Usually, the findings related to the predictive maintenance process are documented in several forms: the measured values in a relational database; the evaluations of measurements/tests in diagnostic reports written in natural language; or the recognized symptoms in photographs. The focus of the work described here are the textual diagnostic reports.

In the domain of predictive maintenance, two parties are involved: the service provider (the company that has the know-how to perform diagnostic procedures and recommend predictive maintenance actions) and the customer (the operator of the machine). As part of their business agreement, the service provider submits to the customer an *official diagnostic report*. Such a report follows a predefined structure template and is written in syntactically correct and parsimonious language. In our case, the language is German.

A report is organized into many sections: summary, reason for the inspection, data of the inspected machine, list of performed tests and measurements, evaluations of measurement and test results, overall assessment and recommendations, as well as several attachments with graphical plots of numerical measurements or photographs of damaged parts.

From a diagnostic point of view, the most important information is found in the evaluations of the measurements and tests performed. As a demonstration, consider the two excerpts in Figure 4.1 (originating from English documents for non-German speaking customers).

At $1.9U_N (= 30kV)$, an insulation breakdown occurred on the upper bar of the slot $N°18$, at the slot exit on the NDE side. The breakdown indicates that the bar insulation is seriously weakened. This may be caused by intense discharges due to a malfunction of the slot anti-corona protection.	The measured bypass currents are in a relatively high range indicating a certain surface conductivity. This is due to the fact that the motor was stored in cold area before it was moved to the high voltage laboratory where the temperature and humidity was much higher so that a certain degree of condensation could occur on the surface of the winding.

Fig. 4.1. Excerpts from two evaluations of isolation current measurements.

As it is often the case with diagnosis, while the quantities that are measured or the components that are inspected are the same, the findings depend on a series of contextual factors, and the reasons for these findings could be quite unique (as the examples of Figure 4.1 demonstrate). Usually, human experts need many years of field experience to gain a degree of expertise that allows them to handle any situation. The goal of our project is to mine the text documents for relevant pieces of knowledge acquired during diagnostic problem solving situations.

4.2.2 Domain Concepts

In some text mining applications, such as text categorization or information retrieval, the goal is often to discover terms specific to the domain that could be used as indices for organizing or retrieving information. Indeed, the excerpts of Figure 4.1 contain several of such domain-specific terms: *insulation, discharge, slot anti-corona protection, conductivity,* or *winding*. Still, using these terms as indices or keywords for representing the documents does not contribute to the purpose of our intended application, which is to find knowledge that supports diagnostic problem solving. To exemplify, consider the sentences in Figure 4.2:

1) The calculated **insulating resistance** values lay in the safe operating area.
2) Compared to the last examination, lower values for the **insulating resistance** were ascertained, due to dirtiness at the surface.

Fig. 4.2. Two sentences with the same domain concept shown in boldface.

In both sentences, the domain concept *insulating resistance* is found, but from a diagnostic point of view only the second sentence is interesting, because it describes a possible cause for lower values. Thus, more than domain concepts are needed to capture the knowledge expressed in the documents. Our solution to this problem is to label the text with semantic annotations expressed in terms of knowledge roles, which are introduced in the following subsection.

4.2.3 Knowledge Roles

Knowledge roles are a concept introduced in CommonKADS [28], a knowledge engineering methodology for implementing knowledge-based systems. More specifically, knowledge roles are abstract names that refer to the role a domain concept plays when reasoning about a knowledge task. Such tasks are, for example, diagnosis, assessment, monitoring, or planning. Although these tasks are found in many domains, their description in CommonKADS is domain-independent. Thus, when describing a diagnosis task, knowledge roles like `finding`, `symptom`, `fault`, `parameter`, or `hypothesis` would be used.

Indeed, if we consider again the sentences in Figure 4.2, it is reasonable to represent the second sentence with knowledge roles as shown in Figure 4.3:

Knowledge Role	Text Phrase
Observed Object:	insulating resistance
Symptom:	lower values
Cause:	dirtiness at the surface

Fig. 4.3. Knowledge roles for sentence 2 of Figure 4.2.

Such a representation can have several advantages. Given a certain value of an *Observed Object*, a list of *Symptoms* that should be checked during the diagnosis could be retrieved. Or, given a certain *Symptom*, possible *Causes* for it could be listed, and so forth.

Understandably, we are interested in performing the text annotation with knowledge roles automatically. To achieve this goal, we draw on research in natural language understanding as described in Section 4.3.

It might be argued that one could simply use a combination of keywords to retrieve the information. For example, for sentences like that in Figure 4.2, one might write a query as below:

[low | small | high | large] && [value] && [insulating resistance]

for retrieving symptoms. Or one can search for:

[due to] | [caused by] | [as a result of] ...

to retrieve sentences containing causes. While this approach may be appealing and in some occasions even successful, there are several reasons why it could not be applied in our application:

- A large number of words (adjectives, nouns, adverbs, or verbs) can be used to describe changes (considered as symptoms in our domain), and no one can know beforehand which of them is used in the text.

- While verbs are very important for capturing the meaning of a sentence, they also abound in numbers. For example, to express an observation, any of the following verbs can be used: *observe, detect, show, exhibit, recognize, determine, result in, indicate*, etc. Furthermore, adverbs and negations can change their meaning and therefore need to be considered. Thus, instead of using verbs as keywords, we use them to bootstrap the annotating process, and incorporate them within semantic frames, like the frame *Observation* for the group above.
- Often, meaning emerges from the relation between different words, instead of the words separately, and this is exactly what we encountered in the diagnostic cases.

The knowledge roles used for annotating cases are abstract constructs in knowledge engineering, defined independently of any natural language constructs. Thus, a contribution of this work lies in trying to bridge the gap between knowledge roles and the natural language constructs whose meaning they capture. For this purpose, frame semantics, as described in the next section, is an ideal place to start.

4.3 Frame Semantics and Semantic Role Labeling

4.3.1 Frame Semantics

In frame semantics theory [12], a frame is a "script-like conceptual structure that describes a particular type of situation, object, or event and the participants involved in it" [24]. Based on this theory, the Berkeley FrameNet Project[1] is creating an online lexical resource for the English language by annotating text from the 100 million words British National Corpus.

The structure of a frame contains lexical units (pairs of a word with its meaning), frame elements (semantic roles played by different syntactic dependents), as well as annotated sentences for all lexical units that evoke the frame. An example of a frame with its related components is shown in Figure 4.4.

Annotation of text with frames and roles in FrameNet has been performed manually by trained linguists. An effort to handle this task automatically is being carried out by research in semantic role labeling, as described in the next subsection.

4.3.2 Semantic Role Labeling

Automatic labeling of semantic roles was introduced in [14]. In this work, after acknowledging the success of information extraction systems that try to fill in domain-specific frame-and-slot templates (see Section 4.3.4), the need for semantic frames that can capture the meaning of text independently of the domain was expressed. The authors envision that the semantic interpretation of text in terms of frames and roles would contribute to many applications, like question answering, information extraction, semantic dialogue systems, as well as statistical machine translation or automatic text summarization, and finally also to text mining.

---

[1] http://framenet.icsi.berkeley.edu/

After this initial work, research on semantic role labeling (SRL) has grown steadily, and in the years 2004 and 2005 [3, 4] a shared task at the CoNLL[2] was defined, in which several research institutions compared their systems. In the meantime, besides FrameNet, another corpus with manually annotated semantic roles has been prepared, PropNet [21], which differs from FrameNet in the fact that it has general semantic roles not related to semantic frames. PropNet is also the corpus used for training and evaluation of research systems on the SRL shared task. A similar corpus to FrameNet for the German language has been created by the Salsa project [10], and a discussion on the differences and similarities among these three projects is found in [9].

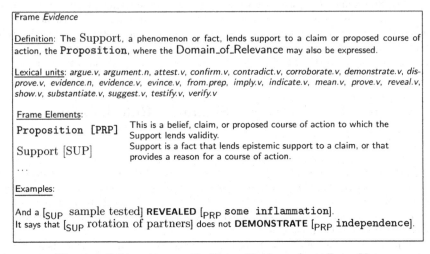

Fig. 4.4. Information on the frame *Evidence* from FrameNet.

SRL is approached as a learning task. For a given target verb in a sentence, the syntactic constituents expressing semantic roles associated to this verb need to be identified and labeled with the right roles. SRL systems usually divide sentences word-by-word or phrase-by-phrase and for each of these instances calculate many features creating a feature vector. The feature vectors are then fed to supervised classifiers, such as support vector machines, maximum entropy, or memory-based learners. While adapting such classifiers to perform better on this task could bring some improvement, better results can be achieved by constructing informative features for learning. A thorough discussion of different features used for SRL can be found in [14, 22].

4.3.3 Frames and Roles for Annotating Cases

On the one hand, in knowledge engineering there are knowledge tasks and knowledge roles to represent knowledge; on the other hand, in natural language understanding there are semantic frames and semantic roles to represent meaning. When knowledge

---

[2] Conference of Natural Language Learning

related to a knowledge task (like diagnosis) is represented by natural language, it is reasonable to expect that some knowledge roles will map to some semantic roles. The question is how to find these mappings, and more importantly, how to label text with these roles?

A knowledge task like diagnosis or monitoring is not equivalent to a semantic frame. The former are more complex and abstract, and can usually be divided into several components, which in turn can be regarded equivalent to semantic frames. By analyzing the textual episodes of diagnostic evaluations, we noticed that they typically contain a list of observations, explanations based on evidence, and suggestions to perform some activities. Thus, we consulted FrameNet for frames like Observation, Change, Evidence, or Activity. Indeed, these frames are all present in FrameNet. For example, Activity is present in 10 subframes, and different meanings of Change are captured in 21 frames. The frame Evidence was shown in Figure 4.4, and besides the two roles of Proposition and Support, it has also roles for Degree, Depictive, Domain_of_Relevance, Manner, Means, and Result. When one carefully reads the definition of the roles Proposition and Support and looks at the examples (Figure 4.4), one can conclude that Proposition is similar to Cause and Support to Symptom in a diagnosis task.

The problem is to determine which frames to look for, given that there are currently more than six hundred frames in FrameNet. The key are the lexical units related to each frame, usually verbs. Starting with the verbs, one gets to the frames and then to the associated roles. This is also the approach we follow. We initially look for the most frequent verbs in our corpus, and by consulting several sources (since the verbs are in German), such as [15], VerbNet,[3] and FrameNet, we connect every verb with a frame, and try to map between semantic roles in a frame and knowledge roles we are interested in. One could also use the roles of FrameNet, but they are linguistically biased, and as such are not understandable by domain users that will annotate training instances for learning (a domain user would directly know to annotate *Cause*, but finds *Proposition* somehow confusing.)

In this work, FrameNet was only used as a lexical resource for consultation, that is, to find out which frames are evoked by certain lexical units, and what the related semantic roles are. Since the language of our corpus is German, we cannot make any statements about how useful the FrameNet frames could be to a learning system based on English annotated data corresponding to the defined frames.

Finally, it should be discussed why such an approach to annotating text cases with frames and roles could be beneficial to text mining. For the purpose of this discussion, consider some facts from the introduced domain corpus. During the evaluation of the learning approach, we manually annotated a subcorpus of unique sentences describing one specific measurement (high-voltage isolation current). In the 585 annotated sentences, the frame Evidence was found 152 times, 84 times evoked by the verb *zurückführen* (trace back to), 40 times by the verb *hindeuten* (point to), and 28 times by 9 other verbs. Analyzing the text annotated with the role *Cause* in the sentences with *zurückführen*, 27 different phrases expressing causes of anomalies pointed to by the symptoms were found. A few of these expressions appeared frequently, some of them occasionally, some others rarely. In Table 4.1, some of these expressions are shown.

---

[3] http://www.cis.upenn.edu/~bsnyder3/cgi-bin/search.cgi

Table 4.1. Some phrases annotated with the role *Cause*.

German Phrase	English Translation	Frequency
Verschmutzungseinflüsse	influences of pollution	10
leitende Verschmutzungen	conducting pollutions	8
Ionisation in Klemmenbereich	ionization in the terminal area	3
äussere Entladungen	external discharges	1

If for every sentence with the frame *Evidence* the text annotated with *Symptom* and *Cause* is extracted, this text can then be processed further with other text mining techniques for deriving domain knowledge, which is not directly available in any of the analyzed texts. For example, one could get answers to questions like: which are the most frequent symptoms and what causes can explain them; what problems (i.e., causes) do appear frequently in a specific type of machine, etc. Thus, such an annotation with frames and roles preprocesses text by generating very informative data for text mining, and it can also be used in the original form for information retrieval. Still, such an approach makes sense in those cases when text contains descriptions of repetitive tasks, which are then expressed by a small number of underlying semantic frames. Since data and text mining try to extract knowledge from data of the same nature in the same domain, we find that annotation of text with knowledge roles could be a valuable approach.

Before explaining in detail the process of learning to automatically annotate text with knowledge roles (based on the SRL task) in Section 4.4, we briefly discuss the related field of information extraction.

4.3.4 Information Extraction

Information extraction (IE), often regarded as a restricted form of natural language understanding, predates research in text mining, although today, IE is seen as one of the techniques contributing to text mining [30]. Actually, the purpose of IE is very similar to what we are trying to achieve with role annotation. In IE it is usually known in advance what information is needed, and part of text is extracted to fill in slots of a predefined template. An example, found in [20], is the job posting template, where, from job posting announcements in Usenet, text to fill slots like: title, state, city, language, platform, etc. is extracted and stored in a database for simpler querying and retrieval.

Usually, methods used by IE have been based on shallow NLP techniques, trying to extract from a corpus different types of syntactic rules that match syntactic roles to semantic categories, as for example in [23].

With the advances in NLP and machine learning research, IE methods have also become more sophisticated. Actually, SRL can also be seen as a technology for performing information extraction, in those cases when text is syntactically and semantically more demanding and expressive. All these technologies are intended to be used for extracting knowledge from text, despite their differences in implementation or scope.

4.4 Learning to Annotate Cases with Knowledge Roles

To perform the task of learning to annotate cases with knowledge roles, we implemented a software framework, as shown in Figure 4.5. Only the preparation of documents (described in Section 4.4.1) is performed outside of this framework. In the remainder of the section, every component of the framework is presented in detail.

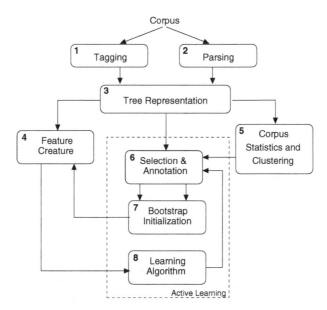

Fig. 4.5. The Learning Framework Architecture.

4.4.1 Document Preparation

In Section 4.2.1 it was mentioned that our documents are official diagnostic reports hierarchically structured in several sections and subsections, written by using MS® Word. Actually, extracting text from such documents, while preserving the content structure, is a difficult task. In completing it we were fortunate twice. First, with MS® Office 2003 the XML based format WordML was introduced that permits storing MS® Word documents directly in XML. Second, the documents were originally created using a MS® Word document template, so that the majority of them had the same structure. Still, many problems needed to be handled. MS® Word mixes formatting instructions with content very heavily and this is reflected also in its XML format. In addition, information about spelling, versioning, hidden template elements, and so on are also stored. Thus, one needs to explore the XML output of the documents to find out how to distinguish text and content structure from unimportant information. Such a process will always be a heuristic one, depending on the nature of the documents. We wrote a program that reads the XML document tree, and for each section with a specified label (from the document template) it extracts the pure text and stores it in a new XML document, as the excerpt in Figure 4.6 shows.

```
<section title="Measurements">
  <subsection title="Stator_Winding">
    <measurement title="Visual_Control">
      <submeasurement title="Overhang_Support">
        <evaluation>
           Die Wickelkopfabsttzung AS und NS befand sich in einem ...
        </evaluation>
        <action>Keine</action>
      </submeasurement>
    ...
```

Fig. 4.6. Excerpt of the XML representation of the documents.

Based on such an XML representation, we create subcorpora of text containing measurement evaluations of the same type, stored as paragraphs of one to many sentences.

4.4.2 Tagging

The part-of-speech (POS) tagger (TreeTagger[4]) that we used [26] is a probabilistic tagger with parameter files for tagging several languages: German, English, French, or Italian. For some small problems we encountered, the author of the tool was very cooperative in providing fixes. Nevertheless, our primary interest in using the tagger was not the POS tagging itself (the parser, as is it shown in Section 4.4.3, performs tagging and parsing), but getting stem information (since the German language has a very rich morphology) and dividing the paragraphs in sentences (since the sentence is the unit of operation for the next processing steps).

The tag set used for tagging German is slightly different from that of English.[5] Figure 4.7 shows the output of the tagger for a short sentence.[6]

As indicated in Figure 4.7, to create sentences it suffices to find the lines containing: ". \$. ." (one sentence contains all the words between two such lines). In general, this is a very good heuristic, but its accuracy depends on the nature of the text. For example, while the tagger correctly tagged abbreviations found in its list of abbreviations (and the list of abbreviations can be customized by adding abbreviations common to the domain of the text), it got confused when the same abbreviations were found inside parentheses, as the examples in Figure 4.8 for the word 'ca.' (circa) show.

If such phenomena occur often, they become a problem for the further correct processing of sentences, although one becomes aware of such problems only in the

---

[4] http://www.ims.uni-stuttgart.de/projekte/corplex/TreeTagger

[5] http://www.ims.uni-stuttgart.de/projekte/corplex/TagSets/stts-table.html

[6] Translation: A generally good external winding condition is present.

Es	PPER	es
liegt	VVFIN	liegen
insgesamt	ADV	insgesamt
ein	ART	ein
guter	ADJA	gut
äusserer	ADJA	äuβer
Wicklungszustand	NN	\<unknown\>
vor	PTKVZ	vor
.	\$.	.

Fig. 4.7. A German sentence tagged with POS-tags by TreeTagger.

course of the work. A possible solution in such cases is to use heuristics to replace erroneous tags with correct ones for the types of identified errors.

an	APR	an		(	\$(	(
ca.	ADV	ca.		ca	NE	\<unknown\>
50	CARD	50		.	\$.	.
%	NN	%		20	CARD	20

Fig. 4.8. Correct and erroneous tagging for the word 'ca.'

The more problematic issue is that of words marked with the stem \<unknown\>. Actually, their POS is usually correctly induced, but we are specifically interested in the stem information. The two reasons for an \<unknown\> label are a) the word has been misspelled and b) the word is domain specific, and as such not seen during the training of the tagger. On the positive side, selecting the words with the \<unknown\> label directly creates the list of domain specific words, useful in creating a domain lexicon.

A handy solution for correcting spelling errors is to use a string similarity function, available in many programming language libraries. For example, the Python language has the function "get_close_matches" in its "difflib" library. An advantage of such a function is having as a parameter the degree of similarity between strings. By setting this value very high (between 0 and 1) one is sure to get really similar matches if any at all.

Before trying to solve the problem of providing stems for words with the \<unknown\> label, one should determine whether the stemming information substantially contributes to the further processing of text. Since we could not know that in advance, we manually provided stems for all words labeled as \<unknown\>. Then, during the learning process we performed a set of experiments, where: a) no stem information at all was used and b) all words had stem information (tagger + manually created list of stems). Table 4.2 summarizes the recall and precision of the learning task in each experiment.

These results show approximately 1% improvement in recall and precision when stems instead of original words are used. We can say that at least for the learning task of annotating text with knowledge roles stem information is not necessarily important, but this could also be due to the fact that a large number of other features (see Section 4.4.5) besides words are used for learning.

Table 4.2. Results of experiments for the contribution of stem information on learning.

Experiment	Recall	Precision
a) no stems (only words)	90.38	92.32
b) only stems	91.29	93.40

Still, the reason for having a list of stems was not in avoiding more data due to word inflections, but in capturing the word composition, a phenomenon typical for the German language. For example, all the words in the first row of Table 4.3 are compound words that belong to the same semantic category identified by their last word 'wert' (value), i.e., they all denote values of different measured quantities, and as such have a similar meaning. This similarity cannot be induced if one compares the words in the original form, something possible by comparing the word representations of the second row.

Table 4.3. Original words (first row), words composed of stems (second row).

Ableitstrom*werte*, Gesamtstrom*werte*, Isolationswiderstands*werte*, Isolationsstrom*werte*, Kapazitäts*werte*, Ladestrom*werte*, Strom*wert*en, Verlustfaktoranfangs*wert*, etc.
Ableit-Strom-Wert,   Gesamt-Strom-Wert,   Isolation-Widerstand-Wert, Isolation-Strom-Wert,   Kapazität-Wert,   Lade-Strom-Wert,   Strom-Wert, Verlustfaktor-Anfang-Wert, etc.

Unfortunately, there are only a few tools available for morphological analysis of German words. We tried Morphy [17], which is publicly available, but it was not able to analyze any of our domain-specific words. Therefore, we had to perform this task by hand.

4.4.3 Parsing

Syntactical parsing is one of the most important steps in the learning framework, since the produced parse trees serve as input for the creation of features used for learning. Since we are interested in getting qualitative parsing results, we experimented with three different parsers: the Stanford parser (Klein 2005), the BitPar parser [27, 25], and the Sleepy parser [7]. What these parsers have in common is that they all are based on unlexicalized probabilistic context free grammars (PCFG) [18], trained on the same corpus of German, Negra[7] (or its superset Tiger[8]), and their source code is publicly available. Still, they do differ in the degree they model some structural aspects of the German language, their annotation schemas, and the infor-

---

[7] http://www.coli.uni-saarland.de/projects/sfb378/negra-corpus/
[8] http://www.ims.uni-stuttgart.de/projekte/TIGER/TIGERCorpus/

mation included in the output. Figure 4.9 shows the output of the same sentence[9] parsed by each parser, and in the following, we discuss each of them.

Stanford Parser	`(ROOT`
	`(NUR`
	`(S`
	`(PP (APPR Auf) (CARD NS))`
	`(VAFIN wurden)`
	`(VP`
	`(AP (ADV ca.)`
	`(NM (CARD 5)`
	`(CARD gerissene)`
	`(CARD Keilsicherungsbandagen)))`
	`(VVPP festgestellt)))`
	`($..)))`

BitPar Parser	`(utt:`
	`(S.fin:`
	`(PP: (APPR: Auf)`
	`(NN: NS))`
	`(VWFIN: wurden)`
	`(AP: (AVP-MAD: (ADV-MAD: ca.))`
	`(CARD: 5))`
	`(NP.nom: (AP: (ADJA%: gerissene))`
	`(NN.nom: Keilsicherungsbandagen))`
	`(VVPP%: festgestellt)))`
	`(\$.: .))`

Sleepy Parser	`(TOP`
	`(S`
	`(PP-MO (APPR-AD Auf)`
	`(NE-NK NS) )`
	`(VAFIN-HD wurden)`
	`(NP-SB`
	`(ADV-MO ca.) (CARD-NK 5)`
	`(ADJA-NK gerissene)`
	`(NN-NK  Keilsicherungsbandagen))`
	`(VP-OC (VVPP-HD festgestellt)))`
	`($. .))`

	Auf NS wurden ca. 5 gerissene Keilsicherungsbandagen festgestellt. On NS were ca. 5 torn wedge's safety bands detected.

Fig. 4.9. Parsing output of the same sentence from the three parsers

Stanford Parser - The Stanford parser is an ambitious project that tackles the task of generating parse trees from unlabeled data independently of the language. For the moment, the parser is distributed with parameter files for parsing English, German, and Chinese. We tested the parser on our data and noticed that

---

[9] English translation: "On NS were detected circa 5 torn wedge's safety bands."

the POS tags were often erroneously induced (in the sentence with only 8 words of Figure 4.9 there are 3 such errors—CARD tags for 2 nouns and 1 adjective), which then resulted in erroneous parse trees. But, in those cases when the tagging was performed correctly, the parse trees were also correct. Still, the parser could not parse long sentences, perhaps due to the fact that it was trained in the part of the Negra corpus with sentences having up to 10 words. Trying the parser with long English sentences instead, produced excellent results. We concluded that at this phase of implementation, the Stanford parser could not be used with our corpus of German sentences that contain an average of up to 18 words per sentence.

BitPar Parser - This parser is composed of two parts, the parser itself [27] and the parameter files (chart rules, lexicon, etc.) from [25]. Published experimental results claim robust performance, due to the use of sophisticated annotation and transformation schemata for modeling grammars. Another advantage of the parser is that its lexicon can be extended very easily with triples of domain-dependent words, their tags, their frequency counts in a corpus, thus avoiding the tagging errors typical for unlexicalised parsers. These tagging errors damage the parse results, as can be seen from the results of the Stanford parser. Our critique for the described BitPar is that it usually produces trees with more nodes than the other parsers and the annotation of nodes contains specialized linguistic information, not very appropriate for creating features for learning.

Sleepy Parser - This parser has been specifically tuned for the German language, and while it is a statistical parser like the others, it uses different annotation schemas and incorporates grammatical functions (SB–subject, OC–clausal object, MO–modifier, HD–head, etc.) or long-distance dependencies between terms. In constrast to the two other parsers, it also has a highly tuned suffix analyzer for guessing POS tags [8], which contributes to more accurate tagging results than the other parsers, although some domain-dependent words are not always correctly tagged. Erroneous parsing is also encountered for very long sentences.

Choosing a Parser

All the tested parsers make errors during parsing. In the end, the criteria upon which we based our choice of the parser were speed and output information. Sleepy was the fastest and had the most informative output (it prints the log value expressing the likelihood of parsing, and it labels the majority of nodes with their grammatical function). Actually, choosing a parser upon these criteria instead of the accuracy of parsing could be regarded as inappropriate. Our justification is that a metric to measure the accuracy of parsing on new data does not exist. These parsers have all been trained on the same corpus, and at least the two German parsers tuned up to the point where their results are almost the same. Thus, *a priori* their expected accuracy in a new corpus should be equal, and accuracy is not a criterion for choosing one over the other. Given the difficulty of evaluating the accuracy of the parse trees and their presumed similarity, we based the choice of parser on the qualities that contributed most to our task, namely speed and informative output.

4.4.4 Tree Representation

The bracketed parse tree and the stem information of tagging serve as input for the step of creating a tree data structure. The tree is composed of terminals (leaf nodes) and non-terminals (internal nodes), all of them known as constituents of the tree. For export purposes as well as for performing exploration or annotation of the corpus, the tree data structures are stored in XML format, according to a schema defined in the TigerSearch[10] tool. The created tree, when visualized in TigerSearch, looks like the one shown in Figure. 4.10.[11] The terminals are labeled with their POS tags and also contain the corresponding words and stems; the inside nodes are labeled with their phrase types (NP, PP, etc.); and the branches have labels, too, corresponding to the grammatical functions of the nodes. The XML representation of a portion of the tree is shown in Figure 4.11.

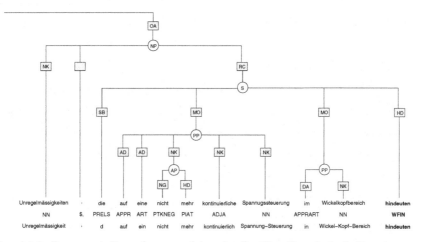

Fig. 4.10. Representation of a parsed tree in the TigerSearch tool. Due to space reasons, only a branch of the tree is shown.

4.4.5 Feature Creation

Features are created from the parse tree of a sentence. A feature vector is created for every constituent of the tree, containing some features unique to the constituent, some features common to all constituents of the sentence, and some others calculated with respect to the target constituent (the predicate verb).

A detailed linguistic description of possible features used by different research systems for the SRL task is found in [22]. In this subsection, we only list the features used in our system and give example values for the leaf node **Spannungssteuerung** of the parse tree in Figure 4.10.

---

[10] http://www.ims.uni-stuttgart.de/projekte/TIGER/TIGERSearch/

[11] English translation: "... irregularities, which point to a not anymore continuous steering of voltage in the area of the winding head."

```
    ...
        <t lemma="Spannung-Steuerung" word="Spannungssteuerung" pos="NN"
            id="sentences._108_28" />
        <t lemma="in" word="im" pos="APPRART"
            id="sentences._108_29" />
        <t lemma="Wickel-Kopf-Bereich" word="Wickelkopfbereich" pos="NN"
            id="sentences._108_30" />
        <t lemma="hindeuten" word="hindeuten" pos="VVFIN" id="sentences._108_31" />
    </terminals>
    <nonterminals>
    <nt id="sentences._108_500" cat="PP">
     <edge idref="sentences._108_3" label="NK" />
     <edge idref="sentences._108_2" label="DA" />
     <edge idref="sentences._108_1" label="DA" />
    </nt>
    ...
```

Fig. 4.11. XML representation of a portion of the parse tree from Figure 4.10.

Phrase type **NN**
Grammatical function **NK**
Terminal (is the constituent a terminal or non-terminal node?) **1**
Path (path from the target verb to the constituent, denoting u(up) and d(down) for the direction)
uSdPPd
Grammatical path (like Path, but instead of node labels, branch labels are considered) **uHDdMOdNK**
Path length (number of branches from target to constituent) **3**
Partial path (path to the lowest common ancestor between target and constituent) **uPPuS**
Relative Position (position of the constituent relative to the target) **left**
Parent phrase type (phrase type of the parent node of the constituent) **PP**
Target (lemma of the target word) **hindeuten**
Target POS (part-of-speech of the target) **VVFIN**
Passive (is the target verb passive or active?) **0**
Preposition (the preposition if the constituent is a PP) **none**
Head Word (for rules on head words refer to [5]) **Spannung-Steuerung**
Left sibling phrase type **ADJA**
Left sibling lemma **kontinuierlich**
Right sibling phrase type **none**
Right sibling lemma **none**
Firstword, Firstword POS, Lastword, Lastword POS (in this case, the constituent has only one word,
thus, these features get the same values: Spannung-Steuerung and NN. For non-terminal constituents
like PP or NP, first word and last word will be different.)
Frame (the frame evoked by the target verb) **Evidence**
Role (this is the class label that the classifier will learn to predict. It will be one of the roles related
to the frame or none, for an example refer to Figure 4.12.) **none**

If a sentence has several clauses where each verb evokes a frame, the feature
vectors are calculated for each evoked frame separately and all the vectors participate
in the learning.

4.4.6 Annotation

To perform the manual annotation, we used the Salsa annotation tool (publicly
available) [11]. The Salsa annotation tool reads the XML representation of a parse
tree and displays it as shown in Figure 4.12. The user has the opportunity to add
frames and roles as well as to attach them to a desired target verb. In the example of
Figure 4.12 (the same sentence of Figure 4.10), the target verb *hindeuten* (point to)
evokes the frame Evidence, and three of its roles have been assigned to constituents of
the tree. Such an assignment can be easily performed using point-and-click. After this

process, an element <frames> is added to the XML representation of the sentence, containing information about the frame. Excerpts of the XML code are shown in Figure 4.13.

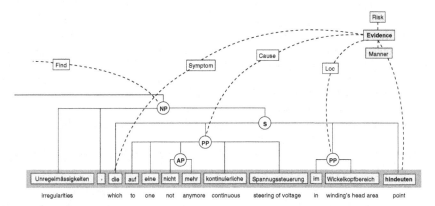

Fig. 4.12. Annotation with roles with the Salsa tool.

```
<frames>
 <frame name="Evidence" id="sentences._108__f1">
  <target><fenode idref="sentences._108_31"/></target>
   <fe name="Symptom" id="sentences._108_f1_e1">
    <fenode idref="sentences._108_22"/>
   </fe>
   <fe name="Cause" id="sentences._108__f1_e2">
    <fenode idref="sentences._108_509"/>
   </fe>
   <fe name="Loc" id="sentences._108__f1_e5">
    <fenode idref="sentences._108_510"/>
   </fe>
...
```

Fig. 4.13. XML Representation of an annotated frame.

4.4.7 Active Learning

Research in IE has indicated that using an active learning approach for acquiring labels from a human annotator has advantages over other approaches of selecting instances for labeling [16]. In our learning framework, we have also implemented an active learning approach. The possibilities for designing an active learning strategy are manifold; the one we have implemented uses a committee-based classification scheme that is steered by corpus statistics. The strategy consists of the following steps:

a) Divide the corpus in clusters of sentences with the same target verb. If a cluster has fewer sentences than a given threshold, group sentences with verbs evoking the same frame into the same cluster.

b) Within each cluster, group the sentences (or clauses) with the same parse sub-tree together.

c) Select sentences from the largest groups of the largest clusters and present them to the user for annotation.

d) Bootstrap initialization: apply the labels assigned by the user to groups of sentences with the same parse sub-tree.

e) Train all the classifiers of the committee on the labeled instances; apply each trained classifier to the unlabeled sentences.

f) Get a pool of instances where the classifiers of the committee disagree and present to the user the instances belonging to sentences from the next largest clusters not yet manually labeled.

g) Repeat steps d)–f) a few times until a desired accuracy of classification is achieved.

In the following, the rationale behind choosing these steps is explained.

Steps a), b), c): In these steps, statistics about the syntactical structure of the corpus are created, with the intention of capturing its underlying distribution, so that representative instances for labeling can be selected.

Step d): This step has been regarded as applicable to our corpus, due to the nature of the text. Our corpus contains repetitive descriptions of the same diagnostic measurements on electrical machines, and often, even the language used has a repetitive nature. Actually, this does not mean that the same words are repeated (although often standard formulations are used, especially in those cases when nothing of value was observed). Rather, the kind of sentences used to describe the task has the same syntactic structure. As an example, consider the sentences shown in Figure 4.14.

[PP Im Nutaustrittsbereich] wurden [NP stärkere Glimmentladungsspuren] festgestellt.
In the area of slot exit stronger signs of corona discharges were detected.

[PP Bei den Endkeilen] wurde [NP ein ausreichender Verkeildruck] festgestellt.
At the terminals' end a sufficient wedging pressure was detected.

[PP An der Schleifringbolzenisolation] wurden [NP mechanische Beschädigungen] festgestellt.
On the insulation of slip rings mechanical damages were detected.

[PP Im Wickelkopfbereich] wurden [NP grossflächige Decklackablätterungen] festgestellt.
In the winding head area extensive chippings of the top coating were detected.

Fig. 4.14. Examples of sentences with the same structure.

What all these sentences have in common is the passive form of the verb *feststellen* (wurden festgestellt), and due to the subcategorization of this verb, the parse tree on the level of phrases is identical for all sentences, as indicated by 4.15. Furthermore, for the frame Observation evoked by the verb, the assigned roles are in all cases: NP—Finding, PP—Observed_Object. Thus, to bootstrap initialization, we assign the same roles to sentences with the same sub-tree as the manually labeled sentences.

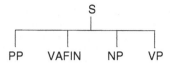

Fig. 4.15. Parse tree of the sentences in Figure 4.14.

Step e): The committee of classifiers consists of a maximum entropy (MaxEnt) classifier from Mallet [19], a Winnow classifier from SNoW [2], and a memory-based learner (MBL) from TiMBL [6]. For the MBL, we selected k=5 as the number of the nearest neighbours. The classification is performed as follows: if at least two classifiers agree on a label, the label is accepted. If there is disagreement, the cluster of labels from the five nearest neighbours is examined. If the cluster is not homogenous (i.e., it contains different labels), the instance is included in the set of instances to be presented to the user for manual labeling.

Step f): If one selects new sentences for manual annotation only based on the output of the committee-based classifier, the risk of selecting outlier sentences is high [29]. Thus, from the instances' set created by the classifier, we select those belonging to large clusters not manually labeled yet.

4.5 Evaluations

To evaluate this active learning approach on the task of annotating text with knowledge roles, we performed a series of experiments that are described in the following. It was explained in Section 4.4.1 that, based on the XML structure of the documents, we created subcorpora with text belonging to different types of diagnostic tests. After such subcorpora have been processed to create sentences, only unique sentences are retained for further processing (repetitive, standard sentences do not bring any new information, they only disturb the learning and therefore are discarded). Then, lists of verbs were created, and by consulting the sources mentioned in Section 4.3.3, verbs were grouped with one of the frames: Observation, Evidence, Activity, and Change. Other verbs that did not belong to any of these frames were not considered for role labeling.

4.5.1 Learning Performance on the Benchmark Datasets

With the aim of exploring the corpus to identify roles for the frames and by using our learning framework, we annotated two different subcorpora and then manually controlled them, to create benchmark datasets for evaluation. Some statistics for the manually annotated subcorpora are summarized in Table 4.4. Then, to evaluate the efficiency of the classification, we performed 10-fold cross-validations on each set, obtaining the results shown in Table 4.5, where recall, precision, and the $F_{\beta=1}$ measure are the standard metrics of information retrieval.

We analyzed some of the classification errors and found that they were due to parsing anomalies, which had forced us in several occasions to split a role among several constituents.

Table 4.4. Statistics for the benchmark datasets.

Subcorpus	Cases No.	Sentences No.	Unique Sentences No.	Annotated Roles No.
Isolation Current	491	1134	585	1862
Wedging System	453	775	602	1751

Table 4.5. Learning results for the benchmark datasets.

Subcorpus	Recall	Precision	$F_{\beta=1}$ measure
Isolation Current	0.913	0.934	0.92
Wedging System	0.838	0.882	0.86

4.5.2 Active Learning versus Uniform Random Selection

In order to evaluate the advantages of active learning, we compared it to the uniform random selection of sentences for manual annotations. Some results for both approaches are summarized in Table 4.6 and Table 4.7. Recall, precision, and $F_{\beta=1}$ measure were calculated after each iteration, in which 10 new sentences manually labeled were added to the training set. The results of active learning ($F_{\beta=1}$ measure) are 5–10 points better than those of random learning. For this experiment, the step d) of the active learning strategy was not applied, since it is very specific to our corpus.

Table 4.6. Random Learning Results.

Sentences No.	Recall	Precision	$F_{\beta=1}$ measure
10	0.508	0.678	0.581
20	0.601	0.801	0.687
30	0.708	0.832	0.765
40	0.749	0.832	0.788

Table 4.7. Active Learning Results.

Sentences No.	Recall	Precision	$F_{\beta=1}$ measure
10	0.616	0.802	0.697
20	0.717	0.896	0.797
30	0.743	0.907	0.817
40	0.803	0.906	0.851

4.5.3 Bootstrapping Based on Other Sets

During the annotation of the two benchmark datasets, we noticed that the two sub-corpora, although different in nature (set_1: *Isolation Current* contains evaluations of numerical measurements performed on the three phases of the machine, set_2: *Wedging System* describes visual inspections on the wedging components of the machine) had very often the frame Observation or Change in common, while the frame Evidence appeared almost only in the first set, and the frame Activity almost always in the second. Thus, we tested whether text annotated with the same roles in one set could bootstrap the learning in the second, and the results are summarized in Table 4.8.

Table 4.8. Results for bootstrapping based on other labeled sets

Training File	Testing File	Recall	Precision
Isolation Current	Wedging System	0.765	0.859
Wedging System	Isolation Current	0.642	0.737

We consider these results as very promising, since they hint at the possibility of using previously annotated text from other subcorpora to bootstrap the learning process, something that would alleviate the process of acquiring manual annotations for new text.

4.6 Conclusions

In this chapter, we have presented an approach for extracting knowledge from text documents containing descriptions of knowledge tasks in a technical domain. Knowledge extraction in our approach is based on the annotation of text with knowledge roles (a concept originating in knowledge engineering), which we map to semantic roles found in frame semantics. The framework implemented for this purpose is based on deep NLP and active learning. Experiments have demonstrated a robust learning performance, and the obtained annotations were of high quality. Since our framework is inspired by and founded upon research in semantic role labeling (SRL), the results indicate that SRL could become a highly valuable processing step for text mining tasks.

In future work, we will consider the advantages of representing annotated text by means of knowledge roles and the related frames. Besides the previously explained uses for semantic retrieval of cases and the extraction of empirical domain knowledge facts, such a representation could also permit looking for potentially interesting relations in text and can be exploited to populate application and domain ontologies with lexical items.

4.7 Acknowledgments

The Insulation Competence Center of ALSTOM Ltd. Switzerland kindly permitted the use of the text documents for research purposes. Katrin Erk, Sebastian Pado, Amit Dubey, Sabine Schulte im Walde, Michael Schiehlen, and Helmut Schmid provided their linguistic tools and were an invaluable source of information and support. We are grateful to all of them.

References

1. A. Blum and T. Mitchell. Combining labeled and unlabeled data with co-training. In *Proc. of the Workshop on Computational Learning Theory, COLT '98, Madison, WI*, pages 92–100, 1998.
2. A. J. Carlson, C. M. Cumby, N. D. Rizzolo, J. L. Rosen, and D. Roth. SNoW: Sparse Network of Winnow. 2004.
3. X. Carreras and L. Màrquez. Introduction to the coNLL shared task: Semantic role labeling. In *Proc. of 8th Conference of Natural Language Learning*, pages 89–97, Boston, MA, 2004.
4. X. Carreras and L. Màrquez. Introduction to the coNLL-2005 shared task: Semantic role labeling. In *Proc. of 9th Conference of Natural Language Learning*, pages 152–165, Ann Arbor, MI, June 2005.
5. M. Collins. *Head-Driven Statistical Models for Natural Language Parsing.* PhD thesis, University of Pennsylvania, 1999.
6. W. Daelemans, J. Zavrel, K. van der Sloot, and A. van den Bosch. TiMBL: Tilburg Memory Based Learner. 2004.
7. A. Dubey. *Statistical Parsing for German.* PhD thesis, University of Saarland, Germany, 2003.
8. A. Dubey. What to do when lexicalization fails: Parsing German with suffix analysis and smoothing. In *Proc. of 43rd Annual Meeting of ACL, Ann Arbor, MI*, pages 314–321, 2005.
9. M. Ellsworth, K. Erk, P. Kingsbury, and S. Padó. PropBank, SALSA, and FrameNet: How design determines product. In *Proc. of the LREC 2004 Workshop on Building Lexical Resources from Semantically Annotated Corpora, Lisbon, Portugal*, 2004.
10. K. Erk, A. Kowalski, and S. Padó. The Salsa annotation tool-demo description. In *Proc. of the 6th Lorraine-Saarland Workshop, Nancy, France*, pages 111–113, 2003.
11. K. Erk, A. Kowalski, S. Padó, and M. Pinkal. Towards a resource for lexical semantics: A large German corpus with extensive semantic annotation. In *Proc. of 41st Annual Meeting of ACL, Saporo, Japan*, pages 537–544, 2003.
12. C. J. Fillmore. Frame semantics and the nature of language. In *Annals of the New York Academy of Sciences: Conf. on the Origin and Development of Language and Speech*, volume 280, pages 20–32, 1976.
13. R. Ghani and R. Jones. A comparison of efficacy of bootstrapping of algorithms for information extraction. In *Proc. of LREC 2002 Workshop on Linguistic Knowledge Acquisition, Las Palmas, Spain*, 2002.
14. D. Gildea and D. Jurafsky. Automatic labeling of semantic roles. In *Computational Linguistics*, volume 23, pages 245–288, 2002.

15. S. Schulte im Walde. *Experiments on the Automatic Induction of German Semantic Verb Classes.* PhD thesis, Universität Stuttgart, Germany, 2003.
16. R. Jones, R. Ghani, T. Mitchell, and E. Riloff. Active learning for information extraction with multiple view features sets. In *Proc. of Adaptive Text Extraction and Mining, EMCL/PKDD-03, Cavtat-Dubrovnik, Croatia*, pages 26–34, 2003.
17. W. Lezius. Morphy - German morphology, part-of-speech tagging and applications. In *Proc. of 9th Euralex International Congress, Stuttgart, Germany*, pages 619–623, 2000.
18. C. Manning and H. Schütze. *Foundations of Statistical Natural Language Processing.* The MIT Press, Cambridge, MA, 1999.
19. A. K. McCallum. MALLET: A machine learning for language toolkit, 2002.
20. R. J. Mooney and R. Bunescu. Mining knowledge from text using information extraction. *SIGKDD Explor. Newsl.*, 7(1):3–10, 2005.
21. M. Palmer and D. Gildea. The proposition bank: An annotated corpus of semantic roles. In *Computational Linguistics*, volume 31, pages 71–106, 2005.
22. S. Pradhan, K. Hacioglu, V. Kruglery, W. Ward, J. H. Martin, and D. Jurafsky. Support vector learning for semantic argument classification. *Machine Learning Journal*, Kluwer Academic Publishers, 59:1–29, 2005.
23. E. Rillof and M. Schelzenbach. An empirical approach to conceptual frame acquisition. In *Proc. of 6th Workshop on Very Large Corpora, Montreal, Canada*, pages 49–56, 1998.
24. J. Ruppenhofer, M. Ellsworth, M. R. L. Petruck, and C. R. Johnson. *FrameNet: Theory and Practice.* 2005.
25. M. Schiehlen. Annotation strategies for probabilistic parsing in German. In *Proc. of CoLing'04, Geneva, Switzerland*, 2004.
26. H. Schmid. Improvement in part-of-speech tagging with an application to German. In *Proc. of the ACL SIGDAT-Workshop, Dublin, Ireland*, pages 47–50, 1995.
27. H. Schmid. Efficient parsing of highly ambiguous context-free grammars with bit vectors. In *Proc. of CoLing'04, Geneva, Switzerland*, 2004.
28. G. Schreiber, H. Akkermans, A. Anjewierden, R. deHoog, N. Shadbolt, W. VandeVelde, and B. Wielinga. *Knowledge Engineering and Management: The CommonKADS Methodology.* The MIT Press, Cambridge, MA, 2000.
29. M. Tang, X. Luo, and S. Roukos. Active learning for statistical natural language parsing. In *Proc. of the ACL 40th Anniversary Meeting, Philadelphia, PA*, pages 120–127, 2002.
30. S. Weiss, N. Indurkhya, T. Zhang, and F. Damerau. *Text Mining: Predictive Methods for Analyzing Unstructured Information.* Springer, New York, NY, 2004.

5

A Case Study in Natural Language Based Web Search

Giovanni Marchisio, Navdeep Dhillon, Jisheng Liang, Carsten Tusk, Krzysztof Koperski, Thien Nguyen, Dan White, and Lubos Pochman

5.1 Introduction

Is there a public for natural language based search? This study, based on our experience with a Web portal, attempts to address criticisms on the lack of scalability and usability of natural language approaches to search. Our solution is based on InFact®, a natural language search engine that combines the speed of keyword search with the power of natural language processing. InFact performs clause level indexing, and offers a full spectrum of functionality that ranges from Boolean keyword operators to linguistic pattern matching in real time, which include recognition of syntactic roles, such as subject/object and semantic categories, such as people and places. A user of our search can navigate and retrieve information based on an understanding of actions, roles and relationships. In developing InFact, we ported the functionality of a deep text analysis platform to a modern search engine architecture. Our distributed indexing and search services are designed to scale to large document collections and large numbers of users. We tested the operational viability of InFact as a search platform by powering a live search on the Web. Site statistics and user logs demonstrate that a statistically significant segment of the user population is relying on natural language search functionality. Going forward, we will focus on promoting this functionality to an even greater percentage of users through a series of creative interfaces.

Information retrieval on the Web today makes little use of Natural Language Processing (NLP) techniques [1, 3, 11, 15, 18]. The perceived value of improved understanding is greatly outweighed by the practical difficulty of storing complex linguistic annotations in a scalable indexing and search framework. In addition, any champion of natural language techniques must overcome significant hurdles in user interface design, as greater search power often comes at a price of more work in formulating a query and navigating the results. All of these obstacles are compounded by the expected resistance to any technological innovation that has the potential to change or erode established models for advertising and search optimization, which are based on pricing of individual keywords or noun phrases, rather than relationships or more complex linguistic constructs.

Nevertheless, with the increasing amount of high value content made available on the Web and increased user sophistication, we have reasons to believe that a segment of the user population will eventually welcome tools that understand a lot more than present day keyword search does. Better understanding and increased search power depend on better parameterization of text content in a search engine index. The most universal storage employed today to capture text content is an inverted index. In a typical Web search engine, an inverted index may register presence or frequency or keywords, along with font size or style, and relative location in a Web page. Obviously this model is only a rough approximation to the complexity of human language and has the potential to be superseded by future generation of indexing standards.

InFact relies on a new approach to text parameterization that captures many linguistic attributes ignored by standard inverted indices. Examples are syntactic categories (parts of speech), syntactical roles (such as subject, objects, verbs, prepositional constraints, modifiers, etc.) and semantic categories (such as people, places, monetary amounts, etc.). Correspondingly, at query time, there are explicit or implicit search operators that can match, join or filter results based on this rich assortment of tags to satisfy very precise search requirements.

The goal of our experiment was to demonstrate that, once scalability barriers are overcome, a statistically significant percentage of Web users can be converted from keyword search to natural language based search. InFact has been the search behind the GlobalSecurity.org site (www.globalsecurity.org) for the past six months. According to the Alexa site (www.alexa.com), GlobalSecurity.org has a respectable overall traffic rank (no. 6,751 as of Feb 14, 2006). Users of the site can perform keyword searches, navigate results by action themes, or enter explicit semantic queries. An analysis of query logs demonstrate that all these non-standard information discovery processes based on NLP have become increasingly popular over the first six months of operation.

The remainder of this chapter is organized as follows. Section 5.2 presents an overview of our system, with special emphasis on the linguistic analyses and new search logic. Section 5.3 describes the architecture and deployment of a typical InFact system. Section 5.4 is a study of user patterns and site statistics.

5.2 InFact System Overview

InFact consists of an indexing and a search module. With reference to Figure 5.1, indexing pertains to the processing flow on the bottom of the diagram. InFact models text as a complex multivariate object using a unique combination of deep parsing, linguistic normalization and efficient storage. The storage schema addresses the fundamental difficulty of reducing information contained in parse trees into generalized data structures that can be queried dynamically. In addition, InFact handles the problem of linguistic variation by mapping complex linguistic structures into semantic and syntactic equivalents. This representation supports dynamic relationship and event search, information extraction and pattern matching from large document collections in real time.

5.2.1 Indexing

With reference to Figure 5.1, InFact's Indexing Service performs in order: 1) document processing, 2) clause processing, and 3) linguistic normalization.

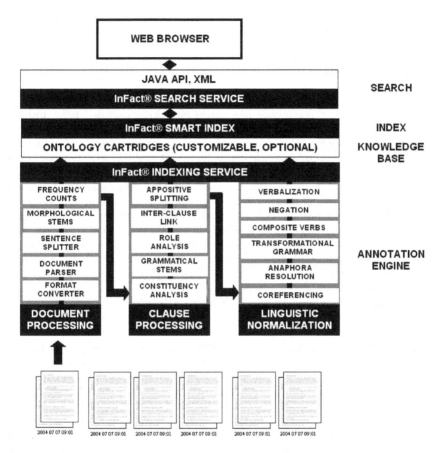

Fig. 5.1. Functional overview of InFact.

Document Processing

The first step in document processing is format conversion, which we handle through our native format converters, or optionally via search export conversion software from Stellant™ (www.stellent.com), which can convert 370 different input file types. Our customized document parsers can process disparate styles and recognized zones within each document. Customized document parsers address the issue that a Web page may not be the basic unit of content, but it may consist of separate sections with an associated set of relationships and metadata. For instance a blog post may contain blocks of text with different dates and topics. The challenge is to automatically recognize variations from a common style template, and segment information in the index to match zones in the source documents, so the relevant section can be displayed in response to a query. Next we apply logic for sentence splitting in preparation for clause processing. Challenges here include the ability to unambiguously recognize sentence delimiters, and recognize regions such as lists or tables that are unsuitable for deep parsing. Last, we extract morphological stems and compute frequency counts, which are then entered in the index.

Clause Processing

The indexing service takes the output of the sentence splitter and feeds it to a deep linguistic parser. A sentence may consist of multiple clauses. Unlike traditional models that store only term frequency distributions, InFact performs clause level indexing and captures syntactic category and roles for each term, and grammatical constructs, relationships, and inter-clause links that enable it to understand events. One strong differentiator of our approach to information extraction [4, 5, 7, 8, 14, 19] is that we create these indices automatically, without using predefined extraction rules, and we capture all information, not just predefined patterns. Our parser performs a full constituency and dependency analysis, extracting part-of-speech (POS) tags and grammatical roles for all tokens in every clause. In the process, tokens undergo grammatical stemming and an optional, additional level of tagging. For instance, when performing grammatical stemming on verb forms, we normalize to the infinitive, but we may retain temporal tags (e.g., past, present, future), aspect tags (e.g., progressive, perfect), mood/modality tags (e.g., possibility, subjunctive, irrealis, negated, conditional, causal) for later use in search.

Next we capture inter-clause links, through: 1) explicit tagging of conjunctions or pronouns that provide the link between the syntactic structures for two adjacent clauses in the same sentence; and 2) pointing to the list of annotated keywords in the antecedent and following sentence. Note that the second mechanism ensures good recall in those instances where the parser fails to produce a full parse tree for long and convoluted sentences, or information about an event is spread across adjacent sentences. In addition, appositive clauses are recognized, split into separate clauses and cross-referenced to the parent clause.

For instance, the sentence: "Appointed commander of the Continental Army in 1775, George Washington molded a fighting force that eventually won independence from Great Britain" consists of three clauses, each containing a governing verb (appoint, mold, and win). InFact decomposes it into a primary clause ("George Washington molded a fighting force") and two secondary clauses, which are related to the primary clause by an appositive construct ("Appointed commander of the Continental Army in 1775") and a pronoun ("that eventually won independence from Great Britain"), respectively. Each term in each clause is assigned a syntactic category or POS tag (e.g., noun, adjective, etc.) and a grammatical role tag (e.g., subject, object, etc.). InFact then utilizes these linguistic tags to extract relationships that are normalized and stored in an index, as outlined in the next two sections.

Linguistic Normalization

We apply normalization rules at the syntactic, semantic, or even pragmatic level. Our approach to coreferencing and anaphora resolution make use of syntactic agreement and/or binding theory constraints, as well as modeling of referential distance, syntactic position, and head noun [6, 10, 12, 13, 16, 17]. Binding theory places syntactic restrictions on the possible coreference relationships between pronouns and their antecedents [2]. For instance, when performing pronoun coreferencing, syntactic agreement based on person, gender and number limits our search for a noun phrase linked to a pronoun to a few candidates in the text. In addition, consistency restrictions limit our search to a precise text span (the previous sentence, the preceding text in the current sentence, or the previous and current sentence) depending upon whether the pronoun is personal, possessive, reflective, and what is its person. In the sentence "John works by himself," "himself" must refer to John, whereas in "John bought him a new car," "him" must refer to some other individual mentioned in a previous sentence. In the sentence, ""You have not been sending money," John said in a recent call to his wife from Germany," binding theory constraints limit pronoun resolution to first and second persons within a quotation (e.g., you), and the candidate antecedent to a noun outside the quotation, which fits the grammatical role of object of a verb or argument of a preposition (e.g., wife). Our coreferencing and anaphora resolution models also benefit from preferential weighting based on dependency attributes. The candidate antecedents that appear closer to a pronoun in the text are scored higher (weighting by referential distance). Subject is favored over object, except for accusative pronouns (weighting by syntactic position). A head noun is favored over its modifiers (weighting by head label). In addition, as part of the normalization process, we apply a transformational grammar to map multiple surface structures into an equivalent deep structure. A common example is the normalization of a dependency structure involving a passive verb form into the active, and recognition of the deep subject of such clause. At the more pragmatic level, we apply rules to normalize composite verb expressions, capture explicit and implicit negations, or to verbalize noun or adjectives in cases where they convey action sense in preference to the governing verb of a clause. For instance, the sentences "Bill did not visit Jane," which contains an explicit negation, and "Bill failed to visit Jane," where the negation is rendered by a composite verb expression, are mapped to the same structure.

5.2.2 Storage

The output of a deep parser is a complex augmented tree structure that usually does not lend itself to a tractable indexing schema for cross-document search. Therefore, we have developed a set of rules for converting an augmented tree representation into a scalable data storage structure.

In a dependency tree, every word in the sentence is a modifier of exactly one other word (called its head), except the head word of the sentence, which does not have a head. We use a list of tuples to specify a dependency tree with the following format:

(Label Modifier Root POS Head-label Role Antecedent [Attributes])

where: **Label** is a unique numeric ID; **Modifier** is a term in the sentence; **Root** is the root form (or category) of the modifier; **POS** is its lexical category; **Head-label** is the ID of the term that modifier modifies; **Role** specifies the type of dependency relationship between head and modifier, such as subject, complement, etc; **Antecedent** is the antecedent of the modifier; **Attributes** is the list of semantic attributes that may be associated with the modifier, e.g., person's name, location, time, number, date, etc.

For instance, the parse tree for our Washington example above is shown in Table 5.1.

Table 5.1. The parse tree representation of a sentence.

Label	Modifier	Root	POS	Head Label	Role	Antecedent	Attributes
1	Appointed	Appoint	V				
2	commander		N	1	Obj		Person/title
3	of		Prep	2	Mod		
4	the		Det	5	Det		
5	Continental Army		N	3	Pcomp		Organization/name
6	in		Prep	1	Mod		
7	1775		N	6	Pcomp		Numeric/date
8	George Washington		N	9	Subj		Person/name
9	molded	mold	V				
10	a		Det	12	Det		
11	fighting		A	12	Mod		
12	force		N	9	Obj		
13	that		N	15	Subj	12	
14	eventually		A	15	Mod		
15	won	win	V				
16	independence		N	15	Obj		
17	from		Prep	16	Mod		
18	Great Britain		N	17	Pcomp		Location/country

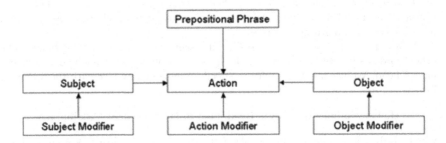

Fig. 5.2. The Subject-Action-Object indexing structure.

The basic idea behind or approach to indexing involves collapsing selected nodes in the parse tree to reduce the overall complexity of the dependency structures.

We model our storage structures after the general notion of subject-action-object triplets, as shown in Figure 5.2. Interlinked subject-action-object triples and their respective modifiers can express most types of syntactic relations between various entities within a sentence.

The index abstraction is presented in Table 5.2, where the additional column *"Dist"* denotes degrees of separations (or distance) between primary *Subject, Verb, Object* and each *Modifier*, and *"Neg"* keeps track of negated actions.

Table 5.2. The index abstraction of a sentence.

Subject	Subject-Modifier	Object	Object-Modifier	Verb	Verb-Modifier	Prep	Pcomp	Dist	Neg
		Washington	George	appoint				1	F
		commander		appoint				1	F
		Army	Continental	appoint				3	F
				appoint		in	1775	2	F
Washington	George	force	fighting	mold				2	F
force	fighting	independence		win				1	F
				win		from	Great Britain	3	F
				win	eventually			1	F

InFact stores the normalized triplets into dedicated index structures that

- are optimized for efficient keyword search
- are optimized for efficient cross-document retrieval of arbitrary classes of relationships or events (see examples in the next section)
- store document metadata and additional ancillary linguistic variables for filtering of search results by metadata constraints (e.g., author, date range), or by linguistic attributes (e.g., retrieve negated actions, search subject modifier field in addition to primary subject in a relationship search)
- (optionally) superimposes annotations and taxonomical dependencies from a custom ontology or knowledge base.

With regard to the last feature, for instance, we may superimpose a *[Country]* entity label on a noun phrase, which is the subject of the verb *"to attack."* The index supports multiple ontologies and entangled multiparent taxonomies.

InFact stores "soft events" instead of fitting textual information into a rigid relational schema that may result in information loss. "Soft events" are data structures that can be recombined to form events and relationships. "Soft events" are pre-indexed to facilitate thematic retrieval by action, subject, and object type. For instance, a sentence like "The president of France visited the capital of Tunisia" contains evidence of 1) a presidential visit to a country's capital and 2) diplomatic relationships between two countries. Our storage strategy maintains both interpretations. In other words, we allow more than one subject or object to be associated with the governing verb of a sentence. The tuples stored in the database are therefore "soft events," as they may encode alternative patterns and relationships found in each sentence. Typically, only one pattern is chosen at search time, in response to a specific user request (i.e., request #1: gather all instances of a president visiting a country; request #2: gather all instances of interactions between any two countries).

5.2.3 Search

Unlike keyword search engines, InFact employs a highly expressive query language (IQL or InFact Query Language) that combines the power of grammatical roles with the flexibility of Boolean operators, and allows users to search for actions, entities, relationships, and events. InFact represents the basic relationship between two entities with an expression of the kind:

$$Subject\ Entity > Action > Object\ Entity,$$

The arrows in the query refer to the directionality of the action, which could be either uni-directional (as above) or bi-directional. For example,

$$Entity\ 1 <> Action <> Entity\ 2$$

will retrieve all relationships involving *Entity 1* and *Entity 2*, regardless of their roles as subject or object of the action. Wildcards can be used for any grammatical role. For instance, the query "* > eat > cake" will retrieve a list of anybody or anything that eats a cake; and a query like "*John > * > Jane*" will retrieve a list of all uni-directional relationships between John and Jane. InFact also supports the notion of entity types. For instance, in addition to entering an explicit country name like "Argentina" as Entity 1 or Entity 2 in a relationship query, a user can enter a wildcard for any country name by using the syntax *[Country]*. InFact comes with a generic ontology that includes *[Location]*, *[Person]*, *[Organization]*, *[Numeric]* as the four main branches. Entity types can be organized hierarchically in a taxonomy. IQL renders hierarchical dependencies by means of taxonomy paths. For instance, in *[Entity/Location/Country]* and *[Entity/Location/City]* both *[Country]* and *[City]* nodes have a common parent *[Location]*. Taxonomy path can encode "is-a" relations (as in the above examples), or any other relations defined in a particular ontology (e.g., "part-of" relation). When querying, we can use a taxonomy node in a relationship search, e.g., *[Location]*, and the query will automatically include all subpaths in the taxonomic hierarchy, including *[City]*, *[Location]*, or narrow the search by expanding the path to *[Location/City]*.

With the InFact query language, we can search for:

- Any relationships involving an entity of interest

For example, the query "*George Bush <> * <> *"* will retrieve any events involving "*George Bush*" as subject or object

- Relationships between two entities or entity types

For example, the query "*China <> * <> Afghan*"* will retrieve all relationships between the two countries. Note in this case a wildcard is used in "*Afghan*"* to handle different spelling variations of Afghanistan. The query "*Bin Laden <>*<> [Organization]*" will retrieve any relationships involving "Bin Laden" and an organization.

- Events involving one or more entities or types

For example, the query "*Pope > visit > [country]*" will return all instances of the Pope visiting a country. In another example, "*[Organization/name] > acquire > [Organization/name]*" will return all events involving a named company buying another named company.

- Events involving a certain action type

"Action types" are groups of semantically linked actions. For example, query *"[Person] > [Communication] > [Person]"* will retrieve all events involving communication between two people.

InFact's query syntax supports Boolean operators (i.e., AND, OR, NOT). For example, the query:

$$Clinton\ NOT\ Hillary > visit\ OR\ travel\ to > [Location]$$

is likely to retrieve the travels of *Bill Clinton*, but not *Hillary Clinton*.

We can further constrain actions with modifiers, which can be explicit entities or entity types, e.g., *Paris* or *[location]*. For example, the query

$$[Organization/Name] > buy > [Organization/Name]\^[money]$$

will only return results where a document mentions a specific monetary amount along with a corporate acquisition. Similarly, the query

$$Bush <> meet<> Clinton\ \^[location]$$

will return results restricted to actions that occur in an explicit geographical location.

We can also filter search results by specifying document-level constraints, including:

- Document metadata tags – lists of returned actions, relationships or events are restricted to documents that contain the specified metadata values.
- Boolean keyword expressions – lists of returned actions, relationships or events are restricted to documents that contain the specified Boolean keyword expressions.

For instance, a query like:

$$[Organization/Name] > buy > [Organization/Name]\^[money];\ energy\ NOT\ oil$$

will return documents that mentions a corporate acquisition with a specific monetary amount, and also contain the keyword "energy" but do not contain the keyword "oil."

InFact also provides a context operator for inter-clause linking. Suppose for instance, that we want to retrieve all events where a plane crash kills a certain number of passengers. The event could be spread over adjacent sentences, as in: *"The plane crashed shortly after take-off. As many as 224 people were killed."* In this case, a query like:

$$* > kill > [numeric] \sim plane\ crash$$

will retrieve all plane crash events, regardless of whether they are contained in a single or multiple, adjacent sentences.

InFact can also support synonyms and query expansion via custom ontologies. In this case, InFact will automatically recognize the equivalence of entities or actions that belong to the same ontology node.

The InFact Query Language rests on a flexible Java Search API. The Java Search API allows us to programmatically concatenate search operators, package and present them to the end user through a simpler interface.

5.3 Architecture and Deployment

We designed both indexing and search as parallel distributed services. Figure 5.3 shows a typical deployment scenario, with an indexing service on the left and a search service on the right. A typical node in each of the diagrams would is a dual processor (e.g., 2.8+GHz Xeon 1U) machine with 4GB of RAM and two 120GB drives.

The Indexing Service (left) processes documents in parallel. Index workers access source documents from external web servers. Multiple index workers can run on each node. Each index worker performs all the "Annotation Engine" analyses described in Figure 5.1. An index manager orchestrates the indexing process across many index workers. The results of all analyses are stored in temporary indices in the index workers. At configurable intervals, the index manager orchestrates the merging of all temporary indices into the partition index components.

A partition index hosts the actual disk based indices used for searching. The contents of a document corpus are broken up into one or more subsets that are each stored in a partition index. The system supports multiple partition indices: the exact number will depend on corpus size, number of queries per second and desired response time. Indices are queried in parallel and are heavily IO bound. Partition indices are attached to the leaf nodes of the Search Service on the right.

In addition to storing results in a temporary index, index workers can also store the raw results of parsing in a Database Management System (DBMS). The database is used almost exclusively to restore a partition index in the event of index corruption. Data storage requirements on the DBMS range between 0.5 and 6x corpus size depending on which recovery options for the InFact system are enabled. Once a document has been indexed and merged into a partition index it is available for searching.

In a typical search deployment, queries are sent from a client application; the client application may be a Web browser or a custom application built using the Search API. Requests arrive over HTTP and are passed through a Web Server to the Search Service layer and on to the top searcher of a searcher tree. Searchers are responsible for searching one or more partition index. Multiple searchers are supported and can be stacked in a hierarchical tree configuration to enable searching large data sets. The top level searcher routes ontology related requests to one or more ontology searchers, which can run on a single node. Search requests are passed to child searchers, which then pass the request down to one or more partition indices. The partition index performs the actual search against the index, and the result passes up the tree until it arrives back at the client for display to the user.

If a particular segment of data located in a partition index is very popular and becomes a search bottleneck, it may be cloned; the parent searcher will load balance across two or three partition indices. In addition, if ontology searches become a bottleneck, more ontology searchers may be added. If a searcher becomes a bottleneck, more searchers can be added. The search service and Web server tier may be replicated, as well, if a load balancer is used.

The example in Figure 5.3 is an example of a large-scale deployment. In the GlobalSecurity.org portal, we currently need only four nodes to support a user community of 100,000 against a corpus of several GB of international news articles, which are updated on a daily basis.

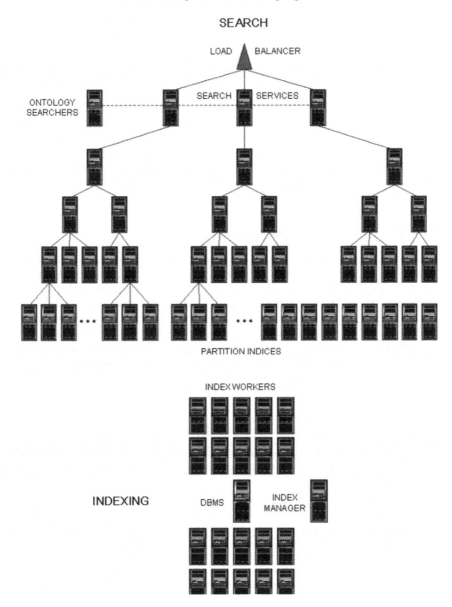

Fig. 5.3. Architectural overview of InFact.

5.4 The GlobalSecurity.org Experience

5.4.1 Site Background

InFact started powering the GlobalSecurity.org Web site on June 22, 2005. Based in Alexandria, VA, and "launched in 2000, GlobalSecurity.org is the most comprehensive and authoritative online destination for those in need of both reliable background information and breaking news ...GlobalSecurity.org's unique positioning enables it to reach both a targeted and large diversified audience. The content of the website is updated hourly, as events around the world develop, providing in-depth coverage of complicated issues. The breadth and depth of information on the site ensures a loyal repeat audience. This is supplemented by GlobalSecurity.org's unique visibility in the mass media, which drives additional growth" [9]. The director of GlobalSecurity.org, John Pike, regularly provides commentary and analysis on space and security issues to PBS, CNN, MSNBC, Fox, ABC, CBS, NBC, BBC, NPR, and numerous print and online publications. In powering this site, InFact serves the information search needs of a well-established user community of 100,000, consisting of news reporters, concerned citizens, subject matter experts, senior leaders, and junior staff and interns.

5.4.2 Operational Considerations

When preparing the GlobalSecurity.org deployment, one of our prime concerns was the response time of the system. For this reason, we kept the data size of the partition indices small enough so that most operations occur in memory and disk access is minimal. We split the GlobalSecurity.org data across two index chunks, each containing roughly 14 GB of data in each partition index. Another concern was having sufficient capacity to handle the user load. To account for future user traffic, we specified the deployment for 2-3 times the maximum expected load of about 11,000 queries per day. This left us with two cloned partition indices per index chunk. In addition, we wanted a hot back up of the entire site, in case of any hardware failures, and to support us each time we are rolling out new features.

Fig. 5.4. The GlobalSecurity.org home page.

Another area of concern was the distribution of query types. Our system has significantly varying average response time and throughput (measured in queries/minute) depending on the type of queries being executed. We assumed that users would take some time to migrate from keyword queries to fact queries. Therefore, we selected a very conservative ratio of 50/50 fact-to-keyword query types with a view to adding more hardware if needed. After automatically generating millions of query files, we heavily loaded the system with the queries to simulate heavy traffic using JMeter, a multi-threaded client web user simulation application from the Apache Jakarta organization. Based on these simulations, we deployed with only four nodes.

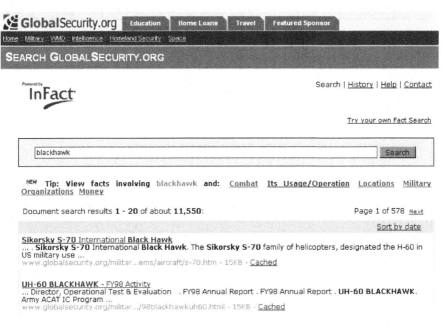

Fig. 5.5. Keyword search result and automatic tip generation with InFact in response to the keyword query "blackhawk."

5.4.3 Usability Considerations

In deploying InFact on the GlobalSecurity.org site, our goal was to serve the information needs of a wide community of users, the majority of which are accustomed to straightforward keyword search. Therefore, on this site, by default, InFact acts as a keyword search engine. However, we also started experimenting with ways to progressively migrate users away from keyword search and towards natural language search or "fact search." With reference to Figure 5.4, users approaching the site can enter InFact queries from the search box in the upper left, or click on the Hot Search link. The latter executes a predefined fact search, which is particularly popular over an extended time period (days or even weeks). The Hot Search is controlled by GlobalSecurity.org staff, and is outside the control of the general user. However, once in the InFact search page (Figure 5.5), the user can execute fact searches explicitly by using the IQL syntax. The IQL syntax is fully documented in the InFact Help page.

Alternatively, by clicking on the "Try your own Fact Search" link on the upper right of the InFact Search page, the user is introduced to a Custom Query Generator (Figure 5.6), which produces the query of Figure 5.7.

Powered by
InFact   Search | History | Help | Contact

Fact Search - Custom query generator

Fact Search is a new way to search for **something that happened,** or **what somebody or something did.**

To use **Fact Search,** you must be looking for something that can be expressed in terms of an **action** or **verb.** You can specify who did the action, or who the action was done to, or both, using the greater-than symbol ('>'). The asterisk ('*') means "anything" or "anyone":

USA > invade > Iraq	- returns links to all sentences mentioning USA invading Iraq
[organization] > win> contract	- returns links to sentences mentioning who won contracts
* > attack > 1st Infantry Division	- returns links to sentences mentioning the division being attacked
iraq war > cost > *	- returns links to sentences discussing what the iraq war is costing
F-22 > * > [money]	- returns links to sentences involving the F-22 and money

You can generate your own query by entering terms in any of the fields below. [learn more]

Source of Action: (e.g., "USA")   Action: (e.g., a verb like "invade")   Target of Action: (e.g., "Iraq")

[   ] → [export   ] → [plutonium   ]

Fact Search can also let you filter out any undesired results, by showing only results from documents that contain a specified keyword.

☐ **Where keywords** (use AND, OR, or NOT): [   ] are found...

  ⦿ Near the relationship ○ Anywhere in document

[Search] [Clear]

Fig. 5.6. Fact search with the InFact Custom Query Generator: the user is looking for facts that involve the export of plutonium.

The most interesting device we employed is guided fact navigation in response to a keyword entry. We call this process "tip generation." In this scenario, we capture keywords entered by a user and try to understand whether these are names of people, places, organization, military units, vehicles, etc. When executing a keyword search, the InFact system can recommend several fact searches which may be of interest to a user based on the keywords entered. These recommendations are presented to the user as a guided navigation menu consisting of links. In the example of Figure 5.5, the user is performing a keyword search for "blackhawk." The user sees a series of links presented at the top of the result set. They read: "Tip: View facts involving blackhawk and: Combat, Its Usage/Operation, Locations, Military Organizations, Money." Each of these links when clicked in turn executes a fact search. For instance, clicking on Military Organizations will generate the list of facts or relationships of Figure 5.8, which gives an overview of all military units that have used the blackhawk helicopter; clicking on Money will generate the list of facts or relationships of Figure 5.9, which gives an overview of procurement and maintenance costs, as well as government spending for this vehicle. The relationships are returned in a table display where each row is an event, and columns identify the three basic semantic

Fig. 5.7. Fact search with the InFact Custom Query Generator: InFact translates the query of Figure 5.6 into the InFact Query Language (IQL) and returns a list of results. IQL operators are fully documented in the Help page.

roles of source (or subject), action (or verb), and target (or object). Note that relationships, by default, are sorted by relevance to a query, but can also be resorted by date, action frequency, or alphabetically by source, action or target. Each of the relationships or facts in the table is in turn hyperlinked to the exact location in the source document where it was found, so the user can quickly validate the findings and explore its context (Figure 5.10).

Usage logs were the primary driver for this customization effort. The personnel at GlobalSecurity.org were very helpful and provided us with many months of user traffic Web logs. We wrote some simple scripts to analyze the logs. For example, we studied the 500 most popular key word searches performed on the site ranked in order of popularity. Next, we began looking for entity types that would be helpful to the most number of users. We found a lot of user interest in weapons, terrorists, and US officials, amongst other things. We then set about creating ontologies for each of these areas. New custom ontologies can easily be mapped into the internal InFact ontology XML format.

5.4.4 Analysis of Query Logs

We wish to quantify the relative popularity of natural language (Fact) search versus keyword search. In addition, we wish to compare the relative success of alternative strategies we adopted to overcome usability issues. This study of log data reflect

Chinook All : BLACK HAWK	include	160th Special Operations Aviation Regiment 101st Airborne Division 10th Mountain Division 82nd Airborne Division
Marine Corps	inspect : across airfield	rigging : on Blackhawk
U.S. Army	install	UH-60 : in future ALQ-211 : on CH-47
U.S. Army	introduce : for example	fly-by-wire : capability : to Army Apache Black Hawk fleet
air force	investigate	Black Hawk fratricide : incident
Troops : from 2nd Battalion 505th Parachute Infantry Regiment 82nd Airborne Division	kick off	Operation Desert Lion : with air assault from Chinook Black Hawk helicopter
Black Hawk : helicopter	land : As part of Operation Falcon Sweep	Shakaria Soldier : of 2nd Battalion 502nd Infantry Regiment
40 : CH-47 UH-60 AH-1	lift	1st Brigade : into
211th Aviation Group	maintain	UH-60 Blackhawk AH-64 Apache
air force : contractor	maintain	Blackhawk : helicopter Army : Apache

Fig. 5.8. Tip Navigation with InFact: facts involving the "blackhawk" helicopter and military organizations.

Date	Source	Action	Target
02/23/2004	$14.6 billion	buy	796 helicopter additional : Black Hawk
10/16/1998	$690 million : appropriation : for fiscal year 1999	buy : for Colombian police extra $190 million for U.S. Customs Service $90 million for enhanced inspection surveillance along U.S.-Mexico border	six UH-60 Black Hawk : helicopter
06/05/1995	Army UH-60 helicopter : trip	almost : cost[2]	more : $1,600 : than car
04/07/2006	Black Hawk : Upgrade - Program	cost	increased : $2,922.5 million
01/02/2004	Blackhawk : helicopter	cost	$8.6 million
06/27/2003	additional : investment : of $331 million for additional spare part	increase[2]	readiness : of Apache Blackhawk helicopter
01/01/2001	FY 2002 : decrease : of $28.2 million	reflect[2]	reduced depot maintenance : requirement : for UH-60 helicopter for UH-1 helicopter retirement pending
02/02/2004	8 new Black Hawk $124.8 : aircraft	upgrade : for 1st	5 : Black Hawk : to UH-60M $78.3 model
06/11/1996	$75,000,000 : for Blackhawk	advance	Rotary Wing Aircraft : blackhawk procurement

Fig. 5.9. Tip Navigation with InFact: facts involving the "blackhawk" helicopter and money.

four ways users submit a natural language query to InFact: 1) they click on the Hot Search link; 2) they click on a keyword tip; 3) they click on an example in the Query Generator or Help page; 4) they attempt to type an explicit relationship or fact search using the IQL syntax.

Date	Source	Action	Target
02/23/2004	$14.6 billion	buy	796 helicopter additional : Black Hawk
10/16/1998	$690 million : appropriation : for fiscal year 1999	buy : for Colombian police extra $190 million for U.S. Customs Service $90 million for enhanced inspection surveillance along U.S.-Mexico border	six UH-60 Black Hawk : helicopter
06/05/1995	Army UH-60 helicopter : trip	almost : cost[2]	more : $1,600 : than car
04/07/2006	Black Hawk : Upgrade - Program	cost	increased : $2,922.5 million
01/02/2004	Blackhawk : helicopter	cost	$8.6 million
06/27/2003	additional : investment : of $331 million for additional spare part	increase[2]	readiness : of Apache Blackhawk helicopter
01/01/2001	FY 2002 : decrease : of $28.2 million	reflect[2]	reduced depot maintenance : requirement : for UH-60 helicopter for UH-1 helicopter retirement pending
02/02/2004	8 new Black Hawk $124.8 : aircraft	upgrade : for 1st	5 : Black Hawk : to UH-60M $78.3 model
06/11/1996	$75,000,000 : for Blackhawk	advance	Rotary Wing Aircraft : blackhawk procurement

In contrast, the unit cost of a P-3 manned aircraft used by U.S.
Immigration and Customs Enforcement is $36 million. **Blackhawk helicopters which are frequently used on the borders cost $8.6 million per unit.** However, the benefit of the Blackhawk's relative low unit cost is diminished by its lack of endurance. Blackhawks have a maximum endurance of 2 hours and 18 minutes.16
Consequently, UAVs longer
dwell time would allow them to patrol the border longer.
The range of UAVs is a significant asset when compared to border agents on patrol or stationery surveillance equipment. If an illegal border entrant attempts to transit through dense woods or mountainous terrain, UAVs would have a greater chance of

Fig. 5.10. Tip Navigation with InFact: each fact is hyperlinked to the exact location where it was found in the source document.

At the time of this writing, an average of 36% of advanced search users click on the hot search link "Iran and Nuclear program," which executes a predefined search like *"Iran > * ~ nuclear."* However, it is difficult to assess what the user experience is like because in 80% of cases the user performs non-search-related tasks, and therefore we don't know how long they spent looking at the results. Note that users clicking on this link may not realize that they are going to a search engine page, since the link title is ambiguous. The results of this search are quite good, and still relevant. The hot search is an important entry point into our search site, as 36% of all the fact search queries executed came from this source. It seems likely that adding more of these hot search links or otherwise accentuating them on the page would significantly increase user exposure to natural language based queries.

Our analysis of query logs shows that keyword tips are the most effective way to migrate users to Fact Search. Users who click on tips frequently follow up with queries of their own. Tip clickers also write better queries, probably because, after seeing the column display, they have a much better sense of how queries can be composed. Keyword tip clickers typically find the results engaging enough to spend an average of 1.5 minutes studying the results: 37% of users go back and click on more than one tip. Even better, 87% follow up by clicking on the "Try your own Fact Search" link and try their own query. All of the queries attempted are queries; 90% produce results; our follow up analysis suggests that for two thirds of these queries the results are relevant to the users search goals. In other words, users who click on the tips are extremely likely not only to try their own fact search, but also to pay enough attention to the format to write both valid and useful queries.

Examples in the Help File or Query Generator are largely ineffective at getting users to try Fact Search. Because the results returned by the examples usually do not necessarily relate to what the user wishes to search on, the column display is more of a distraction than an enticement to try Fact Search. However, those who go on to try Fact Search, after clicking on an example, have a better chance of writing good queries. Example link clickers are less likely to experiment with Fact Search or invest time learning how it works. Seventy-two percent of users end their session after clicking on one or more examples, not even returning to perform the keyword search that presumably brought them to the site in the first place. Of the 28% who did not leave the site after clicking an example, two thirds went on to try a Fact Search. Only 6% of users click on examples after having tried a Fact Search query on their own. Analysis of this user group suggests that examples have a place in the UI, but are not sufficiently compelling to motivate users to try Fact Search alone. However, this evidence does lend support to the hypothesis that users who see the column display are more likely to create valid queries: 60% of the users who click on examples and go on to write their own queries write valid queries and get results, which is still a much higher percentage than for users who blindly try to create queries.

About 75% of users who try Fact Search directly by using the IQL syntax, and without seeing the column display first fail to get results. Forty-five percent of users write invalid queries where nouns are inserted in the action field (the most common error). Another common error is specifying too much information or attaching prepositions to noun phrases. We can detect some of these errors automatically, and we plan to provide automatic guidance to users going forward. About 20% of query creators get impressive results. Most successful users get their queries right on the first shot, and, in general, seem unwilling to invest much time experimenting. Successful users are most likely expert analysts. In reproducing their searches and inspecting their results, we estimate that they have a positive impression of Fact search. In 75% of cases the results of Fact Search take direct the user quickly to the relevant parts of relevant documents, providing a deeper overview and faster navigation of content. However, in 25% of cases, expert users also write queries that return no results. Reasons for this include specifying too much information or including modifiers or prepositional terms in the verb field such as: "cyber attack," "led by," and "go to." In many cases users would be successful by just entering the verb. In some cases, users get lots of fact search results, but lack the experience to refine their query, so they simply go back to keyword search. We should try to communicate how queries can be modified further if there are too many results, perhaps by adding an ontology tag, or a context operator to the query syntax. For instance, the query *"Bush > meet > [person]"* could yield a large number of irrelevant results, if a user is only interested in a list of diplomatic meetings. The query can be refined as *"Bush >meet > [person/name]."* In this case, the addition of an ontology tag restricts the number of meetings to those that are likely to involve named political personalities of some relevance. If the user is primarily interested in meeting that involve talks on nuclear arms control, the query can be further refined as *"Bush > meet > [person/name] ~ nuclear arms control."* Similarly, the query *"[country] > produce > uranium"* can be turned into the query *"[country] > produce >[numeric] uranium"* if a user is after quantities of uranium that are being produced around the world. In general, we observe that users accustomed to keyword search believe that specifying more terms translates into more accurate results. In moving these users to Fact Search we must encourage them to start as simple as possible, since the IQL can express in two words what would take 20 lines using Boolean language.

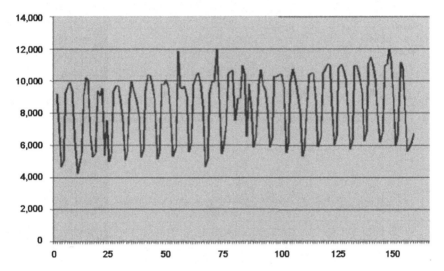

Fig. 5.11. Queries/day vs day of operation (June 22, 2005, to November 30, 2005).

Finally, Figure 5.11 shows overall query volumes (keyword search and Fact Search) as a function of day from the first day of operation (June 22 to November 30, 2005). The cyclic nature of the graph derives from the fact that most user access the site during the working week. Figure 5.12, which displays query volumes vs week of operation, clearly shows a positive trend: overall traffic to the site has increased by almost 40% ever since we introduced InFact search. The most interesting metrics relate to the percentage of users that derive value from Fact Search. The most effective mechanism to promote natural language search, as we have seen, are the tips. Figure 5.13 shows a 60% increase in the number of users that click on the tips automatically generated by InFact's advanced linguistic analysis over our entire period of operation. The overall percentage has increased from 4% to 10%. Our analysis also suggests that the best way to teach users how to write good queries is to first expose them to the summary result displays that ensues from a natural language query. The sooner users become aware of the type of results that a natural language query can yield, the higher the chances that they learn how to use the new search functions correctly. This reinforces the idea that the result display may be a driver of Fact Search.

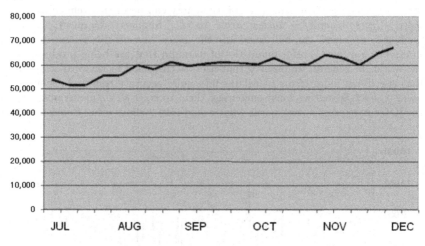

Fig. 5.12. Queries/week vs week of operation (June to November, 2005).

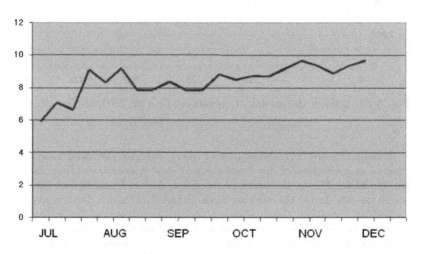

Fig. 5.13. Percentage of tips clicked (June to November, 2005).

5.5 Conclusion

We deployed a natural language based search to a community of Web users, and measured its popularity relative to conventional keyword search. Our work addressed criticisms of NLP approaches to search to the effect that they are not scalable and are too complex to be usable by average end-users. Our approach rests on a sophisticated index parameterization of text content, that captures syntactic and semantic roles, in addition to keyword counts, and enables interactive search and retrieval of events patterns based on a combination of keyword distributions and natural language attributes. Our distributed indexing and search services are designed to scale to large document collections and large numbers of users. We successfully deployed on a Web site that serves a community of 100,000 users. An analysis of query logs shows that, during the first six months of operation, traffic has increased by almost 40%. Even more significantly, we are encountering some success in promoting natural language searches. Our study demonstrates that the percentage of users that avail themselves of guided fact navigation based on natural language understanding has increased from 4% to 10% during the first six months of operation. Going forward, we will focus on increasing this percentage with a more innovative UI.

5.6 Acknowledgments

This work was partially supported by Dr. Joseph Psotka of the US Army Research Institute under contract No. W74V8H-05-C-0016. We are also indebted to John Pike, director of GlobalSecurity.org and his staff for providing us with many months of user traffic Web logs prior to going live.

References

1. D. Appelt and D. Israel. Introduction to information extraction technology. IJCAI-99 tutorial. http://www.ai.sri.com/~appelt/ie-tutorial/ijcai99.pdf.
2. D. Appelt and D. Israel. Semantic approaches to binding theory. In *Proceedings of the Workshop on Semantic Approaches to Binding Theory. ESSLLI*, 2003.
3. A. Arampatzis, T. van der Weide, P. van Bommel, and C. Koster. Linguistically-motivated information retrieval. In M. Dekker, editor, *Encyclopedia of Library and Information Science*, Springer Verlag, volume 69, pages 201–222. 2000.
4. C. F. Baker, C. J. Fillmore, and J. B. Lowe. The Berkeley FrameNet project. In C. Boitet and P. Whitelock, editors, *Proceedings of the Thirty-Sixth Annual Meeting of the Association for Computational Linguistics and Seventeenth International Conference on Computational Linguistics*, pages 86–90, San Francisco, California, 1998. Morgan Kaufmann Publishers.
5. I. Dagan, O. Glickman, and B. Magnini. The pascal recognizing textual entailment challenge. In *Proceedings of the PASCAL Challenges Workshop Recognizing Textual Entailment*, 2005.
6. M. Dimitrov. A light-weight approach to coreference resolution for named entities in text. Master's thesis, University of Sofia, 2002.

7. D. Gildea and D. Jurafsky. Automatic labeling of semantic roles. *Computational Linguistics*, 28(3):245–288, 2002.

8. D. Gildea and M. Palmer. The necessity of parsing for predicate argument recognition. In *Proceedings of the 40th Meeting of the Association for Computational Linguistics (ACL 2002)*, pages 239–246, 2002.

9. GlobalSecurity.org. http://www.globalsecurity.org/org/overview/history.htm.

10. M. Kameyama. Recognizing referential links: An information extraction perspective. In *Proceedings of the ACL'97/EACL'97 Workshop on Operation Factors in Practical, Robust Anaphora Resolution*, pages 46–53, 1997.

11. A. Kao and S. Poteet. Report on KDD conference 2004 panel discussion can natural language processing help text mining? *SIGKDD Explorations*, 6(2):132–133, 2004.

12. C. Kennedy and B. Boguraev. Anaphora for everyone: Pronominal anaphora resolution without a parser. In *Proceedings of the 16th International Conference on Computational Linguistics (COLING'96)*, pages 113–118, 1996.

13. S. Lappin and H. Leass. An algorithm for pronominal anaphora resolution. *Computational Linguistics*, 20(4):535–561, 1994.

14. D. Lin and P. Pantel. DIRT - discovery of inference rules from text. In *Knowledge Discovery and Data Mining*, pages 323–328, 2001.

15. C. Manning and H. Schutze. *Foundation of Statistical Natural Language Processing*. The MIT Press, 2000.

16. R. Miltov. Robust pronoun resolution with limited knowledge. In *Proceedings of the 18th International Conference on Computational Linguistics (COLING'98)/ACL'98*, pages 869–875.

17. R. Miltov. Anaphora resolution: The state of the art. Working paper. University of Wolverhamption, 1999.

18. National Institute of Standards and Technology. Automatic content extraction (ACE). http://www.itl.nist.gov/iaui/894.01/tests/ace.

19. M. Surdeanu, S. Harabagiu, J. Williams, and P. Aarseth. Using predicate-argument structures for information extraction. In *41th Annual Meeting of the Association for Computational Linguistics*, pages 8–15, 2003.

Evaluating Self-Explanations in iSTART: Word Matching, Latent Semantic Analysis, and Topic Models

Chutima Boonthum, Irwin B. Levinstein, and Danielle S. McNamara

6.1 Introduction

iSTART (Interactive Strategy Trainer for Active Reading and Thinking) is a web-based, automated tutor designed to help students become better readers via multimedia technologies. It provides young adolescent to college-aged students with a program of self-explanation and reading strategy training [19] called Self-Explanation Reading Training, or SERT [17, 21, 24, 25]. The reading strategies include (a) comprehension monitoring, being aware of one's understanding of the text; (b) paraphrasing, or restating the text in different words; (c) elaboration, using prior knowledge or experiences to understand the text (i.e., domain-specific knowledge-based inferences) or common sense, using logic to understand the text (i.e., domain-general knowledge based inferences); (d) predictions, predicting what the text will say next; and (e) bridging, understanding the relation between separate sentences of the text. The overall process is called "self-explanation" because the reader is encouraged to explain difficult text to him- or herself. iSTART consists of three modules: Introduction, Demonstration, and Practice. In the last module, students practice using reading strategies by typing self-explanations of sentences. The system evaluates each self-explanation and then provides appropriate feedback to the student. If the explanation is irrelevant or too short, the student is required to add more information. Otherwise, the feedback is based on the level of overall quality.

The computational challenge here is to provide appropriate feedback to the students concerning their self-explanations. To do so requires capturing some sense of both the meaning and quality of the self-explanation. Interpreting text is critical for intelligent tutoring systems, such as iSTART, that are designed to interact meaningfully with, and adapt to, the users' input. iSTART was initially proposed as using Latent Semantic Analysis (LSA; [13]) to capture the meanings of texts and to assess the students' self-explanation; however, while the LSA algorithms were being built, iSTART used simple word matching algorithms. In the course of integrating the LSA algorithms, we found that a combination of word-matching and LSA provided better results than either separately [18].

Our goal in evaluating the adequacy of the algorithms has been to imitate experts' judgments of the quality of the self-explanations. The current evaluation system predicts the score that a human gives on a 4-point scale, where 0 represents an evaluation of the explanation as irrelevant or too short; 1, minimally acceptable; 2, better but including primarily the local textual context; and 3, oriented to a more global comprehension. Depending on the text, population, and LSA space used, our results have ranged from 55 to 70 percent agreement with expert evaluations using that scale. We are currently attempting to improve the effectiveness of our algorithms by incorporating Topic Models (TM) either in place of or in conjunction with LSA and by using more than one LSA space from different genres (science, narrative, and general TASA corpus). We present some of the results of these efforts in this chapter.

Our algorithms are constrained by two major requirements, speedy response times and speedy introduction of new texts. Since the trainer operates in real time, the server that calculates the evaluation must respond in 4 to 5 seconds. Furthermore the algorithms must not require any significant preparation of new texts, a requirement precisely contrary to our plans when the project began. In order to accommodate the needs of the teachers whose classes use iSTART, the trainer must be able to use texts that the teachers wish their students to use for practice within a day or two. This time limit precludes us from significantly marking up the text or gathering related texts to incorporate into an LSA corpus.

In addition to the overall 4-point quality score, we are attempting to expand our evaluation to include an assessment of the presence of various reading strategies in the student's explanation so that we can generate more specific feedback. If the system were able to detect whether the explanation uses paraphrasing, bridging, or elaboration we could provide more detailed feedback to the students, as well as an individualized curriculum based on a more complete model of the student. For example, if the system were able to assess that the student only paraphrased sentences while self-explaining, and never used strategies such as making bridging inferences or knowledge-based elaborations, then the student could be provided additional training to generate more inference-based explanations.

This chapter describes how we employ word matching, LSA, and TM in the iSTART feedback systems and the performance of these techniques in producing both overall quality and reading strategy scores.

6.2 iSTART: Feedback Systems

iSTART was intended from the outset to employ LSA to determine appropriate feedback. The initial goal was to develop one or more benchmarks for each of the SERT strategies relative to each of the sentences in the practice texts and to use LSA to measure the similarity of a trainee's explanation to each of the benchmarks. A benchmark is simply a collection of words, in this case, words chosen to represent each of the strategies (e.g., words that represent the current sentence, words that represent a bridge to a prior sentence). However, while work toward this goal was progressing, we also developed a preliminary "word-based" (WB) system to provide feedback in our first version of iSTART [19] so that we could provide a complete curriculum for use in experimental situations. The second version of iSTART has integrated both LSA and WB in the evaluation process; however, the system still provides only overall quality feedback. Our current investigations aim to provide feedback based on identifying specific reading strategies.

6.2.1 Word Matching Feedback Systems

Word matching is a very simple and intuitive way to estimate the nature of a self-explanation. In the first version of iSTART, several hand-coded components were built for each practice text. For example, for each sentence in the text, the "important words" were identified by a human expert and a length criterion for the explanation was manually estimated. Important words were generally content words that were deemed important to the meaning of the sentence and could include words not found in the sentence. For each important word, an association list of synonyms and related terms was created by examining dictionaries and existing protocols as well as by human judgments of what words were likely to occur in a self-explanation of the sentence. In the sentence "All thunderstorms have a similar life history," for example, important words are *thunderstorm, similar, life*, and *history*. An association list for *thunderstorm* would include *storms, moisture, lightning, thunder, cold, tstorm, t-storm, rain, temperature, rainstorms*, and *electric-storm*. In essence, the attempt was made to imitate LSA.

A trainee's explanation was analyzed by matching the words in the explanation against the words in the target sentence and words in the corresponding association lists. This was accomplished in two ways: (1) Literal word matching and (2) Soundex matching.

Literal word matching - Words are compared character by character and if there is a match of the first 75% of the characters in a word in the target sentence (or its association list) then we call this a literal match. This also includes removing suffix -s, -d, -ed, -ing, and -ion at the end of each words. For example, if the trainee's self-explanation contains 'thunderstom' (even with the misspelling), it still counts as a literal match with words in the target sentence since the first nine characters are exactly the same. On the other hand, if it contains 'thunder,' it will not get a match with the target sentence, but rather with a word on the association list.

Soundex matching - This algorithm compensates for misspellings by mapping similar characters to the same soundex symbol [1, 5]. Words are transformed to their soundex code by retaining the first character, dropping the vowels, and then converting other characters into soundex symbols. If the same symbol occurs more than once consecutively, only one occurrence is retained. For example, 'thunderstorm' will be transformed to 't8693698'; 'communication' to 'c8368.' Note that the later example was originally transformed to 'c888368' and two 8s were dropped ('m' and 'n' are both mapped to '8'). If the trainee's self-explanation contains 'thonderstorm' or 'tonderstorm,' both will be matched with 'thunderstorm' and this is called a soundex match. An exact soundex match is required for short words (i.e., those with fewer than six alpha-characters) due to the high number of false alarms when soundex is used. For longer words, a match on the first four soundex symbols suffices. We are considering replacing this rough and ready approach with a spell-checker.

A formula based on the length of the sentence, the length of the explanation, the length criterion mentioned below, the number of matches to the important words, and the number of matches to the association lists produces a rating of 0 (inadequate), 1 (barely adequate), 2 (good), or 3 (very good) for the explanation. The rating of 0 or inadequate is based on a series of filtering criteria that assesses whether the explanation is too short, too similar to the original sentence, or irrelevant. *Length* is assessed by a ratio of the number of words in the explanation to the number in the target sentence, taking into consideration the length criterion. For example, if the length of the sentence is 10 words and the length priority is 1, then the required length of the self-explanation would be 10 words. If the length of the sentence is 30 words and the length priority is 0.5, then the self-explanation would require a minimum of 15 words. *Relevance* is assessed from the number of matches to important words in the sentence and words in the association lists. *Similarity* is assessed in terms of a ratio of the sentence and explanation lengths and the number of matching important words. If the explanation is close in length to the sentence, with a high percentage of word overlap, the explanation would be deemed too similar to the target sentence. If the explanation failed any of these three criteria (Length, Relevance, and Similarity), the trainee would be given feedback corresponding to the problem and encouraged to revise the self-explanation.

Once the explanation passes the above criteria, then it is evaluated in terms of its overall quality. The three levels of quality that guide feedback to the trainee are based on two factors: 1) the number of words in the explanation that match either the important words or association-list words of the target sentence compared to the number of important words in the sentence and 2) the length of the explanation in comparison with the length of the target sentence. This algorithm will be referred as *WB-ASSO*, which stands for *word-based with association list*.

This first version of iSTART (word-based system) required a great deal of human effort per text, because of the need to identify important words and, especially, to create an association list for each important word. However, because we envisioned a scaled-up system rapidly adaptable to many texts, we needed a system that required relatively little manual effort per text. Therefore, WB-ASSO was replaced. Instead of lists of important and associated words we simply used content words (nouns, verbs, adjectives, adverbs) taken literally from the sentence and the entire text. This algorithm is referred to as *WB-TT*, which stands for *word-based with total text*. The content words were identified using algorithms from Coh-Metrix, an automated tool that yields various measures of cohesion, readability, other characteristics of language [9, 20]. The iSTART system then compares the words in the self-explanation to the content words from the current sentence, prior sentences, and subsequent sentences in the target text, and does a word-based match (both literal and soundex) to determine the number of content words in the self-explanation from each source in the text. While WB-ASSO is based on a richer corpus of words than WB-TT, the replacement was successful because the latter was intended for use together with LSA which incorporates the richness of a corpus of hundreds of documents. In contrast, WB-ASSO was used on its own.

Some hand-coding remained in WB-TT because the length criterion for an explanation was calculated based on the average length of explanations of that sentence collected from a separate pool of participants and on the importance of the sentence according to a manual analysis of the text. Besides being relatively subjective, this process was time consuming because it required an expert in discourse analysis as well as the collection of self-explanation protocols. Consequently, the hand-coded length criterion was replaced with one that could be determined automatically from the number of words and content words in the target sentence (we called this *word-based with total text and automated criteria*, or *WB2-TT*). The change from WB-TT to WB2-TT affected only the screening process of the length and similarity criteria. Its lower-bound and upper-bound lengths are entirely based on the target sentence's length. The overall quality of each self-explanation (1, 2, or 3) is still computed with the same formula used in WB-TT.

6.2.2 Latent Semantic Analysis (LSA) Feedback Systems

Latent Semantic Analysis (LSA; [13, 14]) uses statistical computations to extract and represent the meaning of words. Meanings are represented in terms of their similarity to other words in a large corpus of documents. LSA begins by finding the frequency of terms used and the number of co-occurrences in each document throughout the corpus and then uses a powerful mathematical transformation to find deeper meanings and relations among words. When measuring the similarity between text-objects, LSA's accuracy improves with the size of the objects. Hence, LSA provides the most benefit in finding similarity between two documents. The method, unfortunately, does not take into account word order; hence, very short documents may not be able to receive the full benefit of LSA.

To construct an LSA corpus matrix, a collection of documents are selected. A document may be a sentence, a paragraph, or larger unit of text. A term-document-frequency (TDF) matrix X is created for those terms that appear in two or more documents. The row entities correspond to the words or terms (hence the W) and the column entities correspond to the documents (hence the D). The matrix is then analyzed using Singular Value Decomposition (SVD; [26]), that is the TDF matrix X is decomposed into the product of three other matrices: (1) vectors of derived orthogonal factor values of the original row entities W, (2) vectors of derived orthogonal factor values of the original column entities D, and (3) scaling values (which is a diagonal matrix) S. The product of these three matrices is the original TDF matrix.

$$\{X\} = \{W\}\{S\}\{D\} \tag{6.1}$$

The dimension (d) of $\{S\}$ significantly affects the effectiveness of the LSA space for any particular application. There is no definite formula for finding an optimal number of dimensions; the dimensionality can be determined by sampling the results of using the matrix $\{W\}\{S\}$ to determine the similarity of previously-evaluated document pairs for different dimensionalities of $\{S\}$. The optimal size is usually in the range of 300-400 dimensions.

The similarity of terms is computed by taking the cosine of the corresponding term vectors. A term vector is the row entity of that term in the matrix W. In iSTART, the documents are sentences from texts and trainees' explanations of those sentences. These documents consist of terms, which are represented by term vectors; hence, the document can be represented as a document vector which is computed as the sum of the term vectors of its terms:

$$D_i = \sum_{t=1}^{n} T_{ti} \tag{6.2}$$

where D_i is the vector for the ith document D, T_{ti} is the term vector for the term t in D_i, and n is number of terms in D. The similarity between two documents (i.e., the cosine between the two document vectors) is computed as

$$Sim(D1, D2) = \frac{\sum_{i=1}^{d}(D1_i \times D2_i)}{\sum_{i=1}^{d}(D1_i)^2 \times \sum_{i=1}^{d}(D2_i)^2} \qquad (6.3)$$

Since the first versions of iSTART were intended to improve students' comprehension of science texts, the LSA space was derived from a collection of science texts [11]. This corpus consists of 7,765 documents containing 13,502 terms that were used in two or more documents. By the time the first version of the LSA-based system was created (referred to as *LSA1*), the original goal of identifying particular strategies in an explanation had been replaced with the less ambitious one of rating the explanation as belonging one of three levels [22]. The highest level of explanation, called *"global-focused,"* integrates the sentence material in a deep understanding of the text. A *"local-focused"* explanation explores the sentence in the context of its immediate predecessors. Finally, a *"sentence-focused"* explanation goes little beyond paraphrasing. To assess the level of an explanation, it is compared to four benchmarks or bags of words. The rating is based on formulae that use weighted sums of the four LSA cosines between the explanation and each of the four benchmarks.

The four benchmarks include: 1) the words in the title of the passage ("title"), 2) the words in the sentence ("current sentence"), 3) words that appear in prior sentences in the text that are causally related to the sentence ("prior text"), and 4) words that did not appear in the text but were used by two or more subjects who explained the sentence during experiments ("world knowledge"). While the title and current sentence benchmarks are created automatically, the prior-text benchmark depends on a causal analysis of the conceptual structure of the text, relating each sentence to previous sentences. This analysis requires both time and expertise. Furthermore, the world-knowledge benchmark requires the collection of numerous explanations of each text to be used. To evaluate the explanation of a sentence, the explanation is compared to each benchmark, using the similarity function mentioned above. The result is called a cosine value between the self-explanation (SE) and the benchmark. For example, *Sim(SE, Title)* is called the *title LSA cosine*. Discriminant Analysis was used to construct the formulae that categorized the overall quality as being a level 1, 2, or 3 [23]. A score is calculated for each of the levels using these formulae. The highest of the three scores determines the predicted level of the explanation. For example, the overall quality score of the explanation is a 1 if the level-1 score is higher than both the level-2 and level-3 scores.

Further investigation showed that the LSA1 cosines and the factors used in the WB-ASSO approach could be combined in a discriminant analysis that resulted in better predictions of the values assigned to explanations by human experts. However, the combined approach was less than satisfactory. Like WB-ASSO, LSA1 was not suitable for an iSTART program that would be readily adaptable to new practice texts. Therefore, we experimented with formulae that would simplify the data gathering requirements to develop LSA2. Instead of the four benchmarks mentioned above, we discarded the world knowledge benchmark entirely and replaced the benchmark based on causal analysis of prior-text with one that simply consisted of the words in the previous two sentences. We could do this because the texts were taken from science textbooks whose argumentation tends to be highly linear argumentation in science texts; consequently the two immediately prior sentences worked well as stand-ins for the set of causally related sentences. It should be noted that this approach may not succeed so well with other genres, such as narrative or history texts.

We tested several systems that combined the use of word-matching and LSA2 and the best one is LSA2/WB2-TT. In these combinatory systems, we combine a weighted sum of the factors used in the fully automated word-based systems and LSA2. These combinations allowed us to examine the benefits of using the world knowledge benchmark (in LSA1) when LSA was combined with a fully automated word-based system and we found that world knowledge benchmark could be dropped. Hence, only three benchmarks are used for LSA-based factors: 1) the words in the title of the passage, 2) the words in the sentence, and 3) the words in the two immediately prior sentences. From the word-based values we include 4) the number of content words matched in the target sentence, 5) the number of content words matched in the prior sentences, 6) the number of content words matched in the subsequent sentences, and 7) the number of content words that were not matched in 4, 5, or 6. One further adjustment was made because we noticed that the LSA approach alone was better at predicting higher values correctly, while the word-based approach was better at predicting lower values. Consequently, if the formulae of the combined system predicted a score of 2 or 3, that value is used. However, if the system predicted a 1, a formula from the word-based system is applied. Finally, level 0 was assigned to explanations that had negligible cosine matches with all three LSA benchmarks.

6.2.3 Topic Models (TM) Feedback System

The Topic Models approach (TM; [10, 27]) applies a probabilistic model in finding a relationship between terms and documents in terms of topics. A document is conceived of as having been generated probabilistically from a number of topics and each topic consists of number of terms, each given a probability of selection if that topic is used. By using a TM matrix, we can estimate the probability that a certain topic was used in the creation of a given document. If two documents are similar, the estimates of the topics they probably contain should be similar. TM is very similar to LSA, except that a term-document frequency matrix is factored into two matrices instead of three.

$$\{X_{normalized}\} = \{W\}\{D\} \tag{6.4}$$

The dimension of matrix $\{W\}$ is $W \times T$, where W is the number of words in the corpus and T is number of topics. The number of topics varies, more or less, with the size of corpus; for example, a corpus of 8,000 documents may require only 50 topics while a corpus of 40,000 documents could require about 300 topics. We use the TM Toolbox [28] to generate the $\{W\}$ or TM matrix, using the same science corpus as we used for the LSA matrix. In this construction, the matrix $\{X\}$ is for all terms in the corpus, not just those appearing in two different documents. Although matrix $\{X\}$ is supposed to be normalized, the TM toolbox takes care of this normalization and outputs for each topic, the topic probability, and a list of terms in this topic along with their probabilities in descending order (shown in Table 6.1). This output is easily transformed into the term-topic-probability matrix.

Table 6.1. Results from Topic Models Toolbox: science corpus, 50 topics, seed 1, 500 iteration, default alpha and beta.

TOPIC 2 0.0201963151	TOPIC 38 0.0214418635
earth 0.1373291184	light 0.1238061875
sun 0.0883152826	red 0.0339683946
solar 0.0454833721	color 0.0307797075
atmosphere 0.0418036547	white 0.0262046347
moon 0.0362104843	green 0.0230159476
surface 0.0181062747	radiation 0.0230159476
planet 0.0166343877	wavelengths 0.0230159476
center 0.0148681234	blue 0.0184408748
bodies 0.0147209347	dark 0.0178863206
tides 0.0139849912	visible 0.0170544891
planets 0.0133962364	spectrum 0.0151135492
gravitational 0.0125131042	absorbed 0.0149749106
system 0.0111884060	colors 0.0148362720
appear 0.0110412173	rays 0.0116475849
mass 0.0100108964	eyes 0.0108157535
core 0.0083918207	yellow 0.0105384764
space 0.0083918207	absorption 0.0102611992
times 0.0079502547	eye 0.0095680064
orbit 0.0073614999	pigment 0.0092907293
...	...

To measure the similarity between documents based on TM, the Kullback Liebler distance (KL-distance: [27]) between two documents is recommended, rather than the cosine (which, nevertheless, can be used). A document can be represented by a set of probabilities that this document could contain topic i using the following

$$D_t = \sum_{i=1}^{n} T_{it} \qquad (6.5)$$

where D_t is the probability of topic t in the document D, T_{it} is the probability of topic t of the term i in the document D, and n is number of terms appearing in the document D. The KL-distance between two documents (the similarity) is computed as follows:

$$KL(D1, D2) = \frac{1}{2} \sum_{t=1}^{T} D1_t log_2(D1_t/D2_t) + \frac{1}{2} \sum_{t=1}^{T} D2_t log_2(D2_t/D1_t) \qquad (6.6)$$

Constructing a TM matrix involves making choices regarding a number of factors, such as the number of topics, the seed for random number generation, alpha, beta, and the number of iterations. We have explored these factors and constructed a number of TM matrices in an effort to optimize the resulting matrix; however, for this preliminary evaluation, we use a TM matrix of 50 topics and a seed of 1.

The first TM-based system we tried was simply used in place of the LSA-based factors in the combined-system. The three benchmarks are still the same but similarity is computed in two ways: (1) using cosines — comparing the explanation and the benchmark using the cosine formula (Referred as TM1) and (2) using KL distances — comparing the explanation and the benchmark using the KL distance (Referred as TM2). As before, formulae are constructed using Discriminant Analysis in order to categorize the quality of explanation as Levels 1, 2, or 3.

6.2.4 Metacognitive Statements

The feedback systems include a metacognitive filter that searches the trainees' self-explanations for patterns indicating a description of the trainee's mental state such as "now I see ..." or "I don't understand this at all." While the main purpose of the filter is to enable the system to respond to such non-explanatory content more appropriately, we also used the same filter to remove "noise" such as "What this sentence is saying is ..." from the explanation before further processing. We have examined the effectiveness of the systems with and without the filter and found that they all perform slightly better with than without it. Thus, the systems in this chapter all include the metacognitive filter.

The metacognitive filter also benefits the feedback system. When a metacognitive pattern is recognized, its category is noted. If the self-explanation contains only a metacognitive statement, the system will respond to a metacognitive category such as *understanding, not-understanding, confirmation, prediction,* or *boredom* instead of responding irrelevantly. Regular expressions are used to define multiple patterns for each metacognitive category. If any pattern is matched in the self-explanation, words matching the pattern are removed before evaluation. Examples of regular expression are shown below:

```
NOTUNDERSTAND :i(?:.?m|\W+am)(?:\W+\w+)?\W+\W+(?:(?:not
                (?:\W+\w+)?\W+(?:sure|certain|clear))|
                un(?:sure|certain|clear))
UNDERSTAND :now\W+i\W+(?:know|knew|underst(?:an|oo)d|
                remember(?:ed)?|recall(?:ed)?|recogniz(?:ed)?|get|
                got|see)
CONF :(?:so\W+)?i\W+(?:was|got\W+it)\W+(?:right|correct)
```

The first pattern will include "I'm not sure," "I am uncertain"; second pattern includes "Now I understand," "Now I remembered"; and the last pattern includes "So, I was right." We originally constructed over 60 patterns. These were reduced to 45 by running them on a large corpus of explanations and eliminating those that failed to match and adding those that were missed.

6.3 iSTART: Evaluation of Feedback Systems

Two experiments were used to evaluate the performance of various systems of algorithms that vary as a function of approach (word-based, LSA, combination of word-based and LSA, and combination of word-based TM). In Experiment 1, we compare all eight systems in terms of the overall quality score by applying each system to a database of self-explanation protocols produced by college students. The protocols had been evaluated by a human expert on overall quality. In Experiment 2, we investigated two systems using a database of explanations produced by middle-school students. These protocols were scored to identify particular reading strategies.

6.3.1 Experiment 1

Self-Explanations. The self-explanations were collected from college students who were provided with SERT training and then tested with two texts, Thunderstorm and Coal. Both texts consisted of 20 sentences. The Thunderstorm text was self-explained by 36 students and the Coal text was self-explained by 38 students. The self-explanations were coded by an expert according to the following 4-point scale: 0 = vague or irrelevant; 1 = sentence-focused (restatement or paraphrase of the sentence); 2 = local-focused (includes concepts from immediately previous sentences); 3 = global-focused (using prior knowledge).

The coding system was intended to reveal the extent to which the participant elaborated the current sentence. Sentence-focused explanations do not provide any new information beyond the current sentence. Local-focused explanations might include an elaboration of a concept mentioned in the current or immediately prior sentence, but there is no attempt to link the current sentence to the theme of the text. Self-explanations that linked the sentence to the theme of the text with world knowledge were coded as "global-focused." Global-focused explanations tend to use multiple reading strategies, and indicate the most active level of processing.

Results. Each of the eight systems produces an evaluation comparable to the human ratings on a 4-point scale. Hence, we calculated the correlations and percent agreement between the human and system evaluations (see Table 6.2). Additionally, d primes (d's) were computed for each strategy level as a measure of how well the system could discriminate among the different levels of strategy use. The d's were computed from hit and false-alarm rates. A hit would occur if the system assigned the same self-explanation to a category (e.g., global-focused) as the human judges. A false-alarm would occur if the system assigned the self-explanation to a category (e.g., global-focused) that was different from the human judges (i.e., it was not a global-focused strategy). d's are highest when hits are high and false-alarms are low. In this context, d's refer to the correspondence between the human and system in standard deviation units. A d' of 0 indicates chance performance, whereas greater d's indicate greater correspondence.

One thing to note in Table 6.3 is that there is general improvement according to all of the measures going from left to right. As might be expected, the systems with LSA fared far better than those without LSA, and the combined systems were the most successful. The word-based systems tended to perform worse as the evaluation level increased (from 0 to 3), but performed relatively well at identifying poor self-explanations and paraphrases. All of the systems, however, identified the sentence-focused (i.e., 2's) explanations less successfully. However, the d's for the sentence focused explanations approach 1.0 when LSA is incorporated, particularly when LSA is combined with the word-based algorithms.

Apart from better performance with LSA than without, the performance is also more stable with LSA. Whereas the word-based systems did not perform equally

Table 6.2. Measures of agreement for the Thunderstorm and Coal texts between the eight system evaluations and the human ratings of the self-explanations in Experiment 1.

Thunderstorm Text	WB-ASSO	WB-TT	WB2-TT	LSA1	LSA2	LSA2/WB2-TT	TM1	TM2
Correlation	0.47	0.52	0.43	0.60	0.61	0.64	0.56	0.58
% Agreement	48%	50%	27%	55%	57%	62%	59%	60%
d' of 0's	2.21	2.26	0.97	2.13	2.19	2.21	1.49	2.37
d' of 1's	0.84	0.79	0.66	1.32	1.44	1.45	1.27	1.39
d' of 2's	0.23	0.36	-0.43	0.47	0.59	0.85	0.74	0.70
d' of 3's	1.38	1.52	1.41	1.46	1.48	1.65	1.51	1.41
Avg d'	1.17	1.23	0.65	1.34	1.43	1.54	1.25	1.23

Coal Text	WB-ASSO	WB-TT	WB2-TT	LSA1	LSA2	LSA2/WB2-TT	TM1	TM2
Correlation	0.51	0.47	0.41	0.66	0.67	0.71	0.63	0.61
% Agreement	41%	41%	29%	56%	57%	64%	61%	61%
d' of 0's	4.67	4.73	1.65	2.52	2.99	2.93	2.46	2.05
d' of 1's	1.06	0.89	0.96	1.21	1.29	1.50	1.38	1.52
d' of 2's	0.09	0.13	-0.37	0.45	0.49	0.94	0.74	0.61
d' of 3's	-0.16	1.15	1.28	1.59	1.59	1.79	1.60	1.50
Avg d'	1.42	1.73	0.88	1.44	1.59	1.79	1.54	1.42

well on the Thunderstorm and Coal texts, there is a high-level of agreement for the LSA-based formulas (i.e., the results are virtually identical in the two tables). This indicates that if we were to apply the word-based formulas to yet another text, we have less assurance of finding the same performance, whereas the LSA-based formulas are more likely to replicate across texts.

Figure 6.1.a provides a closer look at the data for the combined, automated system, LSA2/WB2-TT and Figure 6.1.b for the TM2 system. As the d's indicated, both systems' performance is quite good for explanations that were given human ratings of 0, 1, or 3. Thus, the system successfully identifies poor explanations, paraphrases, and very good explanations. It is less successful for identifying explanations that consist of paraphrases in addition to some information from the previous sentence or from world knowledge. As one might expect, some are classified as paraphrases and some as global by the system. Although not perfect, we consider this result a success because so few were misclassified as poor explanations.

6.3.2 Experiment 2

Self-Explanations. The self-explanations were collected from 45 middle-school students (entering 8th and 9th grades) who were provided with iSTART training and then tested with two texts, Thunderstorm and Coal. The texts were shortened versions of the texts used in Experiment 1, consisting of 13 and 12 sentences, respectively. This chapter presents only the data from the Coal text.

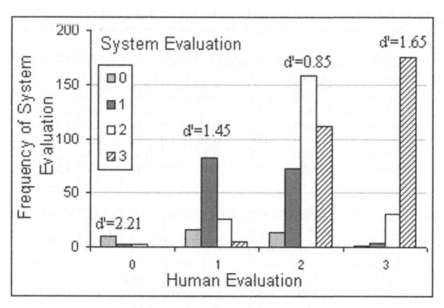

a) LSA2/WB2-TT — LSA with Word-based

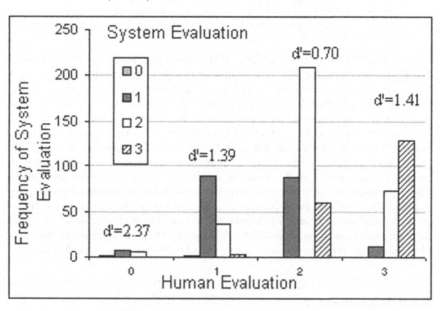

b) TM2 — Topic Models with KL distance

Fig. 6.1. Correspondence between human evaluations of the self-explanations and the combined system (LSA2/WB2-TT and TM2) for Thunderstorm text. Explanations were evaluated by humans as vague or irrelevant (0), sentence-focused (1), local-focused (2), or global (3).

The self-explanations from this text were categorized as paraphrases, irrelevant elaborations, text-based elaborations, or knowledge-based elaborations. Paraphrases did not go beyond the meaning of the target sentence. Irrelevant elaborations may have been related to the sentence superficially or tangentially, but were not related to the overall meaning of the text and did not add to the meaning of the text. Text-based elaborations included bridging inferences that made links to information presented in the text prior to the sentence. Knowledge-based elaborations included the use of prior knowledge to add meaning to the sentence. This latter category is analogous to, but not the same as, the global-focused category in Experiment 1.

Results. In contrast to the human coding system used in Experiment 1, the coding system applied to this data was not intended to map directly onto the iSTART evaluation systems. In this case, the codes are categorical and do not necessarily translate to a 0-3 quality range. One important goal is to be able to assess (or discriminate) the use of reading strategies and improve the system's ability to appropriately respond to the student. This is measured in terms of percent agreement with human judgments of each reading strategy shown in Table 6.3.

Table 6.3. Percent agreement to expert ratings of the self-explanations to the Coal text for the LSA2/WB2-TT and TM2 combined systems for each reading strategy in Experiment 2.

Reading Strategy	LSA2/WB2-TT	TM2
Paraphrase Only	69.9	65.8
Irrelevant Elaboration Only	71.6	76.0
Current Sentence Elaboration Only	71.9	71.2
Knowledge-Based Elaboration Only	94.6	90.3
Paraphrase + Irrelevant Elaboration	79.7	76.6
Paraphrase + Current Sentence Elaboration	68.2	67.3
Paraphrase + Knowledge-Based Elaboration	84.6	81.2

The results show that both systems perform very well, with an average of 77% for the LSA2/WB2-TT system and 75% for the TM2 system. This approaches our criteria of 85% agreement between trained experts who score the self-explanations. The automated systems could be thought of as 'moderately trained scorers.' These results thus show that either of these systems would guide appropriate feedback to the student user.

The score for each strategy score (shown in Table 6.3) can be coded either 0=present or 1=present. With the current coding scheme, only one strategy (out of seven) will be given a value of 1. We are currently redefining the coding scheme so that each reading strategy will have its own scores. For example, if the explanation contains both paraphrase and current sentence elaboration, with the current coding scheme, "Paraphrase + Current Sentence Elaboration" will be coded as a 1. On the other hand, with the new coding scheme, we will have at least 3 variables: (1) "Paraphrase" will be coded as a 1 for *present*, (2) "Elaboration" coded as a 1 for *present*, and (3) "Source of Elaboration" coded as a 2 for *current sentence elaboration*.

6.4 Discussion

The purpose of this chapter has been to investigate the ability of topic model algorithms to identify the quality of explanations as well as specific reading strategies in comparison to word-based and LSA-based algorithms. We found in Experiment 1 that TM systems performed comparably to the combined systems, though not quite as well. In Experiment 2, we found that the TM models performed nearly as well as the combined system in identifying specific strategies. These results thus broaden the scope of NLP models that can be applied to problems such as ours — providing real-time feedback in a tutoring environment. Indeed, the performance of both systems in Experiment 2 was highly encouraging. These results indicate that future versions of iSTART will be able to provide specific feedback about reading comprehension strategy use with relatively high confidence.

Our future work with the TM systems will be to attempt to combine the TM algorithms with the LSA and word-based algorithms. To venture toward that goal, we need to first identify the strengths of the TM algorithms so that the combined algorithm capitalizes on the strengths of the TM — much as we did when we created the combined word-based and LSA-based system. This will require that we analyze a greater variety of protocols, including self-explanations from a greater variety of texts and text genres. We are in the process of completing that work.

These NLP theories and their effectiveness have played important roles in the development of iSTART. For iSTART to effectively teach reading strategies, it must be able to deliver valid feedback on the quality of the self-explanations that a student types during practice. In order to deliver feedback, the system must understand, at least to some extent, what a student is saying in his or her self-explanation. Of course, automating natural language understanding has been extremely challenging, especially for non-restrictive content domains like self-explaining a text in which a student might say one of any number of things. Algorithms such as LSA opened up a horizon of possibilities to systems such as iSTART — in essence LSA provided a 'simple' algorithm that allowed tutoring systems to provide appropriate feedback to students (see [14]). The results presented in this chapter show that the topic model similarly offers a wealth of possibilities in natural language processing.

6.5 Acknowledgments

This project was supported by NSF (IERI Award number: 0241144) and its continuation funded by IES (IES Award number: R305G020018). Any opinions, findings and conclusions or recommendations expressed in this material are those of the authors and do not necessarily reflect the views of NSF and IES.

References

1. Birtwisle, M. (2002) The Soundex Algorithm. Retrieved from:
   http://www.comp.leeds.ac.uk/matthewb/ar32/basic_soundex.htm
2. Bransford, J., Brown, A., & Cocking, R., Eds. (2000). How people learn: Brain, mind, experience, and school. Washington, D.C.: National Academy Press. Online at: http://www.nap.edu/html/howpeople1/

3. Chi, M. T. H., De Leeuw, N., Chiu, M., & LaVancher, C. (1994). Eliciting self-explanations improves understanding. Cognitive Science, 18, 439-477.
4. Chi, M. T. H., Bassok, M., Lewis, M. W., Reimann, R., & Glaser, R. (1989). Self-explanation: How students study and use examples in learning to solve problems. Cognitive Science, 13, 145-182.
5. Christian. P. (1998) Soundex — can it be improved? Computers in Genealogy, 6 (5)
6. Graesser, A. C., Penumatsa, P., Ventura, M., Cai, Z., & Hu, X. (2005). Using LSA in AutoTutor: Learning through mixed-initiative dialogue in natural language. In T. Landauer, D.S., McNamara, S. Dennis, & W. Kintsch (Eds.), LSA: A Road to Meaning. Mahwah, NJ: Erlbaum.
7. Graesser, A. C., Hu, X., & McNamara, D. S. (2005). Computerized learning environments that incorporate research in discourse psychology, cognitive science, and computational linguistics. In A. F. Healy (Ed.), Experimental Cognitive Psychology and its Applications: Festschrift in Honor of Lyle Bourne, Walter Kintsch, and Thomas Landauer. Washington, D.C.: American Psychological Association.
8. Graesser, A. C., Hu, X., & Person, N. (2001). Teaching with the help of talking heads. In T. Okamoto, R. Hartley, Kinshuk, J. P. Klus (Eds.), Proceedings IEEE International Conference on Advanced Learning Technology: Issues, Achievements and Challenges (460-461).
9. Graesser, A. C., McNamara, D. S., Louwerse, M. M., & Cai, Z. (2004). Coh-Metrix: Analysis of text on cohesion and language. Behavior Research Methods, Instruments, and Computers, 36, 193-202.
10. Griffiths, T., & Steyvers, M. (2004). Finding Scientific Topics. Proceedings of the National Academy of Science, 101 (suppl. 1), 5228-5235.
11. Kurby, C.A., Wiemer-Hastings, K., Ganduri, N., Magliano, J.P., Millis, K.K., & McNamaar, D.S. (2003). Computerizing Reading Training: Evaluation of a latent semantic analysis space for science text. Behavior Research Methods, Instruments, and Computers, 35, 244-250.
12. Kintsch, E., Caccamise, D., Dooley, S., Franzke, M., & Johnson, N. (2005). Summary street: LSA-based software for comprehension and writing. In T. Landauer, D.S., McNamara, S. Dennis, & W. Kintsch (Eds.), LSA: A Road to Meaning. Mahwah, NJ: Erlbaum.
13. Landauer, T. K., Foltz, P. W., & Laham, D. (1998). Introduction to Latent Semantic Analysis. Discourse Processes, 25, 259-284.
14. Landauer, T. K., McNamara, D. S., Dennis, S., & W. Kintsch. (2005) LSA: A Road to Meaning, Mahwah, NJ: Erlbaum.
15. Louwerse, M. M., Graesser, A. C., Olney, A., & the Tutoring Research Group. (2002). Good computational manners: Mixed-initiative dialog in conversational agents. In C. Miller (Ed.), Etiquette for Human-Computer Work, Papers from the 2002 Fall Symposium, Technical Report FS-02-02, 71-76.
16. Magliano, J. P., Todaro, S., Millis, K. K., Wiemer-Hastings, K., Kim, H. J., & McNamara, D. S. (2004). Changes in reading strategies as a function of reading training: A comparison of live and computerized training. Submitted for publication.
17. McNamara, D. S. (2004). SERT: Self-explanation reading training. Discourse Processes, 38, 1-30.
18. McNamara, D. S., Boonthum, C., Levinstein, I. B., & Millis, K. K. (2005) Using LSA and word-based measures to assess self-explanations in iSTART. In

T. Landauer, D.S. McNamara, S. Dennis, & W. Kintsch (Eds.), LSA: A Road to Meaning, Mahwah, NJ: Erlbaum.

19. McNamara, D. S., Levinstein, I. B., & Boonthum, C. (2004). iSTART: Interactive strategy training for active reading and thinking. Behavior Research Methods, Instruments, & Computers, 36, 222-233.

20. McNamara, D. S., Louwerse, M. M., & Graesser, A. C. (2002). Coh-Metrix: Automated cohesion and coherence scores to predict text readability and facilitate comprehension. Technical report, Institute for Intelligent Systems, University of Memphis, Memphis, TN.

21. McNamara, D. S., & Scott, J. L. (1999). Training reading strategies. In M. Hahn & S. C. Stoness (Eds.), Proceedings of the Twenty-first Annual Meeting of the Cognitive Science Society (pp. 387-392). Hillsdale, NJ: Erlbaum.

22. Millis, K. K., Kim, H. J., Todaro, S. Magliano, J. P., Wiemer-Hastings, K., & McNamara, D. S. (2004). Identifying reading strategies using latent semantic analysis: Comparing semantic benchmarks. Behavior Research Methods, Instruments, & Computers, 36, 213-221.

23. Millis, K. K., Magliano, J. P., Wiemer-Hastings, K., Todaro, S., & McNamara, D. S. (2005). Assessing comprehension with Latent Semantic Analysis. In T. Landauer, D.S. McNamara, S. Dennis, & W. Kintsch (Eds.), LSA: A Road to Meaning, Mahwah, NJ: Erlbaum.

24. O'Reilly, T., Best, R., & McNamara, D. S. (2004). Self-Explanation reading training: Effects for low-knowledge readers. In K. Forbus, D. Gentner, T. Regier (Eds.), Proceedings of the Twenty-sixth Annual Meeting of the Cognitive Science Society (pp. 1053-1058). Mahwah, NJ: Erlbaum.

25. O'Reilly, T., Sinclair, G. P., & McNamara, D. S. (2004). Reading strategy training: Automated verses live. In K. Forbus, D. Gentner, T. Regier (Eds.), Proceedings of the Twenty-sixth Annual Meeting of the Cognitive Science Society (pp. 1059-1064). Mahwah, NJ: Erlbaum.

26. Press, W.M., Flannery, B.P., Teukolsky, S.A., & Vetterling, W.T. (1986). Numerical recipes: The art of scientific computing. New York, NY: Cambridge University Press.

27. Steyvers, M., & Griffiths, T. (2005) Probabilistic topic models. In T. Landauer, D.S. McNamara, S. Dennis, & W. Kintsch (Eds.), LSA: A Road to Meaning, Mahwah, NJ: Erlbaum.

28. Steyvers, M., & Griffiths, T. (2005) Matlab Topic Modeling Toolbox 1.3. Retrieved from http://psiexp.ss.uci.edu/research/programs_data/toolbox.htm

29. Streeter, L., Lochbaum, K., Psotka, J., & LaVoie, N. (2005). Automated tools for collaborative learning environments. In T. Landauer, D.S., McNamara, S. Dennis, & W. Kintsch (Eds.), LSA: A Road to Meaning. Mahwah, NJ: Erlbaum.

Textual Signatures: Identifying Text-Types Using Latent Semantic Analysis to Measure the Cohesion of Text Structures

Philip M. McCarthy, Stephen W. Briner, Vasile Rus, and
Danielle S. McNamara

7.1 Introduction

Just as a sentence is far more than a mere concatenation of words, a text is far more than a mere concatenation of sentences. Texts contain pertinent information that co-refers across sentences and paragraphs [30]; texts contain relations between phrases, clauses, and sentences that are often causally linked [21, 51, 56]; and texts that depend on relating a series of chronological events contain temporal features that help the reader to build a coherent representation of the text [19, 55]. We refer to textual features such as these as cohesive elements, and they occur within paragraphs (locally), across paragraphs (globally), and in forms such as referential, causal, temporal, and structural [18, 22, 36]. But cohesive elements, and by consequence cohesion, does not simply feature in a text as dialogues tend to feature in narratives, or as cartoons tend to feature in newspapers. That is, cohesion is not present or absent in a binary or optional sense. Instead, cohesion in text exists on a continuum of presence, which is sometimes indicative of the text-type in question [12, 37, 41] and sometimes indicative of the audience for which the text was written [44, 47]. In this chapter, we discuss the nature and importance of cohesion; we demonstrate a computational tool that measures cohesion; and, most importantly, we demonstrate a novel approach to identifying text-types by incorporating contrasting rates of cohesion.

7.2 Cohesion

Recent research in text processing has emphasized the importance of the cohesion of a text in comprehension [5, 44, 43]. Cohesion is the degree to which ideas in the text are explicitly related to each other and facilitate a unified situation model for the reader. As McNamara and colleagues have shown, challenging text (such as science) is particularly difficult for low-knowledge students. These students are cognitively burdened when they are forced to make inferences across texts [22, 34, 35, 38, 44]. Adding cohesion to text alleviates this burden by filling conceptual and structural gaps. Recent developments in computational linguistics and discourse processing have now made it possible to measure this textual cohesion. These developments have come together in a computational tool called *Coh-Metrix* [22] that approximates over 200 indices of textual cohesion and difficulty. Armed with this technology, text-book writers and teachers have the opportunity to better assess the appropriateness of a text for particular students [47], and researchers have the opportunity to assess cohesion patterns in text-types so as to better understand what constitutes a prototypical text from any given domain, genre, register, or even author [37, 42, 12, 14].

7.3 Coh-Metrix

Coh-Metrix assesses characteristics of texts by using parts of speech classifiers [4, 49, 7, 8, 9, 10, 11], and latent semantic analysis [32, 33]. The indices generated from Coh-Metrix offer an assessment of the cohesiveness and readability of any given text . These indices have been used to indicate textual cohesion and difficulty levels in a variety of studies. For example, Ozuru et al. [47] used Coh-Metrix to rate high and low cohesion versions of biology texts, the study showing that participants benefited most from the high cohesion versions. And Best, Floyd, and McNamara [1] used Coh-Metrix to compare 61 third-graders' reading comprehension for narrative and expository texts, the study suggesting that children with low levels of world knowledge were more inclined to have comprehension problems with expository texts. While research into assessing the benefits of cohesion continues apace, the utility of the Coh-Metrix tool has also allowed the pursuit of other avenues of textual investigation.

One of these alternative avenues is text identification. For example, Louwerse et al. [37] used Coh-Metrix to investigate variations in cohesion across written and spoken texts, finding evidence for a significant difference between these modes. McCarthy, Lewis, et al. [42] showed that Coh-Metrix indices were versatile enough to distinguish between authors even within the same register. Crossley et al.[12] used a wide variety of Coh-Metrix indices to show significant differences between authentic English language texts and the simplified versions used in texts designed for English language learners. And McCarthy, Lightman et al. [41] used Coh-Metrix to investigate variations in cohesion and difficulty across units of science and history texts, finding evidence that while difficulty scores for textbooks reflect the grade to which they are assigned, the cohesion rates differed significantly depending upon domain. In this chapter, we build on these approaches to identification of textual characteristics by demonstrating how cohesion indices produced by Coh-Metrix can be used to form prototypical models of text-types that we call *textual signatures*.

7.4 Approaches to Analyzing Texts

Traditional approaches to categorizing discourse have tended to treat text as if it were a homogeneous whole. These wholes, or bodies of text, are analyzed for various textual features, which are used to classify the texts as belonging to one category or another [2, 3, 26, 27, 37, 42]. To be sure, such approaches have yielded impressive findings, generally managing to significantly discriminate texts into categories such as dialect, domain, genre, or author. Such discrimination is made possible because different kinds of texts feature different quantities of features. For example, Biber [2] identified *if clauses* and singular person pronoun use as key predictors in distinguishing British- from American-English. Louwerse et al. [37] used cohesion scores generated from Coh-Metrix to distinguish both spoken from written texts and narratives from non-narratives. And Stamatatos, Fakotatos, and Kokkinakis [50] used a number of style markers including punctuation features and frequencies of verb- and noun-phrases to distinguish between the authors of a variety of newspaper columns. Clearly, discriminating texts by treating them as homogenous wholes has a good track record. However, texts tend to be *heterogeneous*, and treating them as such may substantially increase the power of corpus analyses.

The *parts* of a text serve the textual whole either by function or by form. In terms of *function*, Propp [48] identified that texts can be comprised of fundamental components, fulfilled by various characters, performing set functions. In terms of *form*, numerous theories of text structure have demonstrated how textual elements are inter-related [24, 25, 31, 40]. Labov's narrative theory, to take one example, featured six key components: the abstract (a summary), the orientation (the cast of characters, the scene, and the setting), the action (the problem, issue, or action), the evaluation (the story's significance), the resolution (what happens, the denouement), and the coda (tying up lose ends, moving to the present time and situation).

Unfortunately for text researchers, the identification of the kinds of discourse markers described above has proven problematic because the absence or ambiguity of such textual markers tends to lead to limited success [39]. This is not to say that there has been no success at all. Morris and Hirst [46], for example, developed an algorithm that attempted to uncover a hierarchical structure of discourse based on lexical chains. Although their algorithm was only manually tested, the evidence from their study, suggesting that text is structurally identifiable through themes marked by chains of similar words, supports the view that the elements of heterogeneous texts are identifiable. Hearst [23] developed this idea further by attempting to segment expository texts into topically related parts. Like Morris and Hirst [46], Hearst used term repetition as an indicator of topically related parts. The output of his method is a linear succession of topics, with topics able to extend over more than one paragraph. Hearst's algorithm is fully implementable and was also tested on magazine articles and against human judgments with reported precision and recall measures in the 60th percentile, meaning around 60% of topic boundaries identified in the text are correct (precision) and 60% of the true boundaries are identified (recall).

The limited success in identifying textual segments may be the result of searching for a reliable fine grained analysis before a courser grain has first been established. For example, a courser approach acknowledges that texts have easily identifiable *beginnings*, *middles*, and *ends*, and these *parts* of a text , or at least a sample from them, are not at all difficult to locate. Indeed, textual analysis using such parts has proved quite productive. For example, Burrows [6] found that the introduction section of texts rather than texts as a whole allowed certain authorship to be significantly distinguished. And McCarthy, Lightman et al.[41] divided high-school science and history textbook chapters into sections of beginnings, middles, and ends, finding that reading difficulty scores rose with significant regularity across these sections as a chapter progressed.

If we accept that texts are comprised of parts, and that the text (as a whole) is dependent upon the presence of each part, then we can form the hypothesis that the parts of the text are inter-dependent and, therefore, are likely to be structurally inter-related. In addition, as we know that cohesion exists in texts at the clausal, sentential, and paragraph level [22], it would be no surprise to find that cohesion also existed across the parts of the text that constitute the whole of the text . If this were *not* the case, parts of text would have to exist that bore no reference to the text as a whole. Therefore, if we measure the cohesion that exists across identifiable parts of the text, we can predict the degree to which the parts co-refer would be indicative of the kind of text being analyzed. In Labov's [31] narrative model, for example, we might expect a high degree of coreference between the second section (the orientation) and the sixth section (the coda): Although the two sections are textually distant, they are semantically related in terms of the textual elements with both sections likely to feature the characters, the motive of the story, and the scene in which the story takes place. In contrast, we might expect less coreference between the forth and fifth sections (evaluation and resolution): While the *evaluation* and *resolution* are textually juxtaposed, the *evaluation* section is likely to offer a more global, moral and/or abstracted perspective of the story. The *resolution*, however, is almost bound to be local to the story and feature the characters, the scene, and the outcome. Consequently, semantic relations between these two elements are likely to be less marked.

By forming a picture of the degree to which textual parts inter-relate, we can build a representation of the structure of the texts, a prototypical model that we call *the textual signature*. Such a signature stands to serve students and researchers alike. For students, their work can be analyzed to see the extent to which their paper reflects a prototypical model. Specifically, a parts analysis may help students to see that sections of their papers are under- or over-represented in terms of the global cohesion. For researchers, a text-type signature should help significantly in mining for appropriate texts. For example, the first ten web sites from a Google search for a text about cohesion (featuring the combined keywords of *comprehension, cohesion, coherence,* and *referential*) yielded papers from the field of composition theory, English as a foreign language, and cognitive science, not to mention a disparate array of far less academic sources. While the specified keywords that were entered may have occurred in each of the retrieved items, the organization of the parts of the retrieved papers (and their inter-relatedness) would differ. Knowing the signatures that distinguishes the text types would help researchers to locate more effectively the kind of resources that they require. A further possible benefit of textual signatures involves Question Answering (QA) systems [45, 52]. Given a question and a large collection of texts (often in gigabytes), the task in QA is to draw a list of short answers (the length of a sentence) to the question from the collection. The typical architecture of a modern QA system includes three subsystems: question processing, paragraph retrieval and answer processing. Textual signatures may be able to reduce the search space in the paragraph retrieval stage by identifying more likely candidates.

7.5 Latent Semantic Analysis

To assess the inter-relatedness of text sections we used latent semantic analysis (hereafter, LSA). An extensive review of the procedures and computations involved in LSA is available in Landauer and Dumais [32] and Landauer et al. [33]. For this chapter, however, we offer only an overview of the theory of LSA, its method of calculations, and a summary of some of the many studies that have incorporated its approach.

LSA is a technique that uses a large corpus of texts together with singular value decomposition to derive a representation of world knowledge [33]. LSA is based on the idea that any word (or group of words) appears in some contexts but not in others. Thus, words can be compared by the aggregate of their co-occurrences. This aggregate serves to determine the degree of similarity between such words [13]. LSA's practical advantage over shallow word overlap measures is that it goes beyond lexical similarities such as *chair/chairs* or *run/ran*, and manages to rate the relative semantic similarity between terms such as *chair/table, table/wood*, and *wood/forest*. As such, LSA does not only tell us whether two items are the same, it tells us how similar they are. Further, as Wolfe and Goldman [54] report, there is substantial evidence to support the notion that the reliability of LSA is not significantly different from human raters when asked to perform the same judgments.

As a measure of semantic relatedness, LSA has proven to be a useful tool in a variety of studies. These include computing ratings of the quality of summaries and essays [17, 29], tracing essay elements to their sources [15], optimizing texts-to-reader matches based on reader knowledge and projected difficulty of unread texts [53], and for predicting human interpretation of metaphor difficulty [28]. For this study, however, we adapted the LSA cohesion measuring approach used by Foltz, Kintsch & Landauer [16]. Foltz and colleagues formed a representation of global cohesion by using LSA to analyze the relationship of ever distant textual paragraphs. As the distances increased, so the LSA score of similarity decreased. The results suggested that LSA was a useful and practical tool for measuring the relative degrees of similarity between textual sections. In our study, however, we replace Foltz and colleagues comparison of paragraphs with a comparison of journal sections, and rather than assuming that cohesion would decrease relative to distance, we made predictions based on the relative similarity between the sections of the article.

7.6 Predictions

The *abstract* section was selected as the primary source of comparison as it is the only section whose function is specifically to relate the key elements of each other section of the paper. But the abstract does not relate to each other section of the paper equally. Instead, the abstract outlines the theme of the study (introduction); it can refer to the basic method used in the study (methods); it will briefly state a prominent result from the study (results); and it will then discuss the relevance of the studys findings (discussions). This definition allowed us to make predictions as to the signature generated from such comparisons. Specifically, we predicted that *abstracts* would feature far greater reference to the *introduction* (AI comparison type) and *discussion* sections (AD comparison type), less reference to the results section (AR comparison type), and less reference still to the methods section (AM comparison type). The reason for such predictions is that abstracts would take more care to set the scene of the paper (the introduction) and the significance of the findings (discussions). The results section, although important, tends to see its key findings restated in the discussion section, where it is subsumed into the significance of the paper. We predicted that the abstract to methods comparison type (AM) would form the weakest co-reference as experimental methods, although essential to state clearly in the body of a paper, tend to follow well-established patterns and are of little interest to the reader of an abstract who needs to understand quickly and succinctly the gist of the paper.

7.7 Methods

Using freely available on-line psychology papers from five different journals (see Appendix), we formed a corpus of 100 texts. For the purposes of simplification and consistency, we extracted from this corpus only the texts that were comprised of five author-identified sections: *abstract, Introduction, methods, results, discussion*. This left 67 papers in the analysis. We then removed titles, tables, figures, and footnotes before forming the paired sections outlined above (AI, AM, AR, AD). Each of the pairs from the 67 papers was then processed through the Coh-Metrix version of LSA
.

7.8 Results of Experiment 1

To examine differences in relatedness of the abstract to each of the text sections, we conducted a repeated measures Analysis of Variance (ANOVA) on the LSA cosines including the within-text factors of AI (M=.743, SD=.110), AM (M=.545, SD=.151), AR (M=.637, SD=.143), and AD (M=.742, SD=.101). As shown in Figure 7.1, the results confirmed our predictions. There was a main effect of comparison type, $F(3,66)$= 54.701, MSE=.011, p<.001. Pairwise contrasts (see Table 7.1) indicated that all of the differences were reliable except for the difference between the AI and AD comparisons. The pattern depicted in Figure 7.1 is what we will refer to as the *textual signature* for scientific reports such as those we have analyzed in this study.

Table 7.1. Pairwise Comparisons of the Relatedness of Text Sections to the Abstract

	Method (AM)	Results (AR)	Discussion (AD)
Introduction (AI)	Diff=.198 (.021)*	Diff=.106 (.021)*	Diff=.001(.010)
Method (AM)		Diff=-.092 (.019)*	Diff=-.197(.019)*
Results (AR)			Diff=-.105 (.018)*

Notes: Diff denotes the average difference between the cosines; * *p<.01*

While the signature from Experiment 1 confirmed our prediction, one possibility is that the differences may simply reflect the relative length of the textual sections. To test this possibility, we examined differences in relatedness of the abstract to each of the text sections by conducting a repeated measures ANOVA on

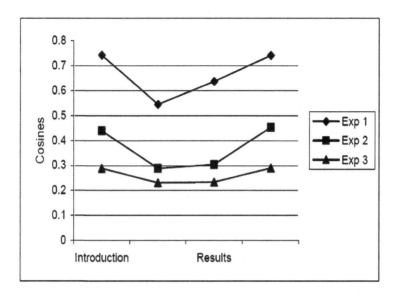

Fig. 7.1. Textual signature formed from means of the abstract to other sections for Experiments 1, 2 and 3.

the number of words in each text section including the within-text factors of Introduction ($M=1598.015$, $SD=871.247$), Method ($M=1295.791$, $SD=689.756$), Results ($M=1408.627$, $SD=841.185$), and Discussion ($M=1361.284$, $SD=653.742$). There was a main effect of comparison type, $F(3,66)= 2.955$, $MSE=382691.182$, p=.034. Pairwise contrasts (see Table 7.2) indicated that the only significant differences were between the AI/AM comparison types and the AI/AD comparison type. The results confirmed that the section *length* signature does not reflect the LSA signature (see Figure 7.2). Removing words that LSA does not account for from this analysis (such as numbers) made no significant difference to the results.

Table 7.2. Pairwise Comparisons of the Relatedness of Text Sections to the Abstract for text length

	Method (AM)	Results (AR)	Discussion (AD)
Introduction (AI)	Diff=302.22 (113.13)*	Diff=189.39 (107.91)	Diff=236.73 (94.37)*
Method (AM)		Diff=-112.84 (120.59)	Diff=-65.49 (105.67)
Results (AR)			Diff=47.34 (97.41)

Notes: Diff denotes the average difference between the lengths; * *p<.01*

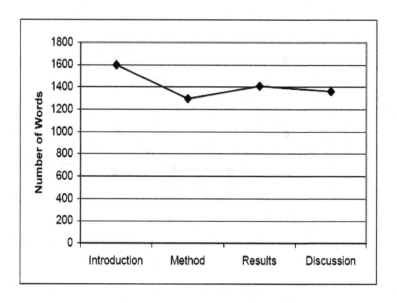

Fig. 7.2. Average length in terms of number of words in each text section.

7.9 Experiment 2

If LSA compares relative similarities between sections, then it is reasonable to assume that comparing similarly *themed* papers would produce signatures similar to those observed in Experiment 1. Because less of a relationship is expected from papers with overlapping themes as compared to those from the same paper, we predicted a relative decline in the LSA comparison scores. We also expected a reduced relationship between the abstract and results section because they are from different studies.

To test this prediction, we composed an entirely new corpus of 20 similar articles: all themed as *working memory and intelligence*. We then extracted the abstracts of these texts from the bodies and randomly reassigned the abstract to a different articles parts. As in Experiment 1, we conducted a repeated measures ANOVA on the LSA cosines including the within-text factors of AI ($M=.439$, $SD=.136$), AM ($M=.289$, $SD=.110$), AR ($M=.304$, $SD=.144$), and AD ($M=.454$, $SD=.162$). There was a main effect of comparison type, $F(3,19)= 16.548$, $MSE=.009$, $p<.001$. Pairwise contrasts (see Table 7.3) indicated that all differences were reliable except between AM and AD and between AM and AR.

As shown in Figure 7.1, the pattern of cosines is similar to that of Experiment 1, with reduced scores overall compared to Experiment 1, and a reduction in the relationship between the abstracts and results section. These results allow us to predict that LSA can produce prototypical signatures that are able to differentiate between sections from the same articles, and those articles that are merely similar in theme.

Table 7.3. Pairwise comparison of abstract to similar-themed body

	Method (AM)	Results (AR)	Discussion (AD)
Introduction (AI)	Diff=.150 (.032)*	Diff=.135 (.032)*	Diff=-.015 (.020)
Method (AM)		Diff=-.015 (.026)	Diff=-.165 (.036)*
Results (AR)			Diff=.150 (.032)*

Notes: Diff denotes the average difference between the cosines; * *p<.01*

7.10 Experiment 2a

One potential weakness of Experiment 2 was the relatively small size of the corpus (i.e., 20 texts). To alleviate the concern that the results were a function of the size of text corpora, we split the original 67-text corpus from Experiment 1 into three random groups of 20 texts and re-analyzed the results. If 20 texts were a sufficiently sized corpus , then the analysis should yield the same pattern as observed in Experiment 1. This analysis produced three sets of scores for each of the four comparison types (AI, AM, AR, and AD). As can be seen from Figure 7.3, the three new signatures map almost perfectly to the original signature from Experiment 1. There were also no significant differences within the corresponding section comparisons from the three 20-text corpora.

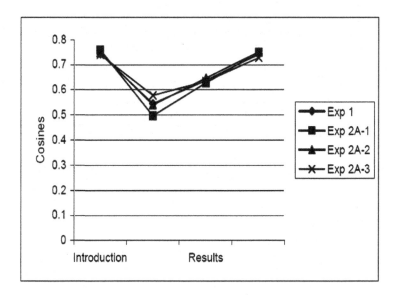

Fig. 7.3. Comparison of Experiment 1 to three sets of 20 texts taken from the original corpora.

7.11 Experiment 3

In Experiment 1, we showed that LSA may be able to provide a textual signature based on the relationships between the abstract of the paper and the sections within the paper. We will refer to this kind of signature as type *same paper* (SP). In Experiment 2 we showed that LSA can also produce prototypical signatures indicative of articles of a similar theme. We will refer to this kind of signature as type *same theme* (ST). In Experiment 3, we show that LSA based signatures can also indicate papers that are differently themed. We will refer to this kind of signature as type *different theme* (DT).

Based on the findings from Experiment 2, we predicted that the DT signature would more closely match that of Experiment 2. However, because the themes of Experiment 3's abstracts are different from the sections they were being compared to, we predicted the differences of the LSA scores for the AI and AD comparison types over the AM and AR comparison types would be less pronounced. To test this prediction, we randomly replaced the abstracts from Experiment 1 with the thematically consistent abstracts from Experiment 2.

To examine differences in relatedness of the abstract to each of the text sections for the DT corpus, we conducted a repeated measures ANOVA on the LSA cosines including the within-text factors of AI (*M*=.289, *SD*=.138), AM (*M*=.231, *SD*=.141), AR (*M*=.234, *SD*=.143), and AD (*M*=.298, *SD*=.150). There was a main effect of comparison type, $F(3,19)= 9.278$, *MSE*=.002, $p<.001$. Pairwise contrasts (see Table 7.4) indicated that the DT signature (like the ST signatures) resulted in the AR and AM comparisons being significantly different from the AI and AD comparison types. However, also like the ST signature, the AI comparisons did not significantly differ from the AD comparisons. Thus, despite the appearance of Figure 7.1 producing a lower cosine signature, we could not be sure from these results whether the DT corpus significantly differed from the ST corpus.

Table 7.4. Pairwise comparison of abstract to dissimilarly themed body

	Method (AM)	Results (AR)	Discussion (AD)
Introduction (AI)	Diff=.058 (.013)*	Diff=.055 (.014)*	Diff=-.002 (.013)
Method (AM)		Diff=-.003 (.015)	Diff=-.060 (.019)*
Results (AR)			Diff=-.056 (.017)*

Notes: Diff denotes the average difference between the cosines; * *p<.01*

To examine whether the SP, ST, and DT corpora were significantly different from one another, we ran mixed ANOVA, including the within-text factor of comparison type and the between-text factor of corpora. Because the SP corpus contained 67 papers, and the other corpora were comprised of 20 papers, we randomly selected a 20-paper corpus from Experiment 2a to represent the SP corpus.

As shown in the previous studies, there was a main effect of comparison type, $F(3,171) = 41.855$, *MSE*=.007, $p<.001$. There was also a main effect of corpus, $F(2,57) = 67.259$, *MSE*=.013, $p<.001$. A post hoc Bonferroni test between the corpora indicated that there was a significant difference between each of the corpora: SP to ST ($p<.001$); SP to DT ($p<.001$); and ST to DT ($p<.05$). Most importantly, the interaction between corpus and section was significant, $F(6,171) = 4.196$, $MSE=.007$, $p<.001$, indicating that the differences between the sections depends on the type of corpora.

The results from this experiment indicate that the corpus using the same papers for the comparisons (SP) shows greater internal difference than do those with either similar or different themes (i.e., ST, DT). This result is largely due to the stronger AR comparison generated in the SP corpus. While the signatures generated from the ST and DT corpora are internally similar, the results of this experiment offer evidence that the degree of similarity between sections within the corpora is significantly different.

These results allowed us to extend our signature assumption to predicting that LSA can differentiate three text-types: the same paper, similarly themed papers, and differently themed papers.

7.12 Discussion

The results of this study suggest that LSA comparisons of textual sections can produce an identifiable textual signature. These signatures serve as a prototypical model of the text-type and are distinguishable from those produced by texts which are merely similar in theme (ST), or similar in field (DT).

Textual signatures of the type produced in this study have the potential to be used for a number of purposes. For example, students could assess how closely the signature of their papers reflected a prototypical signature. The discrepancies between the two LSA cosines may indicate to the student where information is lacking, redundant, or irrelevant. For researchers looking for supplemental material, the signatures method could be useful for identifying texts from the same field, texts of the same theme, and even the part of the text in which the researcher is interested. Related to this issue is a key element in Question Answering systems: as textual signatures stand to identify thematically related material, the retrieval stage of QA systems may be better able to rank its candidate answers.

Future research will focus on developing a range of textual signatures beyond the abstract comparisons outlined in this chapter. Specifically, comparisons of section parts from the perspective of the *introduction, methods, results,* and *discussions* sections need to be examined. This broader scope offers the possibility of greater accuracy in textual identification. For example, papers that were only thematically related would likely have higher overlaps generated from introduction sections than from other sections. Introductions feature a review of the literature which would likely be highly consistent across papers within the same theme, whereas the other sections (especially the results section) would likely be significantly different from paper to paper.

In addition to extending the perspectives of signatures, we also need to consider how other indices may help us to better identify textual signatures. Coh-Metrix generates a variety of alternative lexical similarity indices such as *stem, lemma,* and *word* overlap. While these indices do not compare semantic similarities such as *table/chair* or *intelligence/creativity* (as LSA does), they do compare lexical overlaps such as *produce/production, suggest/suggests* and *investigate/investigated*. Indices such as these, and the signatures they generate, may come to form a web of soft constraints that could help us improve the confidence we have that a retrieved text or textual unit matches a target set of constraints.

If future research offers continued efficacious signatures then an array of indices can be imagined. Once achieved, a discriminant analysis between corpora such as the SP, ST, and DT outlined in this study could be conducted. Such testing would lend substantial support to a textual signatures approach to text identification.

Looking even further ahead, we would also like to extend our signatures research beyond the type of texts presented in this study. For example, we need to consider the signatures generated from articles with multiple experiments as well as articles, essays, and reports from other fields. It is reasonable to expect that any identifiable genre is composed of elements, and that those elements exposed to methods such as those used in this study will produce identifiable and therefore distinguishable signatures.

While a great deal of work remains to be done, we believe that LSA-based textual signatures contributes to the field by offering a useful and novel approach for computational research into text mining.

7.13 Acknowledgments

This research was supported by the Institute for Education Sciences (IES R3056020018-02). Any opinions, findings, and conclusions or recommendations expressed in this material are those of the authors and do not necessarily reflect the views of the IES. We would also like to thank David Dufty and Mike Rowe for their contributions to this study.

References

1. Best, R.M., Floyd, R.G., & McNamra, D.S. (2004). Understanding the fourth-grade slump: Comprehension difficulties as a function of reader aptitudes and text genre. Paper presented at the 85th Annual Meeting of the American Educational Research Association.
2. Biber, D. (1987). A textual comparison of British and American writing. American Speech, 62, 99-119.
3. Biber, D. (1988). Linguistic features: algorithms and functions in variation across speech and writing. Cambridge: Cambridge University Press.
4. Brill, E. (1995). Unsupervised learning of disambiguation rules for part of speech tagging. In Proceedings of the Third Workshop on Very Large Corpora, Cambridge, MA.
5. Britton, B. K., & Gulgoz, S. (1991). Using Kintschs computational model to improve instructional text: Effects of inference calls on recall and cognitive structures. Journal of Educational Psychology, 83, 329-345
6. Burrows, J. (1987). Word-patterns and story-shapes: The statistical analysis of narrative style. Literary and Linguistic Computing, 2, 6170.
7. Charniak, E. (1997) Statistical Parsing with a context-free grammar and word statistics Proceedings of the Fourteenth National Conference on Artificial Intelligence, Menlo Park: AAAI/MIT Press

8. Charniak, E. (2000) A Maximum-Entropy-Inspired Parser. Proceedings of the North-American Chapter of Association for Computational Linguistics, Seattle, WA
9. Charniak, E. & Johnson, M. (2005) Coarse-to-fine n-best parsing and Max-Ent discriminative reranking. Proceedings of the 43rd Annual Meeting of the Association for Computational Linguistics (pp. 173-180). Ann Arbor, MI
10. Collins, M. (1996) A New Statistical Parser Based on Bigram Lexical Dependencies. Proceedings of the 34th Annual Meeting of the ACL, Santa Cruz, CA
11. Collins, M. (1997) Three Generative, Lexicalised Models for Statistical Parsing Proceedings of the 35th Annual Meeting of the Association for Computational Linguistics, Madrid, Spain.
12. Crossley, S., Louwerse, M.M., McCarthy, P.M., & McNamara, D.S. (forthcoming 2007). A linguistic analysis of simplified and authentic texts. Modern Language Journal, 91, (2).
13. Dennis, S., Landauer, T., Kintsch, W. & Quesada, J. (2003). Introduction to Latent Semantic Analysis. Slides from the tutorial given at the 25th Annual Meeting of the Cognitive Science Society, Boston.
14. Duran, N., McCarthy, P.M., Graesser, A.C., McNamara, D.S., (2006). An empirical study of temporal indices. Proceedings of the 28th annual conference of the Cognitive Science Society, 2006.
15. Foltz, P. W., Britt, M. A., & Perfetti, C. A. (1996). Reasoning from multiple texts: An automatic analysis of readers' situation models. In G. W. Cottrell (Ed.) Proceedings of the 18th Annual Cognitive Science Conference (pp. 110-115). Lawrence Erlbaum, NJ.
16. Foltz, P. W., Kintsch, W., & Landauer, T. K. (1998). The measurement of textual Coherence with Latent Semantic Analysis. Discourse Processes, 25, 285-307.
17. Foltz, P. W., Gilliam, S., & Kendall, S. (2000). Supporting content-based feedback in on-line writing evaluation with LSA. Interactive Learning Environments, 8, 111-127.
18. Gernsbacher, M.A. (1990). Language comprehension as structure building. Hillsdale, NJ: Erlbaum.
19. Givn, T. (1995). Coherence in the text and coherence in the mind. In Gernsbacher, M.A. & Givn, T., Coherence in spontaneous text. (pp. 59-115). Amsterdam/Philadelphia, John Benjamins.
20. Graesser, A.C. (1993). Inference generation during text comprehension. Discourse Processes, 16, 1-2.
21. Graesser, A.C., Singer, M., & Trabasso, T. (1994). Constructing inferences during narrative text comprehension. Psychological Review, 101, 371-95.
22. Graesser, A.C., McNamara, D., Louwerse, M., & Cai, Z. (2004). Coh-Metrix: CohMetrix: Analysis of text on cohesion and language. Behavioral Research Methods, Instruments, and Computers, 36, 193-202.
23. Hearst, M.A. (1994) Multi-paragraph Segmentation of Expository Text. Proceedings of the Association of Computational Linguistics, Las Cruces, NM.
24. Hobbs, J.R. (1985). On the coherence and structure of discourse. CSLI Technical Report, 85-37. Stanford, CA.
25. Hovy, E. (1990). Parsimonious and profligate approaches to the question of discourse structure relations. Proceedings of the Fifth International Workshop on Natural Language generation, East Stroudsburg, PA, Association for Computational Linguistics.

26. Karlsgren J. & Cutting, D. (1994). Recognizing text genres with simple metrics using discriminant analysis. International Conference on Computational Linguistics Proceedings of the 15th conference on Computational linguistics - Volume 2 (pp. 1071-1075). Kyoto, Japan.

27. Kessler, Nunberg, G., & Schutze, H. (1997). Automatic detection of text genre. In Proceedings of 35th Annual Meeting of Association for Computational Linguistics, and in 8th Conference of European Chapter of Association for Computational Linguistics (pp. 32-38). Madrid, Spain.

28. Kintsch, W. & Bowles, A. (2002) Metaphor comprehension: What makes a metaphor difficult to understand? Metaphor and Symbol, 2002, 17, 249-262.

29. Kintsch, E., Steinhart, D., Stahl, G., LSA Research Group, Matthews, C., & Lamb, R. (2000). Developing summarization skills through the use of LSA-based feedback. Interactive Learning Environments 8, 87-109.

30. Kintsch, W., & van Dijk, T.A. (1978). Toward a model of text comprehension and production. Psychological Review, 85, 363-394.

31. Labov, W. (1972). The Transformation of Experience in Narrative Syntax, In W. Labov (ed.), Language in the Inner City, 1972, University of Pennsylvania Press, Philadelphia.

32. Landauer, T. K., & Dumais, S. T. (1997). A solution to Plato's problem: The Latent Semantic Analysis theory of the acquisition, induction, and representation of knowledge. Psychological Review, 104, 211-240.

33. Landauer, T. K., Foltz, P. W., & Laham, D. (1998). Introduction to Latent Semantic Analysis. Discourse Processes, 25, 259-284.

34. Lehman, S., & Schraw, G. (2002). Effects of coherence and relevance on shallow and deep text processing. Journal of Educational Psychology, 94, 738-750.

35. Linderholm, T., Everson, M.G., van den Broek, Mischinski, M., Crittenden, A., & Samuels, J. (2000). Effects of causal text revisions on more and less skilled readers comprehension of easy and difficult text. Cognition and Instruction, 18, 525-556.

36. Louwerse, M.M. (2002). Computational retrieval of themes. In M.M. Louwerse & W. van Peer (Eds.), Thematics: Interdisciplinary Studies (pp. 189-212). Amsterdam/Philadelphia: John Benjamins.

37. Louwerse, M. M., McCarthy, P. M., McNamara, D. S., & Graesser, A. C. (2004). Variation in language and cohesion across written and spoken registers. In K. Forbus, D. Gentner, & T. Regier (Eds.), Proceedings of the 26th Annual Meeting of the Cognitive Science Society (pp. 843-848). Mahwah, NJ: Erlbaum.

38. Loxterman, J.A., Beck, I. L., & McKeown, M.G. (1994). The effects of thinking aloud during reading on students' comprehension of more or less coherent text. Reading Research Quarterly, 29, 353-367.

39. Mani, I. & Pustejovsky, J. (2004). Temporal discourse markers for narrative structures.ACL Workshop on Discourse Annotation, Barcelona, Spain. East Stoudsburg, PA, Association for Computational Linguistics.

40. Mann, W. C. & Thompson, S. A. (1988). Rhetorical Structure Theory: Toward a functional theory of text organization. Text, 8 (3). 243-281

41. McCarthy, P.M., Lightman, E.J., Dufty, D.F. & McNamara (in press). Using Coh-Metrix to assess distributions of cohesion and difficulty in high-school textbooks. Proceedings of the 28th annual conference of the Cognitive Science Society.

42. McCarthy, P.M., Lewis, G.A., Dufty, D.F., & McNamara, D.S. (2006). Analyzing Writing Styles with Coh-Metrix. 19th International FLAIRS Conference 2006.

43. McNamara, D.S., Kintsch, E., Songer, N.B., & Kintsch, W. (1996). Are good texts always better? Text coherence, background knowledge, and levels of understanding in learning from text. Cognition and Instruction, 14, 1-43.

44. McNamara, D. S. (2001). Reading both high and low coherence texts: Effects of text sequence and prior knowledge. Canadian Journal of Experimental Psychology, 55, 51-62.

45. Moldovan, D., Harabagiu, S., Pasca, M., Mihalcea, R., Girju, R., Goodrum, R., & Rus, V. (2000): The Structure and Performance of an Open-Domain Question Answering System, in Proceedings of ACL 2000, Hong Kong, October

46. Morris, J., Hirst, G. (1991) Lexical cohesion computed by thesaural relations as an indicator of the structure of text, Computational Linquistics, 17, 21-48.

47. Ozuru, Y., Dempsey, K., Sayroo, J., & McNamara, D. S. (2005). Effects of text cohesion on comprehension of biology texts. Proceedings of the 27th Annual Meeting of the Cognitive Science Society (pp. 1696-1701). Hillsdale, NJ: Erlbaum.

48. Propp, V. (1968). Morphology of the folk tale. Baltimore: Port City Press, pp 19-65.

49. Ratnaparkhi, A. (1996), A maximum entropy model for part-of-speech tagging. Proceedings of Conference on Empirical Methods in Natural Language Processing, University of Pennsylvania.

50. Stamatatos, E., Fakotatos, N., & Kokkinakis, G. (2001). Computer-based authorship attribution without lexical measures. Computers and the Humanities, 35, 193-214.

51. Trabasso, T., & van den Broek, P. (1985). Causal thinking and the representation of narrative events. Journal of Memory and Language, 24, 612-630.

52. Voorhees, E. M. & Tice, D.M. (2000). Building a question answering test collection. Proceedings of the Twenty-Third Annual International ACM SIGIR Conference on Research and Development in Information Retrieval

53. Wolfe, M. B., Schreiner, M. E., Rehder, B., Laham, D., Foltz, P. W., Kintsch, W., & Landauer, T. K. (1998). Learning from text: Matching readers and text by Latent Semantic Analysis. Discourse Processes, 25, 309-336.

54. Wolfe, M. B.W., & Goldman S.R. (2003). Use of latent semantic analysis for predicting psychological phenomena: Two issues and proposed solutions. Behavior Research Methods, Instruments, & Computers, 35, 22-31.

55. Zwaan, R.A.(1996). Processing narrative time shifts. Journal of Experimental Psychology: Learning, Memory, and Cognition, 22, 1196-1207.

56. Zwaan, R.A. & Radvansky, G.A. (1998). Situation models in language comprehension and Memory. Psychological Bulletin, 123, 162-185.

Appendix (Journals Analyzed)

Table 7.5.

Journal Name	Articles	Publication Date Range
Acta Psychologica	11	2000-2004
Biological Psychology	14	2000-2004
Cognition	4	2000-2001
Intelligence	20	2000-2003
Journal of Applied Psychotherapy Research	17	2002-2003

Automatic Document Separation: A Combination of Probabilistic Classification and Finite-State Sequence Modeling

Mauritius A. R. Schmidtler, and Jan W. Amtrup

8.1 Introduction

Large organizations are increasingly confronted with the problem of capturing, processing, and archiving large amounts of data. For several reasons, the problem is especially cumbersome in the case where data is stored on paper. First, the weight, volume, and relative fragility of paper incur problems in handling and require specific, labor-intensive processes to be applied. Second, for automatic processing, the information contained on the pages must be digitized, performing Optical Character Recognition (OCR). This leads to a certain number of errors in the data retrieved from paper. Third, the identities of individual documents become blurred. In a stack of paper, the boundaries between documents are lost, or at least obscured to a large degree.[1]

As an example, consider the processing of loan documents in the mortgage industry: Usually, documents originate at local branch offices of an organization (e.g., bank branches, when a customer fills out and signs the necessary forms and provides additional information). All loan documents finalized at a local office on a given day are collated into one stack of paper (called a *batch*) and sent via surface mail to a centralized processing facility. At that facility, the arriving packets from all over the country are opened and the batches are scanned. In order to define the boundaries and identities of documents, *separator sheets* are manually inserted in the batches. Separator sheets are special pages that carry a barcode identifying the specific loan document that follows the sheet, e.g., Final Loan Application or Tax Form, etc. The separation and identification of the documents is necessary for archival and future retrieval of specific documents. It is also a precondition for further processing, for instance in order to facilitate the extraction of certain key information, e.g., the loan number, property address and the like.

The problem we are addressing in this chapter is the process of manually inserting separator sheets into loan files. A person must take a loan file, leaf through the stack of paper (hundreds of pages), and insert appropriate separators at the correct boundary points. This work is both tedious and challenging. It is tedious, since no important new information is created, but only information that previously

---

[1] Notwithstanding physical markers such as staples, etc. Those are usually removed as a first step in document processing.

existed is re-created. It is challenging, since the person needs to have a fair amount
of knowledge of loan documents (hundreds of document categories) and work with
a high degree of attention to detail. Nevertheless, the error rate for this process can
be as high as 8%. The cost for the insertion is also significant, both in terms of labor
and material; it is estimated that 50% of the document preparation cost is used for
sorting and the insertion of separator sheets. One customer estimates the printing
cost for separator sheets alone to be in excess of $1M per year.

In the automated solution presented here [1], the loan files still need to be collected and shipped to a central facility for processing.[2] At the facility, the batches
are scanned in their entirety, without inserting separator sheets beforehand. The
result of this process is a long sequence of images of pages, up to 2000 images per
batch. Next, the text on each page is read by an OCR engine. A classification engine
(see Section 8.4.2) determines the likely document types of loan documents (e.g.,
Appraisals, Tax Forms, etc.), and a separation mechanism (see Section 8.4.3) inserts
virtual boundaries between pages to indicate where one document ends and the next
one begins. The separated documents are then labeled accordingly and delivered for
further processing, e.g., the extraction of relevant information.

8.2 Related Work

Traditionally, the processing of scanned paper forms has concentrated on the handling of structured forms. These are paper documents that have well-defined physical
areas in which to insert information, such as the social security number and income
information on tax forms. Ideally, for these forms the separation problem does not
even arise, since the documents are of a specified length. If, however, a sequence of
documents needs to be separated, it is usually enough to concentrate a recognition
process on the first page to find out which document is present. This information
defines the number of pages in the document and thus the separation information
with certainty. The recognition process is often done indirectly, coupled with a subsequent extraction system. Extraction rules define areas of interest on a form and
how to gather data from those *zones*. For instance, an extraction rule for a tax form
could first specify how to identify a box on the top left corner of the document that
contains the text "1040." Then the rule would search down the form to find a rect-
angular box labeled "SSN" and extract the nine digits contained in a grid directly
to the right of the label. If this recognition rule succeeds, i.e., text can be found and
recognized with sufficient confidence, the document is identified as a two-page 1040
tax form and the social security number is extracted.

While such local, forms-based rules work extremely well in their area of application, the extension of this approach to less structured forms or even forms that
exist in a large number of variations is highly effort-intensive and error-prone. For
instance, the example above treated federal tax forms, of which there are only a few
varieties. However, there are at least fifty varieties of state tax forms, and defining

---

[2] We do not discuss distributed scanning operations here. The principle in this
case is that no paper documents are ever shipped, but that each local office scans
the documents that are created locally. The images of the documents are then
transferred to a central facility. This operational schema presents some of the
same and some additional complications.

the form and contents of every such form is a major undertaking. But even then, the layout of the forms is known and can, in principle, be described in advance. For other semi-structured forms, this is not the case. For instance, appraisals (as in the case of mortgage loan applications) always contain roughly the same type of information (property address, value, comparable objects in the vicinity of the property in question, etc.). However, recognizing an appraisal based on very local information about specific structural properties of the form is extremely difficult. The layout of appraisals from different sources can not be foreseen. As such, the search for specific items on a page, using this information as an indication of what form is present and, more importantly for the case discussed here, the length of the document, are highly uncertain.

This is even more pronounced for so-called unstructured forms which have no specific layout considerations. Those also appear in concrete business cases, such as legal documents, waivers, riders, etc. Here, a layout-based definition of forms is highly unlikely to succeed.

The conclusion is that for a large variety of important documents, a rule-driven layout-based recognition is possibly inferior to a content-based recognition, as is used in the present solution. This is still true if a subsequent extraction step is used to gather information from the documents. Distinguishing between the separation step and the extraction step can facilitate the process of writing rules for information extraction, since the identity of documents can now be taken for granted.[3]

The cost of maintaining a solution for separation (and extraction) also needs to be considered, since it is highly likely that the layout of forms changes over time. Except in very specific circumstances, the extent and form of the change is out of control of the maintainer of a separation solution. This entails monitoring the incoming forms for such changes and the rules governing recognition must be modified immediately once a change is observed.

From the preceding discussion, it seems to us that treating separation and extraction as two distinct steps is advantageous. Furthermore, we favor content-based and example-based methods over manually written layout rules. The exact form of features used (e.g., image-based or text-based) is unspecified in principle. However, based on the experiences in our application domain, we prefer text-based features (see below).

The most direct approach to document separation would treat the task as a straightforward segmentation problem. Maximum Entropy (ME) methods have proven very successful in the area of segmentation of natural language sentences [2, 3]. Each boundary (in our case the point between two pages) is characterized by features of its environment (e.g., by the words used on the preceding and following page). An ME classifier is then used to solve the binary problem (boundary/non-boundary) for new, unseen page transitions. We are unaware of any publication using this approach for automatic document separation.

Instead of looking for boundaries, one could also attempt to ascertain that two consecutive pages belong in the same document, thus indirectly establishing borders.

---

[3] Note that this still assumes that rules are used to identify local information on a page. It may also be possible to handle the extraction step in a content-based manner, focusing not on the layout of a page, but on the words on it. The respective merits of each of these method is beyond the scope of the present chapter.

An instance of this method is described in [4]. They define a similarity measure between two pages that takes document structure (text in headers and footers, esp. page numbers), layout information (font structure), and content (text on pages) into account. They use a single-linkage agglomerative clustering method to group pages together. The clustering process is bounded by manually set thresholds. They report a maximum separation accuracy of 95.68%, using a metric from [5] that measures the correctness of the number of separation points between non-adjacent pages. Since our data is different and we solve a combined problem of classification and separation ([4] only perform separation), their results cannot directly be compared to ours.

8.3 Data Preparation

The input to our separation solution is the text delivered by an OCR engine of scanned page images. We are primarily reporting on data from the mortgage processing industry, hence the document types (Appraisal, Truth in Lending, etc.). Our sample here contains documents from 30 document types. The quality of the images varies based on their origin (original or photocopy) and treatment (fax). Figures 8.1 and 8.2 show two sample images (one from a Loan Application, one from a Note) and some of the OCR text generated from them.

In order to be prepared for the core classification algorithms (see below), the input text is tokenized and stemmed. Tokenization uses a simple regular expression model that also eliminates all special characters. Stemming for English is based on the Porter algorithm.[6][4]

The stream of stemmed tokens isolated from a scanned image is then converted into a feature vector. We are using a *bag of words* model of text representation; each token type is represented by a single feature and the value of that feature is the number of occurences of the token on the page. In addition, the text is filtered using a stopword list. This filtering removes words that are very common in a language; for instance, in English the list includes all closed-class words such as "the," "a," "in," "he," etc. Table 8.1 shows some of the features and their values extracted from a Note. The entries in the table indicate the processing that the text underwent.

Note that these three processes introduce two significant abstractions over the input text:

- By stemming, we assume that the detailed morphological description of words is irrelevant for the purpose of classification. For instance, we are unable to tell whether the feature "address" in Table 8.1 came from the input "address," "addresses," or "addressing." Inflectional and part-of-speech information is lost.
- Using bags of words, we are abstracting from the linear structure of the input text. We pose that there is little value in knowing which word appeared before or near another and the only important information is in knowing which word appears more frequently than others.
- The application of a stopword list, finally, de-emphasizes the value of syntactic information even further, since many syntactically disambiguating words are ignored.

---

[4] We only apply stemming for English text. Text in other languages is used without morphological processing.

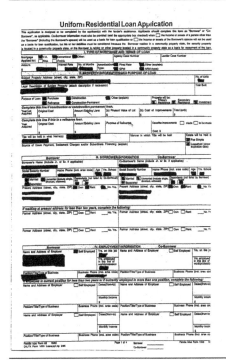

Uniform Residential Loan Application I TYPE GF'MORTGAGE-AHD TERMS OF LOAN Mortgage flvAB—Ccnvniltiai Applied fof: E¿HA Agency Case Number Lender Case Number Amount 5 I No. of Months Amortization Fixed Rate Typo: I Other (explain): I ARM (type): / LOAN Subject Property Adresi (street, city, state, ZIP) Legal Descripllon of Subject Property (attach description If necessary) No. of Units Year Built Purpose of Loan Construction Construction-Permanent Otner (explain): Property will be: Primary " "an. Compl&te this line If construction or construction-permanent loan. Secondary Investment Year Lot Acquired Original Cost S Amount Exjsling Uens $ (a) Present Value of Lot $ (b) Cost o(Improvements $ Total (a+b) S Complete this line if this Is a ra/fiuncfl loan. Year Acquired Original Cost Amount Existing Uens Title will be held in what Name(s) Purpose of Refinance Describe ImprovamanU

Fig. 8.1. Image and OCR text from a sample loan application. While the forms themselves are authentic, we redacted the information contained on them to ensure privacy.

It has been shown [7] that, for certain classifiers and texts, these abstractions do not reduce accuracy. In addition, abstraction reduces the number of parameters that need to be estimated during training, which in turn reduces the number of training samples that need to be provided. This aspect is of particular importance for us. In order to deploy a separation solution, customers must prepare a certain number of samples for each document type. Given the classification technology outlined in section 8.4.2, we achieve acceptable results with as little as twenty to thirty examples per document type. If we were using a classifier that takes word sequence information into account, for instance a Bayesian classifier over word n-grams, we would need hundreds of samples per document type; this would pose a severe entrance barrier for customers.[5]

---

[5] However, for certain types of problems, sequence-aware modeling is superior and even necessary. In one deployment, we encountered a fixed form with two broad columns into which data could be entered. Depending on whether only one column or both were filled out, the documents were categorized as different types. The classification model had difficulties distinguishing between these two document types. In an experiment, we collected enough sample data to train a word n-gram classifier and were then able to reliably assess the correct type.

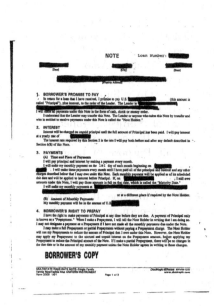

4. BORROWER'S RIGHT TO PREPAY
I have the right to make payments of Principal at any time before they are due. A payment of Principal only is known as a "Prepayment." When I make a Prepayment, I will tell the Note Holder in writing that I am doing so. I may not designate a payment as a Prepayment if 1 have not made all the monthly payments due under the Note. I may make a full Prepayment or partial Prepayments without paying a Prepayment charge. The Note Holder will use my Prepayments to reduce the amount of Principal that I owe under this Note. However, the Note Holder may apply my Prepayment to the accrued and unpaid interest on the Prepayment amount, before applying my Prepayment to reduce the Principal amount of the Note. If I make a partial Prepayment, there willpe no changes in the due date or in the amount of my monthly payment unless the Note Holder agrees in writing to those changes.

Fig. 8.2. Image and OCR text from a sample Note

Table 8.1. Some of the features extracted from a Note

Token	#Occur	Token	#Occur	Token	#Occur
accru	1	chang	2	fanni	1
acm	1	charg	3	fix	1
address	1	check	1	form	3
agre	1	citi	1	freddi	1
ani	3	compani	1	ftill	1
anyon	1	date	5	holder	6
appli	4	day	1	home	1
august	1	dbs	1	howev	1
befor	4	default	1	initi	1
begin	1	describ	2	ink	1
borrow	2	design	1	instrument	1
bowi	1	differ	1	interest	9
box	1	entitl	1	juli	1
burtonsvil	1	everi	2	known	1
cash	1	famili	1	la	1

From the examples in Figures 8.1 and 8.2, it can be seen that the OCR process introduces a significant degree of noise into the textual data that all further processes are operating on. We have not undertaken experiments specifically designed to evaluate the degradation in accuracy of either classification or separation that this OCR noise induces. Such experiments could be set up to work from cleaned-up OCR text. Since this implies a large amount of manual labor, the change in document quality could be simulated by printing electronic documents and manipulating the pages, e.g., by copying them repeatedly.

Table 8.2. Some of the features related to the stem *borrow*

Token	#Occur	Token	#Occur	Token	#Occur
borrnu	1	borronv	4	borrovv	8
borrnwer	1	borrotr	1	borrovvcr	1
borro	92	borrou	3	borrovvef	1
borroa	1	borrov	14	borrovvei	1
borroaer	1	borrovc	1	borrovvfir	1
borroh	4	borrovcf	1	borrovvi	1
borroi	1	borrovd	1	borrovw	1
borroifril	1	borrovi	3		
borrojv	1	borrovj	3		
borrokbr	1	borrovjar	1		
borrom	2	borrovl	1		
borromad	1	borrovrti	1		
borromicrl	1	borrovt	1		
borromr	1	borrovti	1		
borron	1	borrovu	1		

OCR noise also affects the size of training sets negatively. Under the bag-of-words model, the text for each page is converted into a feature vector with a dimensionality equal to the number of distinct words (or stems) in the training corpus. Noise introduced during OCR multiplies this number by generating many seemingly distinct, spurious words. Table 8.2 shows a small number of features related to the stem "borrow."

For some data sets, the number of OCR-induced variations becomes so high that the size of the training set exceeds reasonable memory sizes (e.g., > 2 GB). In those cases, we apply a preliminary feature selection step that removes features with low occurrence counts until we arrive at a small enough feature set. In general, though, we prefer to keep all features available for the classification mechanism and not perform any initial feature selection. Only in cases when size or performance require it, we apply feature selection to reduce the size of the feature set. We use basic frequency filtering and information-gain or mutual information as selection means.

8.4 Document Separation as a Sequence Mapping Problem

Automatic Document Separation adds two pieces of information to a stream of un-labeled pages. It inserts boundaries, so that documents are kept together, and it assigns labels to those documents that indicate their type. The problem can be seen as the mapping of an input sequence to an output sequence, i.e., a sequence of scanned paper pages is mapped to a sequence of document types. The mapping of sequences is a well known problem in Computer Science and there exist many differ-ent applications. For example, compilers, speech recognition, information extraction, and machine translation are all instances that have some aspect that deals with the problem of sequence mapping: A sequence of human readable program statements to a sequence of machine code, a sequence of acoustic signals to a sequence of words, a sequence of words to a sequence of tags, and a sequence of, e.g., Spanish words to a sequence of French words.

In addition, probabilistic models are often employed in order to determine the probabilities of possible output sequences given a particular input sequence. In this chapter, we utilize these concepts to solve the problem of document separation: Map a given sequence of pages to all possible output sequences, i.e., sequences of document types, determine for each output sequence its probability given the input sequence, find the most likely output sequence (sequence of document types), and, thus, effectively separate the sequence of input pages by document type.

8.4.1 Sequence Model

Formally, the procedure described above can be modeled as a Markov chain. De-noting the input sequence of ordered pages[6] p^c by $\mathcal{P} = (p_1^c, \ldots, p_n^c)$ and the output sequence of document types by $\mathcal{D} = (d_1, \ldots, d_n)$, the probability of a specific se-quence of document types $\mathcal{D}$ given the input sequence of pages can be written as

$$p(\mathcal{D}|\mathcal{P}) = \prod_{j=1}^{n} p(d_j|\mathcal{D}_{j-1}, \mathcal{P}), \qquad (8.1)$$

where d_j denotes the document type of the j-th page and $\mathcal{D}_{j-1}$ the output sequence of document types up to the $(j-1)$-th page. In many practical applications, inde-pendence assumptions regarding the different events d_j, $\mathcal{D}_{j-1}$, and $\mathcal{P}$ hold at some level of accuracy and allow estimations of the probability $p(\mathcal{D}|\mathcal{P})$ that are efficient yet accurate enough for the given purpose.

We started by assuming that the document type d_j at time step j only depends on the page content p_j^c at time step j and gradually increased the complexity of the models by taking into account the document types of previous time steps. In particular, we considered

$$p(\mathcal{D}|\mathcal{P}) \approx \prod_{j=1}^{n} p(d_j|p_j^c) \qquad (8.2)$$

as well as the following approximation, which is very common and has been widely used in several fields, e.g., for information extraction [8],

---

[6] The superscript c indicates that the *content* of the pages is considered.

$$p(\mathcal{D}|\mathcal{P}) \approx \prod_{j=1}^{n} p(d_j|d_{j-1}, p_j^c) \tag{8.3}$$

and finally

$$p(\mathcal{D}|\mathcal{P}) \approx \prod_{j=1}^{n} p(d_j|d_{j-1}, d_{j-2}, p_j^c). \tag{8.4}$$

Instead of trying to approximate the probality of $p(\mathcal{D}|\mathcal{P})$ ever more accurately by relaxing the independence assumptions one also can describe pages in more detail by breaking up the document types based on the page position within a document. Functionally, this is achieved by altering the output language. In the extreme, this would lead to a model of the data in which the symbols of the output language are different for each page number within the document. You would have symbols like $TaxForm_1$, $TaxForm_2$, $TaxForm_3$, etc., for the different page numbers within a tax form. Here, we increased the alphabet of the original output language threefold. Every document type symbol is split into three symbols: $Start$, $middle$, and end page of the document type. In our experience, forms often have distinctive first and last pages, e.g., forms ending with signature pages and starting with pages identifying the form, whereas middle pages of forms do not contain as much discriminating information. Accordingly, the sequences of the new output language are now sequences of the type $\mathcal{D}'$, where $\mathcal{D}'$ is given by $\mathcal{D}' = (d'_1, \ldots, d'_n)$ with d'_j denoting the document type as well as the page type. The definitions of the page type events $\{start, middle, end\}$ are:

$$start : \{p_{j,t}^c | t = 1, t \leq l\}$$
$$middle : \{p_{j,t}^c | t > 1, t < l\}$$
$$end : \{p_{j,t}^c | t > 1, t = l\} \tag{8.5}$$

where j is the global page number within the batch and t is the local page number within a document of length l.

One of the models considered using the new output language is

$$p(\mathcal{D}'|\mathcal{P}) \approx \prod_{j=1}^{n} p(d'_j|p_j^c), \tag{8.6}$$

under the constraint that the sequence of page types is consistent with the definitions given by Eq. 8.5, e.g., every document has to end with the end page type with the exception of one-page documents. The last model has, owing to this constraint, many similarities with the model given by Eq. 8.4. The main difference between the two models is that the model of Eq. 8.4 determines boundaries between documents based on the previous document types, whereas the model of Eq. 8.6 relies mainly on the difference of $start$, $middle$, and end pages within the document type to identify boundaries. Accordingly, the model of Eq. 8.6 can separate subsequent instances of the same document type, whereas the model of Eq. 8.4 cannot.

Finally, we also tested models that conditioned the output symbol at a given time step not only on the content of the current page but also on the previous and the next page

$$p(\mathcal{D}|\mathcal{P}) \approx \prod_{j=1}^{n} p(d_j|d_{j-1}, d_{j-2}, p_{j-1}^c, p_j^c, p_{j+1}^c) \qquad (8.7)$$

$$p(\mathcal{D}|\mathcal{P}) \approx \prod_{j=1}^{n} p(d_j'|p_{j-1}^c, p_j^c, p_{j+1}^c), \qquad (8.8)$$

where the model given by Eq. 8.8 has the same constrained output language as the model of Eq. 8.6, i.e., an output language consistent with the definitions of the events $\{start, middle, end\}$ given by Eq. 8.5.

8.4.2 Sequence Model Estimation

The problem of determining the different sequence models introduced in the previous section is given by estimating a probability of the form $p(x|p^c, y)$ with e.g., x denoting a document type and y a history of document types. As outlined in Section 8.3, a *bag of words* model is used for the page content[7] p^c, i.e., $p^c = \{(c_1, w_1), \ldots, (c_n, w_n)\}$ with c_j denoting the number of occurences of word w_j on the page, yielding

$$p(x|p^c, y) = p(p^c|x, y)\frac{p(x, y)}{p(p^c, y)} \propto \prod_{j=1}^{n} p(w_j|x, y)^{c_j} p(x, y), \qquad (8.9)$$

whereby in the last step the constant factor $1/p(p^c, y)$ has been omitted. As can be seen from Eq. 8.9, the sequence model estimation is reduced to the determination of the probabilities $p(w_j|x, y)$ and $p(x, y)$. These probabilities are estimated empirically by using sample documents (training examples) for the various events (x, y). For a typical training corpus , provided by the customer, the statistics for determining the word probabilities $p(w|x, y)$ are very low.[8] Given such statistics, overfitting to the training data is a common problem. Smoothing techniques, like those developed for language modeling [9], are a common tool to address the problem of low statistics by reserving some probability mass for unobserved events. In the case of determining the conditioned word probabilities $p(w|x, y)$, words that have been observed in the training data would be assigned lower probabilites than the maximum likelihood estimates, whereas unobserved words would be assigned higher probabilities than their maximum likelihood estimates. Statistical learning methods, e.g., [10, 11], utilizing methods of regularization theory, allow us to determine the tradeoff between memorization and generalization more principled than the smoothing techniques mentioned above. The learning method adopted here for estimating the sequence model is a Support Vector Machine[10] (SVM). It is commonly known that Support Vector Machines are well suited for text applications given a small number of training examples [12]. This is an important aspect for the commercial use of the system, since the process of gathering, preparing, and cleaning up training examples is time consuming and expensive.

---

[7] Here, p^c indicates both content models we are considering: The page content at a given time step as well as the content of the pages $p_{j-1}^c, p_j^c, p_{j+1}^c$ at a time step j.

[8] For a typical training corpus, almost all words occur rarely with words counts of one to two.

Table 8.3. Classification Results

	Optimized			Not optimized		
	precision	recall	F1-value	precision	recall	F1-value
Micro averages	0.95	0.95	0.95	0.90	0.90	0.90
Macro averages	0.94	0.86	0.87	0.82	0.79	0.78

Support Vector Machines solve a binary classification problem. The SVM score associated with an instance of the considered events is its signed distance to the separating hyperplane in units of the SVM margin. In order to solve multiclass problems, a series of Support Vector Machines have to be trained, e.g., in the case of a one-vs-all training schema, the number of SVMs trained is given by the number of classes. The scores between these different machines are not directly comparable and the scores must be calibrated such that at least for a given classification instance the scores are on an equal scale. In this application, the scores not only must be comparable between classes for a given classification instance (page), but also between different classification instances (pages), i.e., the SVM scores must be mapped to probabilities. Platt [13] uses SVM scores that are calibrated to class membership probabilities by adopting the interpretation of the score being proportional to the logarithmic ratio of class membership probability. He determines the class membership probability as a funcion of the SVM score by fitting a sigmoid function to the empirically observed class membership probabilities as a function of the SVM score. The fit parameters are the slope of the sigmoid function and/or a translational offset. The latter parameter, given the interpretation of the SVM scores discussed above, is the logarithmic ratio of the class prior probabilities. The method used here [14] fixes the translational offset and only fits the slope parameter. In addition, the Support Vector Machines are trained using cost factors for the positive as well as for the negative class and optimize the two costs independently. Empirical studies performed by the authors showed that cost factor optimization in conjunction with fitting the slope parameter of the mapping function from SVM scores to probabilities yields superior probability estimates than fitting the slope and the translational offset without cost factor optimization, fitting the slope and the translational offset with cost factor optimization, and fitting the slope only.

Table 8.3 summarizes the classification results for different loan forms. The results shown in the *Optimized* heading are the classification results obtained with the class membership probabilities using cost factor optimization and fitting the slope of the sigmoid function. Using SVM scores directly without calibration and cost factor optimization yields the results under the heading *Not Optimized*. The macro averages, especially, illustrate the effectiveness of the elected method. The observed improvement is a combined effect of using probabilities instead of SVM scores and cost factor optimization. An added benefit of optimizing the positive and negative cost factors is an improved handling of the OCR noise. As discussed in section 8.3, OCR increases the feature space considerably and cost factor optimization becomes important in order to avoid overfitting to the training corpus.

In summary, the effects of cost factor optimization can be interpreted as follows: The ratio of positive to negative cost factors determines the right class prior prob-

States

	page 1	page 2	page 3	page 4
Appraisal	0.9	0.5	0.5	0.8
TaxForm	0.7	0.9	0.9	0.8
...				
Note	0.5	0.7	0.7	0.3

time

page 1   page 2   page 3   page 4

Fig. 8.3. A trellis for the model of Eq. 8.2.

ability and thus enables an effective mapping of SVM scores to probabilities. The absolute value of the cost factor is an estimate of the optimal tradeoff between memorization and generalization and thus, enables an efficient handling of the noisy data. This together with mapping the scores to probabilities allows us to effectively utilize Support Vector Machines with their superior learning paradigm for the estimation of the sequence models.

8.4.3 Sequence Processing

In the previous two sections, we outlined the different probability models that can be applied to the problem of document separation and the approach to classification that we have taken to arrive at probabilities for categories attached to pages. All probability models were based on viewing the classification and separation process as a sequence mapping problem, described formally as a Markov chain as in Eq. 8.1. Experience from information extraction and speech recognition (e.g., [15]) shows that the results of such mappings and the search for the best sequence can be represented as a *trellis*. A trellis is a two-dimensional graph in which the horizontal axis represents time steps. For speech recognition, this would be incoming acoustic feature vectors. For information extraction, it could be words and, in our case, each time step is an incoming page within a batch. The vertical axis represents the states in which the mapping process may find itself and also the possible output symbols it may generate.

Transitions from states for one time step to the next denote the larger structure of the problem. These transitions can also be annotated with probabilities.

Consider the very simple model of Eq. 8.2, in which the probability of a document type only depends on the content of a page. In the trellis, there are as many states as there are document types. The interesting value for such a state is the probability that the page is of the associated document type. There are transitions from each state for one time step to all states for the next time step, indicating that each following state is equally probable. Figure 8.3 shows part of such a trellis.

The question of what a "best sequence" is can easily be answered: Since the individual scores delivered are probabilities (due to calibration), the probability of the complete sequence can be modeled using the product of all scores encountered on a path from the first page to the last. This sequence can be computed using *Viterbi*

States
Previous Current

Previous	Current	page 1	page 2
Appraisal	Appraisal	(A,A)	(A,A)
TaxForm	Appraisal	(T,A)	(T,A)
Note	Appraisal		(N,A)
Appraisal	TaxForm	(A,T)	(A,T)
TexForm	TaxForm		(T,T)
Note	TaxForm		(N,T)
Appraisal	Note		(A,N)
TexForm	Note	(T,N)	(T,N)
Note	Note		(N,N)

time

page 1   page 2

Fig. 8.4. Partial connection structure for the trellis for model Eq. 8.2.

search. At each time step, it records the locally best path to each state. Due to the independence of each time step, no locally suboptimal path can be part of the global solution. We can use Viterbi search to establish the best sequence of document types according to the model of Eq. 8.2. In fact, in the case of such a simple model, it suffices to identify the best document type for each page, which automatically will be a member of the best overall sequence. However, for any non-trivial model, this is not the case.

The models according to Eq. 8.3 and Eq. 8.4 introduce context into the decision process. This context or history needs to be reflected in the states of the trellis. For instance, the states reflecting the model of Eq. 8.3 are annotated with pairs of document types, the first one denoting the conditioning on the document type of the previous page and the second one denoting the decision for the current page. Moreover, the transition structure of the trellis needs to be modified as to ensure the consistency of paths. For instance, a state marked with "Appraisal" as the current decision can only be connected to following states that have "Appraisal" in their history. Figure 8.4 shows part of the connection structure for the model according to Eq. 8.3.

The extension of the context increases the number of states in a trellis. For the model of Eq. 8.4, we use triples instead of pairs of document types as state names.

Model 8.6 describes pages in more detail, adding a page type (Start, Middle, End) to the document type. Thus, for each document type relevant for a specific problem, we would have three states in the trellis. In addition, the transition structure needs to be carefully crafted as to only allow paths that describe complete documents, i.e., follow Eq. 8.5. For instance, in order to be a valid document boundary, a state associated with an end page must be immediately followed by a state associated with a start page.

For reasons of simplicity and extensibility, it would be advantageous if these sequence constraints could be formulated in isolation from the trellis containing the classification results themselves. Pereira and Riley [16] show that speech recognition

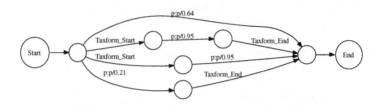

Fig. 8.5. Classification results for one page

can be interpreted as a sequence of weighted finite state transducers (WFSTs) that are combined using the composition operation. We adopt this view by associating our trellis of page classification results with an acoustic model applied to some input in speech recognition. The probabilities for an individual page to be of some class correspond to the emission probabilities represented in the recognition trellis of a speech recognizer. The restriction we placed on only allowing complete documents to be part of a sequence of documents corresponds to the use of a language model that renders certain word sequences more likely than others.[9] The "language model" we use currently only contains binary probability values, modeling hard constraints. However, similar to language models used in speech recognition, we could employ graded constraints represented by probabilities on language model transitions. This could be useful, for instance, in modeling the different likelihoods of sequences of documents, should such sequences exist.

In order to apply this analogy, we need to define the topology and contents of two finite state transducers. For the document type/page type model, the classification results can be represented in an FST as shown in Figure 8.5. The transitions of a classification transducer are of two kinds:

- Transitions that represent physical pages contain a symbol indicating a physical page on the lower and upper level and a classification score as weight. Which score is attached to the page depends on the topology of the transducer, which is defined by the next type of transitions.
- Transitions with an empty lower level denote boundary information about documents. There are transitions for the start and the end of a document. The occurrence of these transitions thus defines the type of page and the type of score that should be used. For instance, in Figure 8.5, the topmost transition (with score 0.64) indicates a middle page, since there are no boundaries given. The second transition chain belongs to a form that contains only a single page and consequently is bounded by both a start indicator and an end indicator. The third and fourth transitions belong to start and end pages respectively.

Figure 8.5 contains the information necessary to represent the classification results for one page with regard to one document type. The complete FST representing a problem with three document types and four pages is shown in Figure 8.6. Note

---

[9] On a more basic level, the document sequence restrictions can also be likened to the use of a pronunciation dictionary within a speech recognizer. However, acoustic modeling and pronunciation dictionary are usually combined into one processing step, while we explicitly distinguish between these.

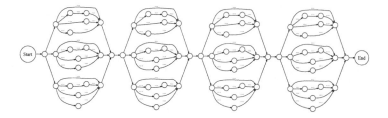

Fig. 8.6. Classification results as an FST

that using this FST, it is still possible to generate invalid page sequences. For instance, a start page for an Appraisal could be followed by another such start page. A restriction transducer plays a role analogous to a language model and ensures that such invalid paths are not present in the final search trellis.

A restriction (or rule) transducer contains labels on both the lower and upper side. The transformation from page content to document type/page type symbols has already been defined by the classification FST. The rule transducer has no informational role anymore, but a pure filtering role of eliminating impossible sequences of document and page types. Figure 8.7 shows the rules for a sequence containing documents of three document types. Note that all weights on the transitions are given as 1.0, so as not to modify the probabilities from the page information.

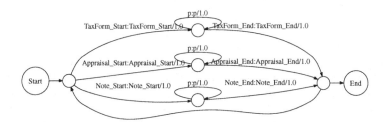

Fig. 8.7. FST for three document types

The composition operation on finite state transducers can now be used to generate a transducer that only contains such sequences of pages that result in a valid sequence of documents. Composition treats the "output" of one transducer (the upper level) as the "input" (lower level) of the other transducer. If we compose the classification FST with the rule FST, we achieve the desired result, an FST that contains the probabilities for specific pages, but only contains valid sequences. The output of this operation can be quite large, though. In the worst case, the composed FST has a number of states that is the product of the number of states of both arguments. In practice, this upper limit is not reached, but the size of the composed FST is still a concern, which we will address below.

Algorithm 1 General document separation

Require: An ordered list of pages (a batch), consisting of pages p_1 to p_n.
Require: An FST *rules* that describes the possible sequences of documents, as in Figure 8.7.
Ensure: An ordered list of documents d_k, each of which consists of an ordered list of pages.
      {Perform Classification}
 2: **for all** pages $p_i, 1 \le i \le n$ in the batch **do**
 3:     **for all** classes c_j **do** {Three classes per document type (start/middle/end)}
 4:         $c_{ij} \leftarrow$ probability that p_i is of class c_j
 5:     **end for**
 6: **end for**
      {Perform Separation}
 8: $pg \leftarrow$ The FST representing the classification results, as in Figure 8.6
 9: $sg \leftarrow pg$ composed with *rules*
10: $sg \leftarrow$ the best path through sg
      {Create documents}
12: $D \leftarrow \emptyset$
13: $d \leftarrow \emptyset$
14: **for all** Transitions in sg, in topological order **do**
15:     **if** The transition is labeled with "_End" **then**
16:         $D{+}=d$
17:     **else if** The transition is labeled with a page **then**
18:         $d{+}=p$
19:     **end if**
20: **end for**

The goal is to find a path through the composed FST from the start state to an end state under the constraint that we are interested in the highest possible overall probability. Any graph search method can be applied. However, the topology of the input graph simplifies the problem somewhat (see below). For convenience, we represent the result of the search also as an FST. The separation algorithm can now be described by Algorithm 1.

Representing rules about the sequence of document types as a graph has more far-reaching applications than just to make sure that document boundaries are observed. For instance, limits about the size of documents can now be easily introduced. Figure 8.8 shows a rule FST that prescribes all Tax forms must be at least two pages and at most five pages long.

Fig. 8.8. A rule FST restricting tax forms to between two and five pages long

Similarly, the rule FST can be used to make demands about the order of documents, depending on the application. For instance, a mortgage application could prescribe that an Appraisal is always directly followed by a Note. Using a powerful representation mechanism such as finite state transducers simplifies the introduction of additional functionality significantly.

However, there are also drawbacks to the naive implementation of operations over finite state transducers. Additional representational power in this case comes at a price, mainly in terms of memory consumption and secondary in processing time. A typical mortgage application defines somewhere between 50 and 200 document types and consequently between 150 and 600 classes for which probabilities and graphs have to be produced. A batch may be as long as 1000 pages. The composition of the resulting classification graph with the rule graph requires a great deal of space to hold and time to construct. We experienced graph sizes of over one gigabyte and runtime reached tens of minutes, clearly insufficient for the successful application in industry.

This situation is again similar to speech recognition with language modeling. A language model represents an extremely large number of possible and probable word sequences. Incorporating this knowledge into the basic recognition trellis is infeasible due to both space and time restrictions. Thus, both knowledge sources are kept separate. The probabilities delivered by the language model are taken into account by the search for the best word sequence. For our problem, we also notice that the composition of the classification and rules FSTs is transient; in the end, we are interested only in the best path through the composition FST. Thus, it is unnecessary to completely unfold the composition. Instead, we use a technique similar to delayed composition [17] combined with beam search [18] to extract the final result. This reduces memory usage significantly for large problems. Table 8.4 shows the memory usage for a few data points, all of which are well within the limits of our requirements. The runtime is also much lower; for 1000 pages and 200 categories, the processing time decreases from roughly 16 minutes for the naive approach to less than 3 minutes for the advanced procedure.

Table 8.4. Memory usage for separation

Batch size in pages	Memory Usage	
	200 categories	300 categories
1000	118 MB	151 MB
2000	211 MB	363 MB

8.5 Results

We evaluated the performance of all probability models for sequences that we described in Section 8.4.2. Table 8.5 shows the $F1$-values for all models. The table suggests three main results:

Table 8.5. Comparison of separation and classifcation results of the various sequence models.

Seqence model Probability		Micro-averaged F1-value
Eq. 8.2	$p(d_j \mid p_j^c)$	0.63
Eq. 8.3	$p(d_j \mid d_{j-1}, p_j^c)$	0.74
Eq. 8.4	$p(d_j \mid d_{j-1}, d_{j-2}, p_j^c)$	0.83
Eq. 8.6	$p(d_j' \mid p_j^c)$	0.84
Eq. 8.7	$p(d_j \mid d_{j-1}, d_{j-2}, p_{j-1}^c, p_j^c, p_{j+1}^c)$	0.86
Eq. 8.8	$p(d_j' \mid p_{j-1}^c, p_j^c, p_{j+1}^c)$	0.87

- The inclusion of a history of document types improves performance. This is not surprising, given the fact that forms are, on average, longer than one page. For instance, using a trigram model instead of a unigram yields an improvement of 31%.
- Specializing page descriptions improves performance. This confirms our earlier reasoning that forms often exhibit specific start and end pages. It also allows the model to separate two consecutive instances of the same document type.
- Conditioning on the content of surrounding pages improves performance. Comparing the last two rows in Table 8.5 with their counterparts without the content of the surrounding pages in the condition indicates a boost of around 3.5% in $F1$-value.

The last model (Eq. 8.8) is the best model in our experiments. However, it presents a serious drawback in that it uses roughly three times the number of features to describe a page (namely, the content of the page itself and that of the two surrounding pages). Given the increased CPU and memory usage during training, this seemed too high a price to pay for a 3% gain in performance. Thus, for deployment into customer production systems, we decided to use the model according to Eq. 8.6. It is the best of the one-page-content models, and the distinction of page types not only makes the model more efficient, but also helps with the integration of the separation workflow in a broader, extraction-oriented system owing to its capability of separating two consecutive identical forms.

Table 8.6 shows detailed results for the final deployment model. For each document type, the table shows the absolute counts of the results, precision, recall, and $F1$-value in two different scenarios. The first six columns show results on the page level: For each page, the predicted document type is compared with the true document type, and results calculated from that. The last six columns show values on the sequence level, taking into account full documents rather than pages. Each document (i.e., the sequence of pages from start page to end page) is compared with a gold standard; if both the extent of the document and its type match, the document is counted as correct. If either the document type or the pages contained in the document do not match, the document is counted as incorrect. These measures are much more strict than the page-level measures, as can be seen from the micro- and macro averages. Note that Table 8.6 reports on an experiment with 30 document types; however, the method scales well, and we achieve similar results with much larger numbers of categories.

Table 8.6. Number of true positive (TP), false positive (FP), false negative (FN), precision (P), recall (R), and F-measure (F) on a page as well as on a sequence level after separation. Final Model.

	Page level						Sequence level					
	TP	FP	FN	P	R	F1	TP	FP	FN	P	R	F1
Form A	207	4	1	0.98	1.00	0.99	108	9	8	0.92	0.93	0.93
Form B	13	0	0	1.00	1.00	1.00	4	0	0	1.00	1.00	1.00
Form C	151	9	7	0.94	0.96	0.95	79	24	13	0.77	0.86	0.81
Form D	171	0	10	1.00	0.94	0.97	108	10	12	0.92	0.90	0.91
Form E	2	0	0	1.00	1.00	1.00	2	0	0	1.00	1.00	1.00
Form F	15	0	0	1.00	1.00	1.00	12	0	0	1.00	1.00	1.00
Form G	100	0	0	1.00	1.00	1.00	22	0	0	1.00	1.00	1.00
Form H	56	0	0	1.00	1.00	1.00	53	0	0	1.00	1.00	1.00
Form I	6	0	0	1.00	1.00	1.00	6	0	0	1.00	1.00	1.00
Form J	14	0	0	1.00	1.00	1.00	14	0	0	1.00	1.00	1.00
Form K	10	3	0	0.77	1.00	0.87	10	3	0	0.77	1.00	0.87
Form L	74	11	12	0.87	0.86	0.87	21	9	7	0.70	0.75	0.72
Form M	52	11	10	0.83	0.84	0.83	18	6	4	0.75	0.82	0.78
Form N	13	0	0	1.00	1.00	1.00	13	0	0	1.00	1.00	1.00
Form O	2	1	3	0.67	0.40	0.50	1	2	3	0.33	0.25	0.29
Form P	167	8	4	0.95	0.98	0.97	106	23	11	0.82	0.91	0.86
Form Q	22	0	0	1.00	1.00	1.00	22	0	0	1.00	1.00	1.00
Form R	51	0	0	1.00	1.00	1.00	16	0	0	1.00	1.00	1.00
Form S	1	5	0	0.17	1.00	0.29	1	5	0	0.17	1.00	0.29
Form T	226	0	0	1.00	1.00	1.00	66	0	0	1.00	1.00	1.00
Form U	64	4	2	0.94	0.97	0.96	48	8	4	0.86	0.92	0.89
Form V	4	2	1	0.67	0.80	0.73	0	6	2	0.00	0.00	0.00
Form W	9	3	1	0.75	0.90	0.82	9	3	1	0.75	0.90	0.82
Form X	55	0	0	1.00	1.00	1.00	28	0	0	1.00	1.00	1.00
Form Y	376	4	13	0.99	0.97	0.98	248	18	15	0.93	0.94	0.94
Form Z	26	0	1	1.00	0.96	0.98	6	3	2	0.67	0.75	0.71
Form AA	326	8	8	0.98	0.98	0.98	26	18	7	0.59	0.79	0.68
Form AB	26	0	0	1.00	1.00	1.00	21	5	1	0.81	0.95	0.88
Form AC	332	0	2	1.00	0.99	1.00	20	2	2	0.91	0.91	0.91
Form AD	17	2	0	0.89	1.00	0.94	17	2	0	0.89	1.00	0.94
Σ	2588	75	75	–	–	—	1105	156	92	–	–	–
Micro averages	–	–	–	0.97	0.97	0.97	–	–	–	0.88	0.92	0.90
Macro averages	–	–	–	0.91	0.95	0.92	–	–	–	0.82	0.89	0.84

The training for this model required at least 20 examples per category, 10 each for the training and as a hold-out set. The maximum number of examples per category was capped at 40. Initially, the feature space had a dimensionality of 620,455. We reduced this number to at most 20,000 features per category by applying mutual information feature selection.

A comparison between the different problems and the models we apply is instructive. In Table 8.3, we reach an $F1$-value of 95% for the classification of documents. There, the boundaries are given, and the classifier is able to use all words from all pages in the document. In the experiments we report in Table 8.5, the problem is more complex: Each page must be classified separately and document boundaries inferred. Applying a comparable model (Eq. 8.2) in this situation, we only reach an $F1$-value of 63%. Only by careful selection of an appropriate probability model, we are able to raise the performance to an $F1$-value of 92% on the page level with model (Eq. 8.6).

One should note that the scores delivered by the SVM multi-class classifier are calibrated and represent class membership probabilities. Thus, thresholding can be applied to control the amount of errors that a customer expects from automatic decisions, and to control the amount of manual review of decisions that have been rejected. Using this technique, we can achieve precision of $> 95\%$ while simultaneously keeping the recall above 80%.

8.5.1 Production Deployments

The deployment of an automatic document separation solution is a lengthy process, as is common for any workflow-changing installation in large organizations. Most often, a proof-of-concept phase precedes the deployment proper. This part of a project can be pre-sales in order to demonstrate the feasibility of the approach to the customer or it can be as the first step in a deployment to find out how much automation can be introduced with high accuracy. In a proof of concept (POC), only a small subset of document types are considered for classification and separation. This poses a set of unique problems to consider: The document separator is normally set up to classify all documents into a set of well-known and well-defined document types. In a POC, only a subset of document types (say, 10 out of 50) is relevant. However, the incoming batches still contain documents of all types. The challenge here is to "actively ignore" the remaining document types without adverse effects on the classification and separation results for the document types on which we are concentrating.

The deployment of the production version of the separation solution can take as long as six months for a medium-sized organization (separating between five and ten million pages per month). Of this time, two to three months are usually spent on configuring the software. This includes the setup of the training data for the separator but also the development of an extraction mechanism that is usually part of the larger workflow. The rest of the time is used for the purchase and installation of hardware (possibly new scanners, processing machines, and review stations) and the retraining of the review personnel. It is good practice to introduce the new workflow and automated solution in increments, first converting one or two production lines to the automated separation solution and reviewing the efficiency of the process. Once the hardware, software and workflow function satisfactorily, the remaining lines are activated.

Using an automated classification and separation solution yields significant benefits for an organization. There are large cost-savings associated with the process (in a manual solution, 50% of the preparation cost is spent on sorting and inserting separator sheets) and the accuracy is superior. In a typical setting with hundreds of document types, at least 95-98% precision can be attained at a recall level of at least 80%. This means that only a fraction of the original data must be reviewed and no operations have to be performed on the physical paper pages that are at the source of the process.

8.6 Conclusion

In this chapter, we presented an automatic solution for the classification and separation of paper documents. The problem is to ingest a long sequence of images of paper pages and to convert those into a sequence of documents with definite boundaries and document types. In a manual setting, this process is costly and error prone. The automatic solution we describe prepares the incoming pages by running them through an OCR process to discover the text on the page. Basic NLP techniques for segmentation and morphological processing are used to arrive at a description of a page that associates stems with occurrence counts for a page (bag-of-words model). An SVM classifier is applied to generate probabilities that pages are of a given document and page type. After obtaining all classification probabilities, we are using a finite state transducer-based approach to detect likely boundaries between documents. Viewing this process as a sequence-mapping problem with well-defined subareas such as probabilistic modeling, classification and sequence processing allows us to fine-tune several aspects of the approach.

There were several major challenges in the development of this set of algorithms. The outside constraints prescribed a solution with high performance, both in terms of process accuracy and resource efficiency (time and hardware in setup and production). These requirements have significant ramifications for the choice of algorithms and models. For instance, Bayesian classifiers based on word n-grams are primarily unsuited due to their high training data demands. Also, the composition and search during separation had to be implemented in an on-demand fashion to comply with memory size requirements.

The overall result is a system that — although relatively simple in its basic components and methods — is very complex in its totality and its optimizations on a component level. We consistently reach high performance of greater than 95% precision with more than 80% recall and use the solution described here in large deployments with several million pages throughput a month.

8.7 Acknowledgments

Developing and validating technology solutions that can eventually be turned into successful products in the marketplace is an endeavor that includes many people. The authors would like to thank all who participated in exploring the technological and engineering problems of automatic document separation, in particular Tristan Juricek, Scott Texeira, and Sameer Samat.

References

1. Schmidtler, M., Texeira, S., Harris, C., Samat, S., Borrey, R., Macciola, A.: Automatic document separation. United States Patent Application 20050134935, US Patent & Trademark Office (2005)
2. Ratnaparkhi, A.: A Simple Introduction to Maximum Entropy Models for Natural Language Processing. IRCS Report 97-08, University of Pennsylvania, Philadelphia, PA (1997)
3. Reynar, J., Ratnaparkhi, A.: A Maximum Entropy Approach to Identifying Sentence Boundaries. In: Proceedings of the ANLP97, Washington, D.C. (1997)
4. Collins-Thompson, K., Nickolov, R.: A Clustering-Based Algorithm for Automatic Document Separation. In: SIGIR 2002 Workshop on Information Retrieval and OCR. (2002)
5. Pevzner, L., Hearst, M.: A Critique and Improvement of an Evaluation Metric for Text Segmentation. Computational Linguistics **28** (2002) 19–36
6. Porter, M.: An Algorithm for Suffix Stripping. Program **14** (1980) 130–130
7. Joachims, T.: Learning to Classify Text using Support Vector Machines: Methods, Theory, and Algorithms. Kluwer (2002)
8. McCallum, A., Freytag, D., Pereira, F.: Maximum entropy markov models for information extraction and segmentation. Technical report, Just Research, AT&T Labs — Research (2000)
9. Goodman, J.: A bit of progress in language modeling. Technical Report MSR-TR-2001-72, Machine Learning and Applied Statistics Group Microsoft Research (2001)
10. Vapnik, V.: Statistical Learning Theory. JOHN WILEY & SONS, INC (1998)
11. Jaakola, T., Meila, M., Jebara, T.: Maximum entropy discrimination. Technical report, MIT AI Lab, MIT Media Lab (1999)
12. Joachims, T.: Text Categorization with Support Vector Machines: Learning with Many Relevant Features. Technical Report LS-8 Report 23, Universitat Dortmund Fachbereich Informatik Lehrstuhl VIII Kunstliche Intelligenz (1997)
13. Platt, J.: Probabilistic outputs for support vector machines and comparison to regularised likelihood methods. Technical report, Microsoft Research (1999)
14. Harris, C., Schmidtler, M.: Effective multi-class support vector machine classification. United States Patent Application 20040111453, US Patent & Trademark Office (2004)
15. Jelinek, F.: Statistical Methods for Speech Recognition. Language, Speech and Communication. MIT Press, Cambridge, Massachusetts (1998)
16. Pereira, F., Riley, M.: Speech recognition by composition of weighted finite automata. Technical report, AT&T Labs — Research (1996)
17. Mohri, M., Pereira, F.C.N., Riley, M.: A Rational Design for a Weighted Finite-State Transducer Library. In: Workshop on Implementing Automata. (1997) 144–158
18. Lowerre, B.T.: The HARPY Speech Recognition System. PhD thesis, Carnegie Mellon University (1976)

9

Evolving Explanatory Novel Patterns for Semantically-Based Text Mining *

John Atkinson

9.1 Motivation

An important problem with mining textual information is that in this unstructured form is not readily accessible to be used by computers. This has been written for human readers and requires, when feasible, some natural language interpretation. Although full processing is still out of reach with current technology, there are tools using basic pattern recognition techniques and heuristics that are capable of extracting valuable information from free text based on the elements contained in it (i.e., keywords). This technology is usually referred to as **Text Mining**, and aims at discovering unseen and interesting patterns in textual databases [8, 19].

These discoveries are useless unless they contribute valuable knowledge for users who make strategic decisions (i.e., managers, scientists, businessmen). This leads then to a complicated activity referred to as **Knowledge Discovery from Texts** (KDT) which, like *Knowledge Discovery from Databases* (KDD), correspond to *"the non-trivial process of identifying valid, novel, useful and understandable patterns in data"* [6].

KDT can potentially benefit from successful techniques from Data Mining or Knowledge Discovery from Databases (KDD) [14] which have been applied to relational databases. However, Data Mining techniques cannot be immediately applied to text data for the purposes of TM as they assume a structure in the source data which is not present in free text. Hence new representations for text data have to be used. Also, while the assessment of discovered knowledge in the context of KDD is a key aspect for producing an effective outcome, the evaluation/assessment of the patterns discovered from text has been a neglected topic in the majority of the KDT approaches. Consequently, it has not been proven whether the discoveries are novel, interesting, and useful for decision makers.

Despite the large amount of research over the last few years, few research efforts worldwide have recognized the need for high-level representations (i.e., not just

---

* This research is sponsored by the National Council for Scientific and Technological Research (FONDECYT, Chile) under grant number 1040469 *"Un Modelo Evolucionario de Descubrimiento de Conocimiento Explicativo desde Textos con Base Semantica con Implicaciones para el Analisis de Inteligencia."*

keywords), for taking advantage of linguistic knowledge, and for special purpose ways of producing and assessing the unseen knowledge. The rest of the effort has concentrated on doing text mining from an *Information Retrieval* (IR) perspective and so both representation (keyword based) and data analysis are restricted.

The most sophisticated approaches to text mining or KDT are characterised by an intensive use of external electronic resources including ontologies, thesauri, etc., which highly restricts the application of the unseen patterns to be discovered, and their domain independence. In addition, the systems so produced have few metrics (or none at all) which allow them to establish whether the patterns are interesting and novel.

In terms of data mining techniques, Genetic Algorithms (GA) for Mining purposes has several promising advantages over the usual learning/analysis methods employed in KDT: the ability to perform global search (traditional approaches deal with predefined patterns and restricted scope), the exploration of solutions in parallel, the robustness to cope with noisy and missing data (something critical in dealing with text information as partial text analysis techniques may lead to imprecise outcome data), and the ability to assess the goodness of the solutions as they are produced.

In this paper, we propose a new model for KDT which brings together the benefits of shallow text processing and GAs to produce effective novel knowledge. In particular, the approach combines *Information Extraction* (IE) technology and multi-objective evolutionary computation techniques. It aims at extracting key underlying linguistic knowledge from text documents (i.e., rhetorical and semantic information) and then hypothesising and assessing interesting and unseen explanatory knowledge. Unlike other approaches to KDT, we do not use additional electronic resources or domain knowledge beyond the text database.

9.2 Related Work

Typical approaches to text mining and knowledge discovery from texts are based on simple bag-of-words (BOW) representations of texts which make it easy to analyse them but restrict the kind of discovered knowledge [2]. Furthermore, the discoveries rely on patterns in the form of numerical associations between concepts (i.e., these terms will be later referred to as *target concepts*) from the documents, which fails to provide explanations of, for example, why these terms show a strong connection. Consequently, no deeper knowledge or evaluation of the discovered knowledge is considered and so the techniques become merely "adaptations" of traditional DM methods with an unproven effectiveness from a user viewpoint.

Traditional approaches to KDT share many characteristics with classical DM but they also differ in many ways: many classical DM algorithms [19, 6], are irrelevant or ill suited for textual applications as they rely on the structuring of data and the availability of large amounts of structured information [7, 18, 27]. Many KDT techniques inherit traditional DM methods and keyword-based representation which are insufficient to cope with the rich information contained in natural-language text. In addition, it is still unclear how to rate the novelty and/or interestingness of the knowledge discovered from texts.

Some people suggest that inadequacy and failure to report novel results are likely because of the confusion between finding/accessing information in texts (i.e., using

IR and data analysis techniques) and text mining: the goal of information access is to help users find documents that satisfy their information needs, whereas KDT aims at discovering or deriving novel information from texts, finding patterns across the documents [17]. Here, two main approaches can be distinguished: those based on Bag-of-Words representations, and those based on more structured representations.

9.2.1 Bag-of-Words-Based Approaches

Some of the early work on TM came from the Information Retrieval community, hence the assumption of text represented as a *Bag-of-Words* (BOW), and then to be processed via classical DM methods [7, 27]. Since there is additional information beyond these keywords and issues such as their order do not matter in a BOW approach, it will usually be referred to as non-structured representation.

Once the initial information (i.e., terms, keywords) has been extracted, KDD operations can be carried out to discover unseen patterns. Representative methods in this context have included *Regular Associations* [6], *Concept Hierarchies* citeFeldman98b, *Full Text Mining* [27], *Clustering, Self-Organising Maps.*

Most of these approaches work in a very limited way because they rely on surface information extracted from the texts, and on its statistical analysis. As a consequence, key underlying linguistic information is lost. The systems may be able to detect relations or associations between items, but they cannot provide any description of what those relations are. At this stage, it is the user's responsibility to look for the documents involved with those concepts and relations to find the answers. Thus, the relations are just a "clue" that there is something interesting but which needs to be manually verified.

9.2.2 High-Level Representation Approaches

Another main stream in KDT involves using more structured or higher-level representations to perform deeper analysis so to discover more sophisticated novel / interesting knowledge. Although in general, the different approaches have been concerned with either performing exploratory analysis for hypothesis formation, or finding new connections/relations between previously analysed natural language knowledge, it has also involved using term-level knowledge for other purposes than just statistical analysis.

Some early research by Swanson on the titles of articles stored in MEDLINE [28] used an augmented low-level representation (the words in the titles) and exploratory data analysis to discover hidden connections [30, 32] leading to very promising and interesting results in terms of answering questions for which the answer was not currently known. He showed how chains of causal implication within the medical literature can lead to hypotheses for causes of rare diseases, some of which have received scientific supporting evidence.

Other approaches using *Information Extraction* (IE) which inherited some of Swanson's ideas to derive new patterns from a combination of text fragments, have also been successful. Essentially, IE is a Natural-Language (NL) technology which analyses an input NL document in a shallow way by using defined patterns along with mechanisms to resolve implicit discourse-level information (i.e., anaphora, coreference, etc.) to match important information from the texts. As a result, an IE task produces an intermediate representation called "templates" in which information relevant has been recognised, for example: names, events, entities, etc., or high-level linguistic entities: noun phrases, etc.

Using IE techniques and electronic linguistic resources, Hearst [19] proposes a domain-independent method for the automatic discovery of WordNet-style lexicose-mantic relations by searching for corresponding lexicosyntactical patterns in unrestricted text collections. This technique is meant to be useful as an automated or semi-automated aid for lexicographers and builders of domain-dependent knowledge bases. Also, it does not require an additional knowledge base or specific interpretation procedures in order to propose new instances of WordNet relations [9]. Once the basic relations (i.e., hyponyms, hypernyms, etc.) are obtained, they are used to find common links with other "similar" concepts in WordNet [9] and so to discover new semantic links [18]. However, there are tasks which need to be performed by hand such as deciding on a lexical relation that is of interest (i.e., hyponym) and a list of word pairs from WordNet this relation is known to hold between.

One of the main advantages of this method is its low cost for augmenting the structure of WordNet and its simplicity of relations. However, it also has some drawbacks including its dependence on the structure of a general-purpose ontology which prevents it from reasoning about specific terminology/concepts, the restricted set of defined semantic relations (i.e., only relations contained in WordNet are dealt with), its dependence on WordNet's terms (i.e., only terms present in WordNet can be related and any novel domain-specific term will be missed), the kind of inference enabled (i.e., it is only possible to produce direct links; what if we wish to relate different terms which are not in WordNet?), etc.

A natural further important step would be using knowledge base such as WordNet to support text inference to extract relevant, unstated information from the text. Harabagiu and Moldovan [15] address this issue by using WordNet as a commonsense knowledge base and designing relation-driven inference mechanisms which look for common semantic paths in order to draw conclusions. One outstanding feature of their method is that from these generated inferences, it is easy to ask for unknown relations between concepts. This has proven to be extremely useful in the context of Question-Answering Systems. However, although the method exhibits understanding capabilities, the commonsense facts discovered have not been demonstrated to be novel and interesting from a KDD viewpoint.

Mooney and colleagues [25] have also attempted to bring together general ontologies, IE technology and traditional machine learning methods to mine interesting patterns. Unlike previous approaches, Mooney deals with a different kind of knowledge, e.g., prediction rules. In addition, an explicit measure of novelty of the mined rules is proposed by establishing semantic distances between rules' antecedents and consequents using the underlying organisation of WordNet. Novelty is then defined as the average (semantic) distance between the words in a rule's antecedent and consequent. A key problem with this is that the method depends highly on WordNet's organisation and idiosyncratic features. As a consequence, since a lot of information extracted from the documents are not included in WordNet the predicted rules will lead to misleading decisions on their novelty.

The discussed approaches to TM/KDT use a variety of different "learning" techniques. Except for cases using Machine Learning techniques such as Neural Networks (e.g., SOM), decision trees, and so on, which have also been used in traditional DM, the real role of "learning" in the systems is not clear. There is no learning which enables the discovery but instead a set of primitive search strategies which do not necessarily explore the whole search space due to their dependence on the kind of semantic information previously extracted.

Although DM tasks have been commonly tackled as learning problems, the nature of DM suggests that the problem of DM (i.e., finding unseen, novel and interesting patterns) should be seen as involving search (i.e., different hypotheses are explored) and optimization (i.e., hypotheses which maximize quality criteria should be preferred) instead.

Despite there being a significant and successful number of practical search and optimization techniques [24, 5], there are some features that make some techniques more appealing to perform this kind of task than others, in terms of representation required, training sets required, supervision, hypothesis assessment, robustness in the search, etc.

In particular, the kind of evolutionary computation technique known as *Genetic Algorithms* (GA) has proved to be promising for search and optimization purposes. Compared with classical search and optimization algorithms, GAs are much less susceptible to getting stuck in local suboptimal regions of the search space as they perform global search by exploring solutions in parallel. GAs are robust and able to cope with noisy and missing data, they can search spaces of hypotheses containing complex interacting parts, where the impact of each part on overall hypothesis fitness may be difficult to model [13].

In order to use GAs to find optimal values of decision variables, we first need to represent the hypotheses in binary strings (the typical pseudo-chromosomal representation of a hypothesis in traditional GAs). After creating an initial population of strings at random, genetic operations are applied with some probability in order to improve the population. Once a new string is created by the operators, the solution is evaluated in terms of its measure of individual goodness referred to as *fitness*.

Individuals for the next generation are selected according to their fitness values, which will determine those to be chosen for reproduction. If a termination condition is not satisfied, the population is modified by the operators and a new (and hopefully better) population is created. Each interaction in this process is called a *generation* and the entire set of generations is called a *run*. At the end of a run there is often one or more highly fit chromosomes in the population.

One of the major contributions of evolutionary algorithms (e.g., GAs) for an important number of DM tasks (e.g., rule discovery, etc.) is that they tend to cope well with attribute interactions. This is in contrast to the local, greedy search performed by often-used rule induction and decision-tree algorithms [3, 14]. Most rule induction algorithms generate (prune) a rule by selecting (removing) one rule condition at a time, whereas evolutionary algorithms usually evaluate a rule as a whole via the fitness function rather than evaluating the impact of adding/removing one condition to/from a rule. In addition, operations such as crossover usually swap several rule conditions at a time between two individuals.

Typical tasks for GAs in DM have included [12, 34]: *Classification*; in which the goal is to predict the value (the class) of a user-defined goal attribute based on the values of other attributes; *Discovery of Association rules*; where binary attributes (items) contained in data instances (i.e., records) are used to discover associations of the form IF-THEN, *Rule discovery/prediction*; in which the system can produce many different combinations of attributes. (even if the original attributes do not have much predictive power by themselves, the system can effectively create "derived attributes" with greater predictive power) to come up with new rules.

A common representation used for this kind of task encodes attributes and values of a rule in a binary string of rule conditions and rule consequent. Suppose that an individual represents a rule antecedent with a single attribute-value condition, where the attribute *Marital_status* and its values can be "single," "married," "divorced," and "widow." A possible representation would be a condition involving this attribute encoded by four bits, so the string "0110" (i.e., the second and third values of the attribute are present) would represent the antecedent *IF marital_status=married OR divorced)* using internal disjunctions (i.e., logical OR).

One general aspect worth noting in applying GAs for DM tasks is that both the representation used for the discovery and the evaluation carried out assume that the source data are properly represented in a structured form (i.e., database) in which the attributes and values are easily handled.

When dealing with text data, these working assumptions are not always plausible because of the complexity of text information. In particular, mining text data using evolutionary algorithms requires a certain level of representation which captures knowledge beyond discrete data (i.e., semantics). Thus there arises the need for new operations to create knowledge from text databases. In addition, fitness evaluation also imposes important challenges in terms of measuring novel and interesting knowledge which might be implicit in the texts or be embedded in the underlying semantics of the extracted data.

Applying evolutionary methods to TM/KDT is a very recent research topic. With the exception of the work of [1] on the discovery of semantic relations no other research effort is under way as far as we know as the most promising KDT techniques have been tackled with more traditional search/learning methods.

The advantage over a similar approach for discovery of unseen relations as in [16], is that this approach provides more robust results in a way that exploits a wider number of possible hypotheses in the search space. In addition, the IE patterns finally used for the extraction are automatically learned, whereas for [16], these need to be handcrafted. Although the obtained relations have been evaluated in terms of their coverage in WordNet, the subjective quality of this unseen knowledge has not been assessed from a KDD viewpoint as no user has been involved in the process.

9.3 A Semantically Guided Model for Effective Text Mining

We developed a semantically guided model for evolutionary Text Mining which is domain-independent but genre-based. Unlike previous approaches to KDT, our approach does not rely on external resources or descriptions hence its domain-independence. Instead, it performs the discovery only using information from the original corpus of text documents and from the training data generated from them. In addition, a number of strategies have been developed for automatically evaluating the quality of the hypotheses ("novel" patterns). This is an important contribution on a topic which has been neglected in most of KDT research over the last years.

We have adopted GAs as central to our approach to KDT. However, for proper GA-based KDT there are important issues to be addressed including representation and guided operations to ensure that the produced offspring are semantically coherent.

In order to deal with issues regarding representation and new genetic operations so to produce an effective KDT process, our working model has been divided into two phases. The first phase is the preprocessing step aimed to produce both training information for further evaluation and the initial population of the GA. The second phase constitutes the knowledge discovery itself, in particular this aims at producing and evaluating explanatory unseen hypotheses.

The whole processing starts by performing the IE task (Figure 9.1) which applies extraction patterns and then generates a rule-like representation for each document of the specific domain corpus. After processing a set of n documents, the extraction stage will produce n rules, each one representing the document's content in terms of its conditions and conclusions. Once generated, these rules, along with other training data, become the "model" which will guide the GA-based discovery (see Figure 9.1).

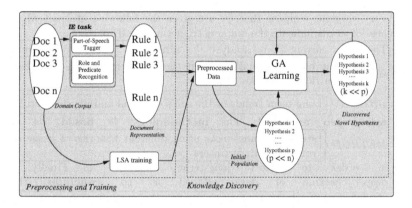

Fig. 9.1. The Evolutionary Model for Knowledge Discovery from Texts

In order to generate an initial set of hypotheses, an initial population is created by building random hypotheses from the initial rules, that is, hypotheses containing predicate and rhetorical information from the rules are constructed. The GA then runs for a number of generations until a fixed number of generations is achieved. At the end, a small set of the best hypotheses are obtained.

The description of the model is organised as follows: Section 9.3.1 presents the main features of the text preprocessing phase and how the representation for the hypotheses is generated. In addition, training tasks which generate the initial knowledge (semantic and rhetorical information) to feed the discovery are described. Section 9.3.2 describes constrained genetic operations to enable the hypotheses discovery, and proposes different evaluation metrics to assess the plausibility of the discovered hypotheses in a multi-objective context.

9.3.1 Text Preprocessing and Training

The preprocessing phase has two main goals: to extract important information from the texts and to use that information to generate both training data and the initial population for the GA.

In terms of text preprocessing (see first phase in Figure 9.1), an underlying principle in our approach is to be able to make good use of the structure of the documents for the discovery process. It is well-known that processing full documents has inherent complexities [23], so we have restricted our scope somewhat to consider a scientific genre involving scientific/technical abstracts. These have a well-defined macro-structure (genre-dependent rhetorical structure) to "summarise" what the author states in the full document (i.e., background information, methods, achievements, conclusions, etc).

Unlike patterns extracted for usual IE purposes such as in [18, 19, 20], this macro-structure and its roles are domain-independent but genre-based, so it is relatively easy to translate it into different contexts.

As an example, suppose that we are given the following abstract where bold sequences of words indicate the markers triggering the IE patterns:

The	current	study	**aims**	**to**	**provide**
$GOAL$ $\{$ the basic information about the fertilisers system, specially in its nutrient dynamics.					
$OBJECT$ $\{$ Long-term trends of the soil's chemical and physical fertility					
were	**also**	**analysed.** The	**methodology**	**is**	**based**	**on**	the
$METHOD$ $\{$ study of lands' plots using different histories of usage of crop rotation with fertilisers					
in	order	to	detect	long-term	changes.	...	Finally,	a
deep	checking	of	data	allowed	us	**to**	**conclude**	**that**
$CONCLUSION$ $\{$ soils have improved after 12 years of continuous rotation.					

From such a structure, important constituents can be identified:

- *Rhetorical Roles (discourse-level knowledge):* these indicate important places where the author makes some "assertions" about his/her work (i.e., the author is stating the goals, used methods, achieved conclusions, etc.). In the example above, the roles are represented by goal, object of study, method and conclusion.
- *Predicate Relations:* these are represented by actions (predicate and arguments) which are directly connected to the role being identified and state a relation which holds between a set of terms (words which are part of a sentence), a predicate and the role which they are linked to. Thus, for the example, they are as follows: **provide('the basic information ..'), analyse('long-term trends ...'), study('lands plot using ...'), improve('soil ..improved after ..')**
- *Causal Relation(s):* Although there are no explicit causal relations in the above example, we can hypothesise a simple rule of the form:
  IF the current goals are G1,G2, .. and the means/methods used M1,M2, .. (and any other constraint/feature) THEN it is true that we can achieve the conclusions C1,C2, ..
  Finally, the sample abstract may be represented in a rule-like form as follows:

```
IF     goal(provide('the basic information ..'))
  AND object(analyse('long-term trends ...'))
  AND method(study('lands plot using   ...'))
THEN   conclusion(improve('soil ..improved after ..'))
```

Note that causal relations are extracted from individual abstracts. In order to extract this initial key information from the texts, an IE module was built. Essentially, it takes a set of text documents, has them tagged through a previously trained Part-of-Speech (POS) tagger (i.e., Brill Tagger), and produces an intermediate representation for every document (i.e., template, in an IE sense) which is then converted into a general rule. A set of hand-crafted domain-independent extraction patterns were written and coded.

In addition, key training data are captured from the corpus of documents itself and from the semantic information contained in the rules. This can guide the discovery process in making further similarity judgements and assessing the plausibility of the produced hypotheses.

- *Training Information from the Corpus:*
  It has been suggested that huge amounts of texts represent a valuable source of semantic knowledge. In particular, in *Latent Semantic Analysis* (LSA) [21] it is claimed that this knowledge is at the word level.
  Following work by [21] on LSA incorporating structure, we have designed a semi-structured LSA representation for text data in which we represent predicate information (i.e., verbs) and arguments (i.e., set of terms) separately once they have been properly extracted in the IE phase. For this, the similarity is calculated by computing the closeness between two predicates (and arguments) based on the LSA data (function $SemSim(P_1(A_1), P_2(A_2))$).
  We propose a simple strategy for representing the meaning of the predicates with arguments. Next, a simple method is developed to measure the similarity between these units.
  Given a predicate P and its argument A, the vectors representing the meaning for both of them can be directly extracted from the training information provided by the LSA analysis. Representing the argument involves summing up all the vectors representing the terms of the argument and then averaging them, as is usually performed in semi-structured LSA. Once this is done, the meaning vector of the predicate and the argument is obtained by computing the sum of the two vectors as used in [33]. If there is more than one argument, then the final vector of the argument is just the sum of the individual arguments' vectors.
  Next, in making further semantic similarity judgements between two predicates $P_1(A_1)$ and $P_2(A_2)$ (i.e., **provide('the basic information ..')**), we take their corresponding previously calculated meaning vectors and then the similarity is determined by how close these two vectors are. We can evaluate this by computing the *cosine* between these vectors which gives us a closeness measure between -1 (complete unrelatedness) and 1 (complete relatedness) [22].
  Note however that training information from the texts is not sufficient as it only conveys data at a word semantics level. We claim that both basic knowledge at a rhetorical, semantic level, and co-occurrence information can be effectively computed to feed the discovery and to guide the GA.
  Accordingly, we perform two kinds of tasks: creating the initial population and computing training information from the rules.

a) *Creating the initial population of hypotheses:*
   once the initial rules have been produced, their components (rhetorical roles, predicate relations, etc.) are isolated and become a separate "database." This information is used both to build the initial hypotheses and to feed the further genetic operations (i.e., mutation of roles will need to randomly pick a role from this database).

b) *Computing training information (in which two kinds of training data are obtained):*

   a) *Computing correlations between rhetorical roles and predicate relations:*
      the connection between rhetorical information and the predicate action constitutes key information for producing coherent hypotheses. For example, is, in some domain, the *goal* of some hypothesis likely to be associated with the *construction* of some component? In a health context, this connection would be less likely than having *"finding* a new medicine for .."* as a *goal*.

      In order to address this issue, we adopted a Bayesian approach where we obtain the conditional probability of some predicate **p** given some attached rhetorical role **r**, namely $Prob(p \mid r)$. This probability values are later used to automatically evaluate some of the hypotheses' criteria.

   b) *Computing co-occurrences of rhetorical information:*
      One could think of a hypothesis as an abstract having text paragraphs which are semantically related to each other. Consequently, the meaning of the scientific evidence stated in the abstract may subtly change if the order of the facts is altered.

      This suggests that in generating valid hypotheses there will be rule structures which are more or less desirable than others. For instance, if every rule contains a "goal" as the first rhetorical role, and the GA has generated a hypothesis starting with some "conclusion" or "method," it will be penalised and therefore, it is very unlikely for that to survive in the next generation. Since the order matters in terms of affecting the rule's meaning, we can think of the p roles of a rule, as a sequence of tags: $< r_1, r_2, ..r_p >$ such that r_i precedes r_{i+1}, so we generate, from the rules, the conditional probabilities $Prob(r_p \mid r_q)$, for every role r_p, r_q. The probability that r_q precedes r_p will be used in evaluating new hypotheses, in terms that, for instance, its coherence.

9.3.2 Knowledge Discovery and Automatic Evaluation of Patterns

Our approach to KDT is strongly guided by semantic and rhetorical information, and consequently there are some soft constraints to be met before producing the offspring so as to keep them coherent.

The GA will start from a initial population, which in this case, is a set of semi-random hypotheses built up from the preprocessing phase. Next, constrained GA operations are applied and the hypotheses are evaluated. In order for every individual to have a fitness assigned, we use a evolutionary multi-objective optimisation strategy based on the *Strength Pareto Evolutionary Algorithm* (SPEA) algorithm [35]. SPEA deals with the diversity of the solutions (i.e., niche formation) and the fitness assignment as a whole in a representation-independent way. An attractive feature of SPEA is that in order to create niches, this does not define a neighborhood by means of a distance metric on the genotypic or phenotypic space. Instead, the classes of solutions are grouped according to the results of a clustering method which uses the vector of objective functions of the individuals, and not the individuals themselves.

Once the offspring is produced, the population update is performed using a steady-state strategy. Here, each individual from a small number of the worst hypotheses is replaced by an individual from the offspring only if the latter are better than the former.

For semantic constraints, judgements of similarity between hypotheses or components of hypotheses (i.e., predicates, arguments, etc.) are carried out using the LSA training data and predicate-level information previously discussed in the training step.

Hypothesis Discovery

Using the semantic measure above and additional constraints discussed later on, we propose new operations to allow guided discovery such that unrelated new knowledge is avoided, as follows:

- *Selection:* selects a small number of the best parent hypotheses of every generation (*Generation Gap*) according to their fitness. Note that the notion of optimum (and *best*) is different here as there is more than one objective to be traded off. Accordingly, this is usually referred to as a *"Pareto Optimum"* [29]. Assuming a minimization problem (i.e., "worse" involves smaller values), a decision vector (i.e., vector of several objectives) is a Pareto optimal if there exists no feasible vector which would increase some objective without causing a simultaneous decrease in at least one other objective. Unfortunately, this concept almost always gives not a single solution, but rather a set of solutions called the *Pareto Optimal set*. The decision vectors corresponding to the solutions included in the Pareto optimal set are called non-dominated, and the space of the objective functions whose nondominated vectors are in the Pareto optimal set is called the *Pareto front* [4, 5, 11].

- *Crossover:* a simple recombination of both hypotheses' conditions and conclusions takes place, where two individuals swap their conditions to produce new offspring (the conclusions remain).

  Under normal circumstances, crossover works on random parents and positions where their parts should be exchanged. However, in our case this operation must be restricted to preserve semantic coherence. We use soft semantic constraints to define two kinds of recombinations:

  a) *Swanson's Crossover:* based on Swanson's hypothesis [30, 31] we propose a recombination operation as follows:

     If there is a hypothesis (AB) such that "IF A THEN B" and another one (BC) such that "IF B' THEN C," (B' being something semantically similar to B) then a new interesting hypothesis "IF A THEN C" can be inferred via LSA if the conclusions of AB have high semantic similarity with the conditions of hypothesis BC.

     The above principle can be seen in Swanson's crossover between two learned hypotheses as shown in figure 9.2

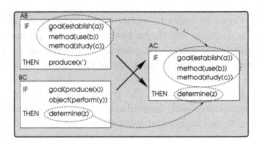

Fig. 9.2. Semantically guided Swanson Crossover

b) *Default Semantic Crossover:* if the previous transitivity does not apply then the recombination is performed as long as both hypotheses as a whole have high semantic similarity which is defined in advance by providing minimum thresholds.

- *Mutation:* aims to make small random changes on hypotheses to explore new possibilities in the search space. As in recombination, we have dealt with this operation in a constrained way, so we propose three kinds of mutations to deal with the hypotheses' different objects:

  a) *Role Mutation:* one rhetorical role (including its contents: relations and arguments) is selected and randomly replaced by a random one from the initial role database.

  b) *Predicate Mutation:* one inner predicate and its argument is selected and randomly replaced with another predicate-argument pair from the initial predicate databases.

  c) *Argument Mutation:* since we have no information about arguments' semantic types, we choose a new argument by following a guided procedure in which the former argument is randomly replaced with that having a high semantic similarity via LSA. [33].

- *Population Update:* we use a non-generational GA in which some individuals are replaced by the new offspring in order to preserve the hypotheses' good material from one generation to other, and so to encourage the improvement of the population's quality.

Evaluation

Since each hypothesis in our model has to be assessed by different criteria, usual methods for evaluating fitness are not appropriate. Hence *Evolutionary Multi-Objective Optimisation* (EMOO) techniques which use the multiple criteria defined for the hypotheses are needed. Accordingly, we propose EMOO-based evaluation metrics to assess the hypotheses' fitness in a domain-independent way and, unlike other approaches, without using any external source of domain knowledge. The different metrics are represented by multiple criteria by which the hypotheses are assessed.

In order to establish evaluation criteria, we have taken into account different issues concerning plausibility (Is the hypothesis semantically sound?, Are the GA operations producing something coherent in the current hypothesis?), and quality itself (How is the hypothesis supported from the initial text documents? How interesting is it?). Accordingly, we have defined eight evaluation criteria to assess the hypotheses (i.e., in terms of Pareto dominance, it will produce a 8-dimensional vector of objective functions) given by: **relevance, structure, cohesion, interestingness, coherence, coverage, simplicity, plausibility of origin**.

The current hypothesis to be assessed will be denoted as H, and the training rules as R_i. Evaluation methods (criteria) by which the hypotheses are assessed and the questions they are trying to address are as follows:

- **Relevance**
  Relevance addresses the issue of how important the hypothesis is to target concepts. This involves two concepts (i.e., terms), as previously described, related to the question:
  What is the best set of hypotheses that explain the relation between $< term1 >$ *and* $< term2 >$?
  Considering the current hypothesis, it turns into a specific question: how good is the hypothesis in explaining this relation?
  This can be estimated by determining the semantic closeness between the hypothesis' predicates (and arguments) and the target concepts[2] by using the meaning vectors obtained from the LSA analysis for both terms and predicates. Our method for assessing relevance takes these issues into account along with some ideas of Kintsch's Predication. Specifically, we use the concept of *Strength* [21]: $strength(A, I) = f(SemSim(A, I), SemSim(P, I)))$ between a predicate with arguments and surrounding concepts (target concepts in our case) as a part of the relevance measure, which basically decides whether the predicate (and argument) is relevant to the target concepts in terms of the similarity between both predicate and argument, and the concepts.
  We define the function f as proposed by [21] to give a relatedness measure such that high values are obtained only if both the similarity between the target concept and the argument (α), and target concept and the predicate (β) exceed some threshold. Next, we highlight the closeness by determining the square difference between each similarity value and the desired value (1.0). If we take the average square difference, we obtain an error metric which is a *Mean Square Error* (MSE). As we want to get low error values so to encourage high closeness, we subtract MSE from 1. Formally, $f(\alpha, \beta)$ is therefore computed as the function:

$$f(\alpha, \beta) = \begin{cases} 1 - MSE(\{\alpha, \beta\}) & \text{if both } \alpha \text{ and } \beta > threshold \\ 0 & \text{Otherwise} \end{cases}$$

where the MSE is the *Mean Square Error* between the similarities and the desired value ($Vd = 1.0$), is calculated as:

$$MSE(\{\text{list of n values } v_i\}) = \frac{1}{n} \sum_{i=1}^{n} (v_i - Vd)^2$$

In order to account for both target concepts, we just take the average of **strength** for both terms. So, the overall relevance becomes:

$$relevance(H) = \frac{\frac{1}{2} \sum_{i=1}^{|H|} strength(P_i, A_i, <term1>) + strength(P_i, A_i, <term2>)}{|H|}$$

---

[2] Target concepts are relevant nouns in our experiment. However, in a general case, these might be either nouns or verbs.

in which $\mid H \mid$ denotes the length of the hypothesis H, that is, the number of predicates.

Note that pairs of target concepts are provided by a domain experts so as to guide the search process.

- **Structure** (*How good is the structure of the rhetorical roles?*): measures how much of the rules' structure is exhibited in the current hypothesis.

Since we have previous pre-processed information for bi-grams of roles, the structure can be computed by following a Markov chain [23] as follows:

$$Structure(H) = Prob(r_1) * \prod_{i=2}^{|H|} Prob(r_i \mid r_{i-1})$$

where r_i represents the $i-th$ role of the hypothesis H, $Prob(r_i \mid r_{i-1})$ denotes the conditional probability that role r_{i-1} immediately precedes r_i. $Prob(r_i)$ denotes the probability that no role precedes r_i, that is, it is at the beginning of the structure (i.e., $Prob(r_i \mid < start >)$).

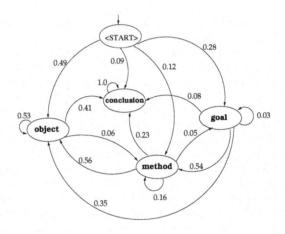

Fig. 9.3. Markov Model for Roles Structure Learned from sampled technical documents

For example, part of a Markov chain of rhetorical roles learned by the model from a specific technical domain can be seen in figure 9.3. Here it can be observed that some structure tags are more frequent than others (i.e., the sequence of rhetorical roles goal-method (0.54) is more likely than the sequence goal-conclusion (0.08)).

- **Cohesion** (*How likely is a predicate action to be associated with some specific rhetorical role?*): measures the degree of "connection" between rhetorical information (i.e., roles) and predicate actions. The issue here is how likely (according to the rules) some predicate relation P in the current hypothesis is to be associated with role r. Formally, *cohesion* for hypothesis H is expressed as:

$$\text{cohesion(H)} = \sum_{r_i, P_i \in H} \frac{Prob(P_i \mid r_i)}{|H|}$$

where $Prob(P_i \mid r_i)$ states the conditional probability of the predicate P_i given the rhetorical role r_i.

- **Interestingness** (*How interesting is the hypothesis in terms of its antecedent and consequent?*):
  Unlike other approaches to measure "interestingness" which use an external resource (e.g., WordNet) and rely on its organisation, we propose a different view where the criterion can be evaluated from the semi-structured information provided by the LSA analysis. Accordingly, the measure for hypothesis H is defined as a degree of unexpectedness as follows:

  ```
  interestingness(H)= <Semantic Dissimilarity between Antecedent
                       and   Consequent>
  ```

  That is, the lower the similarity, the more interesting the hypothesis is likely to be, so the dissimilarity is measured as the inverse of the LSA similarity. Otherwise, it means the hypothesis involves a correlation between its antecedent and consequent which may be an uninteresting known common fact [26].
- **Coherence:** This metrics addresses the question whether the elements of the current hypothesis relate to each other in a semantically coherent way. Unlike rules produced by DM techniques in which the order of the conditions is not an issue, the hypotheses produced in our model rely on pairs of adjacent elements which should be semantically sound, a property which has long been dealt with in the linguistic domain, in the context of *text coherence* [10].
  As we have semantic information provided by the LSA analysis which is complemented with rhetorical and predicate-level knowledge, we developed a simple method to measure coherence, following work by [10] on measuring text coherence.
  Semantic coherence is calculated by considering the average semantic similarity between consecutive elements of the hypothesis. However, note that this closeness is only computed on the semantic information that the predicates and their arguments convey (i.e., not the roles) as the role structure has been considered in a previous criterion. Accordingly, the criterion can be expressed as follows:

$$\text{Coherence(H)}= \sum_{i=1}^{(|H|-1)} \frac{SemSim(P_i(A_i), P_{i+1}(A_{i+1}))}{(|H|-1)}$$

  where $(|\ H\ | -1)$ denotes the number of adjacent pairs, and $SemSim$ is the LSA-based semantic similarity between two predicates.
- **Coverage:** The coverage metric tries to address the question of how much the hypothesis is supported by the model (i.e., rules representing documents and semantic information).
  Coverage of a hypothesis has usually been measured in KDD approaches by considering some structuring in data (i.e., discrete attributes) which is not present in textual information. Besides, most of the KDD approaches have assumed the use of linguistic or conceptual resources to measure the degree of coverage of the hypotheses (i.e., match against databases, positive examples).
  In order to deal with the criterion in the context of KDT, we say that a generated hypothesis H covers an extracted rule R_i (i.e., rule extracted from the original training documents, including semantic and rhetorical information) only if the predicates of H are roughly (or exactly, in the best case) contained in R_i.
  Formally, the rules covered are defined as:

```
RulesCovered(H)={ R_i ∈ RuleSet | ∀P_j ∈ R_i   ∃HP_k ∈ HP :
(SemSim(HP_k, P_j) ≥ threshold ∧ predicate(HP_k)=predicate(P_j))}
```

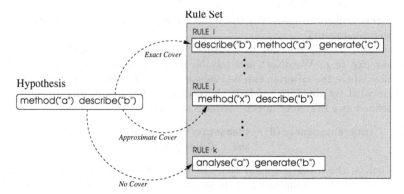

Fig. 9.4. Computing Hypothesis Covering of Documents' rules

Where $SemSim(HP_k, P_j)$ represents the LSA-based similarity between hypothesis predicate HP_k and rule predicate P_j, **threshold** denotes a minimum fixed user-defined value, $RuleSet$ denotes the whole set of rules, HP represents the list of predicates with arguments of H, and P_j represents a predicate (with arguments) contained in R_i. Once the set of rules covered is computed, the criterion can finally be computed as:

$$Coverage(H) = \frac{|RulesCovered(H)|}{|RuleSet|}$$

Where $|\,RulesCovered\,|$ and $|\,RuleSet\,|$ denote the size of the set of rules covered by H, and the size of the initial set of extracted rules, respectively.

- **Simplicity** (*How simple is the hypothesis?*): shorter and/or easy-to-interpret hypotheses are preferred. Since the criterion has to be maximised, the evaluation will depend on the length (number of elements) of the hypothesis.
- **Plausibility of Origin** (*How plausible is the hypothesis produced by Swanson's evidence?*): If the current hypothesis was an offspring from parents which were recombined by a Swanson's transitivity-like operator, then the higher the semantic similarity between one parent's consequent and the other parent's antecedent, the more precise is the evidence, and consequently worth exploring as a novel hypothesis. If no better hypothesis is found so far, the current similarity is inherited from one generation to the next.

Accordingly, the criterion for a hypothesis H is simply given by:

$$Plausibility(H) = \begin{cases} S_p & \text{If H was created from a Swanson's crossover} \\ 0 & \text{If H is in the original population or is a} \\ & \text{result of another operation} \end{cases}$$

Note that since we are dealing with a multi-objective problem, there is no simple way to get independent fitness values as the fitness involves a set of objective functions to be assessed for every individual. Therefore, the computation is performed by comparing objectives of one individual with others in terms of *Pareto dominance* [5] in which non-dominated solutions (Pareto individuals) are searched for in every generation.

We took a simple approach in which an approximation to the Pareto optimal set is incrementally built as the GA goes on. The basic idea is to determine whether a solution is better than another in global terms, that is, a child is better if this is a becomes a non-dominated hypothesis.

Next, since our model is based on a multi-criteria approach, we have to face three important issues in order to assess every hypothesis' fitness: Pareto dominance, fitness assignment and the diversity problem [5]. Despite an important number of state-of-the-art methods to handle these issues [5], only a small number of them has focused on the problem in an integrated and representation-independent way. In particular, Zitzler [35] proposes an interesting method, *Strength Pareto Evolutionary Algorithm* (SPEA) which uses a mixture of established methods and new techniques in order to find multiple Pareto-optimal solutions in parallel, and at the same time to keep the population as diverse as possible. We have also adapted the original SPEA algorithm to allow for the incremental updating of the Pareto-optimal set along with our steady-state replacement method.

9.4 Analysis and Results

In order to assess the quality of the discovered knowledge (hypotheses) by the model a Prolog-based prototype has been built. The IE task has been implemented as a set of modules whose main outcome is the set of rules extracted from the documents. In addition, an intermediate training module is responsible for generating information from the LSA analysis and from the rules just produced. The initial rules are represented by facts containing lists of relations both for antecedent and consequent.

For the purpose of the experiments, the corpus of documents has been obtained from the *AGRIS* database for agricultural and food science. We selected this kind of corpus as it has been properly cleaned-up, and builds upon a scientific area which we do not have any knowledge about so to avoid any possible bias and to make the results more realistic. A set of 1000 documents was extracted from which one third were used for setting parameters and making general adjustments, and the rest were used for the GA itself in the evaluation stage.

Next, we tried to provide answers to two basic questions concerning our original aims:

a) How well does the GA for KDT behave?
b) How good are the hypotheses produced according to human experts in terms of text mining's ultimate goals: interestingness, novelty and usefulness, etc.

In order to address these issues, we used a methodology consisting of two phases: the system evaluation and the experts' assessment.

a) *System Evaluation:* this aims at investigating the behavior and the results produced by the GA.
   We set the GA by generating an initial population of 100 semi-random hypotheses. In addition, we defined the main global parameters such as *Mutation Probability* (0.2), *Crossover Probability* (0.8), *Maximum Size of Pareto set* (5%), etc. We ran five versions of the GA with the same configuration of parameters but different pairs of terms to address the quest for explanatory novel hypotheses.
   The different results obtained from running the GA as used for our experiment are shown in the form of a representative behavior in figure 9.5, where the

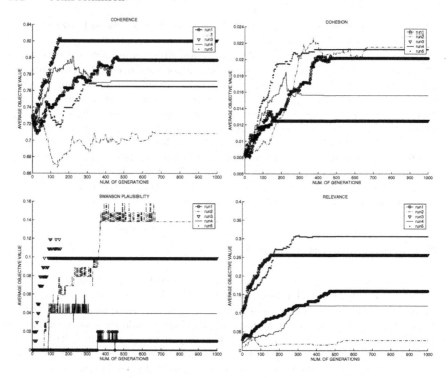

Fig. 9.5. GA evaluation for some of the criteria

number of generations is placed against the average objective value for some of the eight criteria.

Some interesting facts can be noted. Almost all the criteria seem to stabilise after (roughly) generation 700 for all the runs; that is, no further improvement beyond this point is achieved and so this may give us an approximate indication of the limits of the objective function values.

Another aspect worth highlighting is that despite a steady-state strategy being used by the model to produce solutions, the individual evaluation criteria behave in unstable ways to accommodate solutions which had to be removed or added. As a consequence, it is not necessarily the case that all the criteria have to monotonically increase.

In order to see this behavior, look at the results for the criteria for the same period of time, between generations 200 and 300 for run 4. For an average hypothesis, *Coherence*, *Cohesion*, *Simplicity* and *Structure* get worse, whereas *Coverage*, *Interestingness* and *Relevance*, improve and *Plausibility* shows some variability. Note that not all the criteria are shown in the graph.

b) *Expert Assessment:* this aims at assessing the quality (and therefore, effectiveness) of the discovered knowledge on different criteria by human domain experts. For this, we designed an experiment in which 20 human experts were involved and each assessed 5 hypotheses selected from the Pareto set. We then asked the experts to assess the hypotheses from 1 (worst) to 5 (best) in terms of the following criteria: Interestingness (INT), Novelty (NOV), Usefulness (USE) and Sensibleness (SEN).

In order to select worthwhile terms for the experiment, we asked one domain expert to filter pairs of target concepts previously related according to traditional clustering analysis (see Table 9.1 containing target concepts used in the experiments). The pairs which finally deserved attention were used as input in the actual experiments (i.e., **degradation** and **erosive**).

Run	Term 1	Term 2
1	enzyme	zinc
2	glycocide	inhibitor
3	antinutritious	cyanogenics
4	degradation	erosive
5	cyanogenics	inhibitor

Table 9.1. Pairs of target concepts used for the actual experiments

Once the system hypotheses were produced, the experts were asked to score them according to the five subjective criteria. Next, we calculated the scores for every criterion as seen in the overall results in Table 9.2 (for length's sake, only some criterion are shown).

The assessment of individual criteria shows some hypotheses did well with scores above the average (50%) on a 1-5 scale. Overall, this supports the claim that the model indeed is able to find *nuggets* in textual information and to provide some basic explanation about the hidden relationships in these discoveries. This is the case for 3 hypotheses in terms of INT, 2 hypotheses in terms of SEN, 5 hypotheses in terms of USE, and 1 hypothesis in terms of NOV, etc.

	No. of Hypotheses	
Criterion	Negative < Average	Positive ≥ Average
ADD	20/25 (80%)	5/25 (20 %)
INT	19/25 (76%)	6/25 (24 %)
NOV	21/25 (84%)	4/25 (16 %)
SEN	17/25 (68%)	8/25 (32 %)
USE	20/25 (80%)	5/25 (20 %)

Table 9.2. Distribution of Experts' assessment of Hypothesis per Criteria

These results and the evaluation produced by the model were used to measure the correlation between the scores of the human subjects and the system's model evaluation. Since both the expert and the system's model evaluated the results based on several criteria, we first performed a normalisation aimed at producing a single "quality" value for each hypothesis as follows:

- *For the expert assessment:* the scores of the different criteria for every hypothesis[3] are averaged. Note that this will produce values between 1 and 5, with 5 being the best.
- *For the model evaluation:* for every hypothesis, both the objective value and the fitness are considered as follows: whereas the lower the fitness score, the better the hypothesis, the higher the objective value, the better the hypothesis. Therefore, we subtract the fitness from 1 for each hypothesis and then we add this to the average value of the objective values for this hypothesis. Note that this will produce values between 0 and 2, with 2 being the best.

We then calculated the pair of values for every hypothesis and obtained a (Spearman) correlation $r = 0.43$ ($t - test = 23.75, df = 24, p < 0.001$). From this result, we see that the correlation shows a good level of prediction compared to humans. This indicates that for such a complex task (knowledge discovery), the model's behavior is not too different from the experts' (see Figure 9.6).

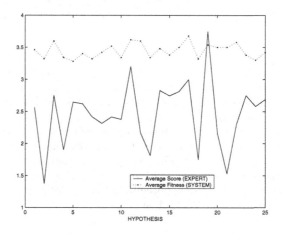

Fig. 9.6. Correlation between human and system evaluation of discovered hypotheses

Note that in Mooney's experiment using simple discovered rules, a lower human-system correlation of $r = 0.386$ was obtained. Considering also that the human subjects were not domain experts as in our case, our results are encouraging as these involve a more demanding process which requires further comprehension of both the hypothesis itself and the working domain. In addition, our model was able to do it better without any external linguistic resources as in Mooney's experiments [26].

In order to show what the final hypotheses look like and how the good characteristics and less desirable features above are exhibited, we picked one of the best hypotheses as assessed by the experts (i.e., we picked one of the best 25 of the 100 final hypotheses) based on the average value of the 5 scores they assigned. For example, hypothesis 65 of run 4 looks like:

---

[3] ADD is not considered here as this does not measure a typical KDD aspect,

```
IF goal(perform(19311)) and goal(analyze(20811))
THEN establish(111)
```

Where the numerical values represent internal identifiers for the arguments and their semantic vectors, and its resulting criteria vector is $[\mathbf{0.92}, 0.09, 0.50, 0.005, 0.7, 0.00, 0.30, 0.25]$ (the vector's elements represent the values for the criteria relevance, structure, coherence, cohesion, interestingness, plausibility, coverage, and simplicity) and obtained an average expert's assessment of 3.74. In natural-language text, this can roughly be interpreted as (each item of the following NL description represents a predicate-level information of hypothesis above):

- IF the work **aims** at **performing** the genetic grouping of seed populations and investigating a tendency to the separation of northern populations into different classes, AND
- The **goal** is to **analyse** the vertical integration for producing and selling Pinus Timber in the Andes-Patagonia region.
- THEN as a **consequence**, the best agricultural use for land lots of organic agriculture must be **established** to promote a conservationist culture in priority or critical agricultural areas.

The hypothesis appears to be more relevant and coherent than others (relevance = 92%). However, this is not complete in terms of cause-effect. For instance, the methods are missing. It is also important to highlight that the high value for the coherence of the pattern (50%) is consistent with the contents of the predicates of the hypothesis. The three key paragraphs containing rhetorical knowledge indeed relate to the same topic: testing and producing specific Pinus trees. Even more important is the fact that despite having zero plausibility (novelty), the pattern is still regarded as interesting by the model (70%) and above the average by the experts. As for the target concepts (**degradant** and **erosive**) and the way the discovered hypothesis attempts to explain the link between them, it can be seen that the contents of this patterns try to relate these terms with "agricultural areas," "seed populations," etc., so the discovery makes a lot of sense.

Another of the discovered patterns is given by hypothesis 88 of run 3, which is represented as follows:

```
IF goal(present(11511)) AND
   method(use(25511))
THEN effect(1931,1932)
```

and has a criteria vector $[0.29, 0.18, 0.41, 0.030, 0.28, \mathbf{0.99}, 0.30, 0.50]$ and obtained an average expert's assessment of 3.20. In natural-language text, this can roughly be interpreted as:

- IF the **goal** is to **present** a two-dimensional scheme for forest restoration in which two regression models with Pinus and without Pinus are identified by inspiring in the natural restoring dynamics, AND
- The **method** is based on the **use** of micro-environments for capturing the kind of farm mice called *Apodemus Sylvaticus*i, and on the use of capture traps at a rate of 1464 traps per night.

- THEN, in vitro digestion of three cutting ages in six ecotypes has an **effect** on "Bigalta" cuttings which got their higher performance in a 63-day period.

This hypothesis looks more complete (goal, methods, etc.) but is less relevant than the previous hypothesis despite its close coherence. Note also that the plausibility is much higher than for hypothesis 65, but the other criteria seemed to be a key factor for the experts.

The hypothesis concerns the production and cutting of a specific kind of tree (Pinus) and forests where these lie. However, the second role ("the method is based...") discusses a different topic (mice capture) which apparently has nothing to do with the main issue and that is the reason for the pattern's coherence to be scored lower than the previous hypothesis (41% vs. 50%). The model also discovered that there are organisms (and issues related to them) which are affecting the Pinus (and forest) restoration (i.e., mice). This fact has received a higher value for *Plausibility of Origin* or the Novelty of the pattern (99%) and consequently, it is correlated with the experts opinion of the pattern (score=3.20).

Another example of discovered patterns is a low-scored hypothesis given by the following hypothesis 52:

```
IF object(perform(20611)) AND
   object(carry_out(2631))
THEN  effect(1931,1932)
```

and has a criteria vector $[\mathbf{0.29}, \mathbf{0.48}, 0.49, 0.014, 0.2, 0, 0.3, 0.5]$ and obtained an average expert's assessment of 1.53.

The structure of this pattern (48%) is better than for hypothesis 88. However, since the hypothesis is not complete, this has been scored lower than the previous one. This might be explained because the difference in structure between object-object and goal-method (Figure 9.3) is not significant and as both hypotheses (88 and 52) become final solutions, the expert scored best those which better explain the facts. Note that as the model relies on the training data, this does not ensure that every hypothesis is complete. In fact, previous experimental analyses of recall show that only 26% of the original rules representing the documents contain some sort of "method."

In natural-language text, the pattern can roughly be interpreted as:

- IF the **object** of the work is to **perform** the analysis of the fractioned honey in Brazil for improving the producers' income and profitability, AND
- The **object** of the work is to **carry out** observations for the study of Pinus hartwegii at the mexican snowed hills so to complement the previously existing information about the development status of *Adjunctus* and its biology.
- THEN in vitro digestion of three cutting ages in six ecotypes has an **effect** on bigalta cuttings which got their higher performance in a 63-day period.

This hypothesis shows the same relevance as the previous one (29%) indicating that both attempt to explain the connection between the target concepts and that contained in the pattern. Note also that coherence is not very high (49%) considering that one part of the pattern discusses the "honey production" and issues, and the other parts deal with the investigation, production and cutting of Pinus trees. Accordingly the degree of interestingness and novelty of the patterns has been low scored which is well-correlated with the expert's assessment. Nevertheless, the hypothesis is successful in detecting hidden relations between certain areas (*Mexican snowed hills*) and the Pinus production and cutting.

9.5 Conclusions

Unlike traditional approaches to Text Mining, in this chapter we contribute an innovative way of combining additional linguistic information and evolutionary learning techniques in order to produce novel hypotheses which involve explanatory and effective novel knowledge.

From the experiments and results, it can be noted that the approach supports the claim that the evolutionary model to KDT indeed is able to find *nuggets* in textual information and to provide basic explanations about the hidden relationships in these discoveries.

We also introduced a unique approach for evaluation which deals with semantic and Data Mining issues in a high-level way. In this context, the proposed representation for hypotheses suggests that performing shallow analysis of the documents and then capturing key rhetorical information may be a good level of processing which constitutes a trade off between completely deep and keyword-based analysis of text documents. In addition, the results suggest that the performance of the model in terms of the correlation with human judgements are slightly better than approaches using external resources as in [26]. In particular criteria, the model shows a very good correlation between the system evaluation and the expert assessment of the hypotheses.

The model deals with the hypothesis production and evaluation in a very promising way which is shown in the overall results obtained from the experts evaluation and the individual scores for each hypothesis. However, it is important to note that unlike the experts who have a lot of experience, preconceived concept models and complex knowledge in their areas, the system has done relatively well only exploring the corpus of technical documents and the implicit connections contained in it.

From an evolutionary KDT viewpoint, the correlations and the quality of the final hypotheses show that the GA operations and the system's evaluation of the individuals may be effective predictions of really useful novel knowledge from a user perspective.

References

1. A. Bergstron, P. Jaksetic, and P. Nordin. Acquiring Textual Relations Automatically on the Web Using Genetic Programming. *EuroGP 2000, Edinburgh, Scotland*, pages 237–246, April 2000.
2. Michael Berry. *Survey of Text Mining: Clustering, Classification, and Retrieval.* Springer, 2004.
3. M. Berthold and D. Hand. *Intelligent Data Analysis.* Springer, 2000.
4. C. Coello. A Short Tutorial on Evolutionary Multiobjective Optimisation. *ACM Computing Surveys*, 2001.

5. Kalyanmoy Deb. *Multi-objective Optimization Using Evolutionary Algorithms.* Wiley, 2001.

6. U. Fayyad, G. Piatesky-Shapiro, and P. Smith. From Data Mining to Knowledge Discovery: An Overview. In *Advances in Knowledge Discovery and Data Mining,* pages 1–36. MIT Press, 1996.

7. R. Feldman. Knowledge Management: A Text Mining Approach. *Proc. of the 2nd Int. Conference on Practical Aspects of Knowledge Management (PAKM98), Basel, Switzerland,* October 1998.

8. R. Feldman and I. Dagan. Knowledge Discovery in textual databases (KDT). *Proceedings of the first international conference on knowledge discovery and data mining (KDD-95), Montreal, Canada,* pages 112–117, August 1995.

9. C. Fellbaum. *WordNet: An Electronic Lexical Database.* MIT Press, 1998.

10. P. Foltz, W. Kintsch, and T. Landauer. The Measurement of Textual Coherence with Latent Semantic Analysis. *Discourse processes,* 25(2):259–284, 1998.

11. C. Fonseca and P. Fleming. An Overview of Evolutionary Algorithms in Multiobjective Optimisation. *Evolutionary Computation,* 3(1):1–16, 1995.

12. A. Freitas. A Survey of Evolutionary Algorithms for Data Mining and Knowledge Discovery. *Advances in Evolutionary Computation, Springer-Verlag,* 2002.

13. D. Goldberg. *Genetic Algorithms in Search, Optimization and Machine Learning.* Addison Wesley, 1989.

14. J. Han and M. Kamber. *Data Mining: Concepts and Techniques.* Morgan-Kaufmann, 2001.

15. S. Harabagiu and D. Moldovan. Knowledge processing on an extended wordnet. In *WordNet: An Electronic Lexical Database,* pages 379–403. MIT Press, 1998.

16. M. Hearst. Automated Discovery of WordNet Relations. In *WordNet: An Electronic Lexical Database,* pages 131–151. MIT Press, 1998.

17. M. Hearst. Text Data Mining: Issues, Techniques and the Relation to Information Access. Technical report, Univerity of California at Berkeley, 1998.

18. M. Hearst. Untangling Text Data Mining. *Proceedings of the 37th Annual Meeting of the ACL, University of Maryland (invited paper),* June 1999.

19. M. Hearst. Text Mining Tools: Instruments for Scientific Discovery. *IMA Text Mining Workshop, USA,* April 2000.

20. C. Jacquemin and E. Tzoukermann. NLP for Term Variant Extraction: Synergy between Morphology, Lexicon, and Syntax. In *Natural Language Information Retrieval.* Kluwer Academic, 1999.

21. W. Kintsch. Predication. *Cognitive Science,* 25(2):173–202, 2001.

22. T. Landauer, P. Foltz, and D. Laham. An Introduction to Latent Semantic Analysis. *Discourse Processes,* 10(25):259–284, 1998.

23. C. Manning and H. Schutze. *Foundations of Statistical Natural Language Processing.* MIT Press, 1999.

24. M. Mitchell. *An Introduction to Genetic Algorithms.* MIT Press, 1996.

25. U. Nahm and R. Mooney. Using Information Extraction to Aid the Discovery of Prediction Rules from Text. *Proceedings of the 6th International Conference on Knowledge Discovery and Data Mining (KDD-2000) Workshop on Text Mining,* August 2000.

26. U. Nahm and R. Mooney. Text Mining with Information Extraction. *AAAI 2002 Spring Symposium on Mining Answers from Texts and Knowledge Bases, Stanford, USA,* 2002.

27. M. Rajman and R. Besancon. Text Mining: Knowledge Extraction from Unstructured Textual Data. *6th Conference of the International federation of classification societies (IFCS-98), Rome, Italy*, July 1998.

28. P. Srinivasan. Text mining: Generating hypotheses from medline. *Journal of the American Society for Information Science*, 55(4):396–413, 2004.

29. W. Stadler. *Fundamentals of Multicriteria Optimization*. Plenum Press, New York, 1988.

30. D. Swanson. Migraine and Magnesium: Eleven Neglected Connections. *Perspectives in Biology and Medicine*, n/a(31):526–557, 1988.

31. D. Swanson. On the Fragmentation of Knowledge, the Connection Explosion, and Assembling Other People's ideas. *Annual Meeting of the American Society for Information Science and Technology*, 27(3), February 2001.

32. M. Weeber, H. Klein, L. de Jong, and R. Vos. Using concepts in literature-based discovery: Simulating swanson's raynaud-fish oil and migraine-magnesium discoveries. *Journal of the American Society for Information Science*, 52(7):548–557, 2001.

33. P. Wiemer-Hastings. Adding Syntactic Information to LSA. *Proceedings of the Twenty-second Annual Conference of the Cognitive Science Society*, pages 989–993, 2000.

34. G. Williams. Evolutionary Hot Spots Data Mining. *3rd Pacific-Asia Conference, PAKDD-99, Beijing, China, April*, pages 184–193, 1999.

35. E. Zitzler and L. Thiele. An Evolutionary Algorithm for Multiobjective Optimisation: The Strength Pareto Approach. Technical Report 43, Swiss Federal Institute of Technology (ETH), Switzerland, 1998.

Handling of Imbalanced Data in Text Classification: Category-Based Term Weights

Ying Liu, Han Tong Loh, Kamal Youcef-Toumi, and Shu Beng Tor

10.1 Introduction

Learning from imbalanced data has emerged as a new challenge to the machine learning (ML), data mining (DM) and text mining (TM) communities. Two recent workshops in 2000 [17] and 2003 [7] at AAAI and ICML conferences respectively and a special issue in ACM SIGKDD explorations [8] are dedicated to this topic. It has been witnessing growing interest and attention among researchers and practitioners seeking solutions in handling imbalanced data. An excellent review of the state-of-the-art is given by Gary Weiss [43].

The data imbalance problem often occurs in classification and clustering scenarios when a portion of the classes possesses many more examples than others. As pointed out by Chawla et al. [8] when standard classification algorithms are applied to such skewed data, they tend to be overwhelmed by the major categories and ignore the minor ones. There are two main reasons why the uneven cases happen. One is due to the intrinsic nature of such events as credit fraud, cancer detection, network intrusion, earthquake prediction and so on [8]. These are rare events presented as a unique category but can only occupy a very small portion of the entire example space. Another case is due to the expense of collecting learning examples and legal or privacy reasons. In our previous endeavor of building a manufacturing centered technical paper corpus [27, 28], due to the costly efforts demanded for human labeling and diverse interests in the papers, we ended up naturally with a skewed collection.

Automatic text classification (TC) has recently witnessed a booming interest, due to the increased availability of documents in digital form and the ensuing need to organize them [40]. In TC tasks, given that most test collections are composed of documents belonging to multiple classes, the performance is usually reported in terms of micro-averaged and macro-averaged scores [40, 46]. Macro-averaging gives equal weights to the scores generated from each individual category. In comparison, micro-averaging tends to be dominated by the categories with more positive training instances. Due to the fact that many of these test corpora used in TC are either naturally skewed or artificially imbalanced especially in the binary and so called 'one-against-all' settings, classifiers often perform far less than satisfactorily for minor categories [24, 40, 46]. Therefore, micro-averaging mostly yields much better results than macro-averaging.

There have been several endeavors in handling imbalanced data sets in TC. Here, we only focus on the approaches adopted in TC and group them based on their primary focus. The first approach is based on sampling strategy. Yang [45] has tested two sampling methods, i.e., proportion-enforced sampling and completeness-driven sampling. Her empirical study using the ExpNet system shows that a global sampling strategy which favors common categories over rare categories is critical for the success of TC based on a statistical learning approach. Without such a global control, the global optimal performance will be compromised and the learning efficiency can be substantially decreased. Nickerson et al. [33] provide a guided sampling approach based on a clustering algorithm called Principal Direction Divisive Partitioning to deal with the between-class imbalance problem. It has shown improvement over existing methods of equalizing class imbalances, especially when there is a large between-class imbalance together with severe imbalance in the relative densities of the subcomponents of each class. Liu's recent efforts [25] in testing different sampling strategies, i.e., under-sampling and over-sampling, and several classification algorithms, i.e., Naïve Bayes, k-Nearest Neighbors (kNN) and Support Vector Machines (SVMs), improve the understanding of interactions among sampling method, classifier and performance measurement.

The second major effort emphasizes cost sensitive learning [10, 12, 44]. In many real scenarios like risk management and medical diagnosis, making wrong decisions are usually associated with very different costs. A wrong prediction of the nonexistence of cancer, i.e., false negative, may lead to death, while the wrong prediction of cancer existence, i.e., false positive, only results in unnecessary anxiety and medical tests. In view of this, assigning different cost factors to false negatives and false positives will lead to better performance with respect to positive (rare) classes [8]. Brank et al. [4] have reported their work on cost sensitive learning using SVMs on TC. They obtain better results with methods that directly modify the score threshold. They further propose a method based on the conditional class distributions for SVM scores that works well when only very few training examples are available.

The recognition based approach, i.e., one-class learning, has provided another class of solutions [18]. One-class learning aims to create the decision model based on the examples of the target category alone, which is different from the typical discriminative approach, i.e., the two classes setting. Manevitz and Yousef [30] have applied one-class SVMs on TC. Raskutti and Kowalczyk [35] claim that one-class learning is particularly helpful when data are extremely skewed and composed of many irrelevant features and very high dimensionality.

Feature selection is often considered an important step in reducing the high dimensionality of the feature space in TC and many other problems in image processing and bioinformatics. However, its unique contribution in identifying the most salient features to boost the performance of minor categories has not been stressed until some recent work [31]. Yang [47] has given a detailed evaluation of several feature selection schemes. We noted the marked difference between micro-averaged and macro-averaged values due to the poor performances over rare categories. Forman [14] has done a very comprehensive study of various schemes for TC on a wide range of commonly used test corpora. He has recommended the best pair among different combinations of selection schemes and evaluation measures. The recent efforts from Zheng et al. [50] advance the understanding of feature selection in TC. They show the merits and great potential of explicitly combining positive and negative features in a nearly optimal fashion according to the imbalanced data.

Some recent work simply adapting existing ML techniques and not even directly targeting the issue of class imbalance have shown great potential with respect to the data imbalance problem. Castillo and Serrano [6], and Fan et al. [13] have reported the success using an ensemble approach, e.g., voting and boosting, to handle skewed data distribution. Challenged by real industry data with a huge number of records and an extremely skewed data distribution, Fan's work shows that the ensemble approach is capable of improving the performance on rare classes. In their approaches, a set of weak classifiers using various learning algorithms are built up over minor categories. The final decision is reached based on the combination of outcomes from different classifiers. Another promising approach which receives less attention falls into the category of semi-supervised learning or weakly supervised learning [3, 15, 16, 23, 26, 34, 48, 49]. The basic idea is to identify more positive examples from a large amount of unknown data. These approaches are especially viable when unlabeled data are steadily available. The last effort attacking the imbalance problem uses parameter tuning in kNNs [2]. The authors expect to set k dynamically according to the data distribution, in which a large k is granted given a minor category.

In this chapter, we tackle the data imbalance problem from a different angle. We present a novel approach assigning better weights to the features from minor categories. Inspired by the merits of feature selection, we base our approach to identifying the most salient features for a category on the classic term weighting scheme, i.e., $tfidf$ and propose several weighting factors called Category-Based Term Weights (CBTW) to replace the idf term in the classic $tfidf$ form. The experiment setup is explained in Section 10.5. We carry out the evaluation and comparison of our CBTWs with many other different weighting forms over two skewed data sets, including Reuters-21578. We explain the experimental findings and discuss their performance in Section 10.6. Finally, we give our conclusions in Section 10.7.

10.2 Term Weighting Scheme

TC is the process of categorizing documents into predefined thematic categories. In its current practice, which is dominated by supervised learning, the construction of a text classifier is often conducted in two main phases [9, 40]:

a) Document indexing - the creation of numeric representations of the documents
   - Term selection - selecting a subset of terms from all terms occurring in the collection to represent the documents in a better way, either to facilitate computing or to achieve best effectiveness in classification
   - Term weighting - assigning a numeric value to each term in order that represents its contribution to making a document stand out from others
b) Classifier learning - the building of a classifier by learning from the numeric representations of the documents

In information retrieval and machine learning, term weighting has long been formulated as *term frequency · inverse documents frequency*, i.e., *tfidf* [1, 36, 38, 39]. The more popular "ltc" form [1, 38, 39] is given by,

$$tfidf(t_i, d_j) = tf(t_i, d_j) \times \log(\frac{N}{N(t_i)}) \tag{10.1}$$

and its normalized version is

$$w_{i,j} = \frac{tfidf(t_i, d_j)}{\sqrt{\sum_{k=1}^{|T|} tfidf(t_k, d_j)^2}} \tag{10.2}$$

where N and $|T|$ denote the total number of documents and unique terms contained in the collection respectively, and $N(t_i)$ represents the number of documents in the collection in which term occurs at least once, and

$$tf(t_i, d_j) = \begin{cases} 1 + \log(n(t_i, d_j)), & \text{if } n(t_i, d_j) > 0; \\ 0, & \text{otherwise.} \end{cases} \tag{10.3}$$

where $n(t_i, d_j)$ is the number of times that the term occurs in the document. In practice, the summation in equation (10.2) is only concerned with the terms occurring in the document.

The significance of the classic term weighting schemes in equation (10.1) and (10.2) is that they have embodied three fundamental assumptions about the term frequency distribution in a collection of documents [9, 40]. These assumptions are:

- Rare terms are no less important than frequent terms - the *idf* assumption
- Multiple appearance of a term in a document are no less important than single appearance - the *tf* assumption
- For the same quantity of term matching, long documents are no more important than short documents - the normalization assumption

Because of these, the "ltc" and its normalized form have been extensively studied by many researchers and show good performance over a number of different data sets [40]. Therefore, they have become the default choice in TC research.

After document indexing, the next phase is classifier induction. Recently, the support vector machine (SVM) [5, 42] has become the most popular learning algorithm in current TC practices mainly due to its leading, consistent performance [11, 19, 24, 40, 46], and its capability of handling a high dimensional input space. Joachims [19, 21] claims that incorporating term selection will weaken the performance of SVM in TC, and therefore recommends skipping term selection. Term selection, one of the two main steps in document indexing, has become less important in SVM-based TC. This has left term weighting as the only step before the induction of an SVM classifier. Furthermore, since current SVM theory is more effective in handling binary problems, the training and testing data sets supplied to SVM are either formed as 'one-category-against-another-category' or 'one-category-against-all-other-categories.' Therefore, instead of answering whether a document belongs to a specific category, the algorithm tries to distinguish the documents of one category from others. To exploit this characteristic of SVM algorithm, our basic idea is to assign weights dynamically to terms in such a way that it helps to differentiate documents of each category under consideration from other categories, rather than giving uniform values, i.e., *idf*, to them across all categories. We explore this problem by merging the power of term selection with term weighting. In other words, we aim to capture the category characteristics of these documents and see whether this can further contribute to the existing performance of SVM.

10.3 Inspiration from Feature Selection

Feature selection serves as a key procedure to reduce the dimensionality of input space in order to save computational cost. It has been integrated as a default step for many learning algorithms, like Artificial Neural Networks, k-Nearest Neighbors, Decision Trees, etc. In the research community of ML, the computational constraints imposed by the high dimensionality of the input data space and the richness of information it provides to maximally identify each individual object is a well known tradeoff. The ability of feature selection to capture the salient information by selecting the most important attributes, and thus making the computing tasks tractable has been shown in IR and ML research [14, 32, 37, 47]. Furthermore, feature selection is also beneficial since it tends to reduce the over-fitting problem, in which the trained objects are tuned to fit very well the data upon which they have been built, but performs poorly when applied to unseen data [40].

In TC, several feature selection methods have been intensively studied to distill the important terms while still keeping the dimensionality low. Table 10.1 shows the general functions of several popular feature selection methods. These methods derive either from the information theory or from the linear algebra literature [40, 47].

Table 10.1. Several feature selection methods and their functions, where t_k denotes a term, c_i stands for a category, $P(t_k, c_i)$ denotes the probability a document is from category c_i when term t_k occurs at least once in it, $P(t_k, \overline{c}_i)$ denotes the probability a document is not from category c_i when term t_k occurs at least once in it, $P(\overline{t}_k, c_i)$ denotes the probability a document is from category c_i when term t_k does not occur in it, $P(\overline{t}_k, \overline{c}_i)$ denotes the probability a document is not from category c_i when term t_k does not occur in it.

Feature Selection Method	Mathematical Form
Information Gain	$P(t_k, c_i) \log \frac{P(t_k, c_i)}{P(t_k)P(c_i)} + P(\overline{t}_k, c_i) \log \frac{P(\overline{t}_k, c_i)}{P(\overline{t}_k)P(c_i)}$
Mutual Information	$\log \frac{P(t_k, c_i)}{P(t_k)P(c_i)}$
Chi-square	$\frac{N[P(t_k, c_i)P(\overline{t}_k, \overline{c}_i) - P(t_k, \overline{c}_i)P(\overline{t}_k, c_i)]^2}{P(t_k)P(\overline{t}_k)P(c_i)P(\overline{c}_i)}$
Correlation Coefficient	$\frac{N[P(t_k, c_i)P(\overline{t}_k, \overline{c}_i) - P(t_k, \overline{c}_i)P(\overline{t}_k, c_i)]}{\sqrt{P(t_k)P(\overline{t}_k)P(c_i)P(\overline{c}_i)}}$
Odds Ratio	$\log \frac{P(t_k|c_i)(1 - P(t_k|\overline{c}_i))}{(1 - P(t_k|c_i))P(t_k|\overline{c}_i)}$
Simplified Chi-square	$P(t_k, c_i)P(\overline{t}_k, \overline{c}_i) - P(t_k, \overline{c}_i)P(\overline{t}_k, c_i)$

Basically, there are two distinct ways to rank and assess the features, i.e., globally and locally.

a) Global feature selection aims to select features which are good across all categories. In this manner, either the sum $f_{sum}(t_k) = \sum_{i=1}^{|c|} f(t_k, c_i)$, or the weighted average of a term t_k, i.e., $f_{avg}(t_k) = \sum_{i=1}^{|c|} P(c_i)f(t_k, c_i)$, is assessed, where f is the specified feature selection method, $P(c_i)$ is the percentage of category c_i and $|c|$ denotes the number of categories.

b) Local feature selection aims to differentiate those terms that are more distinguishable for certain categories only. Usually, terms are ranked and selected based on $f_{max}(t_k) = \max_{i=1}^{|c|} f(t_k, c_i)$, i.e., the maximum of the category specific values.

The sense of either 'global' or 'local' does not have much impact on the selection of method itself, but it does affect the performance of classifiers built upon different categories. In TC, the main purpose is to address whether this document belongs to a specific category. Obviously, we prefer the salient features which are unique from one category to another, i.e., a 'local' approach. Ideally, the salient feature set from one category does not have any items overlapping with those from other categories. If this cannot be avoided, then how to better present them comes into the picture.

While many previous works have shown the relative strengths and merits of these methods [14, 32, 37, 40, 47], our experience with feature selection over a number of standard or ad-hoc data sets shows the performance of such methods can be highly dependant on the data. This is partly due to the lack of understanding of different data sets in a quantitative way, and it needs further research. From our previous study of all feature selection methods and what has been reported in the literature [47], we noted when these methods are applied to text classification for term selection purpose, they are basically utilizing the four fundamental information elements shown in Table 10.2, i.e., A denotes the number of documents belonging to category c_i where the term t_k occurs at least once; B denotes the number of documents not belonging to category c_i where the term t_k occurs at least once; C denotes the number of documents belonging to category c_i where the term t_k does not occur; D denotes the number of documents not belonging to category c_i where the term t_k does not occur.

Table 10.2. Fundamental information elements used for feature selection in text classification

	c_i	$\bar{c}_i$
t_k	A	B
$\bar{t}_k$	C	D

These four information elements have been used to estimate the probabilities listed in Table 10.1. Table 10.3 shows the functions in Table 10.1 as presented by the information elements A, B, C and D.

Table 10.3. Feature selection methods and their formations as represented by information elements in Table 10.2

Method	Mathematical Form Represented by Information Elements
Information Gain	$-\frac{A+C}{N} \log \frac{A+C}{N} + \frac{A}{N} \log(\frac{A}{A+B}) + \frac{C}{N} \log \frac{C}{C+D}$
Mutual Information	$\log(AN/(A+B)(A+C))$
Chi-square	$N(AD - BC)^2/(A+C)(B+D)(A+B)(C+D)$
Correlation Coefficient	$\sqrt{N}(AD - BC)/\sqrt{(A+C)(B+D)(A+B)(C+D)}$
Odds Ratio	$\log(AD/BC)$
Simplified Chi-square	$(AD - BC)/N^2$

10.4 Category-Based Term Weights

10.4.1 Revisit of *tfidf*

As stated before, while many researchers believe that the term weighting schemes in the form as $tfidf$ representing those three aforementioned assumptions, we understand $tfidf$ in a much simpler manner, i.e.,

a) Local weight - the tf term, either normalized or not, specifies the weight of t_k within a specific document, which is basically estimated based on the frequency or relative frequency of t_k within this document.
b) Global weight - the idf term, either normalized or not, defines the contribution of t_k to a specific document in a global sense.

If we temporarily ignore how $tfidf$ is defined, and focus on the core problem, i.e., whether this document is from this category, we realize we need a set of terms to represent the documents effectively and a reference framework to make the comparison possible. As previous research shows that tf is very important [22, 29, 38, 40] and using tf alone can already achieve good performance, we retain the tf term. Now, let us consider idf, i.e., the global weighting of t_k.

The conjecture is that if the term selection can effectively differentiate a set of terms T_k out from all terms T to represent category c_i, then it is desirable to transform that difference into some sort of numeric values for further processing. Our approach is to replace the idf term with the value generated using term selection. Since this procedure is performed jointly with the category membership, this basically implies that the weights of T_k are category specific. Therefore, the only problem left is which term selection method is appropriate to compute such values.

10.4.2 Category-Based Term Weights

We decide to compute the term values using the most direct information, e.g., A, B and C, and combine them in a sensible way which is different from existing feature selection measures. From Table 10.2, two important ratios are noted, i.e., A/B and A/C,

- A/B: it is easy to understand that if term t_k is highly relevant to category c_i only, which basically says that t_k is a good feature to represent category c_i, then the value of A/B tends to be higher.
- A/C: given two terms t_k, t_l and a category c_i, the term with the higher value of A/C, will be the better feature to represent c_i, since a larger portion of it occurs with category c_i.

Obviously, the role of A/B is straightforward and, when A/B is equal, A/C can possibly further differentiate these terms. This has been conjectured to be the contribution of A/C. In fact, these two ratios are nicely supported by probability estimates. For instance, A/B can be extended as $(A/N)/(B/N)$, where N is the total number of documents, A/N is the probability estimate of documents from category c_i where term t_k occurs at least once and B/N is the probability estimate of documents not from category c_i where term t_k occurs at least once. In this manner, A/B can be interpreted as a relevance indicator of term t_k with respect to category

c_i. Surely, the higher the ratio, the more important the term t_k is related to category c_i. A similar analysis can be be made with respect to A/C. The ratio reflects the expectation that a term is deemed as more relevant if it occurs in the larger portion of documents from category c_i than other terms.

Table 10.4. The different combinations of Category-Based Term Weights (CBTW), the mathematical forms are represented by information elements shown in Table 10.2

CBTW_1	$\log(1 + \frac{A}{B}\frac{A}{C})$	CBTW_5	$\log(1 + \frac{A+B}{B}\frac{A+C}{C})$
CBTW_2	$\log(1 + \frac{A}{B} + \frac{A}{C})$	CBTW_6	$\log(1 + \frac{A+B}{B} + \frac{A+C}{C})$
CBTW_3	$\log(1 + \frac{A}{B})\log(1 + \frac{A}{C})$	CBTW_7	$\log(1 + \frac{A+B}{B})\log(1 + \frac{A+C}{C})$
CBTW_4	$\log[(1 + \frac{A}{B})(1 + \frac{A}{C})]$	CBTW_8	$\log[(1 + \frac{A+B}{B})(1 + \frac{A+C}{C})]$

Since the computing of either A/B or A/C has its intrinsic connection with category membership, we propose a new term weighting scheme called Category-Based Term Weights (CBTW) to replace the *idf* part in the classic *tfidf* weighting scheme, and feature selection, a regular step in TC, is skipped in our experiments. Considering the probability foundation of A/B and A/C and the possibility of combining them, the most immediate choice is to take the product of these two ratios. They are named as CBTWn in Table 10.4, where $n = 1, 3, 5, 7$. However, we also include other possibilities by extending them in another four different ways named as CBTWn, where $n = 2, 4, 6, 8$.

Because we are not very sure which one can deliver better performance, these eight combinations are evaluated in the benchmarking experiments reported in Section 10.6.

10.5 Experimental Setup

Two data sets were tested in our experiment, i.e., MCV1 and Reuters-21578. MCV1 is an archive of 1434 English language manufacturing related engineering papers which we gathered by the courtesy of the Society of Manufacturing Engineers (SME). It combines all engineering technical papers published by SME from year 1998 to year 2000. All documents were manually classified [27, 28]. There are a total of 18 major categories in MCV1. Figure 10.1 gives the class distribution in MCV1 . Reuters-21578 is a widely used benchmarking collection [40]. We followed Sun's approach [41] in generating the category information. Figure 10.2 gives the class distribution of the Reuters dataset used in our experiment. Unlike Sun [41], we did not randomly sample negative examples from categories not belonging to any of the categories in our dataset, instead we treated examples not from the target category in our dataset as negatives.

We compared our weighting schemes experimentally with a number of other well established weighting schemes, e.g., TFIDF, 'ltc' and normalized 'ltc,' on MCV1 and Reuters-21578 using SVM as the classification algorithm. We also carried out the benchmarking experiments between our conjectures and many other feature selection methods, e.g., chi-square (ChiS), correlation coefficient (CC), odds ratio (OddsR),

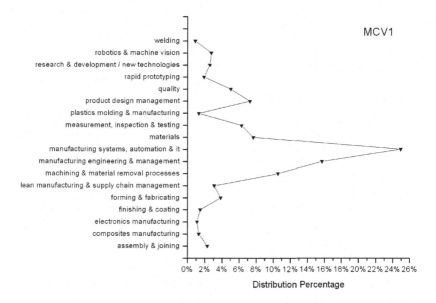

Fig. 10.1. Class distribution in MCV1

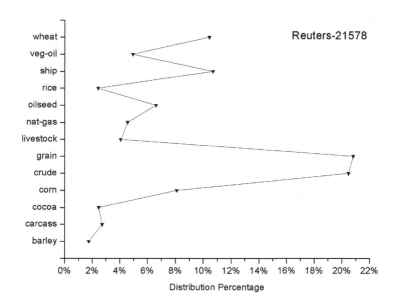

Fig. 10.2. Class distribution in Reuters-21578

information gain (IG) and relevance frequency (RF) [30], by replacing the *idf* term with the feature selection value in the classic *tfidf* weighting schemes. Therefore, schemes are largely formulated in a form as $tf \cdot (feature\ value)$ (TFFV). Table 10.5 shows all 16 weighting schemes tested in our experiments and their mathematic formations. Please note that basically the majority of TFFV schemes are composed of two items, i.e., the normalized term frequency $tf(t_i, d_j)/\max[tf(d_j)]$ and the term's feature value, e.g., $\frac{\sqrt{N}(AD-BC)}{\sqrt{(A+C)(B+D)(A+B)(C+D)}}$ in the correlation coefficient scheme, where $tf(t_i, d_j)$ is the frequency of term t_i in the document d_j and $\max[tf(d_j)]$ is the maximum frequency of a term in the document d_j. The only different ones are TFIDF weighting, 'ltc' form and the normalized 'ltc' form as specified in Table 10.5.

Table 10.5. All weighting schemes tested in the experiments and their mathematic formations, where the normalized term frequency ntf is defined as $\frac{tf(t_i,d_j)}{\max[tf(d_j)]}$

Weighting Scheme	Name	Mathematic Formations
tf·Correlation Coef.	CC	$ntf \cdot \dfrac{\sqrt{N}(AD-BC)}{\sqrt{(A+C)(B+D)(A+B)(C+D)}}$
tf·Chi-square	ChiS	$ntf \cdot \dfrac{N(AD-BC)^2}{(A+C)(B+D)(A+B)(C+D)}$
tf·Information Gain	IG	$ntf \cdot (\frac{A}{N} \log \frac{AN}{(A+B)(A+C)} + \frac{C}{N} \log \frac{CN}{(C+D)(A+C)})$
tf·Odds Ratio	OddsR	$ntf \cdot \log(AD/BC)$
tf·Relevance Freq.	RF	$ntf \cdot \log(1 + \frac{A+B}{B})$
TFIDF [1]	TFIDF	$ntf \cdot \log(\frac{N}{N(t_i)})$
$tfidf$ -ltc	ltc	$tf(t_i, d_j) \cdot \log(\frac{N}{N(t_i)})$
Normalized ltc	nltc	$\dfrac{tfidf_{ltc}}{\sqrt{\sum tfidf_{ltc}^2}}$
Cat. Based Term Wt. 1	CBTW$_1$	$ntf \cdot \log(1 + \frac{A}{B}\frac{A}{C})$
Cat. Based Term Wt. 2	CBTW$_2$	$ntf \cdot \log(1 + \frac{A}{B} + \frac{A}{C})$
Cat. Based Term Wt. 3	CBTW$_3$	$ntf \cdot \log(1 + \frac{A}{B}) \log(1 + \frac{A}{C})$
Cat. Based Term Wt. 4	CBTW$_4$	$ntf \cdot \log[(1 + \frac{A}{B})(1 + \frac{A}{C})]$
Cat. Based Term Wt. 5	CBTW$_5$	$ntf \cdot \log(1 + \frac{A+B}{B}\frac{A+C}{C})$
Cat. Based Term Wt. 6	CBTW$_6$	$ntf \cdot \log(1 + \frac{A+B}{B} + \frac{A+C}{C})$
Cat. Based Term Wt. 7	CBTW$_7$	$ntf \cdot \log(1 + \frac{A+B}{B}) \log(1 + \frac{A+C}{C})$
Cat. Based Term Wt. 8	CBTW$_8$	$ntf \cdot \log[(1 + \frac{A+B}{B})(1 + \frac{A+C}{C})]$

Major standard text preprocessing steps were applied in our experiments, including stopword and punctuation removal, and stemming. However, feature selection was skipped and all terms left after stopword and punctuation removal were kept as features. In our experiments we used the SVM implementation called SVM^{Light} [19, 20]. We used the linear function as its kernel function, since previous work has shown that the linear function can deliver even better performance without tedious parameter tuning in TC [19, 21]. As for the performance measurement, precision, recall and the harmonic combination of precision and recall, i.e., the F_1 value, were calculated [1, 36]. Performance was assessed based on five-fold cross validation. Since we are very concerned about the performance of every category and especially the minor ones, we report the overall performance in macro-averaged scores, to avoid the bias for major categories in imbalanced data associated with micro-averaged scores.

10.6 Experimental Results and Discussion

10.6.1 Overall Performance

Figure 10.3 shows the overall performance of a total of 16 weighting schemes tested over MCV1 and Reuters-21578 . They are reported in terms of macro-averaged F_1 values.

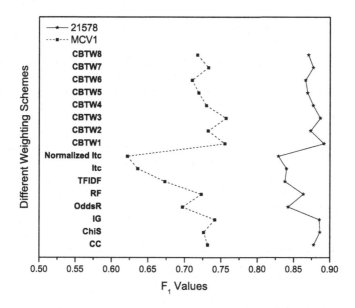

Fig. 10.3. The macro-averaged F_1 values of 16 weighting schemes tested over MCV1 and Reuters-21578

Our first observation is that all TFFV weighting schemes outperform classic ones, i.e., TFIDF, 'ltc,' and normalized 'ltc' schemes. The TFIDF's performance based on Reuters-21578 is in line with the literature [41, 46]. This has shown the overall effectiveness of TFFV-based schemes. In general, the performance patterns of all 16 schemes on MCV1 and Reuters-21578 match very well. For example, CBTW$_1$ and CBTW$_3$ always take the lead among CBTWs, normalized 'ltc' always performs worse than the other two, and the odds ratio does not performe as well as the other TFFVs. Global based classic schemes, i.e., TFIDF, 'ltc', and normalized 'ltc' form, do not work well for either MCV1 or Reuters-21578. A close look at their performance reveals that classifiers built for minor categories, e.g., composites manufacturing, electronics manufacturing and so on, do not produce satisfactory results. This has largely affected the overall performance. Among TFFVs, odds ratio does not work very well. This is a surprise since the odds ratio is mentioned as one of the leading feature selection methods for text classification in the literature [37, 40]. This implies that it is always worthwhile to reassess the strength of a term selection method for a new dataset, even if they have tended to perform well in the past.

From Table 10.5 we also note that RF is actually some sort of simplified version of CBTWs where the ratio of A/C or the information element C is excluded. However, performances generated over MCV1 and Reuters-21578 indicate that CBTWs are not worse than RF. In fact, our experimental results show that the effective combination of A/B and A/C, i.e., CBTW$_1$ and CBTW$_3$, can lead to better performance than RF. This has demonstrated the practical value of A/C and our aforementioned conjectures about how terms can be further distinguished.

10.6.2 Gains for Minor Categories

As shown in Figure 10.1 and Figure 10.2, both MCV1 and Reuters-21578 are skewed data sets. While MCV1 possesses 18 categories with one major category occupying up to 25% of the whole population of supporting documents, there are six categories that own only around 1% of MCV1 each and 11 categories falling below the average, i.e., 5.5%, if MCV1 is evenly distributed. The same case also happens to the Reuters-21578 dataset. While it has 13 categories, grain and crude, the two major categories, share around half of the population. There are eight categories in total falling below the average. Previous literatures did not report successful stories over these minor categories [40, 41, 46].

Since our study shows that TFFV schemes work better than classic approaches, we examine why this is the case. A close analysis shows that TFFVs display much better results over minor categories in both MCV1 and Reuters-21578 . We plot their performances in Figures 10.4 and 10.5, respectively. For all minor categories shown in both figures, we observed a sharp increase of performance occurs when the system's weighting method switches from normalized 'ltc' to CBTWs and from TFIDF to RF.

Based on Figure 10.3, since TFIDF often helps SVM generate the best performance among the three classic ones and CBTW$_1$ has the best overall performance among the 16 weighting candidates, we chose TFIDF and CBTW$_1$ as representative of each group for further analysis. Both precision and recall of each individual category in MCV1 and Reuters-21578 are plotted in Figures 10.6 and 10.7. Looking at both figures reveals why TFFVs, in particular CBTW$_1$, perform better. We observed that in general CBTW$_1$ falls slightly below TFIDF in terms of precision. However, CBTW$_1$ performs far better in terms of recall and as a result surpasses TFIDF in terms of F_1 values. While the averaged precision of TFIDF in MCV1 is 0.8355 which is about 5% higher than CBTW$_1$, the averaged recall of CBTW$_1$ is 0.7443, far superior to TFIDF's 0.6006. The case with Reuters-21578 is even more impressive. While the averaged precision of TFIDF is 0.8982 which is only 1.8%

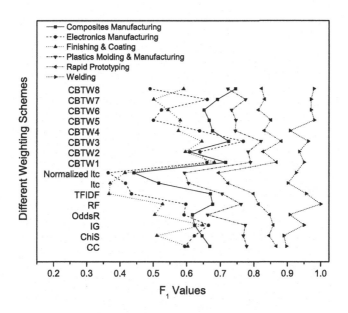

Fig. 10.4. Performance of 16 weighting schemes over 6 minor categories in MCV1, where each of them only occupies around 1% of MCV1

higher than $CBTW_1$, the averaged recall of $CBTW_1$ reaches 0.9080, compared with TFIDF 's 0.7935.

10.6.3 Significance Test

In order to determine whether the performance improvement gained by CBTWs and other TFFVs over these two imbalanced data sets are significant, we performed the macro sign test (S-test) and macro t-test (T-test) on the paired F_1 values. Table 10.6 and 10.7 show the detailed F_1 values of each individual category generated based on different major term weighting approaches over MCV1 and Reuters-21578, respectively. As pointed out by Yang [46], on the one hand, the S-test may be more robust in reducing the influence of outliers, but at the risk of being insensitive or not sufficiently sensitive in performance comparison because it ignores the absolute difference between F_1 values; on the other hand, the T-test is sensitive to the absolute values, but could be overly sensitive when F_1 values are highly unstable, e.g., for the minor categories. Therefore, we adopt both tests here to give a comprehensive understanding of the performance improvement.

Since for both data sets, TFIDF performs better than the other two classic approaches and $CBTW_1$ achieves the best overall performance compared to other CBTWs and TFFVs, we choose them as the representatives of their peers. For

Table 10.6. Macro-averaged F_1 values and detailed performance of each scheme over MCV1

Cat.	TFIDF	CC	ChiS	IG	OddsR	RF	CBTW$_1$
1	0.7351	0.8186	0.7249	0.7463	0.7302	0.7664	0.8029
2	0.6703	0.6684	0.6461	0.6234	0.6172	0.6771	0.7160
3	0.4344	0.5943	0.6232	0.6651	0.5925	0.5978	0.6603
4	0.3670	0.6034	0.5109	0.6476	0.5043	0.5277	0.6825
5	0.7961	0.8202	0.8526	0.8347	0.8252	0.8336	0.8791
6	0.4854	0.6036	0.6346	0.6292	0.5601	0.5997	0.6493
7	0.8554	0.8395	0.8437	0.8280	0.8585	0.8627	0.8643
8	0.7479	0.7470	0.7312	0.7338	0.7488	0.7607	0.7252
9	0.8421	0.8610	0.8522	0.8529	0.8707	0.8597	0.8637
10	0.7628	0.7888	0.7779	0.7915	0.7736	0.7893	0.8274
11	0.7160	0.7230	0.7230	0.7351	0.7073	0.7411	0.7536
12	0.7055	0.7786	0.7689	0.7744	0.6627	0.7618	0.7899
13	0.6162	0.6903	0.6733	0.6753	0.6555	0.6559	0.6657
14	0.4343	0.5499	0.6011	0.5448	0.4651	0.5079	0.4943
15	0.7984	0.8671	0.8455	0.8584	0.8473	0.8141	0.8674
16	0.4411	0.5070	0.5382	0.6190	0.4580	0.4485	0.5730
17	0.7468	0.8122	0.8319	0.8367	0.7643	0.8044	0.8304
18	0.9567	0.8973	0.8892	0.9504	0.9074	1.0000	0.9505
Avg.	0.6729	0.7317	0.7260	0.7415	0.6971	0.7227	0.7553

Table 10.7. Macro-averaged F_1 values and detailed performance of each scheme over Reuters-21578

Cat.	TFIDF	CC	ChiS	IG	OddsR	RF	CBTW$_1$
1	0.7930	0.8144	0.8615	0.8197	0.7466	0.7794	0.8740
2	0.7364	0.8130	0.8139	0.8734	0.6938	0.8044	0.8311
3	0.9465	0.9767	0.9719	0.9721	0.9619	0.9612	0.9814
4	0.8034	0.9030	0.9401	0.9235	0.8881	0.8951	0.9185
5	0.9399	0.9395	0.9151	0.9111	0.9373	0.9385	0.9028
6	0.9472	0.9695	0.9586	0.9491	0.9605	0.9730	0.9630
7	0.8158	0.8457	0.8563	0.8300	0.7446	0.8088	0.8357
8	0.8423	0.8340	0.8481	0.8444	0.8126	0.8648	0.8827
9	0.7648	0.8123	0.8109	0.8073	0.7757	0.7530	0.8423
10	0.7590	0.8463	0.8972	0.9259	0.7727	0.7776	0.8869
11	0.8836	0.9087	0.8840	0.8929	0.9027	0.9135	0.8850
12	0.7962	0.8290	0.8486	0.8290	0.8357	0.8423	0.8546
13	0.8666	0.9186	0.9157	0.9352	0.9173	0.9117	0.9360
Avg.	0.8380	0.8777	0.8863	0.8857	0.8423	0.8633	0.8918

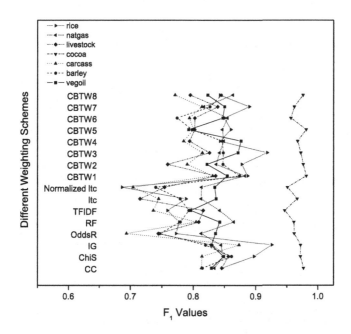

Fig. 10.5. Performance of 16 weighting schemes over 7 minor categories in Reuters-21578, where each of them only occupies between 1% and less than 5% of Reuters-21578

both the S-test and T-test, we actually conduct two sets of tests. One is to test all major schemes against TFIDF and another one is to test $CBTW_1$ against the major schemes. While the first aims to assess the goodness of schemes in the form of TFFVs, the second tests whether CBTWs generate even better results.

Table 10.8. Details of S-test on MCV1 , $P(Z >= k)=p$-Value, where two F_1 values are the same if their difference is not more than 0.01

All vs. TFIDF				CBTW$_1$ vs. All			
Test	n	K	p-Value	Test	n	K	p-Value
CC	16	14	2.090E-03	TFIDF	18	16	6.561E-04
ChiS	18	13	4.813E-02	CC	16	12	3.841E-02
IG	18	14	1.544E-02	ChiS	17	14	6.363E-03
OddsR	15	11	5.923E-02	IG	16	11	1.051E-01
RF	18	18	3.815E-06	OddsR	18	16	6.561E-04
CBTW$_1$	18	16	6.561E-04	RF	16	13	1.064E-02

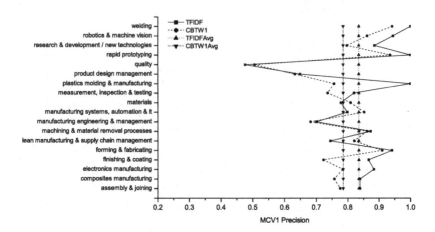

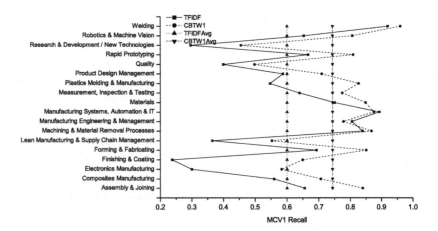

Fig. 10.6. Details of precision and recall for categories in MCV1

Table 10.8 summarizes the S-test results of major schemes against TFIDF and CBTW₁ against others for MCV1. We consider two F_1 values to be the same if their difference is not more than 0.01, i.e., 1%. Table 10.9 summarizes the T-test results of major schemes against TFIDF and CBTW₁ against others for MCV1, where alpha is set as 0.001. Tables 10.10 and 10.11 report the test results for Reuters-21578, where tests are carried out in the same manner conducted in Tables 10.8 and 10.9.

From the results we cam summarize the strength of different schemes. Consider the merits evaluated based on TFFVs against TFIDF, TFFVs have shown they are

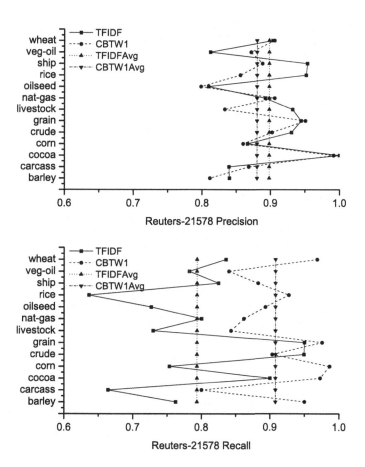

Fig. 10.7. Details of precision and recall for categories in Reuters-21578

the better approach in handling imbalanced data. Among various TFFVs, CBTW$_1$ claims the leading performance in both MCV1 and Reuters-21578. However, the approach based on the odds ratio is not much superior to TFIDF. With respect to the evaluation based on the merits of CBTW$_1$ against the others, it is not surprising to see that CBTW$_1$ still takes the lead. It manages to perform better than the approaches based on information gain and chi-square in the T-test where the absolute difference of F_1 values is considered. Furthermore, CBTW$_1$ always achieves better results than RF in both data sets. This demonstrates the contribution of A/C in handling imbalanced data sets. Finally, the strengths of information gain, chi-square and correlation coefficient shown in the tests are compatible with what is in literature [14, 40, 47]. In general, the more minor categories the dataset possesses, the

Table 10.9. Details of T-test on MCV1 , where $alpha = 0.001$ and degree of freedom $= 34$

All vs. TFIDF, $alpha$=0.001			CBTW$_1$ vs. All, $alpha$=0.001		
Test	t-Value	t-Critical	Test	t-Value	t-Critical
CC	21.509	3.354	TFIDF	30.171	3.354
ChiS	19.634		CC	10.688	
IG	25.879		ChiS	13.465	
OddsR	8.343		IG	6.571	
RF	17.038		OddsR	24.003	
CBTW$_1$	30.171		RF	13.368	
Mean	20.429		Mean	16.378	
StdDev	7.536		StdDev	8.882	

Table 10.10. Details of S-test on Reuters-21578, $P(Z >= k)$=p-Value, where two F_1 values are the same if their difference is not more than 0.01

All vs. TFIDF				CBTW$_1$ vs. All			
Test	n	K	p-Value	Test	n	K	p-Value
CC	12	11	3.174E-03	TFIDF	12	11	3.174E-03
ChiS	12	11	3.174E-03	CC	12	8	1.938E-01
IG	11	10	5.859E-03	ChiS	11	7	2.744E-01
OddsR	12	8	1.938E-01	IG	12	7	3.872E-01
RF	12	9	7.300E-02	OddsR	12	10	1.929E-02
CBTW$_1$	12	11	3.174E-03	RF	13	10	4.614E-02

Table 10.11. Details of T-test on Reuters-21578 , where $alpha = 0.001$ and degree of freedom $= 34$

All vs. TFIDF, $alpha$=0.001			CBTW$_1$ vs. All, $alpha$=0.001		
Test	t-Value	t-Critical	Test	t-Value	t-Critical
CC	19.571	3.467	TFIDF	28.893	3.467
ChiS	25.164		CC	8.587	
IG	24.352		ChiS	3.682	
OddsR	1.692		IG	3.993	
RF	11.338		OddsR	22.619	
CBTW$_1$	28.893		RF	15.139	
Mean	18.501		Mean	13.819	
StdDev	10.214		StdDev	10.326	

better overall performance can be achieved if CBTW$_1$ is chosen as the weighting scheme.

10.7 Conclusion

Handling of imbalanced data sets in TC has become an emerging challenge. In this chapter, we introduce a new weighting scheme which is generally formulated as

$tf \cdot (feature\ value)$ (TFFV) to replace classic $tfidf$-based approaches. We then propose Category-Based Term Weights (CBTWs), which directly make use of two critical information ratios, as a new way to compute the feature value. These two ratios are deemed to possess the most salient information about the category membership of terms and their computation does not impose any extra cost compared to the conventional feature selection methods. Our experimental study and extensive comparisons based on two imbalanced data sets, MCV1 and Reuters-21578, show the merits of TFFV-based approaches and their ability to handle imbalanced data. Among the various TFFVs, $CBTW_1$ offers the best overall performance in both data sets. Our approach has provided an effective choice to improve TC performance for imbalanced data. Furthermore, since CBTWs are derived from the understanding of feature selection, they can also be viewed as new feature selection schemes to reflect the relevance of terms with respect to thematic categories. Their joint application with other algorithms in TC, e.g., Naïve Bayes, k-Nearest Neighbors and Artificial Neural Networks where feature selection is usually performed, needs further exploration.

10.8 Acknowledgment

The authors would like to thank the reviewers for their valuable comments and Ee-Peng Lim and Aixin Sun for much fruitful discussion.

References

1. Baeza-Yates R. & Ribeiro-Neto B. (1999) Modern information retrieval. Addison-Wesley Longman Publishing Co. Inc., Boston, MA, USA
2. Baoli L., Qin L. & Shiwen Y. (2004) An adaptive k-nearest neighbor text categorization strategy. ACM Transactions on Asian Language Information Processing (TALIP) 3:215–226
3. Blum A. & Mitchell T. (1998) Combining Labeled and Unlabeled Data with Co-Training. In: COLT: Proceedings of the Workshop on Computational Learning Theory
4. Brank J., Grobelnik M., Milic-Frayling N. & Mladenic D. (2003) Training text classifiers with SVM on very few positive examples. Report MSR-TR-2003-34
5. Burges C. J. C. (1998) A tutorial on support vector machines for pattern recognition. Data Mining and Knowledge Discovery 2:121–167
6. Castillo M. D. d. & Serrano J. I. (2004) A multistrategy approach for digital text categorization from imbalanced documents. ACM SIGKDD Explorations Newsletter: Special issue on learning from imbalanced datasets 6:70–79
7. Chawla N., Japkowicz N. & Kolcz A. (eds) (2003) Proceedings of the ICML'2003 Workshop on Learning from Imbalanced Data Sets
8. Chawla N., Japkowicz N. & Kolcz A. (eds) (2004) Special Issue on Learning from Imbalanced Data Sets. ACM SIGKDD Explorations Newsletter 6
9. Debole F. & Sebastiani F. (2003) Supervised term weighting for automated text categorization. In: Proceedings of the 2003 ACM Symposium on Applied computing

10. Dietterich T., Margineantu D., Provost F. & Turney P. (eds) (2000) Proceedings of the ICML'2000 Workshop on Cost-sensitive Learning
11. Dumais S. & Chen H. (2000) Hierarchical classification of Web content. In: Proceedings of the 23rd annual international ACM SIGIR conference on Research and development in information retrieval (SIGIR2000)
12. Elkan C. (2001) The Foundations of Cost-Sensitive Learning. In: Proceedings of the Seventeenth International Joint Conference on Artificial Intelligence (IJ-CAI'01)
13. Fan W., Yu P. S. & Wang H. (2004) Mining Extremely Skewed Trading Anomalies. In: Advances in Database Technology - EDBT 2004: 9th International Conference on Extending Database Technology
14. Forman G. (2003) An extensive empirical study of feature selection metrics for text classification. The Journal of Machine Learning Research, Special Issue on Variable and Feature Selection 3:1289–1305
15. Ghani R. (2002) Combining Labeled and Unlabeled Data for MultiClass Text Categorization. In: International Conference on Machine Learning (ICML 2002)
16. Goldman S. & Zhou Y. (2000) Enhancing Supervised Learning with Unlabeled Data. In: Proceedings of 17th International Conference on Machine Learning
17. Japkowicz N. (eds) (2000) Proceedings of the AAAI'2000 Workshop on Learning from Imbalanced Data Sets. AAAI Tech Report WS-00-05, AAAI
18. Japkowicz N., Myers C. & Gluck M. A. (1995) A Novelty Detection Approach to Classification. In: Proceedings of the Fourteenth International Joint Conference on Artificial Intelligence (IJCAI-95)
19. Joachims T. (1998) Text categorization with Support Vector Machines: Learning with many relevant features. In: ECML-98, Tenth European Conference on Machine Learning
20. Joachims T. (2001) A Statistical Learning Model of Text Classification with Support Vector Machines. In: Proceedings of the 24th annual international ACM SIGIR conference on Research and development in information retrieval
21. Joachims T. (2002) Learning to Classify Text Using Support Vector Machines. Kluwer Academic Publishers
22. Leopold E. & Kindermann J. (2002) Text Categorization with Support Vector Machines - How to Represent Texts in Input Space. Machine Learning 46:423–444
23. Lewis D. D. & Gale W. A. (1994) A Sequential Algorithm for Training Text Classifiers. In: Proceedings of SIGIR-94, 17th ACM International Conference on Research and Development in Information Retrieval
24. Lewis D. D., Yang Y., Rose T. G. & Li F. (2004) RCV1: a new benchmark collection for text categorization research. Journal of Machine Learning Research 5:361–397
25. Liu A. Y. C. (2004) The effect of oversampling and undersampling on classifying imbalanced text datasets. Masters thesis. University of Texas at Austin
26. Liu B., Dai Y., Li X., Lee W. S. & Yu P. (2003) Building Text Classifiers Using Positive and Unlabeled Examples. In: Proceedings of the Third IEEE International Conference on Data Mining (ICDM'03)
27. Liu Y., Loh H. T. & Tor S. B. (2004) Building a Document Corpus for Manufacturing Knowledge Retrieval. In: Proceedings of the Singapore MIT Alliance Symposium 2004

28. Liu Y., Loh H. T., Youcef-Toumi K. & Tor S. B. (2005) MCV1: An Engineering Paper Corpus for Manufacturing Knowledge Retrieval. submitted to the Journal of Knowledge and Information System (KAIS)
29. Man L. (2004) A Comprehensive Comparative Study on Term Weighting Schemes for Text Categorization with Support Vector Machines. In: Text Seminar of CHIME Group at the National University of Singapore
30. Manevitz L. M. & Yousef M. (2002) One-class svms for document classification. The Journal of Machine Learning Research 2:139–154
31. Mladenic D. & Grobelnik M. (1999) Feature Selection for Unbalanced Class Distribution and Naive Bayes. In: Proceedings of the Sixteenth International Conference on Machine Learning, ICML'99
32. Ng H. T., Goh W. B. & Low K. L. (1997) Feature selection, perception learning, and a usability case study for text categorization. In: ACM SIGIR Forum, Proceedings of the 20th annual international ACM SIGIR conference on Research and development in information retrieval
33. Nickerson A., Japkowicz N. & Milios E. (2001) Using Unsupervised Learning to Guide Re-Sampling in Imbalanced Data Sets. In: Proceedings of the Eighth International Workshop on AI and Statitsics
34. Nigam K. P. (2001) Using unlabeled data to improve text classification. PhD thesis. Carnegie Mellon University
35. Raskutti B. & Kowalczyk A. (2004) Extreme re-balancing for SVMs: a case study. ACM SIGKDD Explorations Newsletter: Special issue on learning from imbalanced datasets 6:60–69
36. Rijsbergen C. J. v. (1979) Information Retrieval. 2nd edn. Butterworths, London, UK
37. Ruiz M. E. & Srinivasan P. (2002) Hierarchical Text Categorization Using Neural Networks. Information Retrieval 5:87–118
38. Salton G. & Buckley C. (1988) Term Weighting Approaches in Automatic Text Retrieval. Information Processing and Management 24:513–523
39. Salton G. & McGill M. J. (1983) Introduction to Modern Information Retrieval. McGraw-Hill, New York, USA
40. Sebastiani F. (2002) Machine Learning in Automated Text Categorization. ACM Computing Surveys (CSUR) 34:1–47
41. Sun A., Lim E. P., Ng W. K. & Srivastava J. (2004) Blocking Reduction Strategies in Hierarchical Text Classification. IEEE Transactions on Knowledge and Data Engineering (TKDE) 16:1305–1308
42. Vapnik V. N. (1999) The Nature of Statistical Learning Theory. 2nd edn. Springer-Verlag, New York
43. Weiss G. M. (2004) Mining with rarity: a unifying framework. ACM SIGKDD Explorations Newsletter: Special issue on learning from imbalanced datasets 6:7–19
44. Weiss G. M. & Provost F. (2003) Learning when training data are costly: the effect of class distribution on tree induction. Journal of Artificial Intelligence Research 19:315–354
45. Yang Y. (1996) Sampling Strategies and Learning Efficiency in Text Categorization. In: Proceedings of the AAAI Spring Symposium on Machine Learning in Information Access
46. Yang Y. & Liu X. (1999) A re-examination of text categorization methods. In: Proceedings of the 22nd annual international ACM SIGIR conference on Research and development in information retrieval

47. Yang Y. & Pedersen J. O. (1997) A Comparative Study on Feature Selection in Text Categorization. In: Proceedings of ICML-97, 14th International Conference on Machine Learning
48. Yu H., Zhai C. & Han J. (2003) Text Classification from Positive and Unlabeled Documents. In: Proceedings of the twelfth international conference on Information and knowledge management (CIKM 2003)
49. Zelikovitz S. & Hirsh H. (2000) Improving Short Text Classification Using Unlabeled Background Knowledge. In: Proceedings of the Seventeenth International Conference on Machine Learning(ICML2000)
50. Zheng Z., Wu X. & Srihari R. (2004) Feature selection for text categorization on imbalanced data. ACM SIGKDD Explorations Newsletter: Special issue on learning from imbalanced datasets 6:80–89

11

Automatic Evaluation of Ontologies

Janez Brank, Marko Grobelnik, and Dunja Mladenić ,

11.1 Introduction

We can observe that the focus of modern information systems is moving from "data processing" towards "concept processing," meaning that the basic unit of processing is less and less an atomic piece of data and is becoming more a semantic concept which carries an interpretation and exists in a context with other concepts. An ontology is commonly used as a structure capturing knowledge about a certain area by providing relevant concepts and relations between them. Analysis of textual data plays an important role in construction and usage of ontologies, especially with the growing popularity of semi-automated ontology construction (here referred to also as ontology learning). Different knowledge discovery methods have been adopted for the problem of semi-automated ontology construction [10] including unsupervised, semi-supervised and supervised learning over a collection of text documents, using natural language processing to obtain semantic graph of a document, visualization of documents, information extraction to find relevant concepts, visualization of context of named entities in a document collection.

A key factor which makes a particular discipline or approach scientific is the ability to evaluate and compare the ideas within the area. Ontologies are a fundamental data structure for conceptualizing knowledge which is in most practical cases soft and non-uniquely expressible. As a consequence, we are in general able to build many different ontologies conceptualizing the same body of knowledge and we should be able to say which of these ontologies serves better some predefined criterion. Thus, ontology evaluation is an important issue that must be addressed if ontologies are to be widely adopted in the semantic web and other semantics-aware applications. Users facing a multitude of ontologies need to have a way of assessing them and deciding which one best fits their requirements. Likewise, people constructing an ontology need a way to evaluate the resulting ontology and possibly to guide the construction process and any refinement steps. Automated or semi-automated ontology learning techniques also require effective evaluation measures, which can be used to select the best ontology out of many candidates, to select values of tunable parameters of the learning algorithm, or to direct the learning process itself if the latter is formulated as finding a path through a search space.

The remainder of this chapter is structured as follows. In Section 11.2, we present an overview of related work on ontology evaluation. We describe the main approaches to ontology evaluation and show different techniques that are used to evaluate different aspects or levels of an ontology. In Section 11.3, we refer to a formal framework for defining an ontology and show how various aspects of evaluation can be incorporated into such a framework. In Section 11.4, we present our approach to evaluating a hierarchic ontology by comparing it to a gold standard. In Section 11.5, we present experiments that explore how our evaluation measure responds to various modifications in the case of a large real-world topic ontology. Finally, in Section 11.6, we present some guidelines for future work.

11.2 Survey of Ontology Evaluation Approaches

Various approaches to the evaluation of ontologies have been considered in the literature, depending on what kind of ontologies are being evaluated and for what purpose. Broadly speaking, most evaluation approaches fall into one of the following categories:

- approaches based on comparing the ontology to a gold standard (which may itself be an ontology; e.g., [16]);
- approaches based on using the ontology in an application and evaluating the results (e.g., [22]);
- approaches involving comparisons with a source of data (e.g., a collection of documents) about the domain that is to be covered by the ontology (e.g., [2]);
- approaches where evaluation is done by humans who try to assess how well the ontology meets a set of predefined criteria, standards, requirements, etc. (e.g., [15]).

In addition to the above categories of evaluation, we can group the ontology evaluation approaches based on the level of evaluation, as described in the following subsections.

11.2.1 Ontology Evaluation at Different Levels

An ontology is a fairly complex structure and it is often more practical to focus on the evaluation of different levels of the ontology separately rather than trying to directly evaluate the ontology as a whole. This is particularly true if the emphasis is on having the evaluation proceed automatically rather than being entirely carried out by human users/experts. Another reason for the level-based approach is that when automatic learning techniques have been used in the construction of the ontology, the techniques involved are substantially different for the different levels. The individual levels have been defined variously by different authors (e.g., [8, 9, 3, 22, 6]), but these various definitions tend to be broadly similar and usually involve the following levels:

- *Lexical, vocabulary, or data layer.* Here the focus is on which concepts, instances, facts, etc. have been included in the ontology, and the vocabulary used to represent or identify these concepts. Evaluation on this level tends to involve comparisons with various sources of data concerning the problem domain (e.g., domain-specific text corpora), as well as techniques such as string similarity measures (e.g., edit distance).

- *Hierarchy or taxonomy.* An ontology typically includes a hierarchical is-a or subsumption relation between concepts. Although various other relations between concepts may be also defined, the is-a relationship is often particularly important and may be the focus of specific evaluation efforts.
- *Other semantic relations.* The ontology may contain other relations besides is-a, and these relations may be evaluated separately. This typically includes measures such as precision and recall.
- *Context level.* (1) An ontology may be part of a larger collection of ontologies, and may reference or be referenced by various definitions in these other ontologies. In this case it may be important to take this context into account when evaluating it [26, 3, 21]. (2) Another form of context is the application where the ontology is to be used; basically, rather than evaluate the ontology per se, it may be more practical to evaluate it within the context of a particular application, and to see how the results of the application are affected by the use of the ontology in question. Instead of focusing on an individual application, one may also focus on evaluation from the point of view of the individual users or the organization (e.g., company) that will use the ontology [7].
- *Syntactic level.* Evaluation on this level may be of particular interest for ontologies that have been mostly constructed manually. The ontology is usually described in a particular formal language and must match the syntactic requirements of that language (use of the correct keywords, etc.). Various other syntactic considerations, such as the presence of natural-language documentation, avoiding loops between definitions, etc., may also be considered [8]. Of all aspects of ontology evaluation, this is probably the one that lends itself the most easily to automated processing.
- *Structure, architecture, design.* Unlike the first three levels on this list, which focus on the actual sets of concepts, instances, relations, etc. involved in the ontology, this level focuses on higher-level design decisions that were used during the development of the ontology. This is primarily of interest in manually constructed ontologies. Assuming that some kind of design principles or criteria have been agreed upon prior to constructing the ontology, evaluation on this level means checking to what extent the resulting ontology matches those criteria. Structural concerns involve the organization of the ontology and its suitability for further development (e.g., addition of new concepts, modification or removal of old ones) [8, 9]. For some applications, it is also important that the formal definitions and statements of the ontology are accompanied by appropriate natural-language documentation, which must be meaningful, coherent, up-to-date and consistent with the formal definitions, sufficiently detailed, etc. Evaluation of these qualities on this level must usually be done largely or even entirely manually by people such as ontological engineers and domain experts.

The following table summarizes which approaches from the list at the beginning of Section 11.2 are commonly used for which of the levels discussed in this subsection. The next few subsections will present more details about the various approaches and levels of ontology evaluation.

Table 11.1. An overview of approaches to ontology evaluation on different levels.

Level	Approach to ontology evaluation			
	Gold standard	Application based	Data-driven	Assessment by humans
Lexical, vocabulary, concept, data	×	×	×	×
Hierarchy, taxonomy	×	×	×	×
Other semantic relations	×	×	×	×
Context (repository/application)		×		×
Syntactic	×[1]			×
Structure, architecture, design				×

[1] "Gold standard" in the sense of comparing the syntax in the ontology definition with the syntax specification of the formal language in which the ontology is written (e.g., RDF, OWL, etc.).

11.2.2 Evaluation on the Lexical/Vocabulary and Concept/Data Level

An example of an approach that can be used for the evaluation of a lexical/vocabulary level of an ontology is the one proposed by Maedche and Staab [16]. Similarity between two strings is measured based on the Levenshtein edit distance [14], normalized to produce scores in the range [0, 1]. Sometimes background knowledge about the domain can be used to introduce an improved domain-specific definition of the edit distance; for example, when comparing names of persons, one might take into account the fact that first names are often abbreviated [6]. A *string matching* measure between two sets of strings is then defined by taking each string of the first set, finding its similarity to the most similar string in the second set, and averaging this over all strings of the first set. One may take the set of all strings used as concept identifiers in the ontology being evaluated, and compare it to a "gold standard" set of strings that are considered a good representation of the concepts of the problem domain under consideration. The gold standard could be in fact another ontology (as in Maedche and Staab's work), or it could be taken statistically from a corpus of documents (see Section 11.2.4), or prepared by domain experts.

The lexical content of an ontology can also be evaluated using the concepts of precision and recall, as known in information retrieval. In this context, precision would be the percentage of the ontology lexical entries (strings used as concept identifiers) that also appear in the gold standard, relative to the total number of ontology words. Recall is the percentage of the gold standard lexical entries that also appear as concept identifiers in the ontology, relative to the total number of gold standard lexical entries. A downside of the precision and recall measures defined in this way is that they do not allow for minor differences in spelling (e.g., use of hyphens in multi-word phrases, etc.). Another way to achieve more tolerant matching criteria [2] is to augment each lexical entry with its hypernyms from WordNet or some similar resource; then, instead of testing for equality of two lexical entries, one can test for overlap between their corresponding sets of words (each set containing an entry with its hypernyms).

The same approaches could also be used to evaluate the lexical content of an ontology on other levels, e.g., the strings used to identify relations, instances, etc.

Velardi *et al.* [27] describe an approach for the evaluation of an ontology learning system which takes a body of natural-language text and tries to extract from it relevant domain-specific concepts (terms and phrases), and then find definitions for them (using web searches and WordNet entries) and connect some of the concepts by is-a relations. Part of their evaluation approach is to generate natural-language glosses for multiple-word terms. The glosses are of the form "x y = a kind of y, ⟨definition of y⟩, related to the x, ⟨definition of x⟩," where y is typically a noun and x is a modifier such as another noun or an adjective. A gloss like this would then be shown to human domain experts, who would evaluate it to see if the word sense disambiguation algorithm selected the correct definitions of x and y. An advantage of this kind of approach is that domain experts might be unfamiliar with formal languages in which ontologies are commonly described, and thus it might be easier for them to evaluate the natural-language glosses. Of course, the downside of this approach is that it nevertheless requires a lot of work on part of the domain experts.

11.2.3 Evaluation of Taxonomic and Other Semantic Relations

Brewster *et al.* [2] suggested using a data-driven approach to evaluate the degree of structural fit between an ontology and a corpus of documents. (1) Given a corpus of documents from the domain of interest, a clustering algorithm based on expectation maximization is used to determine, in an unsupervised way, a probabilistic mixture model of hidden "topics" such that each document can be modeled as having been generated by a mixture of topics. (2) Each concept c of the ontology is represented by a set of terms including its name in the ontology and the hypernyms of this name, taken from WordNet. (11.3) The probabilistic models obtained during clustering can be used to measure, for each topic identified by the clustering algorithm, how well the concept c fits that topic. (11.4) At this point, if we require that each concept fits at least some topic reasonably well, we obtain a technique for lexical-level evaluation of the ontology. Alternatively, we may require that concepts associated with the same topic should be closely related in the ontology (via is-a and possibly other relations). This would indicate that the structure of the ontology is reasonably well aligned with the hidden structure of topics in the domain-specific corpus of documents. A drawback of this method as an approach for evaluating relations is that it is difficult to take the directionality of relations into account. For example, given concepts c_1 and c_2, the probabilistic models obtained during clustering in step (1) may be enough to infer that they should be related, but they are not really sufficient to infer whether e.g., c_1 is-a c_2, or c_2 is-a c_1, or if they should in fact be connected by some other relation rather than is-a.

Given a gold standard, evaluation of an ontology on the relational level can also be based on precision and recall measures. Spyns [25] discusses an approach for automatically extracting a set of lexons, i.e., triples of the form ⟨*term₁, role, term₂*⟩, from natural-language text. The result can be interpreted as an ontology, with terms corresponding to concepts and roles corresponding to (non-hierarchical) relations between concepts. Evaluation was based on precision and recall, comparing the ontology either with a human-provided gold standard, or with a list of statistically relevant terms. The downside of this approach is again the need for a lot of manual human work involved in preparing the gold standard.

A somewhat different aspect of ontology evaluation has been discussed by Guarino and Welty [11]. They point out several philosophical notions (essentiality, rigidity, unity, etc.) that can be used to better understand the nature of various kinds of semantic relationships that commonly appear in ontologies, and to discover possible problematic decisions in the structure of an ontology. For example, a property is said to be *essential* to an entity if it necessarily holds for that entity. A property that is essential for all entities having this property is called *rigid* (e.g., "being a person": there is no entity that could be a person but isn't; everything that is a person is necessarily always a person); a property that cannot be essential to an entity is called *anti-rigid* (e.g., "being a student": any entity that is a student could also not be a student). A class defined by a rigid property cannot be the subclass of a class defined by an anti-rigid property. This observation allows us to conclude, if we see an ontology in which "person" is a subclass of "student," that this relationship is wrong. Various other kinds of misuse of the is-a relationship can also be detected in a similar way (for example, is-a is sometimes used to express meta-level characteristics of some class, or is used instead of is-a-part-of, or is used to indicate that a term may have multiple meanings). A downside of this approach is that it requires manual intervention by a trained human expert familiar with the above-mentioned notions such as rigidity; at the very least, the expert should annotate the concepts of the ontology with appropriate metadata tags, whereupon checks for certain kinds of errors can be made automatically. As pointed out, e.g., in [12], applications where evaluation of this sort is truly important (and justifies the costs) are probably relatively rare. However, Völker et al. [28] recently proposed an approach to aid in the automatic assignment of these metadata tags.

Maedche and Staab [16] propose several measures for comparing the relational aspects of two ontologies. If one of the ontologies is a gold standard, these measures can also be used for ontology evaluation. Although this is in a way a drawback of this method, an important positive aspect is that once the gold standard is defined, comparison of two ontologies can proceed entirely automatically. The *semantic cotopy* of a term c in a given hierarchy is the set of all its super- and sub-concepts. Given two hierarchies H_1, H_2, a term t might represent some concept c_1 in H_1 and a concept c_2 in H_2. One can then compute the set of terms which represent concepts from the cotopy of c_1 in H_1, and the set of terms representing concepts from the cotopy of c_2 in H_2; the overlap of these two sets can be used as a measure of how similar a role the term t has in the two hierarchies H_1 and H_2. An average of this may then be computed over all the terms occurring in the two hierarchies; this is a measure of similarity between H_1 and H_2.

Similar ideas can also be used to compare other relations besides is-a. Let R_1 be a binary relation in the first ontology, with a domain $d(R_1)$ and a range $r(R_1)$. Analogously, let R_2 be a binary relation in the second ontology. We can consider the relations to be similar if $d(R_1)$ is similar to $d(R_2)$ and $r(R_1)$ is similar to $r(R_2)$. Since $d(R_1)$ and $d(R_2)$ are simply two sets of concepts, they can be compared similarly as in the preceding paragraph: determine the set of terms that occur as names of any concept of $d(R_1)$ or any of its hypernyms; in analogous way, determine the set of terms for $d(R_2)$; then compute the overlap of these two sets. The overlap between ranges $r(R_1)$ and $r(R_2)$ can be computed in an analogous way. If there are several such pairs of relations, the similarity can be computed for each pair and then averaged to obtain an indicator of relational-level similarity between the two ontologies as a whole.

11.2.4 Context-Level Evaluation

Sometimes the ontology is a part of a larger collection of ontologies that may reference one another (e.g., one ontology may use a class or concept declared in another ontology), for example, on the web or within some institutional library of ontologies. This context can be used for evaluation of an ontology in various ways. For example, the Swoogle search engine of Ding *et al.* [5] uses cross-references between semantic-web documents to define a graph and then compute a score for each ontology in a manner analogous to PageRank used by the Google web search engine. The resulting "ontology rank" is used by Swoogle to rank its query results. A similar approach used in the OntoKhoj portal of Patel *et al.* [21]. In both cases an important difference in comparison to PageRank is that not all "links" or references between ontologies are treated the same. For example, if one ontology defines a subclass of a class from another ontology, this reference might be considered more important than if one ontology only uses a class from another as the domain or range of some relation.

Alternatively, the context for evaluation may be provided by human experts; for example, Supekar [26] proposes that an ontology be enhanced with metadata such as its design policy, how it is being used by others, as well as "peer reviews" provided by users of this ontology. A suitable search engine could then be used to perform queries on this metadata and would aid the user in deciding which of the many ontologies in a repository to use. The downside of this approach is that it relies almost entirely on manual human effort to both provide annotations and to use them in evaluating and selecting an ontology.

11.2.5 Application-Based Evaluation

Typically, the ontology will be used in some kind of application or task. The outputs of the application, or its performance on the given task, might be better or worse depending partly on the ontology used in it. Thus one might argue that a good ontology is one which helps the application in question produce good results on the given task. Ontologies may therefore be evaluated simply by plugging them into an application and evaluating the results of the application. This is elegant in the sense that the output of the application might be something for which a relatively straightforward and non-problematic evaluation approach already exists. For example, Porzel and Malaka [22] describe a scenario where the ontology, with its relations (both is-a and others) is used primarily to determine how closely related the meaning of two concepts is. The task is a speech recognition problem, where there may be several hypotheses about what a particular word in the sentence really means; a hypotheses should be coherent, which means that the interpretations of individual words should be concepts that are relatively closely related to each other. Thus the ontology is used to measure distance between concepts and thereby to assess the coherence of hypotheses (and choose the most coherent one). Evaluation of the final output of the task is relatively straightforward, and requires simply that the proposed interpretations of the sentences are compared with the gold standard provided by humans.

An approach like this can elegantly side-step the various complications of ontology evaluation and translate them to the problem of evaluating the application output, which is often simpler. However, this approach to ontology evaluation also has several drawbacks: (1) it allows one to argue that the ontology is good or bad when used in a particular way for a particular task, but it's difficult to generalize this observation (what if the ontology is used for a different task, or differently for the same task?); (2) the evaluation may be sensitive in the sense that the ontology could be only a small component of the application and its effect on the outcome may be relatively small (or depend considerably on the behavior of the other components); (3) if evaluating a large number of ontologies, they must be sufficiently compatible that the application can use them all (or the application must be sufficiently flexible), e.g., as regarding the format in which the ontology is described, the presence and names of semantic relations, etc. If it is necessary to adapt the application somewhat for each ontology that is to be evaluated, this approach to evaluation can quickly become very costly.

11.2.6 Data-Driven Evaluation

An ontology may also be evaluated by comparing it to existing data (usually a collection of textual documents) about the problem domain to which the ontology refers. For example, Patel *et al.* [21] proposed an approach to determine if the ontology refers to a particular topic, and to classify the ontology into a directory of topics: one can extract textual data from the ontology (such as names of concepts and relations, or other suitable natural-language strings) and use this as the input to a text classification model. The model itself can be trained by some of the standard machine learning algorithms from the area of text classification; a corpus of documents on a given subject can be used as the input to the learning algorithm.

Another data-driven approach has been proposed by Brewster *et al.* [2]. First, a set of relevant domain-specific terms are extracted from the corpus of documents, for example using latent semantic analysis. The amount of overlap between the domain-specific terms and the terms appearing in the ontology (e.g., as names of concepts) can then be used to measure the fit between the ontology and the corpus. Measures such as precision or recall could also be used in this context.

In the case of more extensive and sophisticated ontologies that incorporate a lot of factual information (such as Cyc, see, e.g., www.cyc.com), the corpus of documents could also be used as a source of "facts" about the external world, and the evaluation measure is the percentage of these facts that can also be derived from information in the ontology.

11.2.7 Multiple-Criteria Approaches

Another family of approaches to ontology evaluation deals with the problem of selecting a good ontology (or a small short-list of promising ontologies) from a given set of ontologies, and treats this problem as essentially a decision-making problem. Therefore, techniques familiar from the area of decision support systems can be used to help us evaluate the ontologies and choose one of them. Usually, these approaches are based on defining several decision criteria or attributes; for each criterion, the ontology is evaluated and given a numerical score. Additionally a weight is also assigned (in advance) to each criterion, and an overall score for the ontology is then computed as a weighted sum of its per-criterion scores. This approach is analogous to the strategies used in many other contexts to select the best candidate out of many (e.g., tenders, grant applications, etc.). It could be particularly useful in situations where we are faced with a considerable number of ontologies roughly relevant to our domain in interest and wish to select the best ontology (or a few good ones). However, this type of approaches may still have difficulties such as the need for much manual involvement by human experts, for the presence of a gold standard ontology, etc. In effect, the general problem of ontology evaluation has been deferred or relegated to the question of how to evaluate the ontology with respect to the individual evaluation criteria.

Burton-Jones *et al.* [3] propose an approach of this type, with 10 simple criteria such as syntactical correctness, clarity of vocabulary, etc. (a brief description of the way used to compute a numeric score for each attribute is included in parentheses):

- lawfulness (i.e., frequency of syntactical errors),
- richness (how many of the syntactic features available in the formal language are actually used by the ontology),
- interpretability (do the terms used in the ontology also appear in WordNet?),
- consistency (how many concepts in the ontology are involved in inconsistencies),
- clarity (do the terms used in the ontology have many senses in WordNet?),
- comprehensiveness (number of concepts in the ontology, relative to the average for the entire library of ontologies),
- accuracy (percentage of false statements in the ontology),
- relevance (number of statements that involve syntactic features marked as useful or acceptable to the user/agent),
- authority (how many other ontologies use concepts from this ontology),
- history (how many accesses to this ontology have been made, relative to other ontologies in the library/repository).

As can be seen from this list, this methodology involves criteria from most of the levels discussed in Section 11.2.1. A downside of this approach is that there is little in it to help us ascertain to what extent the ontology matches the real-world state of the problem domain to which is refers (or indeed if it really deals with the domain we are interested in; it could be about some entirely unrelated subject; but this problem can be at least partially addressed by text categorization techniques, as used, e.g., in [21]). The accuracy criterion in the list above provides a way to take the accuracy into account when computing the overall ontology score, but it's usually difficult to compute the percentage of false statements otherwise than by examining them all manually. On the positive side, the other criteria listed above can be computed automatically (although some of them assume that the ontology under consideration belongs to a larger library or repository of ontologies, and that metadata such as access history is available for the repository). Fox *et al.* [7] propose another set of criteria, which is however geared more towards manual assessment and evaluation of ontologies. Their criteria involve: functional completeness (does the ontology contain enough information for the application at hand?), generality (is it general enough to be shared by multiple users, departments, etc.?), efficiency (does the ontology support efficient reasoning?), perspicuity (is it understandable to the users?), precision/granularity (does it support multiple levels of abstraction/detail?), minimality (does it contain only as many concepts as necessary?).

An even more detailed set of 117 criteria is described in [15], organized in a three-level framework. The criteria cover various aspects of the formal language used to describe the ontology, the contents of the ontology (concepts, relations, taxonomy, axioms), the methodology used to construct the ontology, the costs (hardware, soft-ware, licensing, etc.) of using the ontology, and the tools available for working with the ontology. Many of the criteria are simple enough that the score of an ontology with respect to these criteria could be computed automatically or at least without much human involvement. The authors also cite several earlier works in the same area, with a more moderate number of criteria.

11.3 A Theoretical Framework for Ontology Evaluation

In this section we present a formal definition of ontologies, provide examples of how various kinds of ontologies may be captured in the context of this formalization, and discuss how evaluation fits into this formal framework.

A reasonable and well thoughtout formal definition of ontologies has been de-scribed recently in the work of Ehrig *et al.* [6]. In this formalization, the on-tology (with datatypes) is defined as a structure $O = (C, T, R, A, I, V, \leq_C, \leq_T, \sigma_R, \sigma_A, \iota_C, \iota_T, \iota_R, \iota_A)$. It consists of (disjoint) sets of concepts (C), types (T), rela-tions (R), attributes (A), instances (I) and values (V). The partial orders $\leq_C$ (on C) and $\leq_T$ (on T) define a concept hierarchy and a type hierarchy. The function $\sigma_R : R \to C \times C$ provides relation signatures (i.e., for each relation, the function specifies which concepts may be linked by this relation), while $\sigma_A : A \to C \times T$ pro-vides attribute signatures (for each attribute, the function specifies to which concept the attribute belongs and what is its datatype). Finally, there are partial instantia-tion functions $\iota_C : C \to 2^I$ (the assignment of instances to concepts), $\iota_T : T \to 2^V$ (the assignment of values to types), $\iota_R : R \to 2^{I \times I}$ (which instances are related by a particular relation), and $\iota_A : A \to 2^{I \times V}$ (what is the value of each attribute for each instance). (Another formalization of ontologies, based on similar principles, has also been described by Bloehdorn *et al.* [1].)

For some types of ontologies, this framework can be further extended, par-ticularly with "concept attributes" in addition to the "instance attributes" men-tioned above. The concept attributes would be a set A', with a signature function $\sigma_{A'} : A' \to T$ and an instantiation function $\iota_{A'} : A' \to 2^{C \times V}$. The value of such an attribute would not be associated to a particular instance of a concept, but would apply to the concept as such. This extension will be useful for some of the evalu-ation scenarios considered later in this section. Other possible extensions, such as relations between concepts (as opposed to between instances), the introduction of metaclasses, or the introduction of relations with arity greater than 2, are probably of less practical interest.

A flexible formal network like this can accommodate various commonly-used kinds of ontologies:

- *Terminological ontologies* where concepts are word senses and instances are words. The WordNet ontology (http://www.cogsci.princeton.edu/~wn/) is an example of this. Attributes include things like natural-language descriptions of word senses (for concepts) and string representations of words (for instances).
- *Topic ontologies* where concepts are topics and instances are documents. Familiar examples include the Open Directory at http://www.dmoz.org/ or the Yahoo! directory at http://dir.yahoo.com/. Concept attributes typically consist of a name and a short description of each topic, and instance attributes consist of a

document title, description, URL, and the main block of the text (for practical purposes, such text is often represented as a vector using, e.g., the TF-IDF weighting under the vector space model of text representation).

- *Data-model ontologies* where concepts are tables in a data base and instances are data records (such as in a database schema). In this setting, datatypes and attributes in the above-mentioned formal definition of an ontology are straight-forward analogies to the types and attributes (a.k.a. fields or columns) in a data base management system.

Evaluation can be incorporated in this theoretical framework as a function that maps the ontology O to a real number, e.g., in the range $[0, 1]$. However, as has been seen in Section 11.2, a more practical approach is to focus the evaluation on individual components of the ontology O (which correspond roughly to the levels of ontology evaluation discussed in Section 11.2). Results of the evaluation of individual components can later be aggregated into a combined ontology evaluation score [6].

- The datatypes and their values (i.e., T, V, $\leq_T$, and ι_T) would typically not be evaluated; they are merely the groundwork on which the rest of the structure can stand.
- A lexical- or concept-level evaluation can focus on C, I, ι_C, and possibly some instance attributes from ι_A.
- Evaluation of the concept hierarchy (is-a relationship) would focus on the $\leq_C$ partial order.
- Evaluation of other semantic relations would focus on R, ι_R, and the concept and instance attributes.
- One could also envision evaluation focusing on particular attributes; for example, whether a suitable natural-language name has been chosen for each concept. This kind of evaluation would take ι_C and the attributes as input and assess whether the concept attributes are suitable given ι_C and the instance attributes.
- Application- or task-based evaluation could be formalized by defining the application as a function $A(D, O)$ which produces some output given its input data D and the ontology O. By fixing the input data D, any evaluation function defined on the outputs of A becomes de facto an evaluation function on O. However, the practical applicability of such a formalization is debatable.
- Evaluation based on comparison to a gold standard can be incorporated into this theoretical framework as a function defined on a pair of ontologies (effectively a kind of similarity measure, or a distance function between ontologies). Similarly, data-driven evaluation can be seen as a function of the ontology and the domain-specific data corpus D, and could even be formulated probabilistically as $P(O|D)$.

11.4 Architecture and Approach

We have developed an approach to ontology evaluation primarily geared to enable automatic evaluation of an ontology that includes instances of the ontology concepts. The approach is based on the gold standard paradigm and its main focus is to compare how well the given ontology resembles the gold standard in the arrangement of instances into concepts and the hierarchical arrangement of the concepts themselves. It is similar to the other existing ontology evaluation methods based on a gold standard (see Section 11.2) with the main difference being that, while it bases the evaluation on instances assigned to the ontology concepts, our approach does not rely on natural-language descriptions of the concepts and instances (unlike e.g., the string edit distance approaches of Maedche and Staab [16]). No assumptions are made regarding the representation of instances, only that we can distinguish one instance from another (and that the ontology is based on the same set of instances as the gold standard).

11.4.1 Task Description

We have tested our approach on a concrete task of evaluating a topic ontology based on the "Science" subtree of the dmoz.org internet directory. The dmoz directory is a topic ontology structured as a hierarchy of topics, and each topic may contain (besides subtopics) zero or more links to external web pages. Each link includes a title and a short description of the external web page. In the context of the ontology learning scenario, each link to an external web page represents an instance of the topic, in a manner similar to the approach to automatic classification of Web documents into a topic ontology defined in [20]. In addition to classifying documents into a topic ontology to populate an existing ontology, we can also define a problem of learning an ontology given only a set of documents. In the case of "Science" subtree of dmoz.org this means given a total of approx. 100,000 instances, arrange the instances into a hierarchy of concepts. In effect, this is similar to an unsupervised hierarchical clustering problem. The resulting hierarchy of concepts (with each instance attached to one of the concepts) is in effect a simple ontology (the hierarchical relationship between concepts can be approximately interpreted as an "is-a" relation). One can evaluate learned ontologies by comparing them to the "Science" subtree of the real dmoz.org directory, which will thus assume the role of a gold standard.

In this evaluation task, each instance is represented by a short document of natural-language text (i.e., the title and description of the external page, as it appears in the dmoz.org directory). The concepts of the learned ontologies, however, are not explicitly represented by any terms, phrases, or similar textual descriptions. The question of how to select a good short textual representation, or perhaps a set of keywords, for a particular learned concept could in itself be a separate task, but is not part of the ontology learning task whose evaluation is being discussed here. Additionally, since the number of instances (as well as concepts) is fairly large, the evaluation must be reasonably fast and completely automated.

11.4.2 Similarity Measures on Partitions

Our approach to evaluation is based on the analogies between this ontology learning task and traditional unsupervised clustering. In clustering, the task is to partition a set of instances into a family of disjoint subsets. Here, the topic ontology can be seen as a hierarchical way of partitioning the set of instances. The clustering community has proposed various techniques for comparing two partitions of the same set of instances, which can be used to compare the output of an automated clustering method with a gold-standard partition. If these distance measures on traditional "flat" partitions can be extended to hierarchical partitions, they can be used to compare a learned ontology to the gold-standard ontology (since both will be, in the context of this ontology learning task, two hierarchical partitions of the same set of instances).

One popular measure of agreement between two flat partitions is the Rand index [24]. Assume that there is a set of instances $O = \{o_1, \ldots, o_n\}$,[1] with two partitions of O into a family of disjoint subsets, $U = \{U_1, \ldots, U_m\}$ and $V = \{V_1, \ldots, V_k\}$, where $\cup_{i=1..m} U_i = O$, $\cup_{j=1..k} V_j = O$, $U_i \cap U_{i'} = \emptyset$ for each $1 \leq i < i' \leq m$, and $V_j \cap V_{j'} = \emptyset$ for each $1 \leq j < j' \leq k$. Then one way to compare the partitions U and V is to count the agreements and disagreements in the placement of instances into clusters. If two items $o_i, o_j \in O$ belong to the same cluster of U but to two separate clusters of V, or vice versa, this is considered a disagreement. On the other hand, if they belong to the same cluster in both partitions, or to separate clusters in both partitions, this is considered an agreement between partitions. The Rand index between U and V is the number of agreements relative to the total number of pairs of instances (i.e., to $n(n-1)/2$).

11.4.3 A Similarity Measure for Ontologies

We can elegantly formulate a similarity measure over ontologies by rephrasing the Rand index as follows. Let us denote by $U(o)$ the cluster of U that contains the instance $o \in O$, and similarly by $V(o)$ the cluster of V that contains the instance $o \in O$. Let $\delta_X(X_i, X_j)$ be some distance measure between clusters X_i and X_j of a partition X. Then we define the OntoRand index by the following formula:

$$OntoRandIdx(U, V) = 1 - \frac{\sum_{1 \leq i < j \leq n} |\delta_U(U(o_i), U(o_j)) - \delta_V(V(o_i), V(o_j))|}{n(n-1)/2}. \quad (11.1)$$

If we define $\delta_U(U_i, U_j) = 1$ if $U_i = U_j$, and $\delta_U(Ui, Uj) = 0$ otherwise and δ_V as well in an analogous manner, we can see that the Rand index is a special case of our OntoRand index. That is, the term bracketed by $|\ldots|$ in eq. (11.1) equals 1 if there is a disagreement between U and V concerning the placement of the pair of instances o_i and o_j. The sum over all i and j therefore counts the number of pairs where a disagreement occurs.

When we apply the OntoRand index for the purpose of comparing ontologies, we must take the hierarchical arrangement of concepts into account. In the original Rand index, what matters for a particular pair of instances is simply if they belong to the same cluster or not. However, when concepts or clusters are organized hierarchically, not any two different clusters are equally different. For example, two concepts with a common parent in the tree are likely to be quite similar even though they are not exactly the same; on the other hand, two concepts that do not have any common ancestor except the root of the tree are probably highly unrelated. Thus, if one ontology places a pair of instances in the same concept while the other ontology places this pair of instances in two different concepts with a common parent, this is a disagreement, but not a very strong one; on the other hand, if the second ontology places the two instances into two completely unrelated concepts, this would

---

[1] In this section, O stands only for the set of instances, not for an entire ontology as in Sec. 11.3. We use O instead of I for the set of instances to prevent confusion with the use of i as an index in subscripts.

be a large disagreement. We use the formula for $OntoRandIdx(U, V)$ given above, where the functions δ_U and δ_V take this intuition into account. That is, rather than returning merely 1 or 0 depending on whether the given two clusters are the same or not, the functions δ_U and δ_V should return a real number from the range $[0, 1]$, expressing a measure of how closely related the two clusters are.

By plugging in various definitions of the functions δ_U and δ_V, we can obtain a family of similarity measures for ontologies, suitable for comparing an ontology with the gold standard in the context of the task that has been discussed in Section 11.4.1. We propose two concrete families of δ_U and δ_V. Since the definitions of δ_U and δ_V will always be analogous to each other and differ only in the fact that each applies to a different ontology, we refer only to the δ_U function in the following discussion.

Similarity Based on Common Ancestors

One possibility is inspired by the approach that is sometimes used to evaluate the performance of classification models for classification in hierarchies (see, e.g., [19]), and that could incidentally also be useful in the context of e.g., evaluating an automatic ontology population system. Given a concept U_i in the ontology U, let $A(U_i)$ be the set of all ancestors of this concept, i.e., all concepts on the path from the root to U_i (including U_i itself). If two concepts U_i and U_j have a common parent, the sets $A(U_i)$ and $A(U_j)$ will have a large intersection; on the other hand, if they have no common parent except the root, the intersection of $A(U_i)$ and $A(U_j)$ will contain only the root concept. Thus the size of the intersection can be taken as a measure of how closely related the two concepts are.

$$\delta_U(U_i, U_j) = |A(U_i) \cap A(U_j)| / |A(U_i) \cup A(U_j)|. \tag{11.2}$$

This measure (also known as the Jaccard coefficient) has the additional nice characteristic that it can be extended to cases where U is not a tree but an arbitrary directed acyclic graph. If the arrows in this graph point from parents to children, the set $A(U_i)$ is simply the set of all nodes from which U is reachable.

Similarity Based on Distance in the Tree

An alternative way to define a suitable function δ_U would be to work directly with the distances between U_i and U_j in the tree U. In this case, let l be the distance between U_i and U_j in the tree (length of the path from U_i to the common ancestor of U_i and U_j, and thence down to U_j), and h be the depth of the deepest common ancestor of U_i and U_j. If l is large, this is a sign that U_i and U_j are not very closely related; similarly, if h is small, this is a sign that U_i and U_j don't have any common ancestors except very general concepts close to the root, and therefore U_i and U_j aren't very closely related. There are various ways of taking these intuitions into account in a formula for δ_U as a function of l and h. For example, Rada et al. [23] have proposed a distance measure of the form:

$$\delta(l, h) = e^{-\alpha l \tanh(\beta h)} \tag{11.3}$$

Here, α and β are nonnegative constants, and tanh is the hyperbolic tangent

$$\tanh(x) = (e^x - e^{-x})/(e^x + e^{-x}) = 1 - 2/(1 + e^{2x}).$$

Thus, if h is small, $th(\beta h)$ is close to 0, whereas for a large h it becomes close to 1. It is reasonable to treat the case when the two concepts are the same, i.e., when $U_i = U_j$ and thus $l = 0$, as a special case, and define $\delta(0, h) = 1$ in that case, to prevent $\delta_U(U_i, U_i)$ from being dependent on the depth of the concept U_i.

Incidentally, if we set α to 0 (or close to 0) and β to some large value, $\delta(l, h)$ will be approx. 0 for $h = 0$ and approx. 1 for $h > 0$. Thus, in the sum used to define the OntoRand index (11.1), each pair of instances contributes the value of 1 if they have some common ancestor besides the root in one ontology but not in other, otherwise it contributes the value of 0. Thus, the OntoRand index becomes equivalent to the ordinary Rand index computed over the partitions of instances implied by the second-level concepts of the two ontologies (i.e., the immediate subconcepts of the root concept). This can be taken as a warning that α should not be too small and β not too large, otherwise the OntoRand index will ignore the structure of the lower levels of the ontologies.

The overlap-based version of d_U from eq. (11.2) can also be defined in terms of h and l. If the root is taken to be at depth 0, then the intersection of $A(U_i)$ and $A(U_j)$ contains $h + 1$ concepts, and the union of $A(U_i)$ and $A(U_j)$ contains $h + l + 1$ concepts. Thus, we see that eq. (11.2) is equivalent to defining

$$\delta(l, h) = (h + 1)/(h + l + 1). \tag{11.4}$$

By comparing the equations (11.3) and (11.4), we see a notable difference between the two definitions of δ: when $h = 0$, i.e., when the two instances have no common ancestor except the root, eq. (11.3) returns $\delta = 0$ while eq. (11.4) returns $\delta = 1/(l + 1) > 0$. When comparing two ontologies, it may often happen that many pairs of instances have no common ancestor (except the root) in either of the two ontologies, i.e., $h_U = h_V = 0$, but the distance between their concepts is likely to be different: $l_U \neq l_V$. In these cases, using eq. (11.3) will result in $\delta_U = \delta_V = 0$, while eq. (11.4) will result in $\delta_U \neq \delta_V$. When the resulting values $|\delta_U - \delta_V|$ are used in eq. (11.1), we see that in the case of definition (11.3), many terms in the sum will be 0 and the OntoRand index will be close to 1. For example, in our experiments with the Science subtree of dmoz.org (Sec. 11.5.3), despite the fact that the assignment of instances to concepts was considerably different between the two ontologies, approx. 81% of instance pairs had $h_U = h_V = 0$ (and only 3.2% of these additionally had $l_U = l_V$). Thus, when using the definition of δ from eq. (11.3) (as opposed to the overlap-based definition from eq. (11.4)), we must accept the fact that most of the terms in the sum (11.1) will be 0 and OntoRand index will be close to 1. This does not mean that the resulting values of OntoRand are not useful for assessing whether, e.g., one ontology is closer to the gold standard than another ontology is, but it may nevertheless appear confusing that OntoRand is always so close to 1. In this case a possible alternative is to replace eq. (11.3) by

$$\delta(l, h) = e^{-\alpha l \tanh(\beta h + 1)} \tag{11.5}$$

The family of δ-functions defined by (11.5) can be seen as a generalization (in a loose sense) of the δ-function from formula (11.4). For example, we compared the values of δ produced by these two definitions on a set of 106 random pairs of documents from the dmoz.org Science subtree. For a suitable choice of α and β, the definition (11.5) can be made to produce values of δ that are very closely correlated with those of definition (11.4) (e.g., correl. coefficient = 0.995 for $\alpha = 0.15, \beta = 0.25$). Similarly, when we compute $|\delta_U - \delta_V|$ for various pairs of documents (when using eq. (11.1) to compare two ontologies in Sec. 11.5.3), definition (11.5) can yield values closely correlated to those of definition (11.4) for suitable values of α and β (e.g., correl. coef. $= 0.981$ for $\alpha = 0.8, \beta = 1.5$). However, note that the fact that δ values of (11.5) are closely correlated with those of (11.4) for some choice of α and β does not imply that the $|\delta_U - \delta_V|$ will also be closely correlated for the same choice of α and β (or vice versa).

The need to select concrete values of α and β is one of the disadvantages of using the definition (11.3) (or (11.5)) rather than the overlap-based definition (11.2) (or equivalently (11.4)).

Further generalizations. The distance measure (11.3) could be further generalized by taking $\delta(l, h) = f(l)g(h)$ for any decreasing function f and increasing function g. Since the values l and h are always integers and are limited by the depth of the tree (or twice the depth in the case of l), the functions f and g (or even $\delta(l, h)$ itself) could even be defined using a table of function values for all possible l and h.

Note that the main part of the OntoRand index formula, as defined in equation (11.1), i.e., the sum $\sum_{1 \leq i < j \leq n} |\delta_U(U(o_i), U(o_j)) - \delta_V(V(o_i), V(o_j))|$, can also be interpreted as a Manhattan (L_1-norm) distance between two vectors of $n(n-1)/2$ components, one depending on the ontology U and the other depending only on the ontology V. Thus, in effect, we have represented an ontology U by a "feature vector" in which the (i, j)-th component has the value $\delta_U(U(o_i), U(o_j))$ describing how closely the instances o_i and o_j have been placed in that ontology. This interpretation opens the possibility of various further generalizations, such as using Euclidean distance instead of Manhattan distance, or even using kernel methods (cf. [13]). However, we leave such extensions for further work.

11.4.4 Approximation Algorithms

As can be seen from eq. (11.1), the computation of our ontology similarity measure involves a sum over all pairs of documents, (i, j) for $1 \leq i < j \leq n$. This quadratic time complexity can be problematic when comparing ontologies with a fairly large number of instances (e.g., on the order of 100,000, as in the case of the dmoz.org "Science" subtree mentioned in Section 11.4.1). One way to speed up the computation of the similarity measure and obtain an approximate result is to use a randomly sampled subset of pairs rather than all possible pairs of documents. That is, eq. (11.1) would then contain the average value of $|\delta_U(U(o_i), U(o_j)) - \delta_V(V(o_i), V(o_j))|$ over some subset of pairs instead of over all pairs.

Another way towards approximate computation of the similarity measure is to try to identify pairs (i, j) for which the difference $|\delta_U(U(o_i), U(o_j)) - \delta_V(V(o_i), V(o_j))|$ is not close to 0. If both ontologies classify the instances o_i and o_j into highly unrelated clusters, the values $\delta_U(U(o_i), U(o_j))$ and $\delta_V(V(o_i), V(o_j))$ will both be close to 0 and their difference will also be close to 0 and will not have a large effect on the sum. (In a typical dmoz-like hierarchy we can expect that a large proportion of pairs of instances will fall unto such relatively unrelated clusters. As an extreme case, consider the definition of δ_U using eq. (3). If a pair of instances has no common ancestor concept except the root, h will be 0 and thus δ_U will be 0. If this happens in both ontologies, the pair will contribute nothing to the sum in eq. (11.1).) Thus it would be reasonable to try identifying pairs (i, j) for which o_i and o_j are in closely related clusters in at least one of the two ontologies, and computing the exact sum for these pairs, while disregarding the remaining pairs (or processing them using the subsampling technique from the previous paragraph). For example, suppose that δ_U is defined by eq. (11.4) as $\delta(l, h) = (h + 1)/(h + l + 1)$. Thus, we need to find pairs of concepts for which $(h + 1)/(h + l + 1)$ is greater than some threshold ε. (Then we will know that detailed processing is advisable for pairs of instances which fall into one of these pairs of concepts.) The condition $(h + 1)/(h + l + 1) > \varepsilon$ can be rewritten as $l < (h+1)(1/\varepsilon - 1)$. Thus, suitable pairs of concepts could be identified by the following algorithm:

Initialize $P := \{\}$.
For each concept c:
    Let h be the depth of c, and let $L = \lfloor (h + 1)(1/\varepsilon - 1) \rfloor$.
    Denote the children of c (its immediate subconcepts) by $c_1, \ldots, c_r$.
    For each l from 1 to L, for each i from 1 to r, let $S_{l,i}$ be the set of
        those subconcepts of c that are also subconcepts of c_i
        and are l levels below c in the tree.
    For each l from 1 to L, for each i from 1 to r,
        add to P all the pairs from $S_{l,i} \times (\cup_{l' \leq L-1} \cup_{i' \neq i} S_{l',i'})$.

In each iteration of the outermost loop, the algorithm processes a concept c and discovers all pairs of concepts c', c'' such that c is the deepest common ancestor of c' and c'' and $\delta_U(c', c'') > \varepsilon$. For more efficient maintenance of the $S_{l,i}$ sets, it might be advisable to process the concepts c in a bottom-up manner, since the sets for a parent concept can be obtained by merging appropriate sets of its children.

For the time being, we have tested random sampling of pairs as outlined at the beginning of this subsection. Separate treatment of pairs with $(h+1)/(h+l+1) > \varepsilon$ will be the topic of future work.

11.5 Evaluation of the Proposed Approach

The idea of evaluating the proposed approach to automatic ontology evaluation is in showing its output on several concrete situations enabling the reader to get an idea of the approach results given a well-defined mismatch in the ontologies (the learned ontology and the "gold-standard" ontology). Namely, instead of learning an ontology that we then evaluate, we use the "gold-standard" ontology, introduce some errors in it and use it to simulate the learned ontology. We have defined several simple and intuitive operations for introducing errors in the "gold-standard" ontology. The aim is to illustrate a kind of mismatch that can be found between the learned ontology and the "gold-standard" ontology and its influence on the evaluation score of the proposed OntoRand index. The following operations are presented below in our evaluation of the proposed approach:

- Removing lower levels of the tree — deleting all concepts below a certain depth in the tree (see Section 11.5.1).
- Swapping a concept and its parent (see Section 11.5.2).
- Reassigning instances to concepts based on their associated natural language text (see Section 11.5.3).

The dataset we used for the evaluation is the dmoz.org directory as of October 21, 2005. It contains 687,333 concepts and 4,381,225 instances. The concepts are organized into a tree; the deepest parts of the hierarchy go 15 levels deep, but in most places it is shallower (85% of all concepts are on levels 5 through 9, and the average node depth is 7.13). Since it would be too time-consuming to compute our OntoRand index over all pairs of documents (there are approx. $9.6 \cdot 10^{12}$ such pairs), we used a random sample of 10^6 pairs of documents.

In the case of the similarity measure (11.3), which is based on the tree distance between two concepts, it is necessary to select the parameters α and β. Recall that α is used in the term $e^{-\alpha l}$, where l is the length of the path from one concept to the other. Since our hierarchy has just 15 levels, we know that $l \leq 28$ for any pair of nodes; but since most nodes are on levels 5 through 9, we can expect l to be around 10–15 for a typical random pair of unrelated concepts. We decided to use $\alpha = 0.3$, which results in $e^{-\alpha l}$ values from 0.74 (for $l = 1$) to 0.22 (for $l = 5$), 0.05 (for $l = 10$) and 0.01 (for $l = 15$).

The parameter β can be chosen using similar considerations. It is used in the term $\tanh(\beta h)$, where h is the level at which the last common ancestor of the two concepts is located. Thus in our case h will be between 0 and 14, and will be close to 0 for two random unrelated concepts. For two very closely related concepts, h will typically be close to the depth of these two concepts, which (as we saw above) is on average around 7. We use $\beta = 0.4$, which results in values of $\tanh(\beta h)$ ranging from 0 (for $h = 0$) and 0.20 (for $h = 1$) to 0.76 (for $h = 5$), 0.89 (for $h = 7$), and 0.96 (for $h = 10$).

In general, the choice of values of α and β depends on the characteristics of the ontologies we are dealing with. A more principled way of choosing α and β might be to set explicit requirements on the value that we want $e^{-\alpha l}$ to have for a pair of two random (i.e., typically unrelated) documents, and on the value that we want $\tanh(\beta h)$ to have for a pair of two very closely related documents.

11.5.1 Removing Lower Levels of the Tree

In this scenario we keep only the upper k levels of the tree, for various values of k. Any concepts located at levels from $k + 1$ on are discarded; instances that used to be assigned to one of the deleted concepts are reassigned to its ancestor on the level $k - 1$ (i.e., the deepest level that was not deleted). We then compare the resulting tree with the original tree. This removal of lower levels of the tree corresponds to the scenario that the ontology is being constructed automatically in a top-down manner (e.g., by hierarchical top-down clustering of instances) and some automatic stopping criterion is used to decide when to stop partitioning the clusters; if we stop too early, the resulting hierarchy will lack the lower levels. The chart in Figure 11.1 shows how the overlap measure (eq. 11.2) and the tree distance measure (eq. 11.3) react to this gradual removal of lower parts of the hierarchy.

We note that the overlap-based similarity measure increases monotonically as more and more levels are kept. The increase is quick at first and slow at the end, which is reasonable because (as has been noted above) the deeper levels of the hierarchy contain relatively few nodes, so discarding them does not alter the hierarchy so dramatically. For instance, if we constructed an ontology in a top-down manner and stopped when the ontology is at most seven levels deep, the OntoRand index

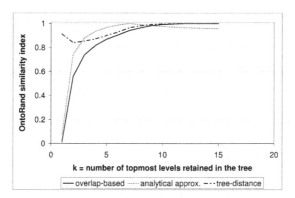

Fig. 11.1. Evaluation of ontologies that lack lower levels, based on the OntoRand index. The overlap-based similarity measure uses eq. (11.2) to define δ_U, while the tree-distance based similarity measure uses eq. (11.3). The dotted line shows an analytical approximation of the OntoRand values based on the overlap similarity measure.

would estimate the similarity of this ontology to the gold standard (having an average node depth of approx. 7) as 0.94. On the other hand, if we stopped after at most three levels, the OntoRand index would be 0.74.

It may be somewhat surprising that the similarity of an ontology to the original one is still as high as 0.74 even if only the top three levels of the ontology have been kept. To understand this, consider a pair of random concepts; in the original hierarchy, they are typically unrelated and are located around the 7th level, so the ancestor sets of eq. (11.2) have an intersection of 1 and a union of around 13, resulting in the overlap measure $\delta \approx 1/13$. In the pruned hierarchy, where only k uppermost levels have been retained, and documents from lower nodes reassigned to the ancestor nodes at level $k - 1$, such a random pair of documents would yield δ around $1/(2k - 1)$. Thus such pairs of documents would push the OntoRand index value towards $1 - |1/13 - 1/(2k - 1)|$. As the "analytical approximation" in the chart shows, this is not an altogether bad predictor of the shape of the curve for the overlap-based measure.

The tree-distance similarity measure is slightly more problematic in this scenario. In the original tree, a typical random pair of instances falls into unrelated concepts that have no common ancestors except the root, i.e., $h = 0$ and thus $\delta = 0$ (or δ close to 0 even if $h > 0$). If a few deepest levels of the tree are removed and instances reassigned to the suitable ancestor concepts, any pair of instances that used to have $h = 0$ will still have $h = 0$, thus its δ according to eq. (11.3) remains unchanged and this pair does not help decrease the similarity measure between the new hierarchy and the original one. This is why the similarity as measured by OntoRand remains relatively high all the time. Only concept pairs with $h > 0$ contribute towards the dissimilarity, because their distance (l in eq. (11.3)) decreases if the lower levels are pruned away and the instances moved to higher-level concepts. Because l is used in the term $e^{-\alpha l}$, decreasing l causes the value of δ to increase for that pair of instances; the more levels we prune away, the larger δ will be compared to its original value, and the OntoRand similarity decreases accordingly. A quirk occurs at the very end, when only one level remains and h drops to 0 even for these pairs of instances; thus δ doesn't increase when we move from two levels to 1: it drops to 0 instead, causing the overall OntoRand similarity to grow again. This non-monotonicity could be addressed by modifying the formula (11.3) somewhat, but it doesn't really have a large practical impact anyway, as in a practical setting the ontology to be compared to the gold standard would certainly have more than one level.

11.5.2 Swapping a Concept and Its Parent

This operation on trees is sometimes known as "rotation." Consider a concept c and its parent concept c'. This operation replaces c and c' so that c' becomes the child of c; all other children of c', which were formerly the siblings of c, are now its grandchildren; all the children of c, which were formerly the grandchildren of c', are now its siblings. If c' formerly had a parent c'', then c'' is now the parent of c, not of c'. The result of this operation is a tree such as might be obtained by an automated ontology construction algorithm that proceeds in a top-down fashion and did not split the set of instances correctly (e.g., instead of splitting the set of instances related to science into those related to physics, chemistry, biology, etc., and then splitting the "physics" cluster into mechanics, thermodynamics, nuclear physics, etc., it might have split the "science" cluster into mechanics, thermodynamics, nuclear physics, and "miscellaneous," where the last group would later be split into chemistry, biology, etc.). How does this operation affect the values of h and l used in eqs. (11.2) and (11.3)? For two concepts that were originally both in the subtree rooted by c, the value of h decreases by 1; if they were both in the subtree of c' but not in the subtree of c, the value of h increases by 1; if one was in the subtree of c and the other outside the subtree of c', the value of l decreases by 1; if one was in the subtree of c' but not in the subtree of c, and the other was outside the subtree of c', the value of l increases by 1; otherwise, nothing changes. The last case includes in particular all those pairs of instances where none belonged to the subtree rooted by c' in the original ontology; this means the vast majority of pairs (unless the subtree of c was very large). Thus the disagreement in the placement of documents is usually quite small for an operation of this type, and OntoRand is close to 1. This phenomenon is even more pronounced when using the similarity measure based on tree distance (eq. 11.3) instead of the overlap measure (eq. 11.2). Therefore, in the charts below (Figures 11.2 and 11.3), we show only the results for the overlap measure and we show $1 -$ OntoRand instead of OntoRand itself.

We performed 640 experiments with this operation, using one of the 640 third-level categories as the category c (e.g., replacing Top/Science/Physics and Top/Science, etc.).

Figure 11.2 shows that the dissimilarity of the ontology after rotation to the original ontology grows with the size of the parent subtree of c, while Figure 11.3 shows that this dissimilarity decreases with the size of c's own subtree. This is reasonable: the more instances there are in c's subtree, the less different it is from its parent, and the less the ontology has changed due to the rotation. For instance, the topmost group of "×" symbols on both charts of Figure 11.3 corresponds to experiments where c was one of the subcategories of the largest second-level category, Top/World. As the right chart on Figure 11.3 shows, the dissimilarity is almost linearly proportional to the difference in the size of the parent subtree and the subtree rooted by c.

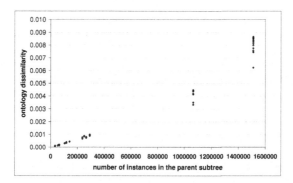

Fig. 11.2. Evaluation of ontologies where a concept c has been swapped with its parent. The chart shows one symbol for each choice of c. The number of instances in the parent subtree (the one rooted by c's parent) is used as the x-coordinate, and the dissimilarity after rotation is used as the y-coordinate.

As we can see, dissimilarity tends to grow approximately linearly with the size of the parent subtree. The groups of symbols on the right represent experiments where c was the child of one of the two largest second-level categories (Top/World and Top/Regional).

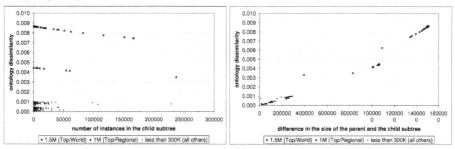

Fig. 11.3. Evaluation of ontologies where a concept c has been swapped with its parent. These charts explore the connection between dissimilarity and the number of instances in c's own subtree. Again each choice of c is represented by one symbol (whose shape depends on the number of instances in the subtree rooted by c's parent). In the left chart, the x-coordinate is the number of instances in c's own subtree; in the right chart, the x-coordinate is the difference in the number of instances between the parent's and c's own subtree.

11.5.3 Reassignment of Instances to Concepts

In the dmoz ontology, each instance is really a short natural-language document consisting of a web page title and description (usually 10–20 words). In this scenario, we follow the standard practice from the field of information retrieval and represent each document by a normalized TF-IDF vector. Based on these vectors, we compute the centroid of each concept, i.e., the average of all documents that belong to this concept or to any of its direct or indirect subconcepts. The cosine of the angle between a document vector and a concept centroid vector is a measure of how closely the topic of the document matches the topic of the concept (as defined by the set of all documents belonging to that concept). We then reassign each document to the category whose centroid is the most similar to the document vector. Thus, the hierarchical relation between concepts remains unchanged, but the assignment of instances to concepts may change considerably. This reassignment of instances to the nearest concepts resembles operations that might be used in an automated ontology construction/population approach (e.g., analogous to k-means clustering). We then measure the similarity of the new ontology (after the reassignment of documents to concepts) to the original one.

For reasons of scalability, the experiments in this section were not performed on the entire dmoz ontology, but only on its "Science" subtree. This consists of 11,624 concepts and 104,853 documents. We compare two reassignment strategies: "thorough reassignment" compares each document vector to the centroids of all concepts, while "top-down reassignment" is a greedy approach that starts with the root concept and proceeds down the tree, always moving into the subconcept whose centroid is the most similar to the document vector. When a leaf is reached, or when none of the subconcept centroids is more similar to the document vector than the current concept's centroid, the procedure stops and assigns the document to the current concept. This is much faster than thorough reassignment, but it has the risk of being derailed into a less promising part of the tree due to bad choices in the upper levels.

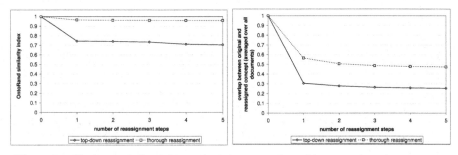

Fig. 11.4. Evaluation of ontology where instances have been reassigned to concepts based on their natural-language descriptions. The number of reassignment steps is used as the x-coordinate. The left chart shows the similarity of the original ontology and the ontology after reassignment. The right chart shows the average distance (as measured by δ_U, eq. (11.2)) between a concept containing an instance in the original ontology and the concept to which the instance has been reassigned.

After documents are reassigned to concepts, new centroids of the concepts may be computed (based on the new assignment of documents to concepts), and a new reassignment step performed using the new centroids. The charts on Figure 11.4 show the results for up to five reassignment steps. The overlap-based definition of δ_U (see eq. (11.2)) was used for both charts.

The left chart in Figure 11.4 shows the similarity of the ontology after each reassignment step to the original ontology. As can be expected, top-down reassignment of documents to concepts introduces much greater changes to the ontology than thorough reassignment. Most of the change occurs during the first reassignment step (which is reasonable as it would be naive to expect a simple centroid-based nearest neighbor approach using 10–20 word descriptions to accurately match the classification of the human editors working for dmoz). In fact, it turns out that 93% of documents are moved to a different concept during the first top-down re-assignment step (or 66% during the first thorough reassignment step). However, the similarity measure between the new ontology and the original one is neverthe-less fairly high (around 0.74). The reasons for this are: firstly, only the assignment of documents to concepts has been changed, but not the hierarchical relationship between the concepts; secondly, if documents are moved to different concepts in a consistent way, δ_U may change fairly little for most pairs of documents, resulting in a high OntoRand index value; thirdly, even though 93% of documents were moved to a different concept, the new concept was often fairly close to the original one. This is shown on the right chart, where the value of δ_U was computed between the concept containing a document in the original ontology and the one containing this document after a certain number of reassignment steps; this was then averaged over all documents. As this chart shows, even though only 7% of documents remained in the same concept during the first step of top-down reassignment, the average (over all documents) δ_U between the original and the new concept is not 0.07 but much higher — approx. 0.31.

11.6 Discussion and Future Work

The main features of our proposed approach are that it focuses on fully automated evaluation of ontologies, based on comparison with a gold standard ontology; it does not make any assumptions regarding the description or representation of instances and concepts, but assumes that both ontologies have the same set of instances. We proposed a new ontology similarity measure, OntoRand index, designed by analogy with the Rand index that is commonly used to compare partitions of a set. We propose several versions of the OntoRand index based on different underlying mea-sures of distance between concepts in the ontology. We evaluated the approach on a large ontology based on the dmoz.org web directory. The experiments were based on several operations that modify the gold standard ontology in order to simulate possible discrepancies that may occur if a different ontology is constructed over the same problem domain (and same set of instances). The experiments show that the measure based on overlap of ancestor sets (Section 11.4.3) is more convenient than the measure based on tree distance (Sec. 11.4.3), because the latter requires the user to define the values of two parameters and it is not obvious how to do this in a principled way. Additionally, the tree-distance based measure is often less successful at spreading similarity values over a greater part of the [0, 1] interval; to address this issue, we propose a modified similarity measure (eq. 11.5), which we will evaluate experimentally in future work. Another issue, which is shared by both sim-ilarity measures proposed here, is that the resulting OntoRand index is sometimes insufficiently sensitive to differences that occur in the upper levels of the ontology (Sec. 11.5.2). Section 11.5.3 indicates another possible drawback of this approach, namely that keeping the structure of the concept hierarchy and modifying only the assignment of instances to concepts may not affect the similarity measure as much as a human observer might expect.

From a purely algorithmic point of view, it would also be interesting to explore if the ontology similarity measure as currently defined in Section 11.4.3 can be accurately computed in sub-quadratic time (in terms of the number of instances).

The experimental evaluation in Section 11.5 could be extended with various other operations. For example, we could split existing leaf concepts into subconcepts, either randomly or using some clustering technique. This is the converse of the operation of removing the leaf concepts described in Section 11.5.1. Another possibly interesting operation would be to merge two or more sibling concepts. As the experiments with switching a concept and its parent showed (Sec. 11.5.2), a rearrangement of concepts in the upper levels of the tree (in our case we were switching a third-level concept and its parent, which is a second-level concept) might have only a very small effect on the similarity measure. Depending on the intended application, this may be undesirable from a human point of view because changes in the upper levels correspond to significantly different decisions regarding the conceptualization of the main concepts (especially the more abstract ones) of the domain of interest. These are important decisions that occur in the early stages of ontology construction; therefore, it might be helpful if our similarity measures could be extended to be more sensitive to such differences in the organization of concepts in the upper levels of the ontology.

11.6.1 Evaluation without Assuming the Same Set of Instances

The proposed approach presented in Section 11.4 assumes that we are comparing two ontologies based on the same set of instances (but with different sets of concepts, different assignment of instances to concepts and different arrangement of concepts into a hierarchy). One way to extend this approach would be to allow for comparison of ontologies based on different sets of instances. In this case it is no longer possible to take a pair of instances and observe where they are placed in one ontology and where in the other, because each ontology has its own separate set of instances. Assuming that each instance is represented by a textual document, some kind of matching would need to be introduced. Given two instances o_i and o_j from the ontology U, one might find a few nearest neighbours of o_i and o_j in the ontology V, and observe δ_V on the pairs of these nearest neighbours. However, this would introduce an additional level of time complexity.

Comparison of two ontologies could also be based on the principle of edit distance. In this case one is looking for a sequence of edit operations that can transform one ontology into the other, while minimizing the total cost (e.g., the number of edit operations). However, if the two ontologies have different sets of concepts (and possibly even different sets of instances), it might be difficult to efficiently find a minimum-cost sequence of edit operations. Some efficient algorithms for comparing ordered trees on the edit distance principle are known (see e.g., [4]), but here we would be dealing with unordered trees.

Another direction that might be promising to explore would be ontology similarity measures based on information-theoretic principles. For example, the variation-of-information metric for comparing two flat partitions of a set of instances [17] has been shown to have a number of desirable and theoretically appealing characteristics [18]. Essentially this metric treats cluster membership as a random variable; two different partitions of a set of instances are treated as two random variables and the mutual information between them is used as a measure of the similarity of the two partitions. This similarity measure could be extended to hierarchical partitions. It would need to roughly answer a question such as: How many bits of information do we need to convey in order to describe, for each instance, where it belongs in the second hierarchy, if we already know the position of all instances in the first hierarchy? A suitable coding scheme would need to be introduced; e.g., for each concept c of the first hierarchy, find the most similar concept c' in the second hierarchy; then, for each instance o from c, to describe its position in the second hierarchy, list a sequence of steps (up and down the is-a connections in the hierarchy) that leads from c' to the concept that actually contains the instance o.

11.6.2 Evaluation without a Gold Standard

It would also be interesting to try evaluating an ontology "by itself" rather than comparing it to a gold standard. This type of evaluation would be useful in many contexts where a gold standard ontology is not available. One possibility is to have a partial gold standard, such as a list of important concepts but not a hierarchy; evaluation could then be based on precision and recall (i.e., observing how many of the concepts from the gold-standard list also appear in the constructed ontology, and vice versa). Another scenario is if a gold standard is not available for our domain of interest but for some other domain, we can use that domain and its gold standard to evaluate/compare different ontology learning algorithms and/or tune their parameters, then use the resulting settings on the actual domain of our interest in the hope that the result will be a reasonable ontology, even though we do not have a gold standard to compare it to.

However, approaches that completely avoid the need for a gold standard could also be considered. In the case of "flat" partitions in traditional clustering, measures such as cluster compactness or inter-cluster distance are often used to evaluate a flat partition: instances from the same cluster should be close to each other, while instances from different clusters should be as far apart as possible. Measures of this sort could also be extended to hierarchical partitions. One could also envision using machine learning methods to evaluate a partition: the partition can be seen as dividing the set of instances into several disjoint classes, and we can try learning a classification model for each class. If the partition of instances into classes was reasonable, one would expect the resulting classifiers to perform better than if the partition was essentially random or unrelated to the attributes of the instances.

11.7 Acknowledgments

This work was supported by the Slovenian Research Agency and the IST Programme of the European Community under SEKT Semantically Enabled Knowledge Technologies (IST-1-506826-IP) and PASCAL Network of Excellence (IST-2002-506778). This publication only reflects the authors' views.

References

1. Bloehdorn S, Haase P, Sure Y, Voelker J, Bevk M, Bontcheva K, Roberts I (2005) Report on the integration of ML, HLT and OM. SEKT Deliverable D.6.6.1, July 2005.
2. Brewster C, Alani H, Dasmahapatra S, Wilks Y (2004) Data driven ontology evaluation. In: Proceedings of the Int. Conf. on Language Resources and Evaluation, Lisbon, Portugal, 26–28 May 2004.
3. Burton-Jones A, Storey V C, Sugumaran V, Ahluwalia P (2004) A semiotic metrics suite for assessing the quality of ontologies. Data and Knowledge Engineering 55(1):84–102.
4. Chawathe S S, Rajaraman A, Garcia-Molina H, Widom J (1996). Change Detection in Hierarchically Structured Information. In: Proc. of the ACM SIGMOD Conference, pp. 493–504, 1996.
5. Ding L, Finin T, Joshi A, Pan R, Cost R S, Peng Y, Reddivari P, Doshi V, Sachs J (2004). Swoogle: A search and metadata engine for the semantic web. In: Proc. ACM Conf. on Information and Knowledge Mgmt, pp. 652–659, 2004.
6. Ehrig M, Haase P, Hefke M, Stojanovic N (2005). Similarity for ontologies — a comprehensive framework. In: Proc. 13th Eur. Conf. Information Sys., 2005.
7. Fox M S, Barbuceanu M, Gruninger M, Lin J (1998). An organization ontology for enterprise modelling. In: Prietula M et al. (eds.) Simulating organizations: Computational models of institutions and groups, AAAI/MIT Press, 1998, pp. 131–152.
8. Gómez-Pérez A (1994) Some ideas and examples to evaluate ontologies. Knowledge Systems Laboratory, Stanford University, 1994.
9. Gómez-Pérez A (1996) Towards a framework to verify knowledge sharing technology. Expert Systems with Applications, 11(11.4):519–529.
10. Grobelnik M, Mladenić D (2005) Automated Knowledge Discovery in Advanced Knowledge Management. Journal of Knowledge Management, 9(5):132–149.
11. Guarino N, Welty C (2002) Evaluating ontological decisions with OntoClean. Communications of the ACM, 45(2):61–65, February 2002.
12. Hartmann J, Spyns P, Giboin A, Maynard D, Cuel R, Suárez-Figueroa M C, Sure Y (2005) Methods for ontology evaluation. KnowledgeWeb Deliverable D1.2.3, January 2005.
13. Haussler, D (1999) Convolution kernels on discrete structures. Technical report, Department of Computer Science, University of California at Santa Cruz, 1999.
14. Levenshtein VI (1966) Binary codes capable of correcting deletions, insertions, and reversals. Soviet Physics Doklady 10(8):707–710.
15. Lozano-Tello A, Gómez-Pérez A (2004) Ontometric: A method to choose the appropriate ontology. Journal of Database Management, 15(2):1–18.
16. Maedche A, Staab S (2002) Measuring similarity between ontologies. In: Proc. 13th Conf. on Information and Knowledge Mgmt. (2002). LNAI vol. 2473.
17. Meila M (2003) Comparing clusterings by the variation of information. In: Proc. of the 16th Annual Conference on Computational Learning Theory, 2003.
18. Meila M (2005) Comparing clusterings — an axiomatic view. In: Proc. of the Int. Conference on Machine Learning, 2005.
19. Mladenić D (1998) Machine Learning on non-homogeneous, distributed text data. Ph. D. thesis, University of Ljubljana, 1998.
20. Mladenić D, Grobelnik M (2003) Feature selection on hierarchy of web documents. Journal of Decision support systems, 35:45–87.

21. Patel C, Supekar K, Lee Y, Park E K (2004) OntoKhoj: a semantic web portal for ontology searching, ranking and classification. In: Proc. of the 5th ACM Workshop on Web Information and Data Mgmt, New Orleans, USA, 2004.
22. Porzel R, Malaka R (2004) A task-based approach for ontology evaluation. In: Proc. ECAI 2004 Workshop on Ontology Learning and Population, pp. 9–16.
23. Rada R, Mili H, Bicknell E, Blettner M (1989) Development and application of a metric on semantic nets. IEEE Trans. on Systems, Man, and Cybernetics, 19(1):17–30.
24. Rand W M (1971) Objective criteria for the evaluation of clustering methods. Journal of the American Statistical Association, 66:846–850.
25. Spyns P (2005) EvaLexon: Assessing triples mined from texts. Technical Report 09, STAR Lab, Brussels, 2005.
26. Supekar K (2005) A peer-review approach for ontology evaluation. In: Proceedings of the Int. Protégé Conf., Madrid, Spain, 2005.
27. Velardi P, Navigli R, Cucchiarelli A, Neri F (2005) Evaluation of OntoLearn, a methodology for automatic learning of domain ontologies. In: Buitelaar P, Cimiano P, Magnini B (eds) Ontology Learning from Text: Methods, Evaluation and Applications, IOS Press, 2005.
28. Völker J, Vrandecic D, Sure Y (2005) Automatic evaluation of ontologies (AEON). In: Proceedings 4th International Semantic Web Conference, 2005.

12

Linguistic Computing with UNIX Tools

Lothar M. Schmitt, Kiel Christianson, and Renu Gupta

12.1 Introduction

This chapter presents an outline of applications to language analysis that open up through the combined use of two simple yet powerful programming languages with particularly short descriptions: **sed** and **awk**. We shall demonstrate how these two UNIX[1] tools can be used to implement small, useful and customized applications ranging from text-formatting and text-transforming to sophisticated linguistic computing. Thus, the user becomes independent of sometimes bulky software packages which may be difficult to customize for particular purposes.

To demonstrate the point, let us list two lines of code which rival an application of "The Oxford Concordance Program OCP2" [21]. Using OCP2, [28] conducted an analysis of collocations occurring with "between" and "through." The following simple UNIX pipe (*cf.* section 12.2.3) performs a similar analysis:

```
#!/bin/sh
leaveOnlyWords $1| oneItemPerLine -| mapToLowerCase -| context - 20|
awk '(($1~/^between$/)||($(NF)~/^between$/))&&($0~/ through /)' -
```

Each of the programs in the above pipe shall be explained in detail in this chapter and contains 3 to 12 essential[2] lines of code.

This chapter is a continuation of [40] where a short, more programming-oriented tutorial introduction to the use of **sed** and **awk** for language analysis can be found including a detailed listing of all operators. A large number of references to [40] including mirror-listings can be found on the internet. A recommended alternative to consulting [40] as supplement to this chapter is reading the manual pages[3] for **sed** and **awk**. In addition, it is recommended (but not necessary) to read [4] and the introductions to **sed** and **awk** in [30].

---

[1] The term UNIX shall stand in the remainder of this chapter for "UNIX or LINUX."

[2] The procedure **leaveOnlyWords** is lengthy because it contains one trivial line of code per single-period-abbreviation such as "**Am.**". It can be computer-generated using **sed** from a list of such abbreviations (*cf.* section 12.3.4).

[3] Type **man sed** and **man awk** in a UNIX terminal window under any shell.

In order to use sed and awk effectively for language analysis, only limited knowledge of UNIX is needed. For proof of this claim and the convenience of the reader, we have listed the minimal number of facts needed to write programs for the Bourne-shell sh such that sed and awk can be combined in the pipe mechanism of UNIX to create very powerful processing devices. See Section 12.2.

An underlying principle in many of the applications presented in this chapter is the fact that the pipe mechanism of UNIX allows the manipulated text to be not only data, but to interact with the UNIX commands/filters in the pipe. From this perspective, the pipe and data are "fluid" rather than static objects. This allows for a very efficient programming style.

Included in this work is a collection of ideas and methods that should enable people to write short, customized applications for language analysis combining the simplicity and the potential of the two programming languages, sed and awk. We shall show that by combining basic components, each containing a few lines of code, one can generate a flexible and powerful customized environment. In addition, more elaborate UNIX tools such as lex [34, 30] or yacc [25, 30], and programming languages such as C [31] or prolog [11] can be used together with the methods presented here. See also [10] for an introduction of certain UNIX tools for language analysis. Note that, e.g., mathematica [47] or some public domain plotting software such as gnuplot [17] can be used to generate graphics from numerical data produced with awk.

The latter parts of this chapter describe methods of application. Some of these applications have been used in [39] which is a system designed to support the teaching of English as a second language by computer means. In particular, we have used sed and awk for analysis and automatic correction of short essays that were submitted as homework by Japanese students of English composition via e-mail. One can use sed and awk to isolate phrases and sentences that were submitted by students and contain critical or interesting grammatical patterns for presentation in class. Other applications of sed and awk in [39] are the analysis of grammatical patterns in students' writings as well as statistical evaluation.

In addition to the applications just described, we can show how to set up a language training environment (cf. [40]), how to develop tools for statistical evaluation of text, be it in regard to concordance (cf. [28] or the example listed above, [38]), in regard to lexical-etymological analysis (cf. [19]), or in regard to judging the readability of text (cf. [22]). In [38], a corpus search for the strings a...òf, an...of, be...to, too...to, for...of, had...of and many...of was conducted. Such a search including the sorting of the results into separate files can also be implemented with a few lines of code. We shall describe how to implement a lexical-etymological analysis on a machine as done in [19] by hand. And, we shall describe how our procedure which counts word frequencies can be used to roughly judge the readability of text (cf. [22]). Finally, we shall indicate how sed and awk can be used to implement special parsers that transform a linear source file for a dictionary (here: [37]) into a multi-dimensional database for the internet. In addition, our exposition contains many comments in regard to other applications using particular features of sed and awk such as identifying Japanese kanji characters in bilingual text or assisting translation.

As outlined above, we present a particularly short and customized introduction to the use of sed and awk under UNIX in language research including a large variety of applications. Scattered reference to sed and awk can be found in descriptions of literary computing, *e.g.*, [18], who uses the tools for literary computing in French. However, we are not aware of any presentation of sed and awk geared toward linguistic analysis with the exception of [39]. We shall demonstrate that sed and awk provide easy-to-understand means to use programming in linguistic research. A genuine alternative to the approach presented in this chapter is using perl [44].

Finally, note that the tools sh, sed and awk which we have used here as well as the pipe mechanism are also available for other operating systems. Consequently, the methods presented here can easily be ported to platforms where these means are available.

12.2 Implementing a Word Frequency Count Using the Bourne-Shell

One can activate the Bourne-shell sh by typing sh↩ in a terminal window on a computer running the UNIX/LINUX operating system. The Bourne-shell sh presents itself with a $ as prompt. It is very important to note that in this state one can test programs for sh interactively line-by-line in the terminal. Typing Control-d in sh causes sh to terminate. For sh, a list of commands that it reads from a file or from a terminal window are indistinguishable. In the remainder of this section, we shall discuss how to set up programs for sh. This is done, in particular, for the purpose of demonstrating how little initial knowledge of UNIX is necessary to start using sed and awk programming in linguistic research.

12.2.1 Creating a UNIX Command Using the Bourne-Shell

Essentially, a sh program is a file containing one sh command per line as well as some multi-line commands. These commands are worked through by sh from top to bottom in the file. Several (single-line) commands can also be separated by semicolons ; and listed on one line. In that case, they are executed from left to right in the line.

Example: Copy the following lines into a file lowerCaseStrings with your favorite text editor:

```
#!/bin/sh
# Comment:  lowerCaseStrings
# (1) Map upper-case characters to lower case.
# (2) Isolate strings of non-white characters on separate lines.
sed  'y/ABCDEFGHIJKLMNOPQRSTUVWXYZ/abcdefghijklmnopqrstuvwxyz/
s/[^a-z][^a-z]*/\
/g' $1
```

Save this file as yourLoginName/lowerCaseStrings directly in your home directory. Then, type cd ; chmod 700 lowerCaseStrings in your currently used shell window[4]. lowerCaseStrings is now a UNIX command just like the built-in ones. Next, type lowerCaseStrings yourTextFile in your shell window to see what the

---

[4] cd sets your working directory to your home directory. chmod 700 lowerCaseStrings makes lowerCaseStrings executable for you in addi-

program does. Here, `yourTextFile` should be a smaller plain-text file in your home directory, and the output of the command will appear in your shell window. It can be redirected to a file (*cf.* Section 12.2.3).

Explanation: The first line `#!/bin/sh` of `lowerCaseStrings` tells whatever shell you are using that the command lines are designed for `sh` which executes the file. The next three lines are comment. Comment for `sh`, `sed` and `awk` starts by definition with a `#` as first character in a line. Note that comment is not allowed within a multi-line `sed` command. The last three lines of `lowerCaseStrings` are one `sh` command which calls `sed` and delivers two arguments (subsequent strings of characters) to `sed`. The first entity following `sed` is a string of characters limited/marked by single-quote characters ' which constitutes the `sed` program. Within that program, the `sed` command `y/ABC...Z/abc...z/` maps characters in the string `ABC...Z` to corresponding characters in the string `abc...z`. In the remainder of this paragraph, the italicized string '*newline*' stands for the "invisible" character that causes a line-break when displayed. The `sed` command `s/[^a-z][^a-z]*/\`*newline*`/g` substitutes(s) every(g) string of non-letters by a single *newline*-character (encoded as[5] `\`*newline*). A string of non-letters (to be precise: non-lower case letters) is thereby encoded as *one non*(^)-*letter* `[^a-z]` followed by *an arbitrary number*(*) *of non-letters* `[^a-z]*`. Consequently, `s/[^a-z][^a-z]*/\`*newline*`/g` puts all strings of letters on separate lines. The trailing `$1` is the second argument to `sed` and stands for the input-file name.[6] In the above example, one has `$1=yourTextFile`.

Remark: We shall refer to a program similar to `lowerCaseStrings` that only contains the first line of the `sed` program invoking the `y` operator as `mapToLowerCase`.

12.2.2 Implementing a Frequency Count Using `awk`

The above `sed` program combined with `awk` makes it easy to implement a simple word frequency count. For that purpose, we need a counting program which we shall name `countFrequencies`. The listing of `countFrequencies` shows the typical use of an array (here: `number`) in `awk` (*cf.* Section 12.4.1.3).

```
#!/bin/sh
# countFrequencies (Counting strings of characters on lines.)
awk '{ number[$0]++ }
     END { for (string in number) { print string , number[string] }}
     ' $1
```

Explanation: `awk` operates on the input (file) line by line. The string/symbol `$0` stands for the content of the line that is currently under consideration/manipulation.

---

tion to being readable and writable. Consult the manual pages entries (*i.e.*, type `man cd` and `man chmod` in your shell window) for further details about `cd` and `chmod`.

[5] `\`*newline* is seen as *newline* character by `sed`. *newline* alone would be interpreted as the start of a new command line for `sed`.

[6] More precisely: the trailing `$1` is the symbol the Bourne-shell uses to communicate the *first* string (*i.e.*, argument) after `lowerCaseStrings` to `sed` (*e.g.*, `yourTextFile` in `lowerCaseStrings yourTextFile` becomes `sed '`*program*`' yourTextFile`). Arguments to a UNIX command are strings separated by white space. Nine arguments `$1...$9` can be used in a UNIX command.

The first `awk` command `{ number[$0]++ }` increments a counter variable `number[`*string*`]` by 1, if the *string* is the content of the current line(=`$0`). For every occurring *string*, the counter `number[`*string*`]` is automatically initiated to 0. The character sequence `++` means "increase by one." If every line contains a single word, then at the end of the file, the counter variable `number[`*word*`]` contains the number of occurrences of that particular *word*. The `awk` command in the last line prints the *string*s which were encountered together with the number of occurrences of these *string*s at the `END` of processing. As in Section 12.2.1, the trailing `$1` stands for the input file.

12.2.3 Using the Pipe Mechanism

Combining `lowerCaseStrings` and `countFrequencies`, we create a UNIX command `wordFrequencyCount` as follows:

```
#!/bin/sh
# wordFrequencyCount
lowerCaseStrings $1 >intermediateFile
countFrequencies intermediateFile
```

The command `wordFrequencyCount` is used as `wordFrequencyCount tFile` where `tFile` is any plain-text file.

Explanation: `lowerCaseStrings $1` applies `lowerCaseStrings` to the first argument (string, filename) after `wordFrequencyCount` (*cf.* Section 12.2.1). The resulting output is then written/redirected via `>` to the file `intermediate File`, which is created if non-existent and *overwritten* if in existence[7]. `inter mediateFile` stays in existence after `wordFrequencyCount` terminates and can be further used. Finally, `countFrequencies intermediateFile` applies the word count to the intermediate result.

Instead of using `intermediateFile`, one can let the UNIX system handle the transfer (piping) of intermediate results from one program to another. The following `sh` program is completely equivalent to the first listing of `wordFrequencyCount` except that the intermediate result is stored nowhere:

```
#!/bin/sh
# wordFrequencyCount (2nd implementation)
lowerCaseStrings $1 | countFrequencies -
```

Explanation: The pipe symbol `|` causes the transfer (piping) of intermediate results from `lowerCaseStrings` to `countFrequencies`. The pipe symbol `|` or the string `|\` can terminate a line, in which case the pipe is continued into the next line. The trailing hyphen symbolizes the virtual file (in UNIX-jargon called "standard input") that is the input file for `countFrequencies`.

We observe that the output of `countFrequencies` is not sorted. The reader may want to replace the last line in the program by

```
lowerCaseStrings $1 | countFrequencies - | sort -
```

employing the UNIX command `sort` as the final step in the processing.

Additional information about programming `sh` and the UNIX commands mentioned above can be obtained using the `man sh` command as well as consulting [30].

---

[7] `>>` instead of `>` appends to an existing file.

12.3 Linguistic Processing with sed

The stream editor sed is the ideal tool to make replacements in texts. This can be used to mark, isolate, rearrange and replace strings and string patterns in texts. In this section, we shall exploit sed's capabilities to present a number of small useful processing devices for linguistic computing which range from preprocessing devices to grammatical analyzers. All of these applications are essentially based upon simple substitution rules.

In our philosophy of text processing, the text itself becomes, *e.g.*, through the introduction of certain markers a program that directs the actions of the UNIX programs that act on it in a pipe.

12.3.1 Overview of sed Programming

A sed program operates on a file line-by-line. Roughly speaking, every line of the input-file is stored in a buffer called the *pattern space* and is worked on therein by every command line of the entire sed program from top to bottom. This is called a *cycle*. Each sed operator that is applied to the content of the pattern space may alter it. In that case, the previous version of the content of the pattern space is lost. Subsequent sed operators are always applied to the current content of the pattern space and <u>not</u> the original input line. After the cycle is over, the resulting pattern space is printed/delivered to output, *i.e.*, the output file or the next process in the UNIX pipe mechanism. Lines that were never worked on are consequently copied to output by sed.

Substitution Programs

The simplest and most commonly used sed programs are short substitution programs. The following example shows a program that replaces the patterns thing and NEWLINE matching the strings thing and NEWLINE in all instances in a file[8] by NOUN and a *newline* character, respectively:

```
#!/bin/sh
sed  's/thing/NOUN/g
s/NEWLINE/\
/g'  $1
```

Explanation: The setup of the entire sed program and the two substitution commands of this program are very similar to the example in section 12.2.1. The first sed command s/thing/NOUN/g consists of four parts: (1) s is the sed operator used and stands for "substitute." (2) thing is the pattern that is to be substituted. A detailed listing of legal patterns in sed substitution commands is given in Appendix A.1. (3) NOUN is the replacement for the pattern. (4) The g means "globally." Without the g at the end only the first occurrence of the pattern would be replaced in a line.

The second substitution command shows the important technique of how to place *newline* characters at specific places in text. This can be used to break pieces of text into fragments on separate lines for further separate processing. There is nothing following the trailing backslash \ which is part of the sed program. See the

---

[8] As before, the symbol/string $1 stands for the filename.

program `lowerCaseStrings` of section 12.2.1 for a non-trivial example using this technique.

We observe that one can also store `sed` commands without the two framing single quotes in a file (say) `sedCommands` and use `sed -f sedCommands` instead of or in any `sh` program as above.

Applications (tagging programs for grammatical analysis): The above example indicates how to examine a text for the overall structure of grammatical patterns occurring in that text. Thereby, lists of verbs, nouns and other grammatical entities can be automatically transformed into `sed` programs that perform identification (see, *e.g.*, the listing of the UNIX command `eliminateList` in Section 12.3.4). Similarly, a dedicated list of words can be automatically formatted into a (search) program in another programming language.

Applications (synonyms/translations through substitution): A custom-de- signed `sed` program similar to the above can be used to replace every word in a file by a bracketed list of synonyms. This can be used as a feedback device to encourage students to use a diversified vocabulary. In addition, note that `sed` can handle Japanese kanji characters. Thus, a custom-designed `sed` program similar to the above where every English word is replaced by a bracketed family of romaji, hiragana/katakana and kanji characters can be used to assist translation of text documents.

Application (cleaning files of control sequences in preprocessing): The replacement in a substitution can be empty. This can, *e.g.*, be used to "clean" a `tex`/`latex` [33] file of control sequences (*e.g.*, \subsection).

The Format of an Addressed sed Command

The format of an addressed `sed` command is   *Address*Command   *Address* can be omitted. In that case, `Command` is then applied to every pattern space. (On first reading, one may think of the pattern space as being the current line of input). If an *Address* is given, then `Command` is applied to the pattern space only if the pattern space matches *Address*. *Address* can be a pattern (regular expression) enclosed within slashes / as described in Appendix A.1, a line number not enclosed within slashes or $ standing for the last line. In addition, a range of addresses in the format *StartActionAddress*,*EndActionAddress*Command   can be used. In that case, `Command` is applied to every pattern space after *StartActionAddress* has been found until and including the pattern space where *EndActionAddress* has been found.

Example: The following program replaces `TX` with `Texas` in all lines that contain the string `USA`.

```
#!/bin/sh
sed  '/USA/s/TX/Texas/g'  $1
```

`sed` commands are terminated by either an immediately following *newline* character, a semicolon, or the end of the program.

One may wish to process the single quote ' using `sed` or `awk`. In a program similar to the one listed above, the single quote ' needs to be encoded as: '\''. This means for `sh`: (1) terminate the string listing the `sed` program temporarily at the first ', (2) concatenate the latter with the literal (\) character ' and (3) continue the string listing the `sed` program by concatenating with the string following the third '. If a `sed` or `awk` program is stored in a file, then the the single quote ' is encoded as itself. The representation of the slash / and backslash characters in **sed** programs are \/ and \\ respectively (*cf.* Appendix A.1).

Application (conditional tagging): A **sed** program similar to the program above can be used for conditional tagging. For example, if a file contains one entire sentence per line, then an *Address* can be used to conditionally tag (or otherwise process) certain items/words/phrases in a sentence depending whether or not that sentence contains a certain (other) key-item that is identified by the *Address* in the **sed** command.

12.3.2 Preprocessing and Formatting Tools

The next simple examples show how text can be preprocessed with small, customized **sed** programs such that the output can be used with much more ease for further processing in a pipe. Alternatively, the code given below may be included in larger **sed** programs when needed. However, dividing processes into small entities as given in the examples below is a very useful technique to isolate reusable components and to avoid programming mistakes resulting from over-complexity of single programs.

Application (adding blanks for easier pattern matching): The following **sh** program adjusts blanks and tabs in the input file (symbolized by **$1**) in such a way that it is better suited for certain searches. This program will be often used in what follows since it makes matching items considerably easier. In what follows, we shall refer to this program as **addBlanks**. All ranges [ ] in the **sed** program contain a blank and a tab.

```
#!/bin/sh
# addBlanks
sed  's/[ ][ ]*/ /g;    s/^ */ /;
      s/ *$/ /;          s/^ *$//'   $1
```

Explanation: First, all strings consisting only of blanks or tabs are normalized to two blanks. Then, a single blank is placed at the beginning and the end of the pattern space. Finally, any resulting white pattern space is cleared in the last substitution command.
Justification: Suppose one wants to search in a file for occurrences of the word "liberal." In order to accurately identify the strings **Liberal** and **liberal** in raw text, one needs the following four patterns (compare Appendix A.1):
```
/[^A-Za-z][Ll]iberal[^A-Za-z]/      /^[Ll]iberal[^A-Za-z]/
/[^A-Za-z][Ll]iberal$/              /^[Ll]iberal$/
```
If one preprocesses the source file with **addBlanks**, only the first pattern is needed. Thus, a **sed**-based search program for **Liberal** and **liberal** is shorter and faster.

Application (Finding words in a text in a crude fashion): The following program is a variation of **addBlanks**. It can be used to isolate words in text in a somewhat crude fashion. In fact, abbreviations and words that contain a hyphen, a slash (*e.g.*, A/C) or an apostrophe are not properly identified.

```
#!/bin/sh
# leaveOnlyWords (crude implementation)
sed   's/[^A-Za-z][^A-Za-z]*/ /g;   s/^ */ /
      s/ *$/ /;                     s/^ *$//'   $1
```

Application (Putting non-white strings on separate lines): The following program is another useful variation of **addBlanks**. It isolates non-white strings of characters in a text and puts every such string on a separate line. This is a very good input format for counting and statistical operations on words. All ranges in the following program [   ] contain a blank and a tab. We shall call this **oneItemPerLine**.

```
#!/bin/sh
# oneItemPerLine
sed '/^[   ]*$/d;    s/^[   ]*//;    s/[   ]*$//;    s/[   ][   ]*/\
/g'  $1
```

Explanation: First, all white lines are removed by deleting the pattern space (**sed** operator d) which includes terminating the cycle[9], *i.e.*, the remainder of the **sed** program is not applied to the current pattern space, the current pattern space is not printed to output, and processing continues with the next line of input. For non-white lines, white characters at the beginning and the end of lines are removed. Finally, all remaining strings of white characters are replaced by newline characters.

Remark: Let us note at this point, that **sed** also has an operator to terminate the program. This is the operator q (quit). For example, **sed '5q' fName** prints the first 5 lines of the file **fName**, since it quits copying lines to the output (no action) at line 5.

Application (Normalizing phrases/items on separate lines): The following **sh** program which removes obsolete blanks and tabs in a file **$1** is somewhat the inverse of **addBlanks**. In what follows, we shall refer to this program as **adjustBlankTabs**. Every range [   ] contains a blank and a tab.

```
#!/bin/sh
# adjustBlankTabs
sed 's/^[   ]*//;    s/[   ]*$//;    s/[   ][   ]*/ /g'  $1
```

Explanation: All leading and trailing white space (blanks and tabs) is removed first. Finally, all white strings are replaced by a single blank in the last substitution command.

Justification: **adjustBlankTabs** standardizes and minimizes phrases (as strings) which may automatically be obtained from e-mail messages with inconsistent typing style or text files that have been justified left and right. This is useful if one wants to analyze sentences or derive statistics for phrases which should be processed as unique strings of characters.

Technique: The following program replaces @ by @@, # by #@, and _ by ## in an input file, *i.e.*, each of the single characters @, #, and _ is replaced by the corresponding pair (consisting of characters @ and # only) in the order of the substitution commands from left to right. In what follows, we shall refer to this program as **hideUnderscore**.

```
#!/bin/sh
# hideUnderscore
sed 's/@/@@/g;    s/#/#@/g;    s/_/##/g'  $1
```

---

[9] See the definition of "cycle" at the beginning of Section 12.3.1.

The following program is the inverse of **hideUnderscore**. In what follows, we shall refer to this inverse program as **restoreUnderscore**. Observe for the verification of the program that **sed** scans the pattern space from left to right.

```
#!/bin/sh
# restoreUnderscore
sed 's/##/_/g;    s/#@/#/g;    s/@@/@/g'  $1
```

Application (using a hidden character as a marker in text): Being able to let a character (here the underscore) "disappear" in text at the beginning of a pipe is extremely useful. That character can be used to "break" complicated, general patterns to mark exceptions. See the use of this technique in the implementations of **leaveOnlyWords** and **markDeterminers** in Section 12.3.3. Entities that have been recognized in text can be marked by keywords of the sort _NOUN_. Framed by underscore characters, these keywords are easily distinguishable from regular words in the text. At the end of the pipe, all keywords are usually gone or properly formatted, and the "missing" character is restored.

Another application is to recognize the ends of sentences in the case of the period character. The period appears also in numbers and in abbreviations. By first replacing the period in the two latter cases by an underscore character and then interpreting the period as a marker for the ends of sentences is, with minor additions, one way to generate a file which contains one entire sentence per line.

12.3.3 Tagging Linguistic Items

The tagged regular expression mechanism is the most powerful programming device in **sed**. This mechanism is not available in such simplicity in **awk**. It can be used to extend, divide and rearrange patterns and their parts. Up to nine chunks of the pattern in a substitution command can be framed (tagged) using the strings \(and \).

Example: Consider the pattern /[0-9][0-9]*\.[0-9]*/ which matches decimal numbers such as 10. or 3.1415. Tagging the integer-part [0-9][0-9]* (*i.e.*, what is positioned left of the period character) in the above pattern yields /\([0-9][0-9]*\)\.[0-9]*/.

The tagged and matched (recognized) strings can be reused in the pattern *and* the replacement in the substitution command as \1, \2, \3 ... counting from left to right. We point out to the reader that the order of \1...\9 standing for tagged regular sub-expressions need not be retained. Thus, rearrangement of tagged expressions is possible in the replacement in a substitution command.

Example: The substitution command s/\(.\)\1/DOUBLE\1/g matches double characters such as oo, 11 or && in the pattern /\(.\)\1/ and replaces them with DOUBLEo, DOUBLE1 or DOUBLE& respectively. More detail about the usage of tagged regular expressions is given in the following three examples.

Application (identifying words in text): The following program shows how one can properly identify words in text. We shall refer to it as **leaveOnlyWords**. (This is the longest program listing in this chapter.)

```
1: #!/bin/sh
```

```
 2: # leaveOnlyWords
 3: sed  's/[^A-Za-z.'\''/-][^A-Za-z.'\''/-]*/ /g
 4: s/\([A-Za-z][A-Za-z]*\)\.\([A-Za-z][A-Za-z]*\)\./\1_\2_/g
 5: s/\([A-Za-z][A-Za-z]*_[A-Za-z][A-Za-z]*\)\./\1_/g
 6: s/Am\./Am_/g;    s/Ave\./Ave_/g;    s/Bart\./Bart_/g;
 7: # The list of substitution commands continues  ...
 8: s/vols\./vols_/g;    s/vs\./vs_/g;    s/wt\./wt_/g;
 9:                                      s/\./ /g;   s/_/./g
10: s/\([A-Za-z]\)\-\([A-Za-z]\)/\1_\2/g;    s/\-/ /g;   s/_/-/g
11: s/\([A-Za-z]\)\/\([A-Za-z]\)/\1_\2/g;    s/\-/ /g;   s/_/\//g
12: s/\([A-Za-z]\)'\''\([A-Za-z]\)/\1_\2/g; s/'\''/ /g; s/_/'\''/g
13: '    $1
```

Explanation: First, all strings which do not contain a letter, a period, an apostrophe, a slash or a hyphen are replaced by a blank (line 3). At this moment, the pattern space does not contain any underscore character which is subsequently used as a marker. The marker (_) is first used to symbolize period characters that are a part of words (abbreviations) and need to be retained. Next (lines 4–5), strings of the type *letters.letters.* are replaced by *letters_letters_*. For example, v.i.p. is replaced by v_i_p. Following that, strings of the type *letters_letters.* are replaced by *letters_letters_*. For example, v_i_p. is then replaced by v_i_p_. Next (lines 6–8) comes a collection of substitution commands that replaces the period in standard abbreviations with an underscore character. Then (line 9), all remaining period characters are replaced by blanks (deleted) and subsequently all underscore characters by periods (restored). Next (line 10), every hyphen which is embedded between two letters is replaced by an underscore character. All other hyphens are then replaced by blanks (deleted), and subsequently all underscore characters are replaced by hyphens (restored). Finally (lines 11–12), the slash (encoded as \/) and the apostrophe (encoded as '\'', *cf.* Section 12.3.1) are treated in a similar way as the hyphen.

Example: The following program finds all four-letter words in a text. The program shows the usefulness of, in particular, **addBlanks** in simplifying pattern matching. We shall refer to it as **findFourLetterWords**.

```
#!/bin/sh
# findFourLetterWords (sed version)
leaveOnlyWords $1  |  addBlanks -  |
sed  's/ \([A-Za-z][a-z][a-z][a-z]\) /_\1/g;    s/ [^_][^_]* //g;
     /^$/d;                                     s/_/ /g;
     =' - |
sed  'N;                                        s/\n/ /' -
```

Explanation: The first **sed** program acts as follows: 1) All four-letter words are marked with a leading underscore character. 2) All unmarked words are deleted. 3) Resulting white pattern spaces (lines) are deleted which also means that the cycle is interrupted and neither the line nor the corresponding line number are subsequently printed. 4) Underscore characters in the pattern space are replaced by blanks. 5) Using the **sed**-operator =, the line number is printed before the pattern space is. This will occur only if a four-letter word was found on a line. The output is piped into the second **sed** program which merges corresponding numbers and lines: 1) Using the **sed**-operator N (new line appended), every second line in the pipe (*i.e.*, every line coming from the original source file $1 which contains at least one four-letter word) is appended via N to the preceding line in the pipe containing solely the corresponding line number. 2) The embedded newline character (encoded as \n) is removed and the two united lines are printed as one.

Application (tagging grammatical entities): The following program shows the first serious linguistic application of the techniques introduced so far. It marks all determiners in an input text file symbolized by $1. We shall refer to it as markDeterminers.

```
 1: #!/bin/sh
 2: # markDeterminers
 3: addBlanks $1 | sed  's/\.\.\./_TRIPLE_PERIOD_/g
 4: s/\([[{(< '"_]\)\([Tt]h[eo]se\)\([]}>> '\''",?!_.]\)/
    \1_DETERMINER_\2_\3/g
 5: s/\([[{(< '"_]\)\([Tt]his\)\([]}>> '\''",?!_.]\)/
    \1_DETERMINER_\2_\3/g
 6: s/\([[{(< '"_]\)\([Tt]hat\)\([]}>> '\''",?!_.]\)/
    \1_DETERMINER_\2_\3/g
 7: s/\([[{(< '"_]\)\([Tt]he\)\([]}>> '\''",?!_.]\)/
    \1_DETERMINER_\2_\3/g
 8: s/\([[{(< '"_]\)\([Aa]n\)\([]}>> '\''",?!_.]\)/
    \1_DETERMINER_\2_\3/g
 9: s/\([[{(< '"_]\)\([Aa]\)\([]}> '\''",?!_]\)/
    \1_DETERMINER_\2_\3/g
10: s/\([[{(< '"_]\)\([Aa]\)\(\. [^A-Za-z]\)/\1_DETERMINER_\2_\3/g
11: s/_TRIPLE_PERIOD_/.../g' -  |  adjustBlankTabs -
```

In the above listing, lines 4–9 are broken at the boundary / of the *pattern* and the *replacement* in the sed substitution commands that are listed. This does not represent correct code. Line 10 shows, in principle, the "correct" code-listing for any of these sed substitution commands.

Explanation of the central sed program: The first substitution command (line 3) replaces the triple period as in "Bill bought...a boat and a car." by the marker _TRIPLE_PERIOD_. This distinguishes the period in front of "a" in "...a boat" from an abbreviation such as "a.s.a.p." The character preceding a determiner[10] is encoded left of the determiner in every pattern (lines 4–10) as range [[{(< '"_], tagged and reused right[11] as \1 in the replacement in the substitution command. The determiner which is specified in the middle of every pattern is reused as \2. It will be preceded by the marker _DETERMINER_ and followed by an underscore character in the output of the above program. The non-letter following a determiner is encoded right of the determiner in the first five patterns (lines 4–8, "those"-"An") as range []}> '\''",?!_.], tagged and reused as \3. The string '\'' represents a single ' (*cf.* section 12.3.1). For the determiner "a" the period is excluded in the characters that are allowed to follow it in the range []}> '\''",?!_] in line 9. If a period follows the character a, then a non-letter must follow in order that a represents the determiner "a". This is encoded as \. [^A-Za-z] in line 10 of the program. The string

---

[10] This means characters that the authors consider legal to precede a word in text.
[11] That is in the continuation of the line below for lines 4–9.

encoded as \. [^A-Za-z] is tagged and reused as \3. After the tagging is completed, the triple period is restored in line 11. For example, the string "A liberal?" is replaced by the program with "_DETERMINER_A_ liberal?".

Application (grammatical analysis): A collection of tagging programs such as markDeterminers can be used for elementary grammatical analysis and search for grammatical patterns in text. If a file contains only one entire sentence per line, then a pattern /_DETERMINER_.*_DETERMINER_/ would find all sentences that contain at least two determiners.

Note that the substitution s/_[A-Za-z_]*_//g eliminates everything that has been tagged thus far.

12.3.4 Turning a Text File into a Program

One can use a sed program to create a program from a file containing data in a convenient format (*e.g.*, a list of words). Such an action can precede the use of the generated program, *i.e.*, one invokes the sed program and the generated program separately. Alternatively, the generation of a program and its subsequent use are part of a single UNIX command. The latter possibility is outlined next.

Application (removing a list of unimportant words): Suppose that one has a file that contains a list of words that are "unimportant" for some reason. Suppose in addition, that one wants to eliminate these unimportant words from a second text file. For example, function words such as *the, a, an, if, then, and, or,* ... are usually the most frequent words but carry less semantic load than content words. See [8, pp. 219–220] for a list of frequent words. The following program generates a sed program $1.sed out of a file $1 that contains a list of words deemed to be "unimportant." The generated script $1.sed eliminates the unimportant words from a second file $2. We shall refer to the following program as eliminateList. For example, eliminateList unimportantWords largeTextFile removes words in $1=unimportantWords from $2=largeTextFile.

```
1: #!/bin/sh
2: # eliminateList
3: # First argument $1 is file of removable material.
4: # Second argument $2 is the file from which material is removed.
5: leaveOnlyWords $1  |  oneItemPerLine -  |
6: sed  's/[./-]/\\&/g
7:      s/.*/s\/\\([^A-Za-z]\\)&\\([^A-Za-z]\\)\/\\1\\2\/g/
8:      ' >$1.sed
9: addBlanks $2  |  sed -f $1.sed  -  |  adjustBlankTabs -
```

Explanation: Line 5 in the program isolates words in the file $1 and feeds them (one word per line) into the first sed program starting in line 6. In the first sed program in lines 6–7 the following is done: 1) Periods, slashes ("A/C"), or hyphens are preceded by a backslash character. Here, the sed-special character & is used which reproduces in the replacement of a sed substitution command what was matched in the pattern of that command (here: the range [./-]). For example, the string built-in is replaced by built\-in. This is done since periods and hyphens are special characters in sed. 2) The second substitution command generates an s-command from a given string on a single line. In fact, out of the pattern space (line) containing solely the string built\-in which is matched by .* and reproduced by & in the substitution command in line 7, the following s-command is generated in $1.sed:

    s/\([^A-Za-z]\)built\-in([^A-Za-z]\)/\1\2/g

Note that all slash and backslash characters occurring in the latter line (except the one in built\-in) have to be preceded by an additional backslash in the replacement

    s\/\\([^A-Za-z]\\)&\\([^A-Za-z]\\)\/\\1\\2\/g

in the generating second substitution command listed above to represent themselves. The list of generated s-commands is stored in a new file $1.sed in line 8. Using sed -f $1.sed in line 9, this file of s-commands is then applied to the file whose name is given to sh as second argument $2.

Application (checking summary writing): With the technique introduced above, one can compare student summaries against the original text by deleting words from the original in the students' writings.

12.3.5 Further Processing Techniques

Processing an input line repeatedly with the same (fragment of the) cycle is an important feature of sed programs and an important technique. This involves the address operator (:) and the loop operator test (t) of sed.   The next example illustrates the basic mechanism in an elementary setup.

Example: The following program moves all characters 0 (zero) to the very right of a line. This shows the typical use of the t operator.

```
#!/bin/sh
# Move all zeroes to the right in a line.
sed ': again;    s/0\([^0]\)/\10/g;    t again' $1
```

Explanation: The first command of the sed program defines the address again. The second command exchanges all characters 0 with a neighboring non-zero to the right. Hereby, the non-zero is encoded as [^0], tagged, and reused as \1 to the left in the replacement in the substitution command. The last command tests whether or not a substitution happened. If a substitution happened, then the cycle is continued at : again. Otherwise, the cycle is terminated.

Application (defining commutation relations and standardization for control sequences in a non plain-text file): In the course of the investigation in [1, 2, 3], techniques were developed by one of the authors to transform the file containing the source file of [37] (which was generated with a What-You-See-Is-What-You-Get Editor) into a prolog database. This raised the following problems:
1) The source is "dirty": it contains many control sequences coming from the wysiwyg-editor which have no meaning, but were used for the format and the spacing in the printed book. Such control sequences had to be removed. This was done using substitution commands with empty replacements.
2) The source cannot be "cleaned" in an easy fashion from the control sequences mentioned in 1). Some of the control sequences in the source are important in regard to the database which was generated. In [37], Japanese words and compounds are

represented using kanji, *on* pronunciation and KUN pronunciation. The *on* pronunciation of kanji is typeset in *italics*. In the source file, the associated text is framed by a unique pair of control sequences. Similarly, the KUN pronunciation of kanji is represented by SMALL CAPS.

3) The source was typed by a human with a regular layout on paper (*i.e.*, in the printed book) in mind. Though quite regular, it contains a certain collection of describable irregularities. For example, the ranges of framing pairs of control sequences overlap sometimes. In order to match *on* and KUN pronunciation in the source file of [37] properly, a collection of commutation rules for control sequences was implemented such that the control sequences needed for pattern matching framed only a piece of text and no other control sequences. These commutation rules were implemented in a similar way as the latter example shows.

Application (sorting results into different files): The following example illustrates how to sort/copy results of text-processing with **sed** into a number of dedicated files. We shall refer to the following program as **sortByVowel**. **sortByVowel** sorts all words in a text file $1=fName into several files depending upon the vowels occurring in the words. For example, all words containing the vowel "a" are put into one file fName.a.

```
1: #!/bin/sh
2: # sortByVowel
3: echo >$1.a;  echo >$1.e;  echo >$1.i;  echo >$1.o;  echo >$1.u;
4: leaveOnlyWords $1  |  oneItemPerLine -  |
5: sed -n  '/a/w '$1'.a
6:         /e/w '$1'.e
7:         /i/w '$1'.i
8:         /o/w '$1'.o
9:         /u/w '$1'.u'
```

Explanation: Line 3 of this **sh** program generates empty files $1.a...$1.u in case the program has been used before on the same file. This is done by *echoing* "*nothing* plus a terminating *newline* character" into the files.[12] First, we observe, that the option[13] **-n** (no printing) suppresses[14] any output of **sed**. Next, observe the use of the single quotes and string concatenation in **sh** in lines 5–9. For example, if the argument $1 to **sh** equals the string fName, then **sh** passes the string /a/w fName.a to **sed** in line 5. Thus, if the current pattern space (input line) contains the vowel "a", then **sed** writes to the file fName.a in line 5. Output by the **w** operator is always appended to an existing file. Thus, the files have to be removed or empty versions have to be created in case the program has been used before on the same file. (Consult **man echo** and **man rm**.) Note that everything after a **w** operator and separating white space until the end of the line is understood as the filename the **w** operator is supposed to write to. Note in addition, that a **w** operator can follow and be part of a substitution command. In that case the **w** operator writes to the named file if a substitution was made.

---

[12] For example, echo 'liberal' >fName overwrites(>) the file fName with the content **liberal***newline*.

[13] When used, options are usually listed directly after a UNIX command with a leading hyphen before the first "real" argument $1 of the command.

[14] Printing can always be triggered explicitly by the print operator **p**. For example, /liberal/p prints the pattern space, if the string **liberal** has been found.

There is no direct output by `sortByVowel`. It is clear how to generalize this procedure to a more significant analysis, e.g., searches for specific patterns or searches for phrases.

12.4 Extending the Capabilities with awk

`awk` is a simple programming language based on pattern recognition in the current line of input and operations on chunks of that line. In that regard, it is very similar to `sed`. In contrast to `sed`, `awk` allows string-variables and numerical variables. Consequently, one can accomplish with much more ease a variety of elaborate manipulations of strings in the current line of input that may depend, in particular, on several previous lines of input. In addition, one can accomplish numerical operations on files such as accounting and keeping statistics of things (*cf.* the example `countFrequencies` in Section 12.2.2). Good introductions to `awk` are [4, 5, 30].

12.4.1 Overview of awk Programming and Its Applications

As mentioned above, `awk` is based on pattern recognition in the current line of input and operations on chunks of that line. `awk` uses pattern recognition as addresses similar to `sed` (*cf.* Section 12.3.1 and Appendix A.1). Furthermore, `awk` partitions the current line of input (input record[15]) automatically in an array of "fields". The fields of the current line of input are usually the full strings of non-white characters in the line. One typical use of `awk` is matching and rearranging the fields in a line similar to the tagging in the substitution command of `sed`. However, the tagging and reuse of tagged expressions in the substitution command of `sed` can usually only be matched by rather complicated programming in `awk`.

The Format of an awk Program

Programs in `awk` need no compilation. An `awk` program looks like the following:

```
awk 'BEGIN     { actionB } ;
     pattern1   { action1 } ;
     pattern2   { action2 } ;
     ...
     END        { actionE }'
```

$action_B$ is executed before the input file is processed. $action_E$ is executed after the input file is processed. The lines with `BEGIN` and `END` can be omitted.

Every line in the above program contains an `awk` command (ignoring the leading string `awk   '` and the trailing `'`). One can store a list of `awk` commands in a file (say) `awkCommands` and use `awk -f awkCommands targetFile` to execute the program on `targetFile`.

`awk` operates on input records (usually lines) in a cycle just like `sed`. $action_1$ is executed if $pattern_1$ matches the original input record. After that, $action_2$ is executed if $pattern_2$ matches the current, possibly altered pattern space and the cycle was not terminated by $action_1$. This continues until the second-to-last line of the `awk` program

---

[15] This is `awk`-jargon. In `sed`-jargon, this was formerly called the pattern space.

is reached. If a *pattern_N*, ($N = 1, 2, ...$), is omitted, then the corresponding *action_N* is executed every time the program reaches that line of code in the cycle. If { *action_N* } is omitted, then the entire input line is printed by default-action. Observe that by default an **awk** program does *not* copy/print an input line (similar to sed -n). Thus, printing has to be triggered by an address *pattern_N* with no corresponding *action_N*, which selects the pattern space, or alternatively, printing can be triggered by a separate **print** statement within *action_N* (similar to the operator **p** in **sed**).

Example: The following program **numberOfLines** prints the number of lines[16] in a file.

```
#!/bin/sh
# numberOfLines
awk  'END {print NR}'  $1
```

numberOfLines prints the built-in counter NR (number of records) at the end of the file. By default setting, which can be changed, records are the lines of input delimited by *newline* characters. The delimiter for records is stored in the built-in variable RS (record separator).

Application (counting the occurrence of word-patterns in text): The following program **countIonWords** counts the occurrence of words ending in "ion" in a text file. Together with a search for the occurrence of words ending in "ment", this gives an indication of the usage of academic vocabulary in the text (*cf.* [13, 14]).

```
#!/bin/sh
# countIonWords
leaveOnlyWords $1| oneItemPerLine -| awk '/ion$/' -| numberOfLines -
```

Explanation: The first two programs of the pipe deliver one word per line into the pipe. The **awk** program[17] /ion$/ invokes the default action **print** the pattern space (*i.e.*, line) for words ending ($) in "ion". The lines which contain such words are then counted by **numberOfLines**.

The Format of an awk Command

As shown above, any **awk** command has the following format:
pattern { *action* } ;
The closing semicolon is optional. If a semicolon follows an **awk** command, then another command can follow on the same line. The commands with the BEGIN and the END pattern must be on separate lines.

If *pattern* matches the input record (pattern space), then *action* is carried out. *pattern* can be very similar to address patterns in **sed**. However, much more complicated address patterns are possible in **awk**. Compare the listings in Appendix A.1 and Appendix A.2. An *action* is a sequence of statements that are separated by semicolons ; or are on different lines.

---

[16] Consult the UNIX manual pages for **wc** in this regard (*i.e.*, type **man wc**).

[17] Alternatively, the **sed** program sed '/ion$/!d' - could be used in the pipe. /ion$/!d does *not* (encoded by the negation operator ! of sed) *delete* (using the deletion operator d) a line (here: word) that ends in "ion". Consult also **man grep** in this regard.

Variables and Arrays

A variable-name or array-name in `awk` is a string of letters. An array-entry has the format `arrayName[index]`. The *index* in `arrayName` is simply a string which is a very flexible format, *i.e.*, any array is by default an associative array and not necessarily a linear array indexed by integers. A *typical example* for use of an associative array showing the power of this concept can be found in Section 12.2.2 of this chapter (`countFrequencies`). Numbers are simultaneously understood as strings in `awk`. All variables or entries of an array that are used are automatically initiated to the empty string. Any string has numerical value zero (0).

Built-In Variables

`awk` has a number of built-in variables some of which have already been introduced. In the next few paragraphs, we shall list the most useful ones. The reader is refered to [4, 5, 40] or the UNIX manual pages for `awk` for a complete listing.

FILENAME: The built-in variable `FILENAME` contains the name of the current input file. `awk` can distinguish the standard input – as the name of the current input file. Using a pattern such as `FILENAME==fName` (*cf.* appendix A.2), processing by `awk` can depend upon one of several input files that follow the `awk` program as arguments and are being processed in the order listed from left to right (*e.g.*, `awk 'awkProgram' fileOne fileTwo fileLast`). See the listing of the program `setIntersection` below in Section 12.4.2.3 for a typical use of `FILENAME`.

FS: The built-in variable `FS` contains the field separator character. Default: sequences of blanks and tabs. For example, the variable `FS` should be reset to `&` (separator for tables in TᴇX), if one wants to partition the input line in regard to fields separated by `&`. Such a resetting action happens often in *action$_B$* matched by the `BEGIN` pattern at the start of processing in an `awk` program.

NF: The built-in variable `NF` contains the number of fields in the current pattern space (input record). This is very important in order to loop over all fields in the pattern space using the `for`-loop construct of `awk`. A typical loop is given by:

　　`for(counter=1;counter<=NF;counter++){ `*actionWith*`(counter) }`.

See the listing of the program `findFourLetterWords` below for a typical use of `NF`. Note that `NF` can be increased to "make room" for more fields which can be filled with results of the current computation in the cycle.

NR: The built-in variable `NR` contains the number of the most recent input record. Usually, this is the line number if the record separator character `RS` is not reset or `NR` itself is not reassigned another value. See the listing of the program `context` below for a typical use of `NR`.

OFS: The built-in variable `OFS` contains the output field separator used in `print`. Default: blank. `OFS` is caused to be printed if a comma "," is used in a `print` statement. See the listing of the program `firstFiveFieldsPerLine` below for an application.

ORS: The built-in variable `ORS` contains the output record separator string. It is appended to the output after each `print` statement. Default: *newline*-character. `ORS` can be set to the empty string through `ORS=""`. In that case, output lines are concatenated. If one sets `ORS="\n\n"`, *i.e.*, two newline characters (see next section), then the output is double-spaced. See the listing of the `awk` program in section 12.5.2 for an application.

RS: The built-in variable RS contains the input record separator character. Default: *newline* character. Note that one can set RS="\n\n". In that case, the built-in variable NR counts paragraphs, if the input text file is single-spaced.

Representation of Strings, Concatenation and Formatting the Output

Strings of characters in awk used in printing and as constant string-values are simply framed by double quotes ". The special character sequences \\, \", \t and \n represent the backslash, the double quote, the tab and the newline character in strings respectively. Otherwise, every character including the blank just represents itself.

Strings or the values of variables containing strings are concatenated by listing the strings or variables separated by blanks. For example, "aa" "bb" represents the same string as "aabb".

A *string* (framed by double quotes ") or a variable var containing *string* can be printed using the statements 'print *string*;' or 'print var;' respectively. The statement print; simply prints the pattern space. Using the print function for printing is sufficient for most purposes. However in awk, one can also use a second printing function printf which acts similar to the function printf of the programming language C. See [40, 31, 4, 5] for further details and consult the manual pages for awk and printf for more information on printf. One may be interested in printf if one wants to print the results of numerical computations, such as statistical evaluations for further processing by a plotting program such as Mathematica [47] or gnuplot [17].

Application (finding a line together with its predecessor in a text): The word "because" is invariably used incorrectly by Japanese learners of English. Because "because" is often used by Japanese learners of English to begin sentences (or sentence fragments), it is necessary to not only print sentences containing the string Because or because, but also to locate and print the preceding sentence as well. The following program prints all lines in a file that match the pattern /[Bb]ecause/ as well as the lines that precede such lines. We shall refer to it as printPredecessorBecause.

```
#!/bin/sh
# printPredecessorBecause
awk  '/[Bb]ecause/ { print previousLine "\n" $0 "\n\n" }
                   { previousLine=$0 }'  $1
```

Explanation: The symbol/string $0 represents the entire line or pattern space in awk. Thus, if the current line matches /[Bb]ecause/, then it is printed following its predecessor which was previously saved in the variable previousLine. Afterwards, two *newline* characters are printed in order to structure the output. Should the first line of the input file match /[Bb]ecause/, then previousLine shall be automatically initiated to the empty string such that the output starts with the first *newline* character that is printed. Finally, every line is saved in the variable previousLine waiting for the next input line and cycle.

Fields and Field Separators

In the default mode, the fields of an input line are the full strings of non-white characters separated by blanks and tabs. They are addressed in the pattern space from left to right as field variables $(1), $(2), ... $(NF) where NF is a built-in variable containing the number of fields in the current input record.   Thus, one can loop over all fields in the current input record using the for-statement of awk and manipulate every field separately. Alternatively, $(1)—$(9) can be addressed as $1—$9. The symbols/strings $0 and $(0) stand for the entire pattern space.

Example: The following program firstFiveFieldsPerLine prints the first five fields in every line separated by one blank. It can be used to isolate starting phrases of sentences, if a text file is formatted in such a way that every line contains an entire single sentence. For example, it enables an educator to check whether his or her students use transition signals such as "First", "Next", "In short" or "In conclusion" in their writing.

```
#!/bin/sh
# firstFiveFieldsPerLine
awk  '{  print $1 , $2 , $3 , $4 , $5  }'  $1
```

Recall that the trailing $1 represents the input file name for the Bourne shell. The commas trigger printing of the built-in variable OFS (output field separator) which is set to a blank by default.

Built-In Operators and Functions

awk has built-in operators for numerical computation, Boolean or logical operations, string manipulation, pattern matching and assignment of values to variables. The following lists all awk operators in decreasing order of precedence, *i.e.*, operators on top of this list are applied before operators that are listed subsequently, if the order of execution is not explicitly set by parentheses.

Note that strings other than those that have the format of numbers all have the value 0 in numerical computations.

• Increment operators ++, --. Comment: ++var increments the variable var by 1 *before* it is used. var++ increments var by 1 immediately *after* it was used (in that particular spot of the expression and the program).

• Algebraic operators *, /, %. Comment: Multiplication, division, and integer division remainder (mod-operator).

• Concatenation of strings. Nothing or white space (*cf.* Section 12.4.1.5).

• Relational operators for comparison >, >=, <, <=, ==, !=, ~, !~. Comment: ==, != stand for "equal" and "not equal," respectively. ~, !~ stand for "matches pattern" and "does not match pattern," respectively. For example, x~/a/ is satisfied, if the string in variable x contains the letter a. If it is not clear what sort of comparison is meant, then awk uses string comparison instead of numerical comparison.

• !. Logical NOT.

• &&. Logical AND.

• ||. Logical OR.

• Assignment operators =, +=, -=, *=, /= and %=. Comment: = is the assignment operator that assigns a value to a variable. The other assignment operators +=, -=, *=, /= and %= exist just for notational convenience as, *e.g.*, in C [31]. For example, var+=d sets var to var+d. This the same as var=var+d.

In addition to the above operators, the following built-in functions can be used in awk programs:

• int, sqrt, exp, log. Comment: int(*expression*) is the integer part of *expression*. sqrt() is the square root function. exp() is the exponential function to base e and log() is its inverse.

- **length**(*string*) returns the length of *string*, *i.e.*, the number of characters in *string*.

- **index**(*bigstring*, *substring*). Comment: This produces the position where *substring* starts in *bigstring*. If *substring* is not contained in *bigstring*, then the value 0 is returned. This allows analysis of fields beyond matching a substring.
- **substr**(*string*, n_1, n_2). Comment: This produces the n_1^{th} through the n_2^{th} character of *string*. If n_2 >**length**(*string*) or if n_2 is omitted, then *string* is copied from the n_1^{th} character to the end.
- **split**(*string*, **arrayName**, **"c"**). Comment: This splits *string* at every instance of the separator character **c** into the array **arrayName** and returns the number of fields encountered.
- **string = sprintf**(*format* , *expr1* , *expr2* ...). Comment: This sets **string** to what is produced by **printf** *format* , *expr1* , *expr2* ... In regard to the printing function **printf** in **awk** or C consult [40, 31, 4, 5] and the manual pages for **awk** and **printf**.

Application (generating strings of context from a file): The next important example shows the use of the functions **index()** and **substr()** in **awk**. It generates all possible sequences of consecutive words of a certain length in a file. We shall refer to it as **context**. Suppose that a file **$1** is organized in such a way that single words are on individual lines (*e.g.*, the output of a pipe **leaveOnlyWords | oneItemPerLine**). **context** uses two arguments. The first argument **$1** is supposed to be the name of the file that is organized as described above. The second argument **$2** is supposed to be a positive integer. **context** then generates "context" of length **$2** out of **$1**. In fact, all possible sequences of length **$2** of consecutive words in **$1** are generated and printed.

```
1: #!/bin/sh
2: # context
3: # First argument $1 is input file name.
4: # Second argument $2 is context-length.
5: awk  'BEGIN { cLength='$2'+0 }
6: NR==1      { c=$0                        }
7: NR>1       { c=c " " $0 }
8: NR>cLength { c=substr(c,index(c," ")+1) }
9: NR>=cLength { print c           }'  $1
```

Explanation: Suppose the above program is invoked as **context sourceFile 11**. Then, **$2**=11. In line 5, the **awk**-variable **cLength** is set to 11. Thereby, the operation +0 forces any string contained in the second argument **$2** to **context**, even the empty string, to be considered as a number in the remainder of the program. In the second command of the **awk** program (line 6), the context **c** is set to the first word (*i.e.*, input line). In the third command (line 7), any subsequent word (input line) other than the first is appended to **c** separated by a blank. The fourth statement (line 8) works as follows: after 12 words are collected in **c**, the first is cut away by using the position of the first blank, *i.e.*, **index(c," ")**, and reproducing **c** from **index(c," ")+1** until the end. Thus, the word at the very left of **c** is lost. Finally (line 9), the context **c** is printed, if it contains at least 11 words **cLength**.

Note that the output of `context` is, essentially, eleven times the size of the input for the example just listed. It may be advisable to incorporate any desired, subsequent pattern matching for the strings that are printed by `context` into an extended version of this program.

Control Structures

`awk` has two special control structures `next` and `exit`. In addition, `awk` has the usual control structures: `if`, `for` and `while`.

`next` is a statement that starts processing the next input line immediately from the top of the `awk` program. `next` is the analogue of the `d` operator in `sed`. `exit` is a statement that causes `awk` to terminate immediately. `exit` is the analogue of the `q` operator in `sed`.

The `if` statement looks the same as in C [31, p. 55]:

      if (*conditional*) { *action1* }
      else { *action2* }

conditional can be any of the types of conditionals we defined above for address patterns including Boolean combinations of comparison of algebraic expressions including the use of variables. If a regular expression /*regExpr*/ is intended to match or not to match the entire pattern space $0 in *conditional*, then this has to be denoted explicitly using the match-operator ˜. Thus, one has to use $0˜/*regExpr*/ or $0!˜/*regExpr*/ respectively. The `else` part of the `if` statement can be omitted or can follow on the same line.

Example: The use of a `for`-statement in connection with an `if`-statement is shown in the next example. We shall refer to the following program as `findFourLetterWords`. It shows a typical use of `for` and `if`, *i.e.*, looping over all fields with `for`, and on condition determined by `if` taking some action on the fields.

```
1: #!/bin/sh
2: # findFourLetterWords (awk version)
3: leaveOnlyWords $1  |
4: awk '        { for(f=1;f<=NF;f++) {
5:                 if($(f)!~/^[A-Za-z][a-z][a-z][a-z]$/) { $(f)="" }
6:               }
7:             }
8:     /[^ ]/ { print NR , $0 }
9:     ' -  |  adjustBlankTabs -
```

Explanation: The `for`-loop in line 4 processes every field (addressed as $(f) in line 5, f the counter variable) from left to right. If a field $(f) does not match the pattern /^[A-Za-z][a-z][a-z][a-z]$/, then it is set to the empty string in line 5. In case the pattern space stays non-white (/[^]/) after this procedure, it is printed in line 8 with a leading line-number NR. Finally, blanks are properly adjusted in the output by `adjustBlankTabs`.

The technique how to loop over associative arrays has already been demonstrated in the listing of the program `countFrequencies` in Section 12.2.2.

Similar to the `for` statement, the `while` statement also looks the same as in C [31, p. 60]: `while ( conditional ) { action }`.

12.4.2 Vectors and Sets

We conclude the section on **awk** by introducing a standard file format called "vectors." For files of this format, we show how to define a large variety of operations such as vector addition/subtraction and statistical operations. In addition, we define set-operations. Such operations are very useful in numerical/statistical evaluations and for comparison of data obtained by methods presented until this point in our exposition.

Definition: Vector (Lists of Type/Token Ratios)

Suppose that one represents frequencies of occurrence of particular words or phrases in the following way in a file: every line of the file consists of two parts where the first part is a word or phrase which may contain digits and the second part (the final field) is a single number which represents and will be called the frequency. A file in this format will be called a *vector (list of type/token ratios)*. An example of an entry of a vector is given by

    limit 55

Mathematically speaking, such a file of word/phrase frequencies is a vector over the free base of character strings [20, p. 13]. The program **countFre- quencies** listed in Section 12.2.2 generates vectors.

Vector Operations

In this section, we show how to implement vector operations using **awk**.

Application (vector addition): The next program **vectorAddition** implements vector addition. If **aFile** and **bFile** are vectors, then **vectorAddition** is used as **cat aFile bFile | vectorAddition -**. The UNIX command **cat aFile bFile** concatenates files **aFile bFile** with the content of **aFile** leading.

vectorAddition can be used, *e.g.*, to measure the cumulative advance of students in regard to vocabulary use.

```
#!/bin/sh
# vectorAddition
adjustBlankTabs $1 |
awk 'NF>1 { n=$(NF); $(NF)=""; sum[$0]+=n                     }
     END { for (string in sum) { print string sum[string] } }
     ' - | sort -
```

Explanation: In the first line of the **awk** program the last field in the pattern space $0 is first saved in the variable **n** before the last field is set to the empty string retaining a trailing blank (*). An array **sum** is generated which uses the altered string $0 in the pattern space as index. Its components **sum[$0]** are used to sum up (**+=**) all frequencies **n** corresponding to the altered string $0. Recall that **sum[$0]** is initiated to 0 automatically. After processing the input this way (at the **END**), the **for**-loop passes through the associative array **sum** with looping index **string**. **string** is printed together with the values of the summations (**sum[string]**). Note that there is no comma in the **print** statement in view of (*). Finally, the overall output is sorted into standard lexicographical order using the UNIX command **sort**.

Application (scalar multiplication): The next program `scalarMultiplica- tion` implements scalar multiplication. If `aFile` is a vector and `n` is a number, then it is used as `scalarMultiplication aFile n`.

```
#!/bin/sh
# scalarMultiplication
# First argument $1 is vector. Second argument $2 is scalar.
awk '{ $(NF)*=('$2'+0) ; print }' $1
```

Explanation: The scalar `$2` is spliced into the `awk` program by `sh` using string concatenation of the strings `'{ $(NF)*=('`, the content of the second argument of the command `$2` and `'+0) ; print }'`. Then, for every input line of the file `$1`, every frequency in the vector which is stored in `$(NF)` is multiplied by the scalar and the resulting pattern space is printed.

Application (absolute value): The next program `computeAbsoluteValue` computes the absolute value of the frequencies of items in a vector.

```
#!/bin/sh
# computeAbsoluteValue
awk '$(NF)<0 { $(NF)=-$(NF) } ;     { print }' $1
```

Explanation: If the last field of an input line is negative, then its sign is reversed. Next, every line is printed.

Application (sign function): Like the previous program, the next program `frequencySign` computes the sign of the frequencies of items in a vector.

```
#!/bin/sh
# frequencySign
awk '$(NF)>0 {$(NF)=1}; $(NF)<0 {$(NF)=-1}; {print}' $1
```

Application (selecting frequencies): The next program cuts away low frequencies from a file `$1` that is a vector. The limit value `$2` is the second argument to the program. We shall refer to it as `filterHighFrequencies`. It can be used to gain files with very common words that are functional in the grammatical sense but not in regard to the context.

```
#!/bin/sh
# filterHighFrequencies
# First argument $1: vector. Second argument $2: cut-off threshold.
awk '$(NF)>='$2 $1
```

Explanation: `$2` stands for the second argument to `filterHighFrequencies`. If this program is invoked with `filterHighFrequencies fname 5`, then `sh` passes `$(NF)>=5` as selecting address pattern to `awk`. Consequently, all lines of `fname` where the last field is larger than or equal to 5 are printed.

Application: The vector operations presented above allow to analyse and compare, *e.g.,* vocabulary use of students in a class in a large variety of ways (vocabulary use of a single student *vs.* the class or *vs.* a dedicated list of words, similarity/distinction of vocabulary use among students, computation of probalility distributions over vocabulary use (normalization), etc.).

Application (average and standard deviation): The following program determines the sum, average and standard deviation of the frequencies in a vector $1.

```
#!/bin/sh
awk  '/[^   ]/ {  s1+=$(NF);  s2+=$(NF)*$(NF)                }
      END     {  print s1 ,  s1/NR ,  sqrt(s2*NR-s1*s1)/NR }'  $1
```

Explanation: The `awk` program only acts on non-white lines since the non-white pattern `/[^   ]/` must be matched. `s1` and `s2` are initiated automatically to value 0 by `awk`. `s1+=$(NF)` adds the last field in every line to `s1`. `s2+=$(NF)*$(NF)` adds the square of the last field in every line to `s2`. Thus, at the end of the program we have $s1=\sum_{n=1}^{NR} \$(NF)_n$ and $s2=\sum_{n=1}^{NR} (\$(NF)_n)^2$. In the END-line, the sum `s1`, the average `s1/NR` and the standard deviation (*cf.* [16, p. 81]) are printed.

Set Operations

In this section, we show how to implement set operations using `awk`. Set operations as well as vector operations are extremely useful in comparing results from different analyses performed with the methods presented thus far.

Application (set intersection): The next program implements set intersection.[18] We shall refer to it as `setIntersection`. If `aFile` and `bFile` are organized such that items (= set elements) are listed on separate lines, then it is used as `setIntersection aFile bFile`. `setIntersection` can be used to measure overlap in use of vocabulary. Consult also `man comm`.

```
#!/bin/sh
# setIntersection
awk  'FILENAME=="'$1'" { n[$0]=1; next };    n[$0]==1'  $1  $2
```

Explanation: `awk` can accept and distinguish more than one input file after the program-string. This property is utilized here. Suppose this command is invoked as `setIntersection aFile bFile`. This means $1=aFile and $2=bFile in the above. As long as this `awk` program reads its first argument `aFile`, it only creates an associative array `n` indexed by the lines $0 in `aFile` with constant value 1 for the elements of the array. If the `awk` program reads the second file `bFile`, then only those lines $0 in `bFile` are printed where the corresponding `n[$0]` was initiated to 1 while reading `aFile`. For elements which occur only in `bFile`, `n[$0]` is initiated to 0 by the conditional which is then found to be *false*.

If one changes the final conditional `n[$0]==1` in `setIntersection` to `n[$0]==0`, then this implements set-complement. If such a procedure is named `setComplement`, then `setComplement aFile bFile` computes all elements from `bFile` that are not in `aFile`.

---

[18] Note that `adjustBlankTabs fName | sort -u -` converts any file `fName` into a set where every element occurs only once. In fact, `sort -u` sorts a file and only prints occurring lines once. Consequently, `cat aFile bFile | adjustBlankTabs - | sort -u -` implements set union.

12.5 Larger Applications

In this section, we describe how these tools can be applied in language teaching and language analysis. We draw on our experience using these tools at the University of Aizu where Japanese students learn English as a foreign language. Of course, any language teacher can modify the examples outlined here to fit a given teaching need.

The tools provide three types of assistance to language teachers: they can be used for teaching, for language analysis to inform teaching, and for language analysis in research. In teaching, the tools can be linked to an email program that informs students about specific errors in their written texts; such electronic feedback for low-level errors can be more effective than feedback from the teacher [43, 45]. The tools can also help teachers identify what needs to be taught. From a database of student writing, a teacher can identify systematic patterns of errors that need to be addressed in class. In addition, one can isolate syntactic structures and lexical items that the students either overuse or avoid using because of their complexity [27].

One can also use the tools to identify (or confirm) the features of expert texts in different research genres. Such texts are organized along similar lines with four sections– Introduction, Methods, Results, and Discussion; further, the Introduction section can be divided into four Moves [42] that use different language structures and lexis. Other features include the location of the thesis sentence [7], the use of hedges such as "perhaps" and "could" [24], and the use of cohesive devices such as repetition to make the text more readable [22]. Since most students are not familiar with such devices, the teacher may need to examine expert texts and use the awk and sed tools to locate similar strings in student writing.

Various commercial tools are currently available for language analysis; however, many of them come in separate packages and are often expensive. Further, they draw on million-word databases that provide accurate results but are overkill for both teachers and students.

The following examples illustrate some of the capabilities of the techniques developed thus far.

12.5.1 Automated Feedback for Spelling and Punctuation

Some of the first mistakes a teacher of English to Japanese students meets are purely mechanical: spelling and punctuation, especially when the students' writing is done on computers with English keyboards (as is the case at the University of Aizu). Japanese university students generally have little experience typing in English, and mechanical mistakes are abundant.

Spelling errors can be identified with the UNIX spell program. In [39], we use sed and awk to reformat the result of the spell check, which is sent back to the student.

More difficult to correct and teach is English punctuation, the rules of which, regarding spacing in particular, are different from Japanese. In fact, written Japanese does not include spaces either between words or after (or before) punctuation marks. At first, this problem may seem trivial. However, hours of class time spent discussing punctuation and yet more hours of manually correcting persistent errors tend to wear on teachers. Persistent errors in English punctuation have even been observed by one of the authors in English printing done by the Japan Bureau of Engraving, the government agency that typesets and prints the entrance examinations for Japanese universities. Clearly, if English punctuation rules (*i.e.*, spacing rules) are not taught explicitly, they will not be learned.

A teacher using an automatic punctuation-correction program such as the one in [39] described below is able to correct nearly all of the students' punctuation problems, thus presenting the spacing rules in an inductive, interactive way. A punctuation-correcting program is one of several tools described in [35].

As a database, we have defined a list of forbidden pairs of characters. This is achieved by listing the matrix M pertaining to the relation R which is given by $char_1$ R $char_2$ $\Leftrightarrow$ "The character sequence $char_1char_2$ is forbidden." During the setup phase of the system used in [39], the matrix M is translated by an **sed** program into a new **sed** program which scans the essays submitted by students via electronic mail for mistakes. Examples for forbidden sequences are *blank,* or *'?*. These mistakes are marked, and the marked essays are sent back to the individual students automatically. The translation into a **sed** program during setup works in the same way as the generation of an elimination program shown above in Section 12.3.4. The resulting marking program is very similar to **markDeterminers**. Suffice it to say that this automated, persistent approach to correcting punctuation has been an immediate and dramatic success [39].

Finally, let us remark that our procedure for identifying mistakes in punctuation can also be used in analyses of punctuation patterns, frequency, and use, as in [36].

12.5.2 Extracting Sentences

In [39], one of the tools reformats student essays in such a way that entire sentences are on single lines. Such a format is very useful in two ways:

Goal 1: To select actual student sentences which match certain patterns. The teacher can then write any number of programs that search for strings identified as particularly problematic for a given group of students. For example, the words "because" and "too" are frequently used incorrectly by Japanese speakers of English. Furthermore, once those strings have been identified, the sentences containing them can be saved in separate files according to the strings and printed as lists of individual sentences. Such lists can then be given to students in subsequent lessons dealing with the problem areas for the students to read and determine whether they are correct or incorrect, and if incorrect, how to fix them.

Goal 2: To analyze example sentences. One example is to measure the complexity of grammatical patterns used by students using components such as **markDeterminers**. This can be used to show the decrease or increase of certain patterns over time using special **sed** based search programs and, *e.g.*, **countFrequencies** as well as **mathematica** for display.

Our procedure for identifying sentences achieves a high level of accuracy without relying on proper spacing as a cue for sentence division, as does another highly accurate divider [26].

The following shows part of the implementation of sentence identification in [39]:

```
#!/bin/sh
hideUnderscore $1 | hideAbbreviations - |
hideNumbers      - | adjustBlankTabs   - |
```

The implementations of **hideUnderscore** and **hideAbbreviations** have been discussed above. Compare also the listing of **leaveOnlyWords** given above **hideNumbers** replaces, *e.g.*, the string $1.000.000 by $1_000_000, thus, "hiding" the decimal points in numbers. The next **sed** program listed below defines the ends of sentences. This is the most important component of the pipe which we show for reference.

```
1: sed 's/\(([^]})'\''".!?][]}).!?]*\)\(([!?]\)
      \(([]})]*\)\(([^]})'\''".!?]\)/\1\2\3__\2__\
2: \4/g
3: s/\(([^]})'\''".!?][]}).!?]*\)\(([!?]\)\(([]})]*\)$/\1\2\3__\2__/
4: s/\(([^]})'\''".!?][]})'\''".!?]*\.
      []})'\''"]*\)\(([^]})'\''".!?]\)/\1__.__\
5: \2/g
6: s/[^]})'\''".!?][]})'\''".!?]*\.[]})'\''"]*$/&__.__/' |
```

Explanation: Line 1 of this listing is broken after \(([!?]\) representing the end of the sentence . In the first two **sed** commands (lines 1–3), the end of the sentence for "?" and "!" are defined. The similar treatment of "?" and "!" is implemented by using a range [!?] which is the second tagged entity in the patterns in lines 1 and 3. Thus, the letter ending the sentence is represented by \2. The range-sequence [^]})'\''".!?] followed by []}).!?]* defines admissible strings before the end of a sentence. It is the first tagged entity \1 in the patterns in lines 1 and 3. The range-sequence represents at least one non-closing character, followed by a possible sequence of allowed closing characters. A sentence may be multiply bracketed in various ways. This is represented by the range []})]* which is the third tagged entity \3 in the patterns in lines 1 and 3. After the possible bracketing is finished, there should not follow another closing (brackets, quotes) or terminating character ".", "?" or "!". (This handles exactly the case of the previous sentence.) The excluded terminating character is encoded as [^]})'\''".!?] in line 1, and is the fourth tagged item \4. In the substitution part of the **sed** command in lines 1–2, the originally tagged sequence (\1\2\3\4) is replaced by \1\2\3__\2__*newline*\4. Thus, after the proper ending of the sentence in \3, a marker __\2__ is introduced for sorting/identification purposes. Then, a *newline* character is introduced such that the next sentence starting in \4 starts on a new line. Line 3 handles the case when the sentence-end in "?" or "!" coincides with the end of the line.

Line 4 of this listing is broken after \. representing the period (and not an arbitrary character) ending the sentence. The last two substitution rules in lines 4–6 for marking sentences that end in a period are different than those for "?" and "!". But the principles are similar. In line 4, the range-sequence [^]})'\''".!?][]})'\''".!?] followed by []})'\''".!?]* defines admissible strings before the end of a sentence. The range-sequence represents at least one non-closing character, followed by a possible sequence of allowed closing characters. Then the closing period is explicitly encoded as \. The range-sequence []})'\''"]* (closing brackets) followed by [^]})'\''".!?] (non-closing character) defines admissible strings after the end of a sentence. Line 7 handles the case when the sentence-end coincides with the end of the line.

Next follows an **awk** program in the pipe which is shown below:

```
awk 'BEGIN    { ORS=" " }
              { print }
```

```
/__[!?.]__$/ { print "\n" }' | ...
```

Explanation: The program merges lines that are not marked as sentence endings by setting the output record separator ORS to a blank. If a line-end is marked as sentence-end, then an extra newline character is printed.

Next, we merge all lines which start, *e.g.*, in a lower case word with its predecessor since this indicates that we have identified a sentence within a sentence. Finally, markers are removed and the "hidden" things are restored in the pipe. By convention, we deliberately accept that an abbreviation does not terminate a sentence. Overall, our procedure creates double sentences on lines in rare cases. Nevertheless, this program is sufficiently accurate for the objectives outlined above in (1) and (2). Note that it is easy to scan the output for lines possibly containing two sentences and subsequently inspect a "diagnostic" file.

Application: The string "and so on" is extremely common in the writing of Japanese learners of English, and it is objected to by most teachers. From the examples listed above such as printPredecessorBecause, it is clear how to connect the output of the sentence finder with a program that searches for and so on.

In [46], 121 very common mistakes made by Japanese students of English are documented. We point out to the reader that a full 75 of these can be located in student writing using the most simple of string-search programs, such as those introduced above.

12.5.3 Readability of Texts

Hoey [22, pp. 35–48, 231–235] points out that the more cohesive a foreign language text, the easier it is for learners of the language to read. One method Hoey proposes for judging relative cohesion, and thus readability, is by merely counting the number of repeated content words in the text (repetition being one of the main cohesive elements of texts in many languages). Hoey concedes though that doing this "rough and ready analysis" [22, p. 235] by hand is tedious work, and impractical for texts of more than 25 sentences.

An analysis like this is perfectly suited for the computer, however. In principle, any on-line text could be analyzed in terms of readability based on repetition. One can use countWordFrequencies or a similar program to determine word frequencies over an entire text or "locally." Entities to search through "locally" could be paragraphs or all blocks of, *e.g.*, 20 lines of text. The latter procedure would define a flow-like concept that could be called "local context." Words that appear at least once with high local frequency are understood to be important. A possible extension of countWordFrequencies is to use spell -x to identify derived words such as Japanese from Japan. Such a procedure aids teachers in deciding which vocabulary items to focus on when assigning students to read the text, *i.e.*, the most frequently occurring ones ordered by their appearance in the text.

Example: The next program implements a search for words that are locally repeated (*i.e.*, within a string of 200 words) in a text. In fact, we determine the frequencies of words in a file $1 that occur first and are repeated at least three times within all possible strings of 200 consecutive words. 200 is an upper bound for the analysis performed in [22, pp. 35–48].

```
#!/bin/sh
leaveOnlyWords $1 | oneItemPerLine   | context - 200 |
quadrupleWords - | countFrequencies -
```

Explanation: `leaveOnlyWords $1 | oneItemPerLine | context - 200` generates all possible strings of 200 consecutive words in the file `$1`. `quadrupleWords` picks those words which occur first and are repeated at least three times within lines. An implementation of `quadrupleWords` is left as an exercise; or consult [40]. `countFrequencies` determines the word frequencies of the determined words.

Note again that `context - 200` creates an intermediate file which essentially is 200 times the size of the input. If one wants to apply the above to large files, then the subsequent search in `quadrupleWords` should be combined with `context - 200`.

We have applied the above procedure to the source file of an older version of this document. Aside from function-words such as *the* and a few names, the following were found with high frequency: *UNIX, address, awk, character, command, field, format, liberal, line, pattern, program, sed, space, string, students, sum,* and *words.*

12.5.4 Lexical-Etymological Analysis

In [19], the author determined the percentage of etymologically related words shared by Serbo-Croatian, Bulgarian, Ukrainian, Russian, Czech, and Polish. The author looked at 1672 words from the above languages to determine what percentage of words each of the six languages shared with each of the other six languages. He did this analysis by hand using a single source. This kind of analysis can help in determining the validity of traditional language family groupings, *e.g.*:
• Is the west-Slavic grouping of Czech, Polish, and Slovak supported by their lexica?
• Do any of these have a significant number of non-related words in its lexicon?
• Is there any other language not in the traditional grouping worthy of inclusion based on the number of words it shares with those in the group?

Information of this kind could also be applied to language teaching/learning by making certain predictions about the "learnability" of languages with more or less similar lexica and developing language teaching materials targeted at learners from a given related language (*e.g.*, Polish learners of Serbo-Croatian).

Disregarding a discussion about possible copyright violations, it is easy today to scan a text written in an alphabetic writing system into a computer to obtain automatically a file format that can be evaluated by machine and, finally, do such a lexical analysis of sorting/counting/intersecting with the means we have described above. The source can be a text of any length. The search can be for any given (more or less narrowly defined) string or number thereof. In principle, one could scan in (or find on-line) a dictionary from each language in question to use as the source-text. Then one could do the following:

1) Write rules using **sed** to "level" or standardize the orthography to make the text uniform.

2) Write rules using **sed** to account for historical sound and phonological changes. (Such rules are almost always systematic and predictable. For example: the German intervocalic "t" is changed in English to "th." Exceptional cases could be included in the programs explicitly. All of these rules already exist, thanks to the efforts of historical linguists over the last century (*cf.* [15]).

Finally, there has to be a definition of unique one-to-one relations of lexica for the languages under consideration. Of course, this has to be done separately for every pair of languages.

12.5.5 Corpus Exploration and Concordance

The following **sh** program shows how to generate the surrounding context for words from a text file **$1**, *i.e.*, the file name is first argument **$1** to the program. The second argument to the program, *i.e.*, **$2**, is supposed to be a strictly positive integer. In this example, two words are related if there are not more that (**$2**)−2 other words in between them.

```
1: #!/bin/sh
2: # surroundingContext
3: leaveOnlyWords $1 | oneItemPerLine - |
4: mapToLowerCase -  | context - $2     |
5: awk '{ for (f=2;f<=NF;f++) { print $1,$(f) } }' |
6: countFrequencies -
```

Explanation: If a file contains the strings (words) **aa**, **ab**, **ac**, ... **zz** and **$2=6**, then the first line of output of the code in lines 3–4 (into the pipe continued at line 5) would be **aa ab ac ad ae af**. That is what the **awk** program in line 5 would see as first line of input. The **awk** program would then print **aa ab**, **aa ac**, ... **aa af** on separate lines as response to that first line of input. The occurrence of such pairs is then counted by **countFrequencies**. This defines a matrix M_d of directed context (asymmetric relation) between the words in a text. M_d is indexed by pairs of words ($word_1$, $word_2$). If the frequency of the entry in M_d pertaining to ($word_1$, $word_2$) is low, then the two words $word_1$ and $word_2$ are distant or unrelated.

Applying the procedure listed above to the source file of an older version of this document and filtering out low frequencies using **filterHighFrequencies - 20** the following pairs of word were found in close proximity among a long list containing otherwise mostly "noise": (address pattern), (awk print), (awk program), (awk sed), (echo echo), (example program), (hold space), (input line), (liberal liberal), (line number), (newline character), (pattern space), (print print), (program line), (range sed), (regular expressions), (sed program), (sh awk), (sh bin), (sh program), (sh sed), (string string), and (substitution command).

Using the simple program listed above or some suitable modification, any language researcher or teacher can conduct basic concordancing and text analysis without having to purchase sometimes expensive and often inflexible concordancing or corpus-exploration software packages. See the example given in the introduction.

In [38], a corpus search for the strings characterized by the following **awk** patterns

```
(a|(an)|(for)|(had)|(many)) [A-Za-z'-]+ of
((be)|(too)) [A-Za-z'-]+ to
```

was conducted. Modifying the program listed in the introduction as follows would allow the user to search for these strings and print the strings themselves and ten words to both the right and left of the patterns in separate files.

```
#!/bin/sh
leaveOnlyWords $1| oneItemPerLine -| mapToLowerCase -| context - 23|
awk '($(11)~/^((an?)|(for)|(had)|(many))$/)&&($(13)=="of") {
                    File="'$1'." $(11) ".of"; print>File }
    ($(11)~/^((be)|(too))$/)              &&($(13)=="to") {
                    File="'$1'." $(11) ".to"; print>File }' -
```

It has been noted in several corpus studies of English collocation ([32, 41, 6]) that
searching for 5 words on either side of a given word will find 95% of collocational co-
occurrence in a text. After a search has been done for all occurrences of word $word_1$
and the accompanying 5 words on either side in a large corpus, one can then search
the resulting list of surrounding words for multiple occurrences of word $word_2$ to
determine with what probability $word_1$ co-occurs with $word_2$. The formula in [12, p.
291] can then be used to determine whether an observed frequency of co-occurrence
in a given text is indeed significantly greater than the expected frequency.

In [9], the English double genitive construction, *e.g.*, "a friend of mine" is
compared in terms of function and meaning to the preposed genitive construction "my friend." In this situation, a simple search for strings containing **of**
((mine)|(yours)|...) (*dative possessive pronouns*) and **of** .*'s would locate all
of the double genitive constructions (and possibly the occasional contraction, which
could be discarded during the subsequent analysis). In addition, a search for *nom-
inative possessive pronouns* and **of** .*'s together with the ten words that follow
every occurrence of these two grammatical patterns would find all of the preposed
genitives (again, with some contractions). Furthermore, a citation for each located
string can be generated that includes document title, approximate page number and
line number.

12.5.6 Reengineering Text Files across Different File Formats

In the course of the investigations outlined in [1, 2, 3], one of the authors developed
a family of programs that are able to transform the source file of [37], which was
typed with a *what-you-see-is-what-you-get* editor into a `prolog` database. In fact,
any machine-readable format can now be generated by slightly altering the programs
already developed.

The source was available in two formats: 1) an RTF format file, and 2) a text
file free of control sequences that was generated from the first file. Both formats
have advantages and disadvantages. As outlined in Section 12.3.5, the RTF format
file distinguishes Japanese *on* and KUN pronunciation from ordinary English text
using *italic* and SMALL CAP typesetting, respectively. On the other hand, the RTF
format file contains many control sequences that make the text "dirty" in regard
to machine evaluation. We have already outlined in Section 12.3.5 how unwanted
control sequences in the RTF format file were eliminated, but valuable information
in regard to the distinction of *on* pronunciation, KUN pronunciation and English
was retained. The second control-sequence-free file contains the standard format of
kanji which is better suited for processing in the UNIX environment we used. In
addition, this format is somewhat more regular, which is useful in regard to pattern
matching that identifies the three different categories of entries in [37]: *radical, kanji*
and *compound*. However, very valuable information is lost in the second file in regard
to the distinction between *on* pronunciation, KUN pronunciation and English.

Our first objective was to merge both texts line-by-line and to extract from every pair of lines the relevant information. Merging was achieved through pattern matching, observing that not all but most lines correspond one-to-one in both sources. Kanji were identified through use of the **sed** operator l[19]. As outlined in Section 12.3.5, control sequences were eliminated from the RTF format file but the information some of them represent was retained.

After the source files were properly cleaned by **sed** and the different pieces from the two sources identified (tagged), **awk** was used to generate a format from which all sorts of applications are now possible. The source file of [37] is typed regularly enough such that the three categories of entry *radical, kanji* and *compound* can be identified using pattern matching. In fact, a small grammar was defined for the structure of the source file of [37] and verified with **awk**. By simply counting all units, an index for the dictionary which does not exist in [37] can now be generated. This is useful in finding compounds in a search over the database and was previously impossible. In addition, all relevant pieces of data in the generated format can be picked by **awk** as fields and framed with, *e.g.*, **prolog** syntax. It is also easy to generate, *e.g.*, English→*kanji* or English→KUN dictionaries from this *kanji→on*/KUN→English dictionary using the UNIX command **sort** and rearrangement of fields. In addition, it is easy to reformat [37] into proper **jlatex** format. This could be used to re-typeset the entire dictionary.

12.6 Conclusion

In the previous exposition, we have given a short but detailed introduction to **sed** and **awk** and their applications to language analysis. We have shown that developing sophisticated tools with **sed** and **awk** is easy even for the computer novice. In addition, we have demonstrated how to write customized filters with particularly short code that can be combined in the UNIX environment to create powerful processing devices particularly useful in language research.

Applications are searches of words, phrases, and sentences that contain interesting or critical grammatical patterns in any machine readable text for research and teaching purposes. We have also shown how certain search or tagging programs can be generated automatically from simple word lists. Part of the search routines outlined above can be used to assist the instructor of English as a second language through automated management of homework submitted by students through electronic mail [39]. This management includes partial evaluation, correction and answering of the homework by machine using programs written in **sed** and/or **awk**. In that regard, we have also shown how to implement a punctuation checker.

Another class of applications is the use of **sed** and **awk** in concordancing. A few lines of code can substitute for an entire commercial programming package. We have shown how to duplicate in a simple way searches performed by large third-party packages. Our examples include concordancing for pairs of words, other more general patterns, and the judgement of readability of text. The result of such searches can be sorted and displayed by machine for subsequent human analysis. Another possibility

---

[19] The **sed** operator l lists the pattern space on the output in an unambiguous form. In particular, non-printing characters are spelled in two-digit ASCII and long lines are folded.

is to combine the selection schemes with elementary statistical operations. We have shown that the latter can easily be implemented with awk.

A third class of application of sed and awk is lexical-etymological analysis. Using sed and awk, dictionaries of related languages can be compared and roots of words determined through rule-based and statistical analysis.

Various selection schemes can easily be formulated and implemented using set and vector operations on files. We have shown the implementation of set union, set complement, vector addition, and other such operations.

Finally, all the above shows that sed and awk are ideally suited for the development of prototype programs in certain areas of language analysis. One saves time in formatting the text source into a suitable database for certain types of programming languages such as prolog. One saves time in compiling and otherwise handling C, which is required if one does analysis with lex and yacc. In particular, if the developed program runs only a few times this is very efficient.

Disclaimer

The authors do not accept responsibility for any line of code or any programming method presented in this work. There is absolutely no guarantee that these methods are reliable or even function in any sense. Responsibility for the use of the code and methods presented in this work lies solely in the domain of the applier/user.

References

1. H. Abramson, S. Bhalla, K.T. Christianson, J.M. Goodwin, J.R. Goodwin, J. Sarraille (1995): Towards CD-ROM based Japanese ↔ English dictionaries: Justification and some implementation issues. IN: *Proc. 3rd Natural Language Processing Pacific-Rim Symp.* (Dec. 4–6, 1995), Seoul, Korea
2. H. Abramson, S. Bhalla, K.T. Christianson, J.M. Goodwin, J.R. Goodwin, J. Sarraille, L.M. Schmitt (1996): Multimedia, multilingual hyperdictionaries: A Japanese ↔ English example. Paper presented at the *Joint Int. Conf. Association for Literary and Linguistic Computing and Association for Computers and the Humanities* (June 25–29, 1996), Bergen, Norway, available from the authors
3. H. Abramson, S. Bhalla, K.T. Christianson, J.M. Goodwin, J.R. Goodwin, J. Sarraille, L.M. Schmitt (1996): The Logic of Kanji lookup in a Japanese ↔ English hyperdictionary. Paper presented at the *Joint Int. Conf. Association for Literary and Linguistic Computing and Association for Computers and the Humanities* (June 25–29, 1996), Bergen, Norway, available from the authors
4. A.V. Aho, B.W. Kernighan, P.J. Weinberger (1978): awk — A Pattern Scanning and Processing Language (2nd ed.). IN: B.W. Kernighanm, M.D. McIlroy (eds.), *UNIX programmer's manual (7th ed.)*, Bell Labs, Murray Hill, http://cm.bell-labs.com/7thEdMan/vol2/awk
5. A.V. Aho, B.W. Kernighan, P.J. Weinberger (1988): *The AWK programming language*. Addison-Wesley, Reading, MA
6. B.T.S. Atkins (1992): *Acta Linguistica Hungarica* **41**:5–71
7. J. Burstein, D. Marcu (2003): *Computers and the Humanities* **37**:455–467

8. C. Butler (1985): *Computers in linguistics*. Basil Blackwell, Oxford
9. K.T. Christianson (1997): *IRAL* **35**:99–113
10. K. Church (1990): Unix for Poets. Tutorial at *13th Int. Conf. on Computational Linguistics, COLING-90* (August 20–25, 1990), Helsinki, Finland, http://www.ling.lu.se/education/homepages/LIS131/unix_for_poets.pdf
11. W.F. Clocksin, C.S. Mellish (1981): *Programming in Prolog*. Springer, Berlin
12. A. Collier (1993): Issues of large-scale collocational analysis. IN: J. Aarts, P. De Haan, and N. Oostdijk (eds.), *English language corpora: Design, analysis and exploitation*, Editions Rodopi, B.V., Amsterdam
13. A. Coxhead (2000): *TESOL Quarterly* **34**:213–238
14. A. Coxhead (2005): Academic word list. Retrieved Nov. 30, 2005, http://www.vuw.ac.nz/lals/research/awl/
15. A. Fox (1995): *Linguistic Reconstruction: An Introduction to Theory and Method*. Oxford Univ. Press, Oxford
16. P.G. Gänssler, W. Stute (1977): *Wahrscheinlichkeitstheorie*. Springer, Berlin
17. GNUPLOT 4.0. Gnuplot homepage, http://www.gnuplot.info
18. J.D. Goldfield (1986): An Approach to Literary Computing in French. IN: *Méthodes quantitatives et informatiques dans l'étude des textes*, Slatkin-Champion, Geneva
19. M. Gordon (1996): What does a language's lexicon say about the company it keeps?: A slavic case study. Paper presented at *Annual Michigan Linguistics Soc. Meeting* (October 1996), Michigan State Univ., East Lansing, MI
20. W. Greub (1981): *Linear Algebra*. Springer, Berlin
21. S. Hockey, J. Martin (1988): *The Oxford concordance program: User's manual (Ver. 2)*. Oxford Univ. Computing Service, Oxford
22. M. Hoey (1991): *Patterns of lexis in text*. Oxford Univ. Press, Oxford
23. A.G. Hume, M.D. McIlroy (1990): *UNIX programmer's manual (10th ed.)*. Bell Labs, Murray Hill
24. K. Hyland (1997): *J. Second Language Writing* **6**:183–205
25. S.C. Johnson (1978): Yacc: Yet another compiler-compiler. IN: B.W. Kernighan, M.D. McIlroy (eds.), *UNIX programmer's manual (7th ed.)*, Bell Labs, Murray Hill, http://cm.bell-labs.com/7thEdMan/vol2/yacc.bun
26. G. Kaye (1990): A corpus builder and real-time concordance browser for an IBM PC. IN: J. Aarts, W. Meijs (eds.), *Theory and practice in corpus linguistics*, Editions Rodopi, B.V., Amsterdam
27. P. Kaszubski (1998): Enhancing a writing textbook: a nationalist perspective. IN: S. Granger (ed.), *Learner English on Computer*, Longman, London
28. G. Kennedy (1991): *Between* and *through*: The company they keep and the functions they serve. IN: K. Aijmer, B. Altenberg (eds.), *English corpus linguistics*, Longman, New York
29. B.W. Kernighan, M.D. McIlroy (1978): *UNIX programmer's manual (7th ed.)*. Bell Labs, Murray Hill
30. B.W. Kernighan, R. Pike (1984): *The UNIX programming environment*. Prentice Hall, Englewood Cliffs, NJ
31. B.W. Kernighan, D.M. Ritchie (1988): *The C programming language*. Prentice Hall, Englewood Cliffs, NJ
32. G. Kjellmer (1989): Aspects of English collocation. IN: W. Meijs (ed.), *Corpus linguistics and beyond*, Editions Rodopi, B.V., Amsterdam
33. L. Lamport (1986): *Latex — A document preparation system*. Addison-Wesley, Reading, MA

34. M.E. Lesk, E. Schmidt (1978): Lex — A lexical analyzer generator. IN: B.W. Kernighan, M.D. McIlroy (eds.), *UNIX programmer's manual (7th ed.)*, Bell Labs, Murray Hill, http://cm.bell-labs.com/7thEdMan/vol2/lex

35. N.H. McDonald, L.T. Frase, P. Gingrich, S. Keenan (1988): *Educational Psychologist* **17**:172–179

36. C.F. Meyer (1994): Studying usage in computer corpora. IN: G.D. Little. M. Montgomery (eds.), *Centennial usage studies*, American Dialect Soc., Jacksonville, FL

37. A.N. Nelson (1962): *The original modern reader's Japanese-English character dictionary (Classic ed.)*. Charles E. Tuttle, Rutland

38. A. Renouf, J.M. Sinclair (1991): Collocational frameworks in English. IN: K. Aijmer, B. Altenberg (Eds.) *English corpus linguistics*, Longman, New York

39. L.M. Schmitt, K. Christianson (1998): *System* **26**:567–589

40. L.M. Schmitt, K. Christianson (1998): ERIC: Educational Resources Information Center, Doc. Service, National Lib. Edu., USA, **ED** 424 729, **FL** 025 224

41. F.A. Smadja (1989): *Literary and Linguistic Computing* **4**:163–168

42. J.M. Swales (1990): *Genre Analysis: English in Academic and Research Setting*. Cambridge Univ. Press, Cambridge

43. F. Tuzi (2004): *Computers and Composition* **21**:217–235

44. L. Wall, R.L. Schwarz (1990): *Programming perl*. O'Reilly, Sebastopol

45. C.A. Warden (2000): *Language Learning* **50**:573–616

46. J.H.M. Webb (1992): 121 *common mistakes of Japanese students of English (Revised ed.)*. The Japan Times, Tokyo

47. S. Wolfram (1991): *Mathematica — A system for doing mathematics by computer (2nd ed.)*. Addison-Wesley, Reading, MA

Appendices

A.1. Patterns (Regular Expressions)

Patterns which are also called regular expressions can be used in sed and awk for two purposes:

(a) As addresses, in order to select the pattern space (roughly the current line) for processing (*cf.* sections 12.3.1 and 12.4.1).

(b) As patterns in sed substitution commands that are actually replaced. Patterns are matched by sed and awk as the *longest, non-overlapping strings* possible.

Regular expressions in sed. The patterns that can be used with sed consist of the following elements in between slashes /:

(1) Any non-special character matches itself.

(2) Special characters that otherwise have a particular function in sed have to be preceded by a backslash \ in order to be understood literally. The special characters are: \\ \/ \^ \$ \. \[\] * \& \n

(3) ^ resp. $ match the beginning resp. the end of the pattern space. They must not be repeated in the replacement in a substitution command.

(4) . matches any single character.

(5) [*range*] matches any character in the string of characters *range*. The following five rules must be observed:

R1: The backslash \ is not needed to indicate special characters in *range*. The backslash only represents itself.

R2: The closing bracket] must be the first character in *range* in order to be recognized as itself.

R3: Intervals of the type a-z, A-Z, 0-9 in *range* are permitted. For example, i-m.

R4: The hyphen - must be at the beginning or the end of *range* in order to be recognized as itself.

R5: The carat ^ must not be the first character in *range* in order to be recognized as itself.

(6) [^*range*] matches any character not in *range*. The rules *R1–R4* under 5) also apply here.

(7) *pattern** stands for 0 or any number of concatenated copies of *pattern* where *pattern* is a specific character, the period . (meaning any character) or a range [...] as described under 5) and 6).

(8) *pattern*\{α,ω\} stands for α to ω concatenated copies of *pattern*. If ω is omitted, then an arbitrarily large number of copies of *pattern* is matched. Thus, the repitor * is equivalent to \{0,\}.

Regular expressions in awk. Regular expressions are used in awk as address patterns to select the pattern space for an action. They can also be used in the if statement of awk to define a conditional. Regular expressions in awk are very similar to regular expressions in sed. The regular expressions that can be used with awk consist of the following elements in between slashes /:

(1) Any non-special character matches itself as in sed.

(2) Special characters that otherwise have a particular function in awk have to be preceded by a backslash \ in order to be understood literally as in sed. A *newline* character in the pattern space can be matched with \n. The special characters are: \\ \/ \^ \$ \. \[\] * \+ \? \(\) \| \n.

Observe that & is not special in awk but in sed. In contrast, + and ? are special in awk serving as repitors similar to *. Parentheses are allowed in regular expressions in awk for grouping. Alternatives in regular expressions in awk are encoded using the vertical slash character |. Thus, the literal characters \+, \?, \(, \) and \| become special in awk but are not in sed. Note that there is no tagging using \(and \) in awk.

(3) ^ resp. $ match the beginning resp. the end of the pattern space as in sed.

(4) . matches any single character as in sed.

(5) [*range*] matches any character in the string of characters *range*. The following five rules must be observed:

R1: The backslash \ is not used to indicate special characters in *range* except for \] and \\.

R2: The closing bracket] is represented as \]. The backslash \ is represented as \\.

R3: Intervals of the type a-z, A-Z, 0-9 in *range* are permitted. For example, 1-9.

R4: The hyphen - must be at the beginning or the end of *range* in order to be recognized as itself.

R5: The carat ^ must not be the first character in *range* in order to be recognized as itself.

(6) [^*range*] matches any character not in *range*. The rules *R1–R4* set under 5) also apply here.

(7) *pattern*? stands for 0 or 1 copies of *pattern* where *pattern* is a specific character, the period . (meaning any character) or a range [...] as described under 5) and 6) or something in parentheses. *pattern** stands for 0 or any number of concatenated copies of *pattern*. *pattern+* stands for 1 or any number of concatenated copies of *pattern*.

(8) The ordinary parentheses (and) are used for grouping.

(9) The vertical slash | is used to define alternatives.

A.2. Advanced Patterns in awk

Address patterns in awk that select the pattern space for action can be

(1) regular expressions as described in A.1,

(2) algebraic-computational expressions involving variables[20] and functions, and

(3) Boolean combinations of anything listed under 1) or 2).

Essentially, everything can be combined in a sensible way to customize a pattern.

Example: In the introduction, the following is used:

```
awk '(($1~/^between$/)||($(NF)~/^between$/))&&($0~/ through /)' -
```

This prints every line of input where the first or (||) last field equals between and (&&) there exits a field that equals through on the line by invoking the default action (*i.e.*, printing). It is assumed that fields are separated by blanks. This is used in the very first example code in the introduction.

---

[20] For example, the variable fields of the input record can be matched against patterns using the tilde operator.

Index